THE PATH OF VIRTUE

The classic route traveled by
all Great Souls of the East and the West

Jonathan Murro

Ann Ree Colton Foundation
336 West Colorado Street
Post Office Box 2057
Glendale, California 91209

Copyright © 1980

by Ann Ree Colton Foundation of Niscience, Inc.

All rights reserved, including the right to
reproduce this book or portions thereof in
any form.

First Edition

Library of Congress Card Catalog
Number: 79-54382

Printed in the United States of America
by Book Graphics, Inc., Marina del Rey, California

DEDICATED
TO
THE
DIMENSIONAL
HEALING POWER
OF THE
CHRIST

And the whole multitude sought to touch Him: for there went virtue out of Him, and healed them all.
—St. Luke 6:19

My reverent gratitude:

To God for His patience, mercy and love;

To the Great Teachers for their sublime virtues;

To the Saints for their spiritual nobility;

To my beloved Teacher, Ann Ree Colton, for her courage, wisdom and beauty of soul;

To each individual, past and present, who has inspired me to see in virtues the Divine Essence.

CONTENTS

FOREWORD BY ANN REE COLTON   ix

PART I

1 SACRED SOURCES   3
Love... The Path... Vedas... Upanishads... Mahabharata... Bhagavad Gita... Egypt... Old Testament ... Talmud Torah... Talmud... Midrash... Dhammapada... Zoroaster... Yoga Sutras of Patanjali... Lao Tzu... Confucius... Pythagoras... Socrates... Plato... Aristotle... Cicero... New Testament... Seneca... Plutarch... Plotinus... Koran... Saints and Mystics... Literature... Statesmen... Golden Rule

2 THE GLORY OF GOD   33
Time... The Great Teachers... The Stars... Time Cycles... 500-Year Cycles... The Meek and the Galaxy Consciousness... Meekness... Time as Truth

3 WORSHIP   51
Worship... The Desire to Worship... Virtue-Clusters... The Freedom of Worship... Sabbath Cycles... Martyrdom ... Lady Poverty His Spouse

4 THE SECRET OF THE SAINTS   75
God... The Sacrament-Light of the Soul... The Virtue-Ladder of Illumination... The Mediation-Host Working with the Christ... Table of Virtues and Anti-virtues... The Praises of the Virtues... The Birth of a Virtue

5 THE GODHEAD   97
   Godhead...Divine Union: Parables and Prayers...
   Righteousness...The Devotee and the Ocean of Divine
   Grace...Beauty and the Anointing Spirit...Beauty...
   Bliss and Revelation...Ring-Pass-Not...Compassion
   ...Fulness

6 THE HOLY GHOST   121
   Holy Ghost...Ten-Year Cycles...The Whole Armour
   ...Diamond of Illumination...Nirvana-Points...
   Virtue-Diamonds...The Nirvana-Point Within a Virtue-
   Diamond...Virtue-Diamonds and the Anointing Spirit
   of God...Androgynous Virtues

7 MEMORY TREASURES   141
   Memory...Energy and the Soul...The Principle of
   Gradation...The Record of the Soul...The Memory of
   God...Magnification...The Power of Blessing...The
   Candelabra of the Soul

8 THE ROYAL GIFT OF PROPHECY   163
   Prophecy...The Relativity of Illumination...Archetypal
   Prophecies...Detachment...Dedicated Fasting...
   Moderation: The Golden Mean

9 THE ANOINTED CONSCIENCE   187
   Conscience...Virginity and Morality...Integrity...
   Integrity-Lens of the Conscience...Character...The
   Kiss of the Christ...Faithfulness...The Conscience of
   the Cosmos

PART II

10 JOY IN MARRIAGE   205
Marriage...Dowry of Virtues: Preparation for Marriage...Kindness...Cheerfulness...The Altar in the Home...Giving...Friendship...Dedication and the Tester...Courage...The Divine Mother...Wholesome Sense of Humor

11 MEDITATION AND THE LAW   237
Silence...The Quality of Silence...The Importance of Enthusiasm...Love and Simplicity...Simplicity...The Virtue of Honesty...Honesty...Meditation-Adoration...Meditation and the Cosmos...The Galaxy Consciousness and the New Covenant

12 PRAYERS FOR THE DEDICATED HEART   265
Prayer...Dedication of the Day...Prayers to Overcome Faults...Praise...Gratitude...Guidance...Punctuality...Obedience and Diligence...Diligence...Teaching the Word of God in Public

13 THE IMAGE OF GOD   297
Self-Mastery...Quickenings...The Ten Commandments and the Sermon on the Mount...The Indwelling and Overdwelling Image of God..."The House of the Lord"...Divine-Image Electricities...Kundalini, Chakras and Virtues...Ancestral Armageddon

14 THE MERCY OF GOD   325
Mercy...Repentance...Forgiveness...Humility...Ladder of Repentance: Levels of Prototypal Progression on the Path of Virtue...Virtue of Discernment...Discernment...Confession...The Snowflake and the Six...Cardinal-Virtue Energies and the Commandments

15 RESTITUTION AND MIRACLES   361
    Charity. . .Honorableness. . .Remission of Sins. . .The Dimensional Healing Power of the Christ. . .Atom Energy-Field of Illumination. . .The Tree of One's Being in the Present Life. . .Faith. . .Prayer of Repentance: The Desire to Make Restitution. . .Equanimity and the Moon. . . Equanimity

16 PURE LOVE AND THE PROTOTYPES   387
    The Sun. . .The Countenances of God. . .Purity. . .Prototypal Illuminations. . .The Gift of Healing. . .Modesty . . .Proteges of the Saints, Proteges of the Hierarchs

17 SOUL-COVENANTS AND
    REINCARNATION-CYCLES   413
    Reincarnation. . .Learning and the Universe. . .Pre-Solar-System Covenant. . .Pre-Birth Covenant. . .Pre-Day Covenant. . .Good

18 THE REALITY OF ETERNALITY   439
    Eternal and Everlasting. . .Constants in the Cosmos. . . The Great Logics. . .Patience. . .The Virtue of Holy Poverty. . .The Nature of God

BIBLIOGRAPHY   461

INDEX . . . *Inclusive of Quotation References*   465

LIST OF BOOKS   489

FOREWORD
BY
ANN REE COLTON

The knowledge of the virtues is a virtue.

    Jonathan Murro's writing involves one with his ecstasy. It is a writing of ecstatic intensity, involving the reader to share—and to expand his own powers of anointing, sealing and quickening.
    In the physical world, God encases the soul in a physical body. In God-Realization, one is first anointed; secondly, sealed; and last, quickened. The benediction of God is with the anointed through purification. To be *sealed* exceeds encasement. When the initiate is sealed, he is forever in the state of God-Realization, inviolate within the Kingdom and the Power of the Will of God.
    To be quickened after one is sealed, is to be in a state of eternity, inexhaustibly spreading the God-Realization Light to the world.
    Jesus was anointed by Baptism by John the Baptist through the Holy Spirit. His Great Sealing came during His Crucifixion. His Quickening Spirit is eternal through Christ. So is the initiate initiated through God-Realization.

PART I

. . . add to your faith virtue.

—Saint Peter

LOVE

Beloved, let us love one another: for love is of God; and every one that loveth is born of God, and knoweth God. He that loveth not knoweth not God; for God is love.
—Saint John the Beloved

The Lord make you to increase and abound in love one toward another, and toward all men. —Saint Paul

When the evening of this life comes, we shall be judged on Love. —Saint John of the Cross

You are one, forever. You are love. —Katha Upanishad

To him in whom love dwells, the whole world is but one family. —Buddha

Love covereth all sins. —Solomon

Love thy neighbor as thyself. —Moses

Love your enemies. —Jesus

Kindle in the heart the flame of love. —Rumi

Life is a flower of which love is the honey. —Victor Hugo

We are put in training for a love which knows not sex or person, nor partiality, but which seeks virtue and wisdom everywhere. —Ralph Waldo Emerson

There will be no true freedom without virtue, no true science without religion, no true industry without the fear of God and love to your fellow-citizens. —Charles Kingsley

Jesus lived in vain if he did not teach us to regulate the whole of life by the eternal law of love. —Mohandas K. Gandhi

Where there is Love and Wisdom, there is neither fear nor ignorance. —Saint Francis of Assisi

1
SACRED SOURCES

Take up, read! Take up, read!
—Saint Augustine

A room without books is as a body without a soul.
—Cicero

Study to shew thyself approved unto God.
—Saint Paul

The Path

The steep path of virtue.
—Horace

Virtue, difficult to the human race, noblest pursuit in life.
—Aristotle

How far from easy is virtue! How difficult is even a continual pretence of virtue.
—Cicero

Virtue proceeds through toil.
—Euripides

> Virtue is nothing if not difficult.
> —Ovid

> Sages say the path is narrow and difficult to tread, narrow as the razor's edge.
> —Katha Upanishad

> Strait is the gate, and narrow is the way, which leadeth unto life, and few there be that find it.
> Jesus
> —*St. Matthew 7:14*

The Scriptural, philosophical and poetic words of the Great Souls of the past reveal that the Path of Virtue is the way to union with God. The wisdom of the ages related to this classic Path lives in the present time through the inspired words of the Great Teachers, Saints, Sages, Philosophers and Poets of the East and the West. All generations of devotees and initiates of the higher life may draw upon this timeless wisdom for inspiration, guidance and enlightenment.

The Path of Virtue is a *Universal* Path. All Truth-seekers —regardless of their different races, nations and religions— must walk the same Path of Virtue and climb the same Mountain of Illumination. Even as the physical laws governing mountain climbing or space travel are the same impersonal laws for all nations, so are the holy laws governing an illuminative union with God the same laws for all individuals.

All true teachers in each age and time are teachers of Love and Love-Commandments. Love is the only cradle in which the Babe of Truth will rest with serene contentment. Where Love is, Truth is; where Love is not, Truth does not have its perfect place for growth. As Truth grows, Freedoms expand—and the cradle of Love is transformed into a castle of Love wherein may be found the treasures of the soul and the spirit.

The sole purpose of Scriptural study, devotional practices and all other aspects of the higher life is to make one's love pure and perfect. Through pure love, all virtues are united in harmonious rapport with the Creator's Will. The numerous tests one experiences in life are designed to purify his love and to expand his virtues. As his love and virtues increase, his union with the Glory and Love of God prospers.

Each person has his own ideas and attitudes regarding disciplines and virtues. These ideas and attitudes, if not motivated by pure love, hinder his progress on the Path. God-Realization occurs through one's dedication to daily worship-observances, the continuous purification of his love, and his unceasing efforts to emulate the attitudes and virtues of the Great Teachers.

Virtues, when planted in the soil of love and discipline, become as plants with healthy roots. The love of discipline heralds the birth of Wisdom through the marriage of Virtue and Life.

When a seeker after Truth first learns about a cardinal virtue, he may be likened to the discoverer of a new country and a vast ocean. To gain firsthand knowledge of a new country, one must explore its mountains, rivers, plains and valleys; so must a cardinal virtue be explored in order to discover its beauty, breadth and height. An ocean, when discovered, leads one to the shores of new lands; a virtue, as an ocean, guides an alert individual to the shores of new understanding. This process of discovery, knowledge and understanding pertains to each virtue that God is asking His children to perfect through life on earth.

The *exalted* or *divine* degrees of each virtue are on the purest levels of the soul. Earnest devotees on the Path of Virtue give freedom to their souls by working to attain the highest degrees of all virtues. The Scriptures of the East and the West contain numerous references to sacred Laws and divine virtues—however, many secrets of enlightenment remain for every sincere devotee to discover for himself regarding each Law of God and each cardinal virtue.

> Although virtue receives some of its excellence from nature, yet it is perfected by education.
> —Quintilian

> Virtue, though in rags, will keep me warm.
> —Dryden

> Through virtue lies the one and only road to a life of peace.
> —Juvenal

> There is no attribute of the superior man greater than his helping men to practice virtue.
> —Mencius

The Vedas

The word "Veda" means *knowledge*. Some historians believe that the *Vedas,* the oldest religious books in the world, were composed from 10–20,000 years before the Christ. These ancient books of the Hindus contain hymns, rules of sacrifice, and philosophical discourses. The word *Vedic* is thought by many to refer to all literature which orthodox Hindus believe to be sacred, inclusive of the Brahmanas, Upanishads and Sutras, as well as the Vedic Hymns.

There are four Vedas: *Rig Veda,* the earlier hymns and

discourses of the sages and Rishis; *Sama Veda,* a book of hymns, including those from the Rig Veda; *Yajur Veda,* a book presenting the rules of sacrifice; *Atharva Veda,* a fourth book compiled at a later date, containing the then existing hymns and rules of sacrifice.

> Well, O people, let us all sit together and sing the praises of the Lord and worship the same God.
> —Yajur Veda

> Heaven is my Father, Progenitor! There is my origin.
> —Rig Veda

> In the beginning there arose the Golden Child. As soon as he was born he alone was the lord of all that is. He established the earth and this heaven.
> —Vedic Hymn

The Upanishads

The *Upanishads* are philosophical discourses taken from the Vedas; these discourses relate to the Supreme Being, the nature of man, the human soul, and immortality. The word "Upanishad" means *that which brings us near to God,* or *to sit down near,* signifying the importance of learning the principles of the higher life from an enlightened teacher.

The various Upanishads are from one hundred and fifty to one hundred and seventy in number; twelve are well-known. The Upanishads are also called *Vedanta,* meaning the end of the Vedas or the climax of knowledge. The date of the earliest Upanishad is about 600 B.C.

> Lead me from the unreal to the real!
> Lead me from darkness to light!
> Lead me from death to immortality!
> —Brihadaranyaka Upanishad

> The pathways of the spirit
> Run like spokes
> To the hub of the heart,
> Where from the one light irradiate
> A thousand shining shafts.
> —Mundaka Upanishad

> In the faith of 'He is' his existence must be preserved, in his essence. When he is perceived as 'He is' then shines forth the revelation of his essence.
> —Katha Upanishad

THE MAHABHARATA

The *Mahabharata* is an epic poem of India with over 90,000 couplets. Historians offer different dates as to its origin: 5000 B.C., 1400–1000 B.C., the Third Century B.C. The Mahabharata, compiled around 400 A.D., contains the *Ramayana* and the *Bhagavad Gita*.

> From virtue arises happiness.

> Virtue protects him who protects her.

> Virtue is the only friend that accompanies man beyond death.

THE BHAGAVAD GITA

The *Bhagavad Gita*—the *Lord's Song* or *Song Celestial*—has seven hundred verses divided into eighteen chapters. The central figures are Krishna and his friend and devotee, Arjuna. The wisdom of the Gita, offering solutions to the problems of life, is based upon logic, reason, and religious philosophy.

Divine virtues are regarded as conducive to liberation and demoniacal properties as conducive to bondage. Grieve not, Arjuna, for you are born with divine virtues.

Who sees Me in all,
And sees all in Me,
For him I am not lost,
And he is not lost for Me.

I am easily attainable by that steadfast spiritual aspirant who remembers Me constantly and daily, with a single mind.
—Bhagavad Gita

Egypt

During its early dynasties, Egypt contributed to the world great wisdom, beauty and understanding. Certain pharaohs and priests comprehended many mysteries of Nature and secrets of the soul. The building of the pyramids, the philosophy of Ikhnaton, the artistry of the craftsmen, and the perceptive symbolism passed from dynasty to dynasty testify to the greatness of olden Egypt.

More acceptable is the virtue of the upright man than the ox of him that doeth iniquity.
—Instruction to Prince
Merikere from his father,
a Pharaoh of Heracleopolis
(c. 2200 B.C.)

A man's virtue is his monument, but forgotten is the man of evil repute.
—Egyptian tombstone
inscription (c. 2100 B.C.)

> How manifold are thy works!
> They are hidden from before (us),
> O sole God, whose powers no other possesseth.
> —Ikhnaton
> Pharaoh, 1300 B.C.

The Old Testament

The *Old Testament* contains thirty-nine books written by Hebrew prophets and holy men. These sacred writings describe the developmental rise of a people graced with inspired leadership and an abiding faith in God.

Moses, the first writer in the Old Testament, lived 1200 years before the time of Jesus. The Ten Commandments, received by Moses on Mount Sinai, have been revered and practiced over the centuries by countless persons in different races, nations and religions.

> In the beginning God created the heaven and the earth.
> Moses
> —*Genesis 1:1*

> For the righteous Lord loveth righteousness; his countenance doth behold the upright.
> David
> —*Psalm 11:7*

> For the Lord is our judge, the Lord is our lawgiver, the Lord is our king; he will save us.
> —*Isaiah 33:22*

> A virtuous woman is a crown to her husband.
> Solomon
> —*Proverbs 12:4*

> I know that my redeemer liveth, and that he shall stand at the latter day upon the earth.
> —*Job 19:25*

THE TEN COMMANDMENTS

1. Thou shalt have no other gods before me.

2. Thou shalt not make unto thee any graven image, or any likeness of any thing that is in heaven above, or that is in the earth beneath, or that is in the water under the earth:

   Thou shalt not bow down thyself to them, nor serve them: for I the LORD thy God am a jealous God, visiting the iniquity of the fathers upon the children unto the third and fourth generation of them that hate me;

   And shewing mercy unto thousands of them that love me, and keep my commandments.

3. Thou shalt not take the name of the LORD thy God in vain; for the LORD will not hold him guiltless that taketh his name in vain.

4. Remember the sabbath day, to keep it holy.

   Six days shalt thou labour, and do all thy work:

   But the seventh day is the sabbath of the LORD thy God: in it thou shalt not do any work, thou, nor thy son, nor thy daughter, thy manservant, nor thy maidservant, nor thy cattle, nor thy stranger that is within thy gates.

   For in six days the LORD made heaven and earth, the sea, and all that in them is, and rested the seventh day; wherefore the LORD blessed the sabbath day, and hallowed it.

5. Honour thy father and thy mother: that thy days may be long upon the land which the LORD thy God giveth thee.

6. Thou shalt not kill.

7. Thou shalt not commit adultery.

8. Thou shalt not steal.

9. Thou shalt not bear false witness against thy neighbour.

10. Thou shalt not covet thy neighbour's house, thou shalt not covet thy neighbour's wife, nor his manservant, nor his maidservant, nor his ox, nor his ass, nor any thing that is thy neighbour's.
—Exodus 20:3-17

APOCRYPHA

The word "apocrypha" comes from a Greek word meaning "hidden away" or "secret." The *Apocrypha*—written by Scriptural scribes, prophets and poet-philosophers—is important for its historical record and also for its inspired teachings on the sanctity of marriage, the resurrection of the dead, eternal life, and other vital subjects. The fifteen books in the Apocrypha are sometimes included in printings of the Old Testament.

> Uphold the truth, and lead the virtuous life:
> Virtue brings rich rewards.
> —Ben Sira 51:30

> All things were lying in peace and silence and night in her swift course was half spent, when thy almighty Word leapt from the royal throne in heaven.
> —Wisdom 18:14, 15

> Hear, O Israel, the commandments of life, be attentive to Wisdom and understanding.
> —1 Baruch 3:9

TALMUD TORAH AND TALMUD

The *Talmud Torah* is the name given to the first five books (Pentateuch) in the Old Testament.

The *Talmud* contains the transcripts of symposiums held by Hebrew scholars, rabbis and sages from the Fifth Century B.C. to the Eighth Century A.D. These transcripts constitute Jewish civil and religious law.

> A man should endeavor to be as pliant as a reed, yet as hard as cedar-wood.
> —Talmud

The development of the Talmud evolved into two vast bodies of legal knowledge: the *Mishnah* (Repetition) and the *Gemara* (Learning). The Mishnah is a compilation of the Laws decided on by the Sanhedrin during its years as the highest court in the land. Its contents are organized into six sections that relate to Seeds, Feasts, Women, Damages, Sacred Things, and Purification.

In the Mishnah, codified around 200 A.D., sincerity and enthusiasm are taught to be as essential in study as in prayer. Humility also is important, and the scholar is warned against intellectual pride. Study should . . .

> Clothe him in meekness and reverence; it fits him to become just, pious, upright and faithful; it keeps him from sin, and brings him near to virtue.
> —Mishnah

While the Mishnah is a commentary on an elaboration of the Torah, the Gemara is a commentary on an elaboration of the Mishnah. There is a *Babylonian Gemara* and a *Jerusalem Gemara;* thus, the Talmud is two similar and yet different sets of volumes, known either as the Babylonian Talmud or the Jerusalem Talmud. The Babylonian Talmud is approximately nine times larger than the Jerusalem Talmud. Each Talmud is divided into six main divisions or books.

> Repent one day before your death.
> —Babylonian Talmud

MIDRASH

The *Midrash,* dating from the Fifth Century B.C., contains collections of Hebrew moral and ethical commentaries on the Old Testament. The major collection was compiled from the Sixth Century A.D. to the Twelfth Century. The illustrative stories, parables, allegories, homilies and pithy sayings in the Midrash had great popular appeal.

> He used to say: Better one hour of repentance and good works in this world than all the life in the world to come; and better one hour of calmness of spirit in the world to come than all the life in this world.
> —Midrash

DHAMMAPADA

The *Dhammapada* is a collection of ethical sayings of the Buddha (563–483 B.C.). These sayings were first gathered in northern India in the Third Century B.C., and originally written down in Ceylon in the First Century B.C. The Dhammapada, divided into twenty-six chapters, is the principal Scripture for Buddhists in Ceylon and Southeast Asia.

Dhamma* means law, virtue, justice, righteousness, religion, discipline, truth; *pada* means path, step, foot, foundation. The word *Dhammapada* is interpreted either as the Way of the Law or the Path to Virtue.

> The virtuous man is happy in this world, and he is happy in the next; he is happy in both. He is happy when he thinks of the good he has done; he is still more happy when going on the good path.
>
> He who possesses virtue and intelligence, who is just, speaks the truth, and does what is his own business, him the world will hold dear.
>
> Happy is virtue lasting to old age; happy is faith firmly rooted; happy is the attainment of wisdom; happy is the avoidance of sins.
>
> Buddha
—*Dhammapada*

THE EIGHTFOLD PATH

The essence of Buddha's wisdom is contained within his teaching of the *Eightfold Path*.

1. Right views
2. Right aspirations
3. Right speech
4. Right actions
5. Right living
6. Right exertion
7. Right recollection
8. Right meditation.

**Dhamma,* in the Pali language, has the same meanings as the Sanskrit word *Dharma.*

Zoroaster

The birth of Zoroaster is believed to have occurred between the Sixth Century B.C. and 1000 B.C. Zoroaster strongly influenced religious thought in Persia; presently, the majority of his followers live in India. The most highly prized single virtue in Zoroastrianism is purity. The sacred writings of this religion teach that there is one Deity, *Ahura Mazda,* meaning Wise Lord or Lord of Wisdom; the power of light, life, truth, goodness. The chief Scripture is the *Zend-Avesta.*

> Ahura, the creator, radiant, glorious, greatest and best, most beautiful, most firm, wisest, most perfect, the most bounteous Spirit!
>
> The will of the Lord is the law of righteousness.
>
> Holiness is the best of all good. Happy, happy the man who is holy with perfect holiness.
> —Zend-Avesta

Yoga Sutras of Patanjali

The *Yoga Sutras of Patanjali* are believed to have been written either during the period around 200 B.C. or 700 B.C. Patanjali's work is essentially a mental discipline in eight stages for the attainment of spiritual freedom. Physical and moral preparation are integral parts of his teaching. Patanjali presents one hundred and ninety-five aphorisms; these are divided into four chapters. For successful results, his followers are expected to practice daily meditation on Divine qualities or virtues.

He who remains undistracted even when he is in possession of all the psychic powers, achieves, as the result of perfect discrimination, that samadhi which is called the "cloud of virtues."

Undisturbed calmness of mind is attained by cultivating friendliness toward the happy, compassion for the unhappy, delight in the virtuous, and indifference toward the wicked.

—Patanjali

Lao Tzu

Some authorities believe that Lao Tzu lived in China from 604 B.C. to 531 B.C.; others, the Fourth Century B.C. For hundreds of years, the essence of his teachings of the Tao (Way) provided one of the major influences in Chinese thought and culture. Taoism, imbued by a reverence for the mystic and the meditative, opened to ancient man the way to inner tranquility and enlightenment.

> With virtue and quietness one may conquer the world.

> The good I meet with goodness, the bad I also meet with goodness. For virtue is goodness throughout.

> Cultivate Virtue in yourself,
> And Virtue will be real.
> Cultivate it in the family,
> And Virtue will abound.
> Cultivate it in the village,
> And Virtue will grow.
> Cultivate it in the nation,
> And Virtue will be abundant.
> Cultivate it in the universe,
> And Virtue will be everywhere.

—Lao Tzu

Confucius

The wisdom of Confucius (556–479 B.C.) has remained throughout the centuries as a source of inspiration related to ethics, learning, moral perfection, and decency in behavior. Confucius urged his followers to live in harmony with themselves so that they might live in harmony with the universe.

In Confucianism, the virtues are grouped under five: *love*, the root of all the others; justice; reverence; wisdom; sincerity. The outstanding virtue is filial loyalty, which also includes loyalty and is the outgrowth of reverence. For men, Confucius emphasized the importance of loyalty and good faith; for women, chastity and docility. In many of his sayings, Confucius describes the qualities of "the superior man."

> The way of the superior man is threefold: Virtuous, he is free from anxieties; Wise, he is free from perplexities; Bold, he is free from fear.
>
> The superior man, in the world, does not set his mind either for anything, or against anything; what is right he will follow. The superior man thinks of virtue; the small man thinks of comfort. The superior man thinks of the sanctions of law; the small man thinks of favours which he may receive.
>
> What the superior man seeks is in himself; what the small man seeks is in others.
>
> There are three things which the superior man guards against. In youth . . . lust. When he is strong . . . quarrelsomeness. When he is old . . . covetousness.

ity Library and Archives
(16) 251-3503

te charged: 8/16/2007,15:25
em ID: 0005100245856
tle: The path of virtue : the classic ro
e traveled b
te due: 9/13/2007,23:59

te charged: 8/16/2007,15:25
em ID: 0005100336053
tle: God-realization journal
te due: 9/13/2007,23:59

te charged: 8/16/2007,15:25
em ID: 0005100335704
tle: Nine faces of Christ : a narrative
nine great
e due: 9/13/2007,23:59

e charged: 8/16/2007,15:25
m ID: 0005100234859
le: Prophet for the archangels
e due: 9/13/2007,23:59

nk you!
.unityonline.org/library

Without recognizing the ordinances of Heaven, it is impossible to be a superior man.

The determined scholar and the man of virtue will not seek to live at the expense of injuring their virtue. They will even sacrifice their lives to preserve their virtue complete.

To be able to practice five things everywhere under heaven constitutes perfect virtue . . . (they are) gravity, generosity of soul, sincerity, earnestness, and kindness.
—Confucius

Pythagoras

Pythagoras (582–507? B.C.) combined rational science with religious mysticism. He is credited with having discovered the importance of numbers in music. Pythagoras influenced Plato and Plotinus, and, through them, many mystics and metaphysicians up to the present time. In the teachings of Pythagoras, the demand for purity in life was deeply grounded.

Virtue is harmony.

Wealth is a weak anchor, and glory cannot support a man; this is the law of God, that virtue only is firm, and cannot be shaken by a tempest.

Before thou act, advise;
Nor suffer sleep at night
   to close thine eyes,
Til thrice thy acts that day
   thou hast ore-run.

> How slipt? what deeds?
>   what duty left undone?
> Thus thy account summ'd up
>   from first to last,
> Grieve for the ill,
>   joy for what good hath past.
> These study, practice these,
>   and these affect;
> To sacred virtue
>   these thy steps direct.
>
> —Pythagoras

SOCRATES

The Greek philosopher Socrates (469–399 B.C.) insisted on the belief in moral values, an austere conduct of life, and the unity of wisdom, knowledge and virtue.

> There is only one good, knowledge,
> and one evil, ignorance.

> And so if the virtues, however many and different they may be, they all have a common nature which makes them virtues . . .

> Then, Meno, the conclusion is that virtue comes to the virtuous by the gift of God.
>
> —Socrates

PLATO

Plato (427–347 B.C.) derived the rules of rightful conduct of human life from the laws that govern the universe. His brilliance as a philosopher has contributed to many areas of scientific, philosophical and metaphysical thought.

Love is the eldest and noblest and mightiest of the gods and chiefest author and giver of virtue in life and of happiness after death.

Beauty, goodness, justice, and the like, each exists in and for itself.

Virtue, if she could be seen, would win great love and affection.

Virtue of herself is sufficient for happiness.
—Plato

Aristotle

Aristotle (384-322 B.C.) had an inspired philosophic insight combined with keen powers of observation. He was a great thinker, systematic historian and natural scientist, contributing to the worlds of physics and metaphysics. Aristotle conceived the perfect state to be a democracy where education is aimed at the development of the body and the virtues.

Even if happiness is not sent by the gods, but is the result of virtue and of learning of discipline of some kind, it is apparently one of the most divine things in the world; for it would appear that that which is the prize and end of virtue is the supreme good, and in its nature divine and blessed.

The chief good is the exercise of virtue in a perfect life.
—Aristotle

Cicero

Cicero (106–43 B.C.) was a Roman orator, statesman and philosopher whose writings influenced the works of the early Christians, Petrarch, Erasmus and Copernicus. The founding fathers of the United States were ardent in their admiration of Cicero.

> Virtue is a habit of the mind, consistent with nature and moderation and reason.
>
> In virtue are riches.
>
> In our dispositions the seeds of the virtues are implanted by nature.
>
> In virtue there are many grades, and the highest glory is won by the highest virtue.
>
> —Cicero

New Testament

The twenty-seven books of the *New Testament* were written by disciples and apostles of the Christ. The wisdom of Jesus is recorded in the Gospels (Good Tidings) of Matthew, Mark, Luke and John. The New Testament also contains the epistles of Paul, Peter, James, Jude, and John the Beloved. The latter wrote the profound book of *Revelation*.

The New Testament has contributed to the establishing and spreading of the teachings of Jesus relating to Worship, Ethics, Principles, Virtues, Commandments, Spiritual Gifts and the Kingdom of God.

> Be ye therefore perfect, even as your Father which is in heaven is perfect.
>
> Jesus of Nazareth
> —*Saint Matthew 5:48*

Finally, brethren, whatsoever things are true, whatsoever things are honest, whatsoever things are just, whatsoever things are pure, whatsoever things are lovely, whatsoever things are of good report, if there be any virtue, and if there be any praise, think on these things.

Saint Paul
—Philippians 4:8

Grace and peace be multiplied unto you through the knowledge of God, and of Jesus our Lord, according as his divine power hath given unto us all things that pertain unto life and godliness, through the knowledge of him that hath called us to glory and virtue.

Saint Peter
—2 Peter 1:2, 3

THE BEATITUDES

The Sermon on the Mount contains the quintessence of all pure teachings. The *Beatitudes* are nine stanzas spoken by Jesus at the beginning of the Sermon on the Mount.

1. Blessed are the poor in spirit: for theirs is the kingdom of heaven.
2. Blessed are they that mourn: for they shall be comforted.
3. Blessed are the meek: for they shall inherit the earth.
4. Blessed are they which do hunger and thirst after righteousness: for they shall be filled.
5. Blessed are the merciful: for they shall obtain mercy.
6. Blessed are the pure in heart: for they shall see God.
7. Blessed are the peacemakers: for they shall be called the children of God.
8. Blessed are they which are persecuted for righteousness' sake: for theirs is the kingdom of heaven.

9. Blessed are ye, when men shall revile you, and persecute you, and shall say all manner of evil against you falsely, for my sake. Rejoice, and be exceeding glad: for great is your reward in heaven: for so persecuted they the prophets which were before you.

—*Saint Matthew 5:3-12*

Seneca

Seneca (4 B.C.-65 A.D.), Roman dramatist and statesman, wrote treatises on the natural sciences, psychology, and moral questions. He was a prominent jurist, and was acknowledged by his contemporaries to be an authority on geology, meteorology, and marine biology.

> You ask what I seek from virtue?
> Itself. For virtue has nothing better
> to give; its value is in itself.

> It is the edge and temper of the blade that make a good sword, not the richness of the scabbard; and so it is not money or possessions that make man considerable, but his virtue.

> How well it would be if men would but exercise their brains as they do their bodies, and take as much pains for virtues as they do for pleasure.

> Virtue is that perfect good which is the complement of a happy life; the only immortal thing that belongs to mortality.

—Seneca

Plutarch

Over the centuries, Plutarch (50-120 A.D.) has been held in high esteem as a moralist and as a biographer of great individuals. Plutarch served as a priest in the temple of the Academy founded by Plato; his spiritual life was centered in Athens and Delphi. The prolific writings of Plutarch contain a treasury of knowledge for modern-day psychologists, sociologists, educators, historians, philosophers, and students of religion.

> Divinity has three elements of superiority, incorruption, power and virtue, and the most reverend of these is virtue; for in fundamental justice nothing participates except through the exercise of intelligent reasoning powers.
>
> Virtue, the most pleasing and valuable possession in the world.
>
> Virtue, like a strong and hardy plant, takes root in any place, if she finds there a generous nature and a spirit that shuns no labor.
> —Plutarch

PLOTINUS

Plotinus (205–270 A.D.), an Egyptian Neoplatonist, was a student of the wisdom of India. He believed that asceticism and ecstasy lead to wisdom. Saint Augustine stated that Plotinus, in order to become a Christian, would have to change "only a few words." Christian theology and philosophy of the Middle Ages adopted many of Plotinus' thoughts. From 245 until his death, Plotinus taught philosophy in Rome, where he was consulted on different occasions by the Emperor.

> Virtue is the beauty of the soul.
>
> Some bodies are beautiful by a kind of participation; others appear to be essentially beautiful in themselves—such is the nature of virtue.
> —Plotinus

The Koran

The Koran was written by Muhammad (570–632), the Founder of the Islam religion. Muhammad believed that he received the words of the Koran from the Archangel Gabriel. He wrote his inspirations on the ribs of palm leaves, the shoulder-blades of sheep, and on parchment.

The Koran, meaning Recitations, consists of twenty-nine chapters. The first third of its 144 sections (Surus) was conceived in Mecca and deals with the creation and future fate of the world, the proofs of the omnipotence of Allah, and the teachings of a moral conduct of life as a preparation for standing the test on the Day of Judgment. The remainder of the Koran, accomplished in Medina, disputes other religious and civil legislation.

The Koran is a book of precepts and laws in matters of religion, such as prayer, fasting and pilgrimage. There also are laws regarding the civil life: marriage, the possession and bequeathing of property, and the administration of justice.

> Spiritual virtue is to adore God as if thou sawest Him; and if thou seest Him not, He nevertheless sees thee.
>
> Verily, God is pure and loves the pure, is clean, and loves the clean, is beneficent and loves the beneficent, is generous and loves the generous.
>
> If all the trees in the earth were pens, and the sea, with seven more seas to help it, (were ink), the words of Allah could not be exhausted. Lo! Allah is Mighty, Wise.
>
> Muhammad
—The Koran

Saints and Mystics

The gentleness and faith of Saint Francis of Assisi and other Saints have inspired many persons to live with the spirit of kindness and love toward their fellow man. All true Saints and pure Mystics of the East and the West are enlightened wayshowers toward the attaining of an illuminative union with God.

> All holy virtues,
>   God keep you,
> God, from whom you proceed and come.
> —Saint Francis of Assisi
> 1182-1226

What, then, is real virtue? Anything wrought in the soul by divine love alone.
—Meister Eckhart
1260-1327

If this man would overcome his fickleness, he must learn to rest above all virtues in God and in the most high Unity of God.
—Blessed John Ruysbroeck
1293-1381

Some also at first do offer all, but afterwards, being assailed with temptation, they return again to their own ways, and therefore make no progress in the ways of virtue.
—Saint Thomas á Kempis
1380-1471

The Cross is the abyss of wonders, the centre of desires, the school of virtues, the house of wisdom, the throne of love, the theatre of joys, and the place of sorrows; It is the root of happiness, and the gate of Heaven.
—Thomas Traherne
c. 1637–1674

Bow down and worship where others kneel, for where so many have been paying the tribute of adoration, the kind Lord must manifest himself, for he is all mercy.
—Sri Ramakrishna
1836–1886

LITERATURE

Great writings contain numerous themes related to the beauty and importance of virtues. Inspired authors, poets, artists and musicians as well as philosophers and religious leaders have worked unceasingly to preserve and to prosper the knowledge of virtues in the world.

Love kindled by virtue always kindles another, provided that its flame appears outwardly.
—Dante
1265–1321

Our life is short, but to expand that span to vast eternity is virtue's work.
—William Shakespeare
1564–1616

Mortals that would follow me,
Love virtue; she alone is free;
She can teach ye how to climb

Higher than the sphery chime;
Or if virtue feeble were,
Heav'n itself would stoop to her.
—John Milton
1608-1674

Virtue may choose the high or low degree,
'T is just alike to Virtue and to me;
Dwell in a monk, or light upon a king,
She's still the same belov'd contented thing.
—Alexander Pope
1688-1744

Statesmen

National leaders devoted to spiritual values and moral principles influence the attitudes and actions of their countrymen for many generations. The courage, faith and wisdom of honorable statesmen continue to live in the hearts of those who also recognize the relationship between virtues and Divine Providence.

> To be innocent is to be not guilty; but to be virtuous is to overcome our evil feelings and intentions.
> —William Penn
> 1644-1718

Hast thou virtue? acquire also the graces and beauties of virtue.
—Benjamin Franklin
1706-1790

And if Wise be the happy man, as these sages say, he must be virtuous too; for without virtue happiness cannot be.
—Thomas Jefferson
1743-1826

To see the universal and all-pervading Spirit of Truth face to face one must be able to love the meanest of creation as oneself.
—Mohandas K. Gandhi
1869–1948

THE GOLDEN RULE

What you do not want done to yourself, do not do to others.
—Confucius

Hurt not others with that which pains thyself.

Since, for each one of us, our own self is the most important, respect the self of your fellow man as you respect your own.
—Buddha

Do not unto others all that which is not well for oneself.
—Zoroaster

In happiness and suffering, in joy and grief, we should regard all creatures as we regard our own self, and should therefore refrain from inflicting upon others such injury as would appear undesirable to us if inflicted upon ourselves.   —Jainism

May I do to others as I would that they should do unto me.
—Plato

We should behave to our friends as we would wish our friends to behave to us.   —Aristotle

Do naught to others which if done to thee would cause thee pain.   —Mahabharata

What is hateful to you, never do to a fellow man: that is the whole Law—all the rest is commentary.   —Talmud

Sacred Sources

What you do not want done to you, do not do to anyone else.
—Apocrypha

What is hateful to yourself, do not do to your fellow man.
—Rabbi Hillel
First Century, B.C.

Therefore, all things whatsoever ye would that men should do to you, do ye even so to them: for this is the law and the prophets. —Jesus

In your dealings with others, harm not that you be not harmed.

Treat your inferiors as you would be treated by your betters.
—Seneca

Do unto all men as you would wish them to have done unto you.

No man is a true believer unless he desireth for his brother what he desires for himself.

No man can be called a believer until he loves for his brother what he loves for himself. —Muhammad

Treat others as thou wouldst be treated. —Sikhism

Do unto others as you would have them do unto you.
—Modern

TIME

Time was created as an image of eternity. —Plato

Time discovers truth. —Seneca

Time will explain it all, He is a talker, and needs no questioning before he speaks. —Euripides

Time is the most valuable thing a man can spend. —Theophrastus

Pythagoras, when he was asked what time was, answered that it was the soul of this world. —Plutarch

Wait for that wisest of all counselors, Time. —Pericles

The best preacher is the heart; the best teacher is time; the best book is the world; the best friend is God. —The Talmud

Is there not an appointed time to man upon earth? —Job 7:1

The irresistible course of Time affects all mortals. —The Mahabharata

To everything there is a season, and a time to every purpose under heaven.
Solomon
—*Ecclesiastes 3:1*

Time is fulfilled when time is no more. He who in time has his heart established in eternity and in whom all temporal things are dead, in him is the fullness of time. —Meister Eckhart

And the angel which I saw stand upon the sea and upon the earth lifted up his hand to heaven, and sware by him that liveth for ever and ever, who created heaven, and the things that therein are, and the earth, and the things that therein are, and the sea, and the things which are therein, that there should be time no longer. Saint John the Beloved
—*Revelation 10:5, 6*

2

THE GLORY OF GOD

The heavens declare the glory of God.
—Psalm 19:1

The earth shall be filled with the knowledge of the glory of the Lord, as the waters cover the sea.
—Habakkuk 2:14

THE GREAT TEACHERS

There is one glory of the sun, and another glory of the moon, and another glory of the stars: for one star differeth from another star in glory.
Saint Paul
—*1 Corinthians 15:41*

The night sky, thick with the ever-present lights of countless stars, testifies to the Glory of God in the Cosmos. The Great Teachers of the world testify to the Glory of God in the Soul. Even as each star has its individual and unique Glory, so does each soul created by God have a special and powerful Glory. The Glory of God in the soul manifests itself on earth through a broad spectrum of virtues. Wherever this resplendent Glory is given freedom in the world, mankind progresses through virtue-inspired accomplishments.

The Scriptures of all faiths contain voluminous references to the value and necessity of virtues. The knowledge of virtues is a light that glows in lands and in hearts where love and goodness are cherished and expressed. Individuals and nations that recognize and follow this light are mankind's hope for the present and for the future.

The welfare and survival of a nation are dependent upon the integrity of its leaders and the moral character of its people. The success and happiness of a marriage are determined by the love and virtues of husband and wife. The spiritual enlightenment of an individual is in direct degree to the nobility of his virtues and the purity of his love.

When one studies and applies the knowledge of virtues presented by the Great Teachers, his life comes into order and harmony; his physical body experiences health and vigor; and beautiful inspirations fill his mind. These physical and spiritual blessings are received due to his uniting with the Healing and Illuminating Presence of God within virtues.

Albert Einstein, when asked to choose one word to describe the myriad stars and galaxies moving and turning in the Cosmos, selected the word "Harmony." Pythagoras, who lived fourteen centuries earlier, said: "Virtue is harmony." Present-day mankind is on the brink of discovering the relationship between virtue's harmony and the harmony of the stars and the galaxies.

In recent decades, astronomers have opened new doors to a scientific understanding of the harmony of the Universe. Numerous discoveries about the wonders of space are awakening the minds of men to the deep meanings and vast potentials of the Eternal Drama being enacted by the multitudes of stars.

The Glory of God

Photographs of the distant heavens disclose that billions of galaxies of varying sizes are within the Cosmos. Through these remarkable photographs, astronomers have identified "rich" clusters of galaxies and "great" clusters of galaxies. A rich cluster contains hundreds of galaxies; a great cluster, thousands of galaxies. The Milky Way is in a cluster of about twenty galaxies.

The planet Earth is part of the Milky Way, a spiral-shaped galaxy with approximately two-hundred billion stars. The number of stars in the Milky Way is small in comparison to a supergiant galaxy containing more than ten trillion stars.

All galaxies in the Cosmos are moving at incredible rates of speed. The Milky Way is traveling 1.3 million miles an hour. The Sun and its planets, located on the rim of the Milky Way, are part of this continuous movement and velocity. The Earth, as a spinning planet, is traveling 66,600 miles an hour during its orbit around the Sun.

The Great Teachers of the East and the West have spoken of the *eternal* and the *everlasting*. All Sacred Scriptures contain dynamic passages related to the eternal and the everlasting. Perceptive scientists in the world today are contemplating words such as *infinity,* an *expanding universe,* the *relativity* of Time and Space. Mankind now stands on the threshold of new eras of understanding regarding the eternal, the everlasting and the infinite. A **Cosmos Logic** is coming to birth in the minds of men. This Logic is the flowering forth of the wisdom-seeds planted by the Great Teachers—a wisdom based on their knowledge of eternal life.

The pure logic of eternal life, as a laser-like light in the consciousness, activates powerful breakthroughs in understanding and in creative expression. Through this extended and perceptive logic, one sees life on earth as a priceless opportunity to increase his knowledge of Eternal Truths and

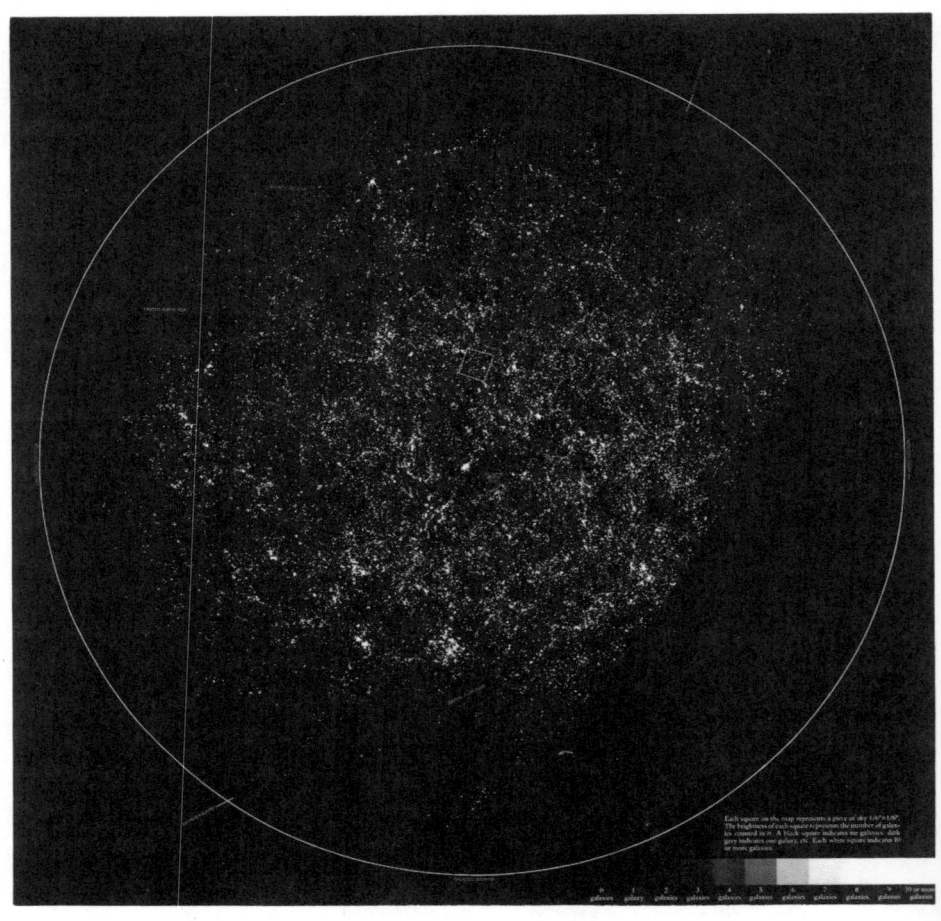

Computer photo-map* of one million *galaxies*. This view of the heavens was taken by telescope from Earth's Northern Hemisphere. Galaxies form in clusters, super clusters and super super-clusters.

---

*Courtesy of the Co-Evolution Quarterly, Sausalito, California and P. James E. Peebles of Princeton University, Princeton, New Jersey.

Universal Laws, and to increase his degrees of love and virtues.

The closest star and the farthest star known to mankind are within the One Plan of God. The consciousness mind of man is being prepared by the Creator to discover great secrets of Cosmos Creation. The clues to each discovery related to the Glory of God in the Cosmos are concealed within Virtues. Even as a high-powered telescope reveals new and greater ranges of the Universe, so do sanctified virtues act as high-powered telescopes through which the consciousness mind may perceive Cosmos Truths and Eternal Verities.

Over the centuries the Great Teachers, Saints and Sages of the East and the West have sought to inspire their fellow men to live according to spiritual laws, virtues and ethics. In the present era, the knowledge of sacred statutes and moral precepts is leading the human spirit to a scientific-spiritual understanding of Time, Space and the Universe.

The Commandments revealed by Moses and Jesus are the *Rosetta Stone* for mankind's decoding the hieroglyphics of the heavens. Each Commandment is a law of harmony seeking to unite life on earth with the Intelligence of God creating the stars and the galaxies.

Man lives in a Morality Universe, a Righteousness Universe, a Truth Universe, a Universe of Love-Energies— therefore, all Great Teachers emphasized the importance of Morality, Righteousness, Truth and Love. When these mighty principles direct one's life, he is lifted to higher plateaus of understanding from which he can view the Earth and the Cosmos as *One* in God.

THE STARS

Two things fill the mind with ever new and increasing wonder and awe—the starry heavens above me and the moral law within me.
—Immanuel Kant

Let your soul stand cool and composed
Before a million universes.
—Walt Whitman

Heaven's ebon vault
Studded with stars unutterably bright.
—Shelley

Silently one by one, in the infinite meadows of heaven,
Blossomed the lovely stars, the forget-me-nots of the angels.
—Longfellow

If the stars should appear one night in a thousand years, how men would believe and adore, and preserve for many generations the remembrance of the City of God which had been shown. But every night come out these envoys of beauty, and light the Universe with their admonishing smile. —Emerson

The celestial order and beauty of the universe compel me to admit that there is some excellent and eternal Being, who deserves the respect and homage of man. —Cicero

Astronomy compels the world to look upwards and leads us from this world to another. —Plato

The glory of Him who moves everything, penetrates through the universe, and is resplendent in one part more and in another less. —Dante

The fact that the whole of reality is like celestial space without any differentiating attributes, radiant and pure from its very beginning, is the formation of an attitude directed toward enlightenment. —Buddha

One universe made up of all things; and one God in it all, and one principle of Being, and one Law, one Reason, shared by all thinking creatures, and one Truth. —Marcus Aurelius

The Glory of God

O ancient spirit, it is within you the cosmos rests in safety.
—Bhagavad Gita

Praise ye Him, sun and moon: praise Him, all ye stars of light.
—Psalm 148:3

Mortal I know I am, short-lived; and yet, whenever
I watch the multitude of swirling stars,
Then I no longer tread this earth, but rise to feast
With God, and enjoy the food of the immortals. —Ptolemy

Time Cycles

> Philosophy is written in this grand book—I mean the universe—which stands continually open to our gaze, but it cannot be understood unless one first learns to comprehend the language and interpret the characters in which it is written. It is written in the language of mathematics, and its characters are triangles, circles, and other geometrical figures, without which it is humanly impossible to understand a single word of it; without these, one is wandering about in a dark labyrinth.
> —Galileo Galilei
> 1564–1642

And as for the revolution of these heavenly bodies, there may very well be other principles which lie behind them.
—Aristotle

It is not for the sun to overtake the moon, nor doth the night outstrip the day. They float each in an orbit.
Muhammad
—Koran XXXVI. 40

>   All the cyclic heavens around me spun.
>   —E.B. Browning

The Sun came to birth and the Earth was formed. The Earth came to birth and Mankind began its pilgrimage to Truth. Each step toward Truth is marked by the birth of a Virtue. The births of many virtues herald the birth of the Conscience, Logic and Love. With the births of the Conscience, Logic and Love, the Gifts of the Soul and the Spirit come to birth. With the births of the Gifts of the Soul and the Spirit, Man works with the Creator toward the time of birth for a new Sun and a new Earth.

> For as the new heavens and the new earth, which I will make, shall remain before me, saith the Lord, so shall your seed and your name remain.
>   —Isaiah 66:22

> Nevertheless we, according to His promise, look for new heavens and a new earth, wherein dwelleth righteousness.
>   —2 Peter 3:13

> And I saw a new heaven and a new earth: for the first heaven and the first earth were passed away.
>   Saint John the Beloved
>   —*Revelation 21:1*

The creation of Man in the Image of God is based upon a mathematical system of Time Cycles. The galaxies and their stars are being created through Celestial or Galaxy Cycles. Each Celestial Cycle is part of the Ongoing Spirit of God, ever expanding, creating, perfecting. The creation of the Milky Way Galaxy is in perfect harmony with the creation of all other galaxies.

The creation of Man through Galaxy Cycles and Solar Cycles is one of movement and energies. All stars and galaxies in the Cosmos are synchronized in their movements and energies. This perfect synchronization is occurring through interrelated and harmonious Cycles. Each galaxy is cycling around a central axis; each star has its individual Cycle within the Galaxy Cycle. The Cycle of the planet Earth is moving in perfect harmony within the Cycle of its Sun and the Cycle of the Milky Way Galaxy. Man is being shaped, formed and enlightened by these mathematical energy-processes and cyclic harmonics.

The life-span of each star is governed by the Laws of God that determine its purpose and placement in the Cosmos. These immutable Laws establish the numerous Cycles through which the star fulfills its functions as a radiating light in the Universe.

The creation of each solar system in the Universe is *holy,* for God, the Universal I Am, is holy. The movement of each Galaxy, Star, Moon and Planet in the Universe is *sacred;* therefore, the movement of Life on Earth is sacred.

Enlightenment begins for man on Earth when his consciousness mind identifies with the Laws and Commandments revealed by the Great Teachers. With each identification of Holy Law, Divine Virtues experience a process of birth and illumination. Gradually, the Presence of God within Divine Virtues prepares the heart and the mind to comprehend and to experience the sacredness and the holiness of Cycles.

The Path of Virtue is one of Cycles within Cycles: Dedication Cycles, Worship Cycles, Sabbath Cycles, Sacrament Cycles, Soul Cycles, Holy Ghost Cycles, and other Sacred Cycles. Through faith in God and reverence for His Laws, one's life comes into harmonious accord with all Galaxy Cycles and all *Commandment Cycles.* Each Commandment of God is a cyclic Law fulfilling an important role in the creation of the Cosmos and in the creation of Man as a child of the Cosmos.

Virtues progress in Cycles due to the cyclic nature of God's Holy Laws. Each time one fulfills a major Commandment, his virtues are naturally and automatically expressed in devotion to God; the Creator, in turn, anoints, quickens and expands the virtues being used in service to Him.

The Sun, a medium-sized star, has completed the first half of its Life Cycle.* For milleniums, the Sun has provided its energies for the evolution of all forms of life on Earth. During the remaining ages and epochs, mankind will utilize the Sun's life-giving energies through evolutionary expansions of Love, Virtues, Conscience and Logic. These expansions will occur through the flawless and uninterrupted action of the Time Cycles.

500-YEAR CYCLES

c. 3000 B.C.	City-states first established in southern Mesopotamia.
c. 2500 B.C.	The building of the Great Pyramid of Giza. Height of the Indus Valley culture. Golden Age of Ur.
c. 2000 B.C.	Birth of Abraham, Patriarch and Founder of the Hebrew nation.
c. 1500 B.C.	Aryan invasion of India.
c. 1000 B.C.	Kingdom of Israel established. Reigns of David and Solomon. Vedic period in India.
6th Century B.C.	The flowering of the Babylonian and Persian empires. The time of Pythagoras and Heraclitus in Greece; Zoroaster in Persia; Confucius, Lao Tzu and Chuang Tzu in China; Gautama Buddha and Mahavir the Jain in India; Old Testament Prophets in Israel.

*The life of a medium-sized star is estimated to be 9–10 billion years.

5th Century B.C.	The Age of Pericles.
1st Century B.C., A.D.	Birth of the Christ. Height of the Roman empire.
6th Century A.D.	Birth of Muhammad. Byzantine empire.
1000 A.D.	Age of exploration by Vikings. First landing on North America.
1500 A.D.	Second great age of exploration. Height of the Renaissance. Cultural explosion throughout Europe.
c. 1500 A.D.	Leonardo Da Vinci. Michelangelo. Raphael. Copernicus. Columbus. Magellan. Martin Luther.
2000 A.D.	Third great age of exploration. Age of Science. Space exploration. The beginning of the Age of Niscience or Knowing: the Galaxy Consciousness.

THE MEEK AND THE GALAXY CONSCIOUSNESS

I am meek and lowly in heart.

Jesus
—*St. Matthew 11:29*

Jesus, through divine-degrees of the Virtue of Meekness, had command of miracle-producing energies and powers. As one proves meek in the sight of God, his faith, gentleness and dedication to ethics are his keys to freeing the supernatural energies of his soul and spirit.

The increasing knowledge of powerful energy resources —atomic, oceanic, solar and celestial—will require that nations and individuals learn of ethics on levels of national and cosmic comprehension. This knowledge will enable the human spirit to discern the truth of its divinity and the reality of its potentialities as sons and daughters of God.

Nations tempted to use their scientific understanding of destructive energies to annihilate or conquer other nations are deterred only by the fear of retaliation. When love and meekness replace fear on national levels, mankind will begin to take gigantic strides toward the Golden Age. In the Golden Age, the knowledge and use of Galaxy Energies will mark for man the dawn of the *Galaxy Consciousness.*

The Galaxy Consciousness—a Gift from God to humankind—will be gained through love, meekness, and the other cardinal virtues. Many centuries of Time Cycles will be required before the Galaxy Consciousness becomes a perfected instrument of discernment, perception and creation.

"And other sheep I have, which are not of this fold: them also I must bring, and they shall hear my voice; and there shall be one fold, and one shepherd." (St. John 10:16) If a devotee of the higher life—regardless of his race or religion—has meekness, conscience, purity of heart and love for God, he is a sheep of the Great Shepherd. He is working in his polarity-placement in the world to change darkness into light; to be an example to others; and to become adept in the ethical use of spiritual energies and soul powers.

"I am the door." (St. John 10:9) Jesus is the Door to the Glory of God in the Galaxies and the Eternals. He is the Door to the Glory of God within Time and Timelessness. Truth-seekers who strive to emulate the virtues of the Lord Jesus are the meek of the earth. The meek serve God as enlightened participants in the great drama of Universal Creation.

MEEKNESS

Now the man Moses was very meek, above all the men which were upon the face of the earth.   —Numbers 12:3

The Glory of God

The meek will he guide in judgment: and the meek will he teach his way. —Psalm 25:9

For the Lord taketh pleasure in his people: he will beautify the meek with salvation. —Psalm 149:4

The meek also shall increase their joy in the Lord.
—Isaiah 29:19

Seek ye the Lord, all ye meek of the earth, which have wrought his judgment; seek righteousness, seek meekness.
—Zephaniah 2:3

But thou, O man of God . . . follow after righteousness, godliness, faith, love, patience, meekness.
Saint Paul
—*1 Timothy 6:11*

Wherefore lay apart all filthiness and superfluity of naughtiness, and receive with meekness the engrafted word, which is able to save your souls. —James 1:21

The meek shall inherit the earth; and shall delight themselves in the abundance of peace. —Psalm 37:11

Blessed are the meek: for they shall inherit the earth.
Jesus
—*St. Matthew 5:5*

Time as Truth

Great is the power of truth.
—Cicero

Those who love the Truth in each thing are to be called lovers of wisdom and not lovers of opinion.
—Plato

> Above all things truth beareth away the victory.
> Apocrypha
> —*1 Esdras 3:12*

> He who harbors in his heart love of truth will live and not die, for he has drunk the water of immortality.
> —Buddha

> Teach me thy way, O Lord; I will walk in thy truth.
> —Psalm 86:11

> Buy the truth, and sell it not; also wisdom, and instruction, and understanding.
> —Proverbs 23:23

> Sanctify them through thy truth: thy word is truth.
> Jesus
> —*St. John 17:17*

The second, the minute, the hour, the day, the month, the season, the year, the decade, the century, the lesser ages and the greater ages are major factors in the Time Cycles. Through these rhythms and energies of Time, Man is being created in the Image of God. When one contemplates *Time* as a Gift from God—and lives each moment with reverence and gratitude—the Creator opens his understanding of the mysteries and secrets of Time.

Union with God as the Supreme and Absolute Truth begins with one's first serious thoughts or meditations about his present placement in the *Eternal* Plan of God. Clarity in thought enables one to see each day and night as being the Truth, each person in his life as being the Truth, each of his physical senses as being the Truth. He also perceives that

THE GLORY OF GOD 47

the theme of the Universe is *Harmony* and that this Harmony is based upon *Law*.

All spiritual Laws and Commandments revealed by the Great Teachers are Cosmos Laws of Universal Harmony. The laws of Nature are based upon cycles in perfect harmony with the Cosmos and its laws. When one contemplates the Time Cycles within Nature, he discovers his first clues to the purpose of life in the physical world and in the Cosmos.

The cycles of Nature pertain to the four seasons of the year, the twelve months of the year, the hours, minutes and seconds of each day and night. All cycles relating to one's self, Nature, and Time are *Truth Cycles*. These cycles *are*—therefore, they are Truth; they are of God. That which *Is* is the Omnipresence of God. The Creator's Omnipresence is everywhere and in everyone; His Omnipresence is revealing itself in and through each cycle being experienced by Man, the Earth, the Solar System, the Universe. Thus, he who would make a Truth-union with God turns his attention to the obvious, the seen, the known; that which is being experienced physically, emotionally, mentally and spiritually.

During one's quest for union with God as the Truth, he becomes keenly aware of the obvious cycles of Time within Truth. The cycles of Time within Truth affect the physical body, emotional nature, mental expansion and soul qualities. These different aspects of one's being are responding each moment of the day and the night to the cycles of the Sun, the Moon, the Planets, the Stars and the Galaxies.

"Thy will be done in earth, as it is in heaven." (St. Matthew 6:10) This stanza in the Lord's Prayer discloses the interrelationship between heaven and earth: As above, so below. The Eternal Spiritual—the *above*—is creating the physical in its Image. Man is being created in the Image of God; the Earth is being created in the Image of Heaven.

God, as Pure Truth, first reveals His Truth-Presence in the natural or physical world. The thread of His Truth-Presence in the physical world leads one to His Truth-Presence in the dimensions of the soul and the spirit.

Time is Truth. He who loves Truth reveres Time. And he who reveres Time unites with the One who created Time and the Time Cycles.

> A leaf, a drop, a crystal, a moment of time, each partakes of the perfection of the whole.
> —Emerson

> Time is but a stream I go a-fishin-in. I drink at it; but while I drink I see the sandy bottom and detect how shallow it is. Its thin current slides away, but eternity remains. I would drink deeper, fish in the sky, whose bottom is pebbly with stars.
> —Thoreau

> See ever so far, there is limitless space
>   around that,
> Count ever so much, there is limitless time
>   around that.
> —Whitman

> Prolific, thousand-eyed, and undecaying, a horse
>   with seven reins, Time bears us onward.
> Sages inspired with holy knowledge mount him:
>   his chariot wheels are all the worlds of
>   creatures.

> This Time hath seven rolling wheels and seven
>   naves: immortality is the chariot's axle.
> This Time brings hitherward all worlds about
>   us: as primal deity is he entreated.
> —Atharva Veda

WORSHIP

Four types of virtuous men worship me, Arjuna—the seeker of worldly objects, the sufferer, the seeker of knowledge, and the man of wisdom. But those men of virtuous deeds whose sins have come to an end, being freed from delusion in the shape of pairs of opposites, worship Me with a firm resolve in every way. —Bhagavad Gita

Gather ye in thousands, and worship God and chant His praises. —Rig Veda

The highest worship is to feel the presence of Brahman, the omnipresent Being, constantly shining. —Upanishads

O come, let us worship and bow down: let us kneel before the Lord our Maker. —Psalm 95:6

Give unto the Lord the glory due unto his name: bring an offering, and come before him: worship the Lord in the beauty of holiness. —1 Chronicles 16:29

Thou shalt worship the Lord thy God, and him only shalt thou serve.
Jesus
—*St. Matthew 4:10*

The four and twenty elders fall down before him that sat on the throne, and worship him that liveth for ever and ever, and cast their crowns before the throne, saying, Thou art worthy, O Lord, to receive glory and honour and power: for thou hast created all things, and for thy pleasure they are and were created.
Saint John the Beloved
—*Revelation 4:10, 11*

Thou, even thou, art Lord alone; thou hast made heaven, the heaven of heavens, with all their host, the earth, and all things that are therein, the seas, and all that is therein, and thou preservest them all; and the host of heaven worshippeth thee. —Nehemiah 9:6

3

WORSHIP

> Every devoted thing is most holy unto the Lord.
> Moses
> —*Leviticus 27:28*

THE DESIRE TO WORSHIP

> But the hour cometh, and now is, when the true worshippers shall worship the Father in spirit and in truth: for the Father seeketh such to worship Him. God is a Spirit: and they that worship Him must worship Him in spirit and in truth.
> Jesus
> —*St. John 4:23, 24*

The Path of Virtue is a Path of Laws, Principles, Ethics, Virtues and Daily Worship of God. Even as a blind man cannot see light, a spiritually-blind person cannot perceive wisdom in worship. As one increases in virtue, he increases in wisdom—a wisdom in earth matters and a wisdom in worship dedications.

The virtues with which one is born are priceless inheritances bequeathed to himself from past lives. During childhood, these virtues provide him with an invaluable intuition regarding the difference between right and wrong. If important virtues are weak or missing, a child or young adult is not fortified by a sense of rightness and goodness, nor does he have a desire to worship God. Each person's lessons in life during his early years are determined by the virtues present or absent.

The virtues of Jesus drew Him to two pure parents who loved and protected Him—and instructed Him in the ways of God. Each person blessed with loving parents who teach him of holy laws and virtues is richly endowed with grace of the soul earned during his past lives. If this grace manifests at birth, one is born to reverent parents devoted to God and His Truth. The example set by such parents enables his innate virtues to flower forth with naturalness and beauty during his childhood and youth.

After one's last breath in each life, the mathematical Laws of God determine the type of parents who will give him birth in his next life on earth. His physical body, emotions, mentality, reflexes, talents, skills, gifts, desires, aspirations, virtues, memory and conscience in the new life are direct results of the soul's record of his actions, feelings and thoughts in previous lives.

A love of good, a love of ethics, a love of worship, a love of God, a love of people, a love of animals and a love of Nature denote that one has earned a number of key virtues in former lives—and these light-filled virtues are producing sweet fruits in the present life. When there is true and pure love, all virtues are present in the heart and mind; it is this love that a devotee gives as his most holy gift to God.

The *year* of one's life when he first turns to the Almighty contains an important clue to understanding the past lives that are influencing his present-life attitudes and decisions. All painful trials previous to the time one turns to God are his soul's ways of urging him to walk the Path of Virtue toward union with the Creator. These soul-promptings occurring through various crises seek to awaken beauty's light within his consciousness, that he may know in heart and mind that union with the Beauty of God is the true goal in life.

If one turns to God during childhood, adolescence, young adulthood, his middle years, or later in life, he is responding to a rhythm and desire established in former lives. Whenever this important cycle reasserts itself in his present life, he experiences the return of memory-cells that reawaken in him the desire to worship God. In many instances, the desire to worship God does not occur until one experiences pain, suffering, affliction, sorrow, loneliness or loss by death. *The soul uses whatever means is necessary in order to place one's feet on the Path of Virtue and Illumination.*

After one begins the daily worship of God, his lessons in life pertain to his attaining the higher degrees of the virtues. The soul assists the devotee by sending its grace-essences into his heart and mind during the Cycles of sleep and dreaming and during Daily Worship-Cycles of prayer and meditation. Gradually, a sincere devotee is prepared to receive the sacred anointings of Divine Grace that open his understanding of the Kingdoms of Heaven and their Mediation-Host.

> Heaven means to be one with God.
> —Confucius

> O Thou great incomprehensible God. Who fillest all, be Thou indeed my heaven. Let my spirit be indeed the music and the joy of Thy spirit. Do Thou make music in me and may I make harmony in the Divine Kingdom of Thy joy, in the great love of God, in the wonders of Thy glory and splendour, in the company of Thy holy angelic harmonies.
> —Jacob Boehme
> 1624 A.D.

> Exalt us with Thee, O Lord, to know the mystery of life, that we may use the earthly as the appointed expression and type of the heavenly, and by using to Thy glory the natural body may befit it to be exalted to the use of the spiritual body.
>
> —Charles Kingsley
> 1819–1875 A.D.

VIRTUE-CLUSTERS

> Giving birth and nourishing,
> Bearing yet not possessing,
> Working yet not taking credit,
> Leading yet not dominating,
> This is the Primal Virtue.
>
> —Lao Tzu

While hundreds of millions of persons living in the world have no desire to worship God, there are multitudes who heed the instruction of the Great Teachers to reverently worship and serve the Creator. When one desires to worship God, the energies of the Virtues of Faith, Reverence, Devotion, Dedication and other cardinal virtues are present and active in his heart and mind. These important virtues operative during worship form a beauteous *cluster* of virtues. As one purifies his love, the energy-fields of these powerful virtues and correlating virtue-clusters are expanded and extended.

Even as God creates stars and galaxies in clusters, so does He create virtues in clusters. The consciousness mind of man may be likened to the sky with its scintillating stars. Virtues are the stars in one's consciousness—and, as stars, produce energy and light. However, even as voids are in the Cosmos-sky, so may there be voids in the

Consciousness-sky. Each void in the Consciousness-sky is yet to be filled by the energy and light of a starlike virtue. As each virtue-void is transformed into a starry light in the consciousness, its light is brightened by correlating virtues in its cluster.

When the Spirit of God energizes a void in the Cosmos, a new star undergoes the process of birth—from an unformed or uncongealed energy mass into a mighty light illuminating the heavens. When the Spirit of God energizes a void in the consciousness, a new virtue experiences different stages of birth—until the void becomes filled with the blazing light of an Illumined Virtue.

If many virtue-voids are in the consciousness, one behaves, thinks and feels in ways that are harmful to himself and to others. Even as the light of many stars contributes to the birth of a new star, so does the virtue-light of one's fellow men contribute to the birth of new virtues in his consciousness mind and heart.

From time to time, the Creator sends to the earth enlightened personages whose hearts and minds are filled with the light of Illumined Virtues. These enlightened individuals become the Great Teachers of mankind, guiding the human spirit toward the highest and noblest values of each virtue.

A person's desires, attitudes and goals in life are due to the virtue-clusters present or absent in his consciousness. The Spirit of God quickens individual virtues and virtue-clusters through the mathematical process of *Initiations*. Each Initiation is a necessary step in one's birth to virtues, conscience, logic, love, and soul-skills.

If one has worshipped God in many previous lives, the luminous energies of Faith, Reverence, Devotion, Dedication and other radiant virtues are integral parts of his basic nature. As each cluster of cardinal virtues increases its energization of the heart and the mind, the flow of light and grace from the soul becomes an expanding source of strength, healing and inspiration.

If certain virtue-clusters have yet to become energy-presences in one's being, he is naturally atheistic, agnostic, irreligious, nonreligious or anti-religious. When these virtue-clusters make their appearance in the heart and mind, one becomes a reverent worshipper devoted to God and His Commandments.

While there are virtue-clusters that fill one with the desire to worship God, there are other virtue-clusters that produce a moral conscience, a giving heart, and a sacrificial love for mankind. Each virtue-cluster fulfills an important function in the creation of man in the Image of God. The purpose of life on earth pertains to the quickening and illuminating of all virtue-clusters related to all aspects of man's physical and spiritual life.

Each cardinal virtue—such as Reverence, Humility, Honesty, Integrity, Character, Sincerity, Gratitude, etc.—is part of a virtue-cluster. When the various starlike clusters of virtues are activated by the Spirit of God, they become receivers and transmitters of the soul's grace and Divine Grace. Through the combined action of numerous virtue-clusters, one lives in a state of expanding grace blessed by the Creator.

An enlightened teacher of the higher life presents to his students the knowledge of holy laws, virtues and worship-procedures. If an alert student applies this instruction with love and dedication to God, all virtue-clusters begin an immediate activation in his heart and mind—and the aspirant makes rapid progress on the Path of Virtue toward the first stages of Illumination.

"Ask, and it shall be given you." (*St. Matthew 7:7*) Progress on the Path is accelerated each time a devotee reverently

asks God that he be spiritually quickened so that he may better serve Him. Spiritual quickenings gained through worship combined with selfless asking manifest the ever-increasing light of important virtue-clusters.

". . . whatsoever ye do, do all to the glory of God." (1 Corinthians 10:31) The moment one desires to do all things for the Glory of God, he begins to unite with the Glory of God. The Glory of God is powerful in its Sweetness and awesome in its Beauty and Truth. A sincere devotee seeks to qualify for union with the holiness and righteousness of God's Glory. Each step of progress toward this supernal goal is timed according to the virtue-clusters being quickened in his heart and mind.

> Persons who are so devoted to Me that their whole heart and mind go unto Me without thinking of anything else, they who worship Me in all beings and meditate on Me: out of grace I guard what they have and I secure what they have not; their welfare is assured through Me.
> —Bhagavad Gita

The Freedom of Worship

> Worship is transcendent wonder.
> —Carlyle

> Worship the Lord in the beauty of holiness.
> —Psalm 29:2

Each race, religion, nation and family has a potential spiritual-creative uniqueness and beauty sealed into it by the Creator. Through the expression of virtues, the latent uniqueness and beauty are discovered and manifested in remarkable ways of creativity, charitableness, compassion and love. The worship of God by a race, religion, nation or family provides the reverent atmosphere in which virtues flourish, freedoms manifest and pure-creations abound.

Divine laws determine the placement of each house of worship in the world. These laws preserve the knowledge of God's Word from generation to generation, century to century, age to age. Whenever one experiences a compelling desire to worship the Almighty, he is guided by the perfect Law of Attraction to the worship-home that will answer his devotional needs.

The desire to worship God is being fulfilled in the numerous churches, temples, sancturaries and synagogues protected by God's Love and filled with His Presence. Each house of worship is mathematically positioned by the Creator in nations and communities where individuals are experiencing the birth of virtues and the birth of the conscience related to the freedom of worship and other freedoms.

The Hand of God may place one in a nation governed by despots and tyrants or in a nation graced with religious and spiritual freedoms. If one is humbly grateful to God for the freedom of worship and for all other freedoms—a gratitude spoken often in his prayers—he works toward the day when all nations will experience the rare grace of sacred freedoms.

There is a vast difference between ingratitude and gratitude to God. To be ungrateful, careless or neglectful regarding the freedom of worship is to lose the freedom of worship, either in the present life or in coming lives. Gratitude for each spiritual freedom—when accompanied by Humility, Reverence and Love—gives one the peace of serene contentment that comes with a trust in God to bless his present life and all lives to come.

Men will be ruled by God or ruled by tyrants.
—William Penn

And what greater calamity can fall upon a nation than the loss of worship.
—Emerson

Sabbath Cycles

Remember the Sabbath Day, to keep it holy.
Fourth Commandment
—Exodus 20:8

And it shall come to pass, that, from one new moon to another, and from one Sabbath to another, shall all flesh come to worship before me, saith the Lord.
—Isaiah 66:23

The Sabbath-Day Commandment of worship is based upon a seven-day Time Cycle mathematically synchronized with the Soul's Grace and Divine Grace. As one establishes the rhythm of Daily Worship-Cycles and the Sabbath-Day Worship-Cycle, he comes into timing with the Clockwork of Universal Creation. Each New Moon becomes a time of New Beginning; each Full Moon, a Time of Harvesting or Reaping.

If one has sown seeds of love for God over many lifetimes, the sacred cycles of New Moon to Full Moon and Full Moon to New Moon manifest many surprise blessings of Grace and Truth. These beautiful blessings wash upon the shore of his life and consciousness in tides of grace activated and perpetuated by Sabbath-Day Worship-Cycles.

70-YEAR LIFE-SPAN

MONDAY	TUESDAY	WEDNESDAY	THURSDAY	FRIDAY	SATURDAY	SUNDAY
10 YEARS	10 YEARS	10 YEARS	10 YEARS	10 YEARS	10 YEARS	10 YEARS

A person who reaches the age of 70 has lived 10 years on each Day of the Week. Union with the Glory of God in *Time* is determined by one's dedication to Daily Worship-Cycles and Sabbath-Day Worship-Cycles.

The Glory of God within Time is sealed into each Day of the Week: Monday, Tuesday, Wednesday, Thursday, Friday, Saturday and Sunday. Each Day has its unique Glory. When one begins to make union with the Glory of God within each of the seven Days, he is blessed with powerful illuminations related to Time, the Commandments and the Cosmos.

Each Commandment is based upon the cyclic Law of Sowing and Reaping: The Law of Cause and Effect or Karma (Deeds). Whatever one sows in his use of Time, he reaps—from day to day, year to year and life to life.

> Be not deceived; God is not mocked: for whatsoever a man soweth, that shall he also reap.
> Saint Paul
> —*Galatians 6:7*

> What you sow that will you reap.
> —Buddha

The Sabbath, hallowed by the Creator with a special blessing, contains the spark of holy fire that frees into one's life the Glory of God within the seven Days of the

Week. The Sabbath spark unites one with the Illuminating Glory of God within the Commandments and within Virtues.

Union with the Glory of God within the Sabbath Day is necessary before one can ascend the Pyramid of Time to the apex-points of Illumination. The Glory of God within the Sabbath Day is a mighty dynamo of spiritual light and power that sends its creation-energies throughout the other Days of the Week.

The Sabbath Day for Moslems (Friday), Hebrews (Saturday) and Christians (Sunday)* is kept as a memorial feast of the Creation. The followers of Jesus also observe the Sabbath as a memorial of the Resurrection.

The Sabbath-Day Commandment is a powerful law with far-reaching consequences in the life of the individual, his family, nation and religion. Complacency, carelessness or wilful disobedience regarding this mandatory statute attract many penalties, sorrows and afflictions. The reverent and obedient Truth-seeker observes each Sabbath-Day as a love-tryst with God; in this, he receives the priceless blessings of freedom, grace and spiritual enlightenment.

In the sin of adultery, one is unfaithful to his mate. In the failure to worship on the Sabbath Day, one is unfaithful to God. The sins of adultery in marriage and unfaithfulness to God on the Sabbath Day stain the soul's record and produce pain and suffering in one's self, his loved ones and in the world.

The freedom of worship is difficult to earn and easy to lose. Persons in a free land who fail to worship God on each Sabbath Day face the laborious task in future lives of re-earning the freedom of worship. If one reveres and cherishes the priceless freedom of worship, his coming lives will be graced with increasing measures of freedom blessed by God.

*In certain Christian denominations, the Sabbath is observed on Saturday.

The soul works through the Holy Law of Reincarnation to bring all virtues to birth. Thus, one may continue to reincarnate in atheistic or agnostic nations or families in life after life until he experiences his first heart-stirrings toward the worship of God.

"Take fast hold of instruction; let her not go: keep her; for she is thy life." (Proverbs 4:13) It is one thing to be untaught and another thing to be unteachable. To be blessed with spiritual instruction and to reject it, is to invite serious consequences for many lifetimes. If a student of the higher life learns of the importance of the Ten Commandments—and then disregards the Sabbath Cycle as a spiritual dedication—it is inevitable that the Spirit of God will harden the hearts of others toward him. This hardness of heart and other unhappy personal, marriage and family problems are healed after one proves faithful to the Sabbath-Day Time Cycle and to the other Commandments.

"Verily My sabbaths ye shall keep: for it is a sign between Me and you throughout your generations; that ye may know that I am the Lord that doth sanctify you." (Exodus 31:13) The Sabbath Day, as the *sign* of "a perpetual covenant"* between God and man, is the key to attaining sanctified virtues. Each time one enters a sanctuary of worship, the Angel of the Presence protecting the Altar blesses and anoints his soul's record. Over the years of faithful worship in the sanctuary of God, a reverent devotee receives numerous Sabbath-Day anointings by the Angel of the Presence. Through these and other sacred anointings, his virtues become sanctified instruments for communion with the Creator's Glory and Love.

> The angel of His presence saved them.
> —Isaiah 63:9

*Exodus 31:16

WORSHIP

In the present era, atheism, agnosticism, selfishness, complacency, and the pursuit of pleasure keep many persons from observing the Sabbath-Day Commandment. Through the Cycles of Time and the Holy Law of Reincarnation, God extends to each of His children endless opportunities to perceive the wisdom in worship as the door to union with His Grace and Glory.

The Lord blessed the sabbath day, and hallowed it.
—Exodus 20:11

Ye shall keep my sabbaths, and reverence my sanctuary: I am the Lord. —Leviticus 19:30

For the Son of Man is Lord even of the sabbath day.
Jesus
—*St. Matthew 12:8*

Take the Sunday with you through the week,
And sweeten with it all the other days. —Longfellow

O what their joy and their glory must be,
Those endless sabbaths the blessed ones see!
—Peter Abelard
1079-1142

On the seventh day there are spread before the people in every city innumerable lessons in prudence, justice and all other virtues . . . and so the lives of all are improved.
—Philo of Alexandria

Sunday is the golden clasp that binds together the volume of the week. —Longfellow

The Sunday is the core of our civilization, dedicated to thought and reverence—it invites to the noblest solitude and to the noblest society. —Emerson

The Sabbaths of Eternity,
One Sabbath deep and wide.
    —Tennyson

A Sabbath well spent brings a week of content,
And health for the toils of the morrow;
 But a Sabbath profan'd
 Whatso'er may be gained,
Is a certain forerunner of sorrow.
    —Sir Matthew Hale

If one does not keep the Sabbath, God will take it away.
    —Ann Ree Colton

A world without a Sabbath would be like a man without a smile, like a summer without flowers, and like a homestead without a garden. It is the joyous day of the whole week.
    —H.W. Beecher

Where there is no Christian Sabbath, there is no Christian morality; and without this, free institutions cannot long be sustained.   —McLean

The longer I live the more highly do I estimate the Christian Sabbath, and the more grateful do I feel to those who impress its importance on the community.
    —Daniel Webster

Martyrdom

  Greater love hath no man than this, that a man lay down his life for his friends.
    Jesus
    —St. John 15:13

Painting by Jonathan Murro

> And they stoned Stephen, calling upon God, and saying, Lord Jesus, receive my spirit. And he kneeled down, and cried with a loud voice, Lord, lay not this sin to their charge. And when he had said this, he fell asleep.
> —Acts 7:59, 60

Since the martyrdom of Jesus and His early Apostles, such as Saint Stephen, numerous Saints and other followers of the Gentle Shepherd-Lord have been martyred. With each martyrdom suffered in His Name, the conscience of the world has experienced a new spark of holiness. The many martyrdom-sparks of holiness are lighting inextinguishable flames in the world-conscience. From these flames will come the *Illumination* of the world.

The ending of pain, suffering and tyranny on earth will occur in direct correlation to the increasing of virtues and conscience within the human spirit. The virtue-examples of the Saints are pointing to this inevitable victory for mankind.

"Blessed are they which are persecuted for righteousness' sake: for theirs is the kingdom of heaven." (St. Matthew 5:10) All religions, races and nations have their martyred Saints, leaders and courageous individuals who have sacrificed their lives for the sake of righteousness, integrity, justice, and freedom. Those who suffer persecution, imprisonment, dismemberment or martyrdom due to their faithfulness to spiritual values and moral principles are bountifully rewarded by God in the afterlife and in coming lives.

Martyrdom, when suffered by the just at the hands of the unjust, awakens in empathetic persons the buds of conscience and accelerates the birth of virtues. Individuals who suffer martyrdom or persecution for righteousness' sake are rendering an invaluable service to the world, for they inspire others to live with more devotion to God through the expression of virtues and conscience.

The martyrdom of Jesus is a painful memory in the conscience of the world. His martyrdom is as an increasing fire in the world-conscience—a fire that will gradually burn away all that stands between the human spirit and Pure Truth.

Jesus, while suffering martyrdom, said: *"Father, forgive them; for they know not what they do."* (St. Luke 23:34) Persons whose consciences are yet unawakened "know not what they do"—therefore, they persecute and martyr the righteous. When the conscience begins to pulsate its living embers into the consciousness, the conscienceless become the conscience-stricken; the conscience-stricken, in time, begin to revere and to emulate the virtues of the one or ones they have persecuted and martyred.

A continuous procession of martyrs in nations, races and religions is marching on the Path of Virtue through the centuries and the ages. Each martyr is contributing to the birth process of virtues and conscience within the human spirit.

†Since the Crucifixion of Jesus, numerous followers of the Christ have worn the robe of Martyrdom, beginning with Saint James, the Apostle of Jesus who died under the hand of Herod Agrippa I in 44 A.D. Saint Andrew was martyred in Greece when Roman authorities tied him to a cross shaped as an X. Saint Peter was crucified head-downward in Rome.

†Saint Philip was scourged, thrown into prison, and later crucified. Saint Thomas was martyred in southeastern India. Today, certain churches in India call themselves "Thomas Christians," claiming Thomas as their founder. Saint Jude, martyred about 80 A.D., was clubbed to death; thus, paintings of this great Apostle sometimes show him carrying a club.

†Saint Matthew was martyred in Ethiopia. James the Less died a martyr's death after fruitful years of service as an Apostle. Bartholomew preached in several countries and translated the Gospel of Matthew into the language of India, the place of his martyrdom.

†Simon Zelotes was crucified in 74 A.D. Matthias, who was elected to replace Judas, was stoned at Jerusalem and then beheaded.

†Saint Mark, author of one of the four Gospels in the New Testament, was martyred in Egypt. Saint Luke, another Gospel writer, died a martyr's death in Greece. Saint Paul wore the robe and jeweled crown of martyrdom in Rome, where he was beheaded.

The early Apostles of Jesus who suffered persecution and martyrdom heralded the coming of other Saints. Many of these dedicated servants of God died a martyr's death because they refused to worship idols or to renounce their faith in God and the Christ.

†Timothy, the disciple of Saint Paul, and bishop of Ephesus until 97 A.D., was beaten with clubs by idol-worshippers, and died of the bruises two days later. Dionysius, bishop of Athens, suffered martyrdom because of his steadfast faith, as did many other followers of the Lord Jesus during the First Century.

†Saint Ignatius, Bishop of Antioch who succeeded Peter, was sentenced by the emperor to be thrown to wild beasts in the arena at Rome. In a letter to his friends, he wrote: "Now I begin to be a disciple. I care for nothing, of visible or invisible things, so that I may but win Christ. Let fire and the cross, let the companies of wild beasts, let breaking of bones and tearing of limbs, let the grinding of the whole body, and all the malice of the devil come upon me; be it so, only may I win Christ Jesus!" Shortly before his martyrdom, Ignatius said: "God's wheat am I and I shall be

ground by the teeth of the beasts, that I may become the pure bread in Christ."

†Saint Polycarp, venerable bishop of Smyrna, was told by one of his captors, "Swear, and I will release thee; reproach Christ." Polycarp answered, "Eighty and six years have I served him, and he never once wronged me; how then shall I blaspheme my King, Who hath saved me?" Saint Polycarp was tied to a stake and the stake was set afire; however, the flames encircled his body and would not touch him. Then he was stabbed in the heart and his dead body was burned.

†Saint Lucian was thrown into prison and condemned to torture for twelve days. He finished his days in prison, dying with these words on his lips: "I am a Christian."

†Saint Sebastian was an officer in the Roman army in the Third Century. He cured the sick through his prayers and led multitudes to faith in God. In his martyrdom, Sebastian was pierced with arrows and left for dead; after God raised him up again, he was beaten by clubs until dead, thus experiencing a double martyrdom.

†Saint Vincent was stretched on a rack and his flesh torn with hooks. He was bound in a chair of red-hot iron; lard and salt were rubbed into his wounds. During the cruelties inflicted upon him, his eyes remained toward Heaven.

†Saint Venantius, condemned to be scourged, was saved by an angel. While Venantius was being burned with torches and placed over a slow fire, an angel robed in white trampled out the fire and again set free the youthful martyr. The Saint was then cast into prison, where his faith was tested. The governor ordered his teeth and jaws to be broken and had him thrown into a furnace, from which the angel once more delivered him. Venantius was dragged through a heap of brambles and thorns, but again God preserved him. The soldiers were thirsty, so the Saint knelt on a

rock and signed it with a cross. A jet of clear, cool water spurted up from the spot. After this miracle in the year 250, Venantius was beheaded.

†Saint Felicitas and her seven sons were martyrs because they would not answer the command to turn away from Christ as their Lord. One son, Januarius, was scourged to death with whips loaded with plummets of lead. Two sons, Felix and Philip, were beaten with clubs until they died. Sylvanus, the fourth son, was thrown down a steep precipice. The three youngest, Alexander, Vitalis and Martialis, were beheaded, as was their mother a few months later.

†Saint Blase, first a physician, later became a servant of God. In the year 316, he was scourged and beheaded.

†When Saint Agatha refused to sin in order to save her life, the govenor of Sicily gave the order for her to have her breasts cut off. After she was miraculously healed, Agatha was rolled naked upon pieces of broken pottery. God heard her prayer for help and she passed out of the body.

†Saint Dorothy was buffeted in the face, and her sides were burned with plates of hot iron; after this, she was sentenced to be beheaded. A lawyer employed to persecute Christians asked her mockingly to send him "apples or roses from the garden of her Spouse." Before Saint Dorothy died, a little child stood by her side bearing three apples and three roses. She asked the child to take them to the lawyer and tell him this was the present which he sought from the garden of the Spouse. When the lawyer saw that the child was an angel in disguise, and the fruit and flowers of no earthly growth, he was converted to faith in the Christ—and shared in the martyrdom of Saint Dorothy.

†Saint Fulgentius was scourged around the year 508. His hair and beard were plucked out, and he was left naked, his body one bleeding sore. He did not seek revenge, saying: "A Christian must not seek revenge in this world. God knows how to right His servants' wrongs."

†The enemies of Saint John Chrysostom exposed him to hardship, cold, wet, and semi-starvation; however, his adversaries could not overcome his cheerfulness and consideration for others. Finally, he passed away with these words on his lips: "Glory be to God for all things. Amen."

†Saint Barachisius had two red-hot iron plates and two red-hot hammers applied under each arm, and melted lead dropped into his nostrils and eyes. He then was carried into prison and hung up by one foot.

†Saint Vitalis was stretched on the rack. After suffering other torments, he was buried alive.

†Saint Victor, when ordered to offer incense to a statue of Jupiter, kicked it down; the emperor ordered Victor's foot to be chopped off. The emperor then condemned him to be put under the grindstone of a hand-mill and crushed to death. After the mill broke down, Saint Victor was beheaded.

†Saint Laurence was roasted over a slow fire. He made sport of his pains, saying, "I am done enough, eat if you will." Finally, he passed into the kingdom awaiting him.

†Saint Julia was hung on a cross. Saint Agnes was beheaded. Saint Joan of Arc was burned to death. Savonarola was placed on a rack, tortured and burned to death.

The voices of all martyred Saints are never still. Their voices, testifying to the greatness of God and the mightiness of His Plan, are the voices leading the human spirit from the labyrinths of darkness into the hallowed splendor of Virtue and Truth.

> Precious in the sight of the Lord is the death of His saints.
> —Psalm 116:15

> Twelve lives as a martyr produce a perfected Saint.
> —Ann Ree Colton

He who dies for virtue does not perish.
—Plautus

Do ye not know that the saints shall judge the world?
Saint Paul
—*1 Corinthians 6:2*

LADY POVERTY HIS SPOUSE
By Saint Francis of Assisi

Behold, LORD JESUS, Poverty is the queen of virtues, for her Thou didst leave the throne of the angels and camest down to this earth; in Thine eternal love Thou hast espoused her in order to have, by her, in her and of her perfect sons. . . . When Thou camest forth from the Virgin's womb, she received Thee in the holy manger, in a stable, and during Thy sojourn in the world she deprived Thee of all things in such a manner that Thou hadst not where to lay Thy head. Inseparable companion, when Thou didst begin the battle of our redemption, she followed Thee faithfully; in the height of Thy Passion she alone stood beside Thee like a squire. Thy disciples forsook Thee and denied Thee; she did not go away, but faithfully at that time supplied Thee with the whole escort of her sisters. Even Thy Mother, who alone remained steadfastly attached to Thee and shared Thy Passion with so much anguish, Thy Mother because of the height of the cross could not reach Thee. But Lady Poverty, with all her privations, like a gentle maiden embraced Thee more chastely than ever, she was more intimately united with Thee in Thy Crucifixion. She did not furnish—will it be believed?—nails enough to pierce Thee; they were neither sharp nor polished; she prepared but three, and they were rough, big and blunt to make Thee suffer more. And while Thou were dying of thirst, this faithful spouse took care that Thou shouldst be denied even a little water, and that impious soldiers should offer Thee a draught so bitter that far from drinking it scarcely wouldst Thou taste it. Thou didst give up Thy soul in the close embrace of this spouse. But, faithful spouse, she did not leave Thee at the scene of Thy burial; sepulchre, spices, linen, she only allowed you what was borrowed. Neither was this most holy spouse absent from Thy resurrection; she rejoiced in Thy kisses when Thou didst rise gloriously from the tomb, leaving there what had been given or lent. Thou didst take her with Thee to the skies, leaving to the world all that is of the world. And then to Lady Poverty Thou hast given the seal of the kingdom of heaven wherewith to mark those beings who desire to walk in the way of perfection.

GOD

God is a Spirit. —Jesus of Nazareth

God is Love. —Saint John the Beloved

God is a sea of infinite substance. —Saint John of Damascus

God is that, the greater than which cannot be perceived.
—Saint Anselm

God is truth and light his shadow.

God is a geometrician. —Plato

God, under whose guidance everything proceeds. —Seneca

God, the ruler of all. —Tacitus

There is nothing which God cannot effect. —Cicero

His being cannot be accurately described by any of the names we call Him. —Hermes

Since God is the universal cause of all Being, in whatever region Being can be found, there must be the Divine Presence. —Saint Thomas Aquinas

This is the goodness of God: He bestoweth it on whom He will: God is of immense goodness! —Muhammad

Put God behind everything. —Buddha

Who denies God, denies himself. Who affirms God, affirms himself. —Taittiriya Upanishad

Now unto the King eternal, immortal, invisible, the only wise God, be honour and glory for ever and ever. —Saint Paul

4

THE SECRET OF THE SAINTS

Let the saints be joyful in glory.
—Psalm 149:5

The Sacrament-Light of the Soul

> The world is imprisoned in its own activity, except when actions are performed as worship of God. Therefore you must perform every action sacramentally, and be free from all attachments to results.
>
> —Bhagavad Gita

All Saints in heaven and on earth have attained union with the Glory of God through the sacramental use of the energies apportioned to them by the Creator. When one becomes a protege of the ascended Saints in heaven, his eyes begin to perceive the importance of doing all things sacramentally. This inspired perception begins his union with the sacred dimensions of the Divine Presence.

The living Saints within a religion inspire their fellow worshippers to observe a loving and sacramental use of physical energies, emotional energies, mental energies, and spiritual energies. Those who follow the reverent examples of the Saints in their religion experience the Glory of God through the *sacrament-light* of their souls.

The sacrament-light of the soul and the sacrament-degrees of the virtues are one. The sacrament-degrees of the virtues are energy-charged reservoirs of wisdom, peace, love and joy. These pure degrees of the Creator's Glory within the soul and within virtues inspire the noble works, pure creations and charitable deeds of His Saints and their proteges.

As one uses life's energies sacramentally, the importance of virtues is magnified in his consciousness. This increasing magnification denotes that he is earning a high degree of union with the Glory of God within his soul. After attaining this vital stage of enlightenment on the Path of Virtue, all of one's actions on earth become sacraments; all disciplines become sacraments; all creations become sacraments.

The light of the soul is a holy, effulgent light. All soul-light degrees of *holiness* are filled with a fulness blessed by God. Thus, when a devotee is at one with the sacrament-light of his soul, he is rewarded with full measures of grace and truth. *"And of His fulness have all we received, and grace for grace."* (St. John 1:16)

When one unites with the sacrament-light of the soul, he knows with an inspired certainty that life is sacred and that all souls created by God are precious. This knowing produces a reverence that unites him with the Presence of God in the souls of others—and he is able to work efficaciously for their healing good. Through the sacrament-light of the soul, one's prayers for those in need are answered on soul-grace levels of answering—and miracles occur!

The Creator moves each of His children from life to life, age to age, trial to trial, victory to victory, until the sacrament-light of the soul is free to fill the heart and the mind.

When the sacrament-light of the soul is free, the Presence of God becomes an *abiding* Presence—and the Door opens to new expanses of logic and love within the Glory of God.

The holy joys and sacred ecstasies experienced by the Saints and their proteges are virtue-joys and virtue-ecstasies attained through union with the sacrament-light of the soul. The sacrament-light of the soul is a prophetic light, a light of realization and revelation, a light illuminating one's way into an enlightened understanding of God's Holy Laws. Through the sacrament-light of the soul, one moves into the deeper waters of God's Laws, where may be found the priceless treasures of Pure Truth.

The sacrament-light of the soul produces holy inspirations, dynamic realizations and radiant revelations related to the Presence of God and His Eternal Plan. The Saints bask in this light of holiness, enlightenment and illumination—and the crosses they carry become light through the sacrament-light of their souls.

Whenever a Saint on earth makes a sacrifice, he does not consider it to be a burden; to him, the sacrifice is a joy, an expression of his love for God and the human spirit. To a Saint, sacrifice, self-denial, humility and renunciation are pure joy, for the sacrament-degrees of these virtues are soul-degrees of joy, wisdom and inspiration.

> The ETERNAL, the all-permeating, is ever present in sacrifice.
> —Bhagavad Gita

> The only true religion is sacrifice and humility.
> —Ann Ree Colton

The Presence or Glory of God within the sacrament-degrees of the virtues rewards the Saints of the East and the West with fulness-anointings of grace and truth. When a devotee of the higher life seeks to express all virtues sacramentally with love for God and for his fellow man, he has in his hand the Saint's key to a fruitful and illuminative union with the Creator.

Creative mastercraftsmen in the worlds of music, art and literature—drawing their inspiration from the exalted virtues of Jesus and the Saints—have blessed the earth with their beautiful inspirations and creations. These dedicated individuals expressed with naturalness the higher or sacrament-degrees of one or more virtues; thus, their works and words contain a soul-beauty that continues to inspire each new generation.

Johann Sebastian Bach was graced with prolific musical compositions that testify to his faith in God and his love for the Lord Jesus. At the beginning of each page of manuscript, Bach wrote the initials J.J., for the words *Jesus Juva*—Jesus help me! On the final page of each composition, he wrote S.D.G., the first letters in *Soli Deo Gloria*—To God alone the Glory!

Bach, a genius of music, was also a genius of humility. His beautiful, innovative music is a direct result of his expressing the sacrament-degrees of the Virtue of Humility. *"God . . . giveth grace unto the humble." (James 4:6)*

The dedication of Dr. Albert Schweitzer to minister to poverty-stricken natives in Africa stemmed from his philosophy of "reverence for life." His inspired understanding of reverence embraced all forms of animal, insect and plant life as well as human life. The sacrament-degrees of the Virtue of Reverence enabled Dr. Schweitzer to express himself as a versatile craftsman in several fields of creative-spiritual endeavor.

> Reverence for Life contains in itself resignation, an affirmative attitude toward the world, and

ethics—the three essential elements in a philosophy of life, as mutually interrelated results of thinking.

Having its origin in realistic thinking, the ethic of Reverence for Life is realistic, and brings man to a realistic and steady facing of reality.

The ethic of Reverence for Life is the ethic of Love widened into universality. It is the ethic of Jesus, now recognized as a logical consequence of thought.
—Albert Schweitzer

The way of reverence and righteousness is the way of harmlessness. From the reverence of Ikhnaton of Egypt to Saint Francis of Assisi to Mohandas K. Gandhi of India, a line of *harmless ones* has continued to grace the earth with their gentleness and wisdom. These and other saintly souls are noble examples of the exalted or sacrament-degrees of the mighty Virtues of Harmlessness and other beautiful Virtues.

> Be ye therefore wise as serpents, and harmless as doves.
> —Jesus

> Moreover, brethren, though robbers, who are highwaymen, should with a two-handed saw carve you in pieces limb by limb, yet if the mind of any one of you should be offended thereat, such an one is no follower of my gospel.
> —Buddha

> In the presence of him who has perfected harmlessness, all enmity ceases.
> —Patanjali

> Nothing is so strong as gentleness; nothing so gentle as real strength.
>
> —Saint Francis de Sales

The Path of Virtue presents each aspirant with many tests and trials related to Reverence, Righteousness, Harmlessness, and the other cardinal virtues. Each initiatory trial is seeking to lift a Truth-seeker closer to the divine or sacrament-degrees of the virtues. The sacrament-degrees of all virtues are as great radio-telescopes receiving the sounds and tones of the Cosmos. As these sounds and tones become decoded through one's love for God, mysteries and secrets of the Universe are perceived with a clarity blessed by the Christ.

Virtues are the stepping-stones to the stars. The sacrament-degrees of the virtues are man's true hope for communing with the Cosmos, for the energy-units of virtues are *soul* energy-units. The soul, beyond Time and Space, blesses one with spiritual gifts, skills and graces that enable him to unite with dimensions beyond Time and Space. The Door of the Soul leads to the Door of the Christ; the Door of the Christ leads to the dimensional glories of God in the inner Universe and the outer Universe.

"The Son quickeneth whom He will." (St. John 5:21) When a seeker after Truth is called, chosen and spiritually quickened by the Christ, he awakens to the reality of God's Glory within many different levels of Creation. If the Creator reveals His Glory within His Laws and within virtues, one's understanding opens regarding the beauty and purpose of Holy Laws and virtues, the mediative work of the Saints, and the importance of the Sacrament of Communion.

> And as they were eating, Jesus took bread, and blessed it, and brake it, and gave it to the disciples, and said, Take, eat; this is my body. And he took the cup, and gave thanks, and gave it to them, saying, Drink ye all of it; for this is my blood of the new testament, which is shed for many for the remission of sins.
> —Saint Matthew 26:26-28

When Jesus gave the Bread and the Wine to His disciples, He said: "*. . . this do in remembrance of me.*"* Saint Ambrose refers to the Eucharist as "the medicine of immortality." All who offer and receive the Sacrament of Communion are participating in a great Drama related to the Illumination of the heart and the mind, the overcoming of Time and Space, and the uniting of Heaven and Earth.

Each time one receives the Sacrament of Communion with reverence and gratitude, a great blessing is sealed into him. If he accepts this blessing and sealing with selfless love—*and immediately sends the blessing out into the world and into the Cosmos for God to use as He will*—he is expressing the sacrament-degrees of the Virtue of Self-Denial and other cardinal virtues. The sacrament-degrees of Self-Denial, quickened through the Sacrament of Communion, unite one with the higher states of Grace and Truth under command of the Christ.

To return all blessings to God is a wholehearted expression of love and trust; the Creator always reciprocates by rewarding His selfless devotees with blessings that continuously increase in magnitude and spiritual worth. In this, one becomes knowledgeable in the wonders of God and His Expanding Love; through His Expanding Love, God

---
*St. Luke 22:19

is creating and governing each star and galaxy in the Expanding Universe.

When one who walks the Path seeks enlightenment for self, the Path turns into slippery ice. When one seeks enlightenment so that he may better serve God and his fellow man, the Path becomes a grassy lane filled with flowers of Grace.

Every worship dedication and sacrifice observed by a devotee in the spirit of love, reverence and self-denial is rewarded bountifully by the Divine Presence. Through attitudes of self-denial and acts of restitution for past offenses, one gains the freedom to bathe and swim in the sacred waters of wisdom and revelation.

The Sacrament of Communion received in the Name of the Christ; the sacramental eating of food during each meal; sacramental meditation, prayer, fasting and alms-giving; the sacrament of dedicated creativity—these and other reverent Sacraments observed with love for God draw one steadily toward the sacrament-light of his soul. Thus, he who does all things selflessly and sacramentally is blessed by the Creator with expanding fulnesses of joy, grace and truth. This is the secret of the Saints in heaven and on earth.

> The spiritual virtue of a sacrament is like light: although it passes among the impure, it is not polluted.
> —Saint Augustine

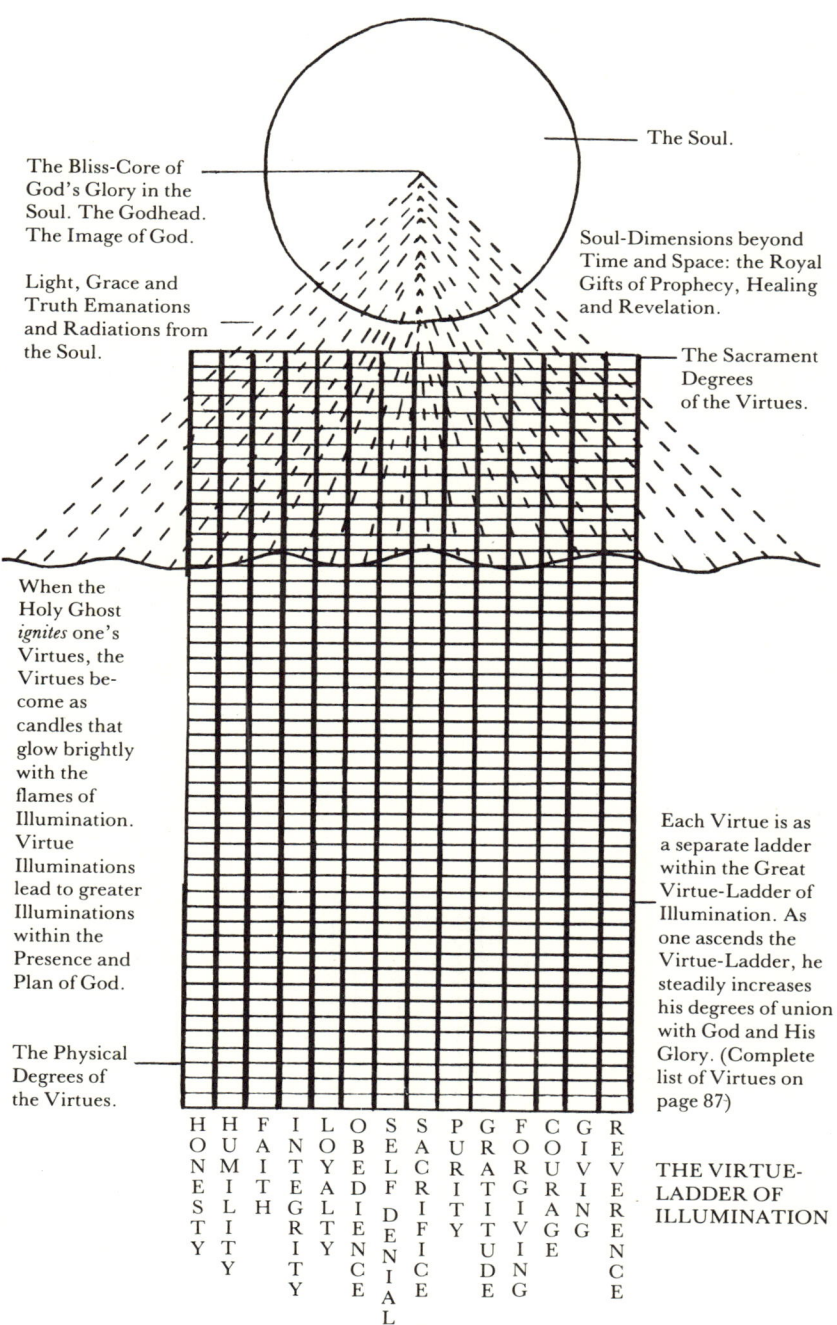

THE VIRTUE-LADDER OF ILLUMINATION

84 The Path of Virtue

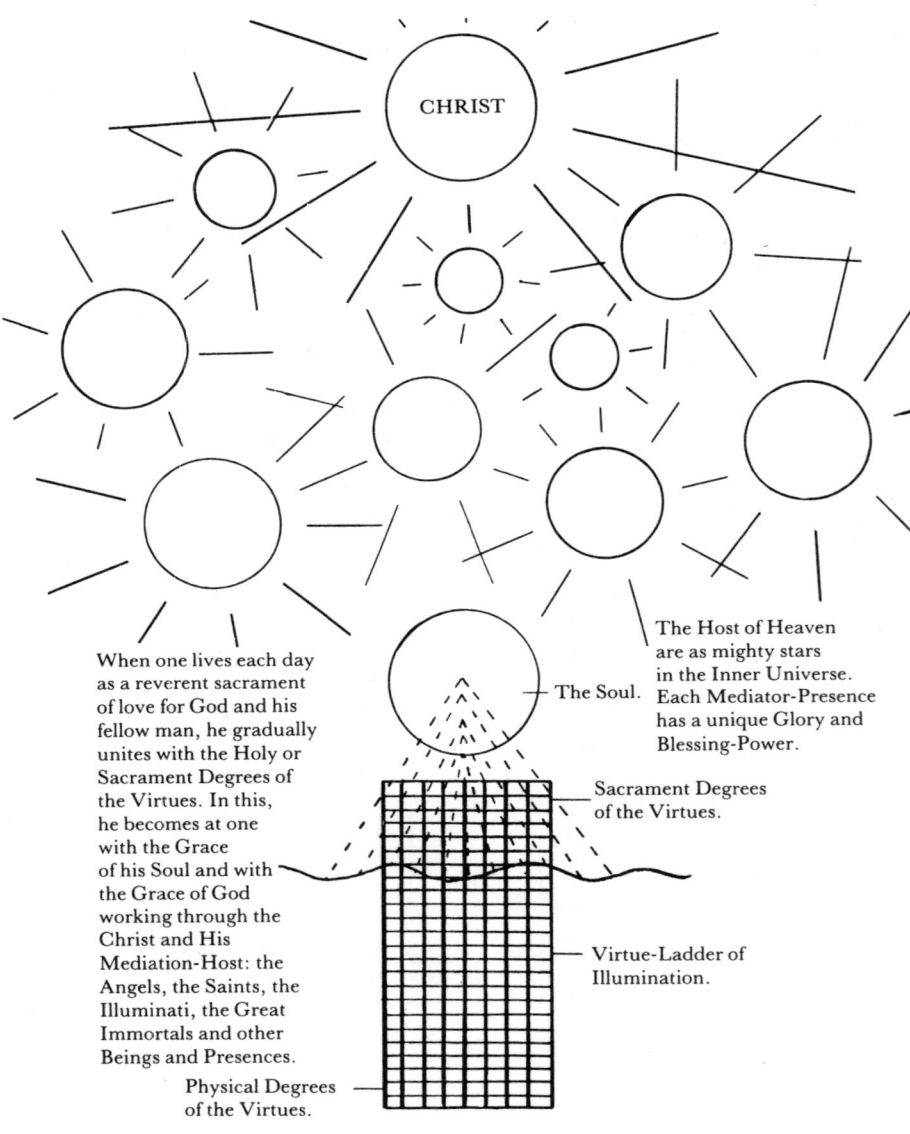

When one lives each day as a reverent sacrament of love for God and his fellow man, he gradually unites with the Holy or Sacrament Degrees of the Virtues. In this, he becomes at one with the Grace of his Soul and with the Grace of God working through the Christ and His Mediation-Host: the Angels, the Saints, the Illuminati, the Great Immortals and other Beings and Presences.

Physical Degrees of the Virtues.

The Soul.

The Host of Heaven are as mighty stars in the Inner Universe. Each Mediator-Presence has a unique Glory and Blessing-Power.

Sacrament Degrees of the Virtues.

Virtue-Ladder of Illumination.

THE MEDIATION-HOST WORKING WITH THE CHRIST

Table of Virtues and Anti-Virtues

> When a man's knowledge is sufficient to attain, and his virtue is not sufficient to enable him to hold, whatever he may have gained, he will lose again.
> —Confucius

> I cannot praise a fugitive or cloistered virtue, unexercised and unbreathed, that never sallies out and sees her adversary, but slinks out of the race, where that immortal garland is to be run for, not without dust and heat.
> —Milton

> If every year we rooted out one vice, we should soon become perfect men.
> —Saint Thomas á Kempis

> The amiableness of virtue consisteth in this, that by it all happiness is either attained or enjoyed.
> —Thomas Traherne

In the Plan of God for the planet Earth, there is a Christ and an Antichrist; there are Virtues and Anti-virtues. As man overcomes the darkness within anti-virtues, he gains the light of virtues. The Antichrist works through anti-virtues; the Christ works through virtues. The darkness within anti-virtues is mastered and overcome through Love combined with Law. All Sacred Scriptures describe this monumental drama that has absorbed mankind since its birth to consciousness.

The raw or crude energies within anti-virtues, when transformed and purified, become the powerful energies of virtues. All Great Teachers, Saints and Sages of the East and the West stress the importance of transforming pride, an anti-virtue, into the virtue of humility; selfishness, into selflessness; greed, into giving; hate, into love; dishonesty, into honesty; lust, into purity; cruelty, into compassion, etc.

Wherever there is human life—from the most primitive to the most civilized—there are codes of conduct. In some cultures, there are strict moral codes; if the knowledge of God's Laws is present, there are *Commandments* that serve as guidelines to conduct. Commandments and moral codes, when observed, provide protection from the destructive nature of anti-virtues and assure progress through the creative energies of virtues.

Meditation, Prayer, Fasting and Almsgiving—when based upon Love, Law and Virtue—are the Great Processors through which the dark energies of anti-virtues are purified and changed into refined energies used by the soul in the illumination of the heart and the mind. Meditation, Prayer, Fasting and Almsgiving are sacred sciences that lift one into the transcendent peace of Divine Grace.

Even as the element carbon experiences a slow transformation before becoming a beautiful diamond, so do anti-virtues undergo a lengthy energy-transformation process until they become diamond-like virtues. During each stage of this mighty transformation, new degrees of virtue-light are added to one's being, the human spirit and the Cosmos. Virtue-light, when dedicated to God, becomes the energy for *pure creations.* Pure creations by the hands and hearts of reverent individuals are manifestations of God's Spirit of Creation. Thus, the cycle of birth—from anti-virtue to virtue—is a vital contribution to the overall Creation of the Universe.

VIRTUES

Adaptability
Amiability
Appreciativeness
Benevolence
Carefulness
Character
Charitableness
Chaste Speaking
Chastity
Childlikeness
Cleanliness
Compassion
Congeniality
Conscientiousness
Considerateness
Contentment
Cordiality
Courage
Courteousness
Craftsmanship
Decency
Dedication
Dependability
Detachment
Devotion
Dignity
Diligence
Discernment of the True and the False
Dispassion
Earnestness
Equanimity

Ethicalness
Faith
Felicity
Fidelity
Flexibility
Forbearance
Forgiveness
Fortitude
Friendliness
Generosity
Gentleness
Giving
Godliness
Good Cheer
Goodness
Graciousness
Gratitude
Guilelessness
Harmlessness
Holy Concern
Holy Enthusiasm
Holy Poverty
Honesty
Honorableness
Hope
Hospitality
Humaneness
Humility
Integrity
Just
Keeping One's Word
Kindness

Love of Study
Love of Work
Love of Worship
Loyalty
Magnanimity
Meekness
Mercy
Mindfulness
Moderation
Modesty
Morality
Neatness
Obedience
Optimism
Patience
Perseverance
Persistence
Philosophical
Politeness
Prudence
Punctuality
Purity
Reliability
Renunciation

Reverence
Righteousness
Sacrifice
Self-Control
Self-Denial
Selflessness
Sense of Responsibility
Serenity
Simplicity
Sincerity
Stewardship
Tact
Teachableness
Temperance
Tenderness
Tranquility
Trust in God
Trustworthiness
Truthfulness
Veracity
Vigilance
Wholesome Sense of
    Humor

ANTI-VIRTUES

Adultery
Aggressive, Overly
Agnosticism
Ambivalence
Amorality
Anger
Antisocial

Arrogance
Atheism
Attachment
Avariciousness
Belligerence
Bigotry
Bitterness

Boastfulness
Brutality
Cheating
Competitive, Overly
Constant Complaining
Contemptuousness
Contrariness
Covetousness
Critical-mindedness
Cunning
Cupidity
Cynicism
Deceitfulness
Depression
Despair
Despondence
Disagreeableness
Dishonesty
Disobedience
Disrespect
Egotism
Envy
Evil
Fault-finding
Fear
Fecklessness
Fickleness
Forcefulness
Furtiveness
Gluttony
Gossip
Greed
Harmful Habits
Hate

Haughtiness
Hostility
Hypocrisy
Impatience
Impracticality
Impulsiveness
Inconsideration
Infidelity
Ingratitude
Insincerity
Intolerance
Irresponsibility
Irreverence
Irritability
Jealousy
Judging of others
Laziness
Lethargy
Licentiousness
Lust
Lying
Malice
Meanness
Mercenariness
Miserliness
Murder
Nagging Nature
Narrow-mindedness
Non-reverence
Parasiticalness
Parsimony
Perversion
Pettiness
Petulance

Possessiveness
Prejudice
Pride
Procrastination
Rapaciousness
Resentfulness
Retaliation
Revengefulness
Rudeness
Ruthlessness
Scandal-spreading
Self-delusion
Self-deprecation
Selfishness
Self-love
Self-pity
Sensuality
Sloth
Spitefulness
Stealing
Sullenness
Surliness
Uncharitableness
Unchaste Speaking
Uncleanness
Uncontrolled Tongue
Undisciplined
Unfaithfulness
Unforgiveness
Unjustness
Unlovingness
Unmercifulness
Unthoughtfulness
Untrustworthiness
Vanity
Vindictiveness
Vulgarity
Wickedness
Willfulness
Wrathfulness

O Lord, come quickly and reign on thy throne, for now oft-times something rises up within me and tries to take possession of thy throne; pride, covetousness, uncleanness and sloth want to be my kings; and then evil-speaking, anger, hatred and the whole train of vices join with me in warring against myself and try to reign over me. I resist them, I cry out against them, and say, "I have no other king but Christ!" O King of Peace, come and reign in me, for I will have no king but thee. Amen.
—Saint Bernard

THE PRAISES OF THE VIRTUES
By Saint Francis of Assisi

Hail, Queen Wisdom! The Lord save you,
   with your sister, pure, holy Simplicity.
Lady Holy Poverty, God keep you,
   with your sister, holy Humility.
Lady Holy Love, God keep you,
   with your sister, holy Obedience.
All holy virtues,
   God keep you,
   God, from whom you proceed and come.
In all the world there is not a man
   who can possess any one of you
   without first dying to himself.
The man who practices one and does not offend against
   the others
   possesses all;
The man who offends against one,
   possesses none and violates all.
Each and every one of you
   puts vice and sin to shame.
Holy Wisdom puts satan
   and all his wiles to shame.
Pure and holy Simplicty puts
   all the learning of this world,
   all natural wisdom, to shame.
Holy Poverty puts to shame
   all greed, avarice,
   and all the anxieties of this life.
Holy Humility puts pride to shame,
   and all the inhabitants of this world
   and all that is in the world.
Holy Love puts to shame all the temptations
   of the devil and the flesh
   and all natural fear.

Holy Obedience puts to shame
   all natural and selfish desires.
It mortifies our lower nature
   and makes it obey the spirit
   and our fellow men.
Obedience subjects a man
   to everyone on earth,
And not only to men,
   but to all the beasts as well
   and to the wild animals,
So that they can do what they like with him,
   as far as God allows them.

THE BIRTH OF A VIRTUE

> Let a man overcome anger by love, let him overcome evil by good; let him overcome the greedy by generosity, and a liar by the truth. For hatred does not cease by hatred at any time; hatred ceases by love, this is an old rule.
>
>   Buddha
>   —*Dhammapada*

> The real problem is in the hearts and minds of men. It is not a problem of physics but of ethics. It is easier to denature plutonium than to denature the evil spirit of man.
>
>   —Albert Einstein

In the present era, the stage of life on earth is the scene of virtues coming to birth in masses of persons. In certain periods and phases of the human experience, the slower-than-slow pace of virtue-births is a testimony to the thoroughness with which God is creating man in His Image.

The birth of a virtue is heralded in heaven as a time of utmost importance. Even as the discovery of atomic energy marked the beginning of a new era for the earth, the birth of a virtue is a new beginning for the soul—for with the birth of each virtue new energies are added to the heart and the mind.

The soul is a dynamo of dimensional energies. The Great Teachers of the past, at one with their souls, lived in the dimensional energy-worlds of understanding, prophecy and revelation. The Glory of God in their souls—freed into outer expression through love and selflessness—filled their words and works with a creative holiness radiating from starlike virtues.

A virtue, being a portion of the soul and an energy-facet of the Spirit of God, is precious. Each action, feeling and thought motivated by one's virtues becomes a light in the world of man and in the world of God. This light never dies; it continues to expand through the actions, feelings and thoughts of persons whose lives are touched by one's virtues.

Acts of charitableness, humaneness, benevolence, mercy, kindness and love add increasing measures of virtue-light to the world, for numerous persons are inspired to follow the examples of those who are expressing these and other virtues. The Creation of the Universe prospers with the birth of each new virtue within an individual called to life on Earth. The birth pains caused by each virtue-birth are quickly forgotten after the virtue begins to add its warming and wondrous light to the heart and the mind.

Even as the birth of an infant is followed by years of growth and maturing, so is the birth of a virtue followed by stages of growth until maturation is attained. The growth stages of a virtue may require many ages of time before the virtue becomes an unwavering, permanent energy-light in the consciousness mind and heart.

An individual may have all virtues except one. God will continue to send him to the world so that he might give birth to the missing virtue. This important birth may require hundreds or thousands of lives on earth before the virtue becomes an integral part of his being.

When a Great Teacher comes to the earth, he accelerates the birth-process of the cardinal virtues in the lives of individuals, nations, races and religions. Each virtue-birth adds a new degree of light to the heart and mind of the individual; a new degree of light to the human spirit as a whole; and a new degree of light to the Cosmos. The earth, centered in Cosmos, is daily adding new degrees of light to the Creation of the Universe. These new degrees of light are virtues coming to birth and virtues being expressed in varying degrees on physical and spiritual levels.

While many ages may be required for an individual to give birth to the *physical* degrees of a virtue, many additional aeons may be necessary before he frees the *spiritual* or *sacrament* degrees of the same virtue. The timing of the birth of each physical or spiritual degree of a virtue is determined by the Wisdom of God, for each virtue-birth is part of the mathematics of the Creation of the solar system in which mankind is experiencing life. The solar system and its planet Earth, in turn, are part of the mathematics of the Creation of the Cosmos.

In the higher life, one prays for patience, for through patience he gains an eternal overlook—and the billions of years marking the beginning and end of human life on earth become as small drops of water in the endless Ocean of Eternal Life and Universal Creation. Countless solar systems have created Man as he is today; innumerable solar systems will be the future homes of his soul and spirit. Only when the spiritual or sacrament-degrees of all virtues come to full maturation will the hearts and minds of men be able to comprehend the magnitude and infinitude of Everlasting Life. The Great Teachers, as Cosmos Revelators, are preparing the human spirit to attain this lofty goal within the Will and Plan of God.

> Consider your origin; you were not born to live like brutes, but to follow virtue and knowledge.
> —Dante

> We make a ladder of our vices, if we trample those same vices underfoot.
> —Saint Augustine

> There is great difference between the absence of a vice and the possession of the contrary virtue.
> —Saint Francis de Sales

> A few vices are sufficient to darken many virtues.
> —Plutarch

> The greatest minds are capable of the greatest vices as well as of the greatest virtues.
> —Descartes

> The virtues of society are vices of the saints.
> —Emerson

> To flee vice is the beginning of virtue, and to have got rid of folly is the beginning of wisdom.
> —Horace

GODHEAD

We worship with reverent silence the unutterable Truths and, with the unfathomable and holy veneration of our mind, approach that Mystery of Godhead which exceeds all Mind and Being. —Saint Dionysius

May God, the uncreated abyss, vouchsafe to call unto Himself our Spirit, the created abyss, and make it one with Him, that our spirit, plunged in the deep sea of the Godhead, may happily lose itself in the Spirit of God. —Saint Blasius

Forasmuch then as we are the offspring of God, we ought not to think that the Godhead is like unto gold, or silver, or stone, graven by art and man's device. —Saint Paul

If we fail to find God it is because we seek in semblance what has no resemblance . . . On merging into the Godhead all definition is lost. —Meister Eckhart

For in him dwelleth all the fulness of the Godhead bodily.
—Saint Paul

Love and Light build all arts and all gifts in expression. And Love alone bringeth these to the height of creation of which men shall ultimately share in the Fountainhead and Godhead.
—Ann Ree Colton

O Jesus, Thou King of Saints, whom all adore: and the Holy imitate, I admire the perfection of Thy love in every soul! . . . It is my privilege that I can enter with Thee into every soul, and in every living Temple of Thy manhood and Thy Godhead behold again, and enjoy Thy glory. —Thomas Traherne

5

THE GODHEAD

DIVINE UNION: PARABLES AND PRAYERS

> For the invisible things of Him from the creation of the world are clearly seen, being understood by the things that are made, even His eternal power and Godhead.
>
> <div align="right">Saint Paul
—<i>Romans 1:20</i></div>

Oh, Abyss! Oh, Eternal Godhead! Oh, Sea Profound! What more couldst Thou give me than Thyself? Thou art the fire which ever burns, without being consumed; Thou consumest in Thy heat all the soul's self-love; Thou art the fire which takes away all cold; with Thy light Thou dost illuminate me so that I may know all

> Thy truth; Thou art that light above all light which illuminates supernaturally the eye of my intellect, and so perfectly that I may see that my soul is alive, and in this light receive Thee—the true light.
> —Saint Catherine of Siena

The Godhead is the Eternal Wellspring from which all galaxies and solar systems draw their energies. The composite energy of all seen and unseen galaxies with their myriad stars is but a portion of the energy radiating from the Godhead. In the solar system containing the planet Earth, the energy-radiations from the Godhead are received by the human spirit as holiness, righteousness, love, light, grace and truth.

In the Sacred Scriptures, the Illumination Process is likened to one's walking a Path, climbing a Mountain, sailing an Ocean, or scaling a Ladder. Each of these parables is an ages-old picturization of the progressive steps toward union with the Godhead.

The Earth, 8000 miles in diameter, has a fiery-hot core. The different layers between the Earth's outer crust and its inner core symbolize the initiatory stages on the Path of Virtue. The fiery core of the Earth may be likened to the Bliss-Fire of the Godhead. The Scriptures of the East and the West describe the illuminations that occur upon one's reaching the jewel-like splendor of the Godhead.

From the sages of India and Tibet have come the words *Om Mani Padme Hum,* an inspired parable and prayer relating to "the Jewel in the Lotus." For thousands of years, this sacred chant has been spoken and sung by enlightened personages and by those desiring enlightenment. One interpretation of *Om Mani Padme Hum* is: Hail to the Jewel in the Lotus. The word *Om* links man with the Divine

The Godhead

Essence within the Universe. *Mani* means jewel; *padme,* in the lotus of the heart. *Hum* is the equivalent to Aum and usually occurs at the end of a mantra; it also correlates to the throat chakra from which comes forth the gift of speech.

The Jewel in the Lotus is the Godhead. Every law, principle, ethic, virtue, person and thing imaged and created by God follows and fulfills the basic pattern of a Lotus opening numerous outer and inner petals that surround the Central Jewel of the Godhead. Sincere devotees of the higher life seek to qualify for union with this mighty Jewel; through worship, purification and dedication, mysteries and secrets related to the Godhead are gradually discovered and experienced.

The Jewel in the Lotus is as an *Ocean* in its action. This vast and deep Ocean of Divine Grace has increasing intensities of power and light within its Bliss-Core. Moving outward from the Bliss-Core of the Godhead are scintillating energy-radiations of multitudinous degrees of Sacred Ecstasy. As the powerful-sweet degrees of Sacred Ecstasy move closer to the human spirit, they become gradated into countless manifestations of Holy Inspiration and Holy Joy.

When one worships God each day through sacramental meditation and prayer, his heart and mind open to the numerous joys of Holy Inspiration. Gradually, an earnest devotee qualifies for entry into the ecstasy-waters of Sacred Realization; and, in time, supernal degrees of bliss are experienced as Divine Revelation. Thus, each step on the Path is a progressive step toward the Godhead, the Central Jewel in the Lotus of Life Everlasting.

The Holy Inspirations received by a devotee on the Path of Virtue are nuggets of gold leading him to the Mother Lode of the Godhead. Holy Inspirations may be received as poems, parables, insights, new songs, beautiful thoughts, wisdom-sayings, and other forms of spiritual creation. These *touches of grace* are manifestations of the Creator's Love, rewarding and blessing the efforts of those who seek Him.

The Spirit of God reveals itself through many different kinds of Holy Inspiration, Sacred Realization and Divine Revelation. Divine Revelation signifies that one has attained the fulness of grace that comes through continuous union with the Creator. When this occurs, the Spirit of God is as a dove resting serenely in the nest of the heart.

One's progress toward the Godhead may be likened to a musician who begins by playing an instrument with one octave. As he becomes more skillful, new octaves are added. In the higher life, the first octaves relate to Holy Inspiration; when octaves of Sacred Realization are added, one's capacities and capabilities are expanded and extended. Eventually, the servant of God qualifies for union with the octaves of Divine Revelation. This high level of attainment on the Path of Virtue enables one to create works of beauty and truth that glorify God and bless the human spirit.

> We must praise thy goodness that thou has left nothing undone to draw us unto thyself. But one thing we ask of thee, our God, not to cease thy work in our improvement. Let us tend toward thee, no matter by what means, and be fruitful in good works. Amen.
>
> —Ludwig van Beethoven
> 1770–1827

> I thank Thee, my Creator and Lord, that thou has given me these joys in thy creation, this ecstacy over the works of thy hands.
>
> I have made known the glory of thy works to men as far as my finite spirit was able to comprehend thy infinity.
>
> If I have said anything wholly unworthy of Thee, or have aspired after my own glory, graciously forgive me. Amen.
> —Johannes Kepler
> Astronomer 1571–1630.
> Prayer after finishing his work on "the harmony of worlds."

From the time of early Christianity until the present day, the symbol for a dedicated follower of the Christ has been the *fish*. Individuals who apply the principles and precepts of the Lord Jesus swim as fish in the Ocean of Divine Grace.

Each devotee on the Path of Virtue may be likened to a salmon. If an aspirant is halfhearted or self-deceived, he will not apply himself to the disciplines necessary for the arduous and difficult journey toward the Godhead. If a seeker after Truth is sincerely dedicated, he will meet each obstacle with perseverance and integrity; and he will continue on his course regardless of the strong rapids or currents of the world trying to pull him in the opposite direction. Major initiatory trials require that one exert all his energy so that, as a determined salmon, he may overcome the rapids and leap up waterfalls testing the sincerity of his desire to reach the Godhead.

The salmon, on reaching its goal, spawns and dies. A devotee-initiate who is bathed and purified in the pristine Bliss-Fire of the Godhead dies to his lesser self and is born to his Higher or Selfless Self, for the Righteousness-flames of God's Holy Fire have burned away or consumed all shadows of unrighteousness within him. To stand in the Presence or Auric Glow of the Godhead is to experience the Greater Illuminations of Grace and Truth.

The Righteousness-light of God's Holy Presence presses more powerfully upon those who approach the sacred dimensions of the Godhead—thus, the closer a devotee is to the Bliss-Glory of God, the more intensive become his *Righteousness Initiations.* Each Righteousness Initiation is a test of his integrity, character, faith and love.

RIGHTEOUSNESS

But seek ye first the kingdom of God, and His righteousness; and all these things shall be added unto you.

Jesus
—St. Matthew 6:33

The Lord rewarded me according to my righteousness.

David
—Psalm 18:20

If a man each month repeat a thousand sacrifices and give offerings without ceasing, he is not equal to him who but for a moment fixes his mind upon righteousness.

—Buddha

As for me, I will behold Thy face in righteousness.

—Psalm 17:15

The company of just and righteous men is better than wealth and a rich estate.

—Euripides

THE GODHEAD

Righteousness exalteth a nation.

Solomon
—*Proverbs 14:34*

I will fetch my knowledge from afar, and will ascribe righteousness to my Maker. —Job 36:3

Mercy and truth are met together; righteousness and peace have kissed each other. —Psalm 85:10

And the work of righteousness shall be peace; and the effect of righteousness quietness and assurance for ever.
—Isaiah 32:17

And they that be wise shall shine as the brightness of the firmament; and they that turn many to righteousness as the stars for ever and ever. —Daniel 12:3

But unto you that fear my name shall the Sun of righteousness arise with healing in his wings. —Malachi 4:2

And that ye put on the new man, which after God is created in righteousness and true holiness.

Saint Paul
—*Ephesians 4:24*

And the fruit of righteousness is sown in peace of them that make peace. —James 3:18

If ye know that He is righteous, ye know that every one that doeth righteousness is born of Him. —1 John 2:29

A literal interpretation of the word *Nirvana* is "the extinction of self." On the Path of Virtue, the self that is overcome is the prodigal-son self—the lesser self. The death of the lesser self heralds the birth of the Higher or

Grace Self, which is at home in the Nirvana-degrees of the Godhead.

Each sincere devotee steadily increases his degree of righteousness through the gradual or rapid overcoming of the lesser self and the attaining of the Virtue of Selflessness and other cardinal virtues. With each increase of righteousness, he experiences new insights and inspirations related to the *Holiness* of God.

> Exalt the Lord our God, and worship at His holy hill; for the Lord our God is holy.
> —Psalm 99:9

> Wherefore the law is holy, and the commandment holy, and just, and good.
> Saint Paul
> —*Romans 7:12*

The Holy Laws and Commandments of God are Great Lights of Wisdom and Truth moving upon mankind from the Godhead. An enlightened teacher continually emphasizes to his students the importance of fulfilling each of God's Laws and Commandments with the right spirit of love, reverence and devotion, for the energy-emanations of the Divine Presence within each Holy Law provide protection, inspiration and enlightenment.

Before an aspirant of the higher life can unite with the Holiness Degrees and Dimensions of God's Presence, he must have the cardinal Virtues of Dedication, Reverence, Devotion and Faith present and active in his heart and mind. If these virtues are weak or absent, he will be unable to experience the Holiness of God, the Holiness of His Commandments, or the Holiness of Spiritual Gifts.

The Godhead

Enlightenment comes when one experiences the Holiness Degrees of God's Presence within His Commandments and within Virtues.

As one is shepherded by the Lord Jesus toward the Godhead, he becomes increasingly aware of the importance of each cardinal Commandment and each cardinal virtue. In time, the Path of Virtue and Righteousness becomes the Path of Revelation and Illumination.

Illumination prospers through love for Holy Law and love for one's fellow man. He who becomes illumined through righteousness and love is in harmonious accord with the Laws governing the Universe and with the holiness-degrees of Inspiration, Realization and Revelation radiating from the Godhead.

In modern times, many persons desiring to experience the Divine Presence are experimenting with various forms of drugs, yoga postures, meditation procedures, and other techniques. However, the only way to attain union with the Glory and Love of God is through the righteousness-light of love and virtues.

Virtues are love's voices. As one purifies his love, he unites with finer degrees of God's Love. Through continuous purifications, one's virtues become vortices of love-energies. Into these virtue-vortices, God places His Anointing Spirit—and the Truth-seeker receives the sweet nectars and sacred elixirs of Divine Love.

> May we know Thee more clearly, love Thee more dearly, and follow Thee more nearly.
> —Saint Richard

> O Lord, Thou desirest my spirit in the inward parts, that I may see Thee as Thou seest me, and love Thee as Thou lovest me.
> —Ruysbroeck
> 1293–1381 A.D.

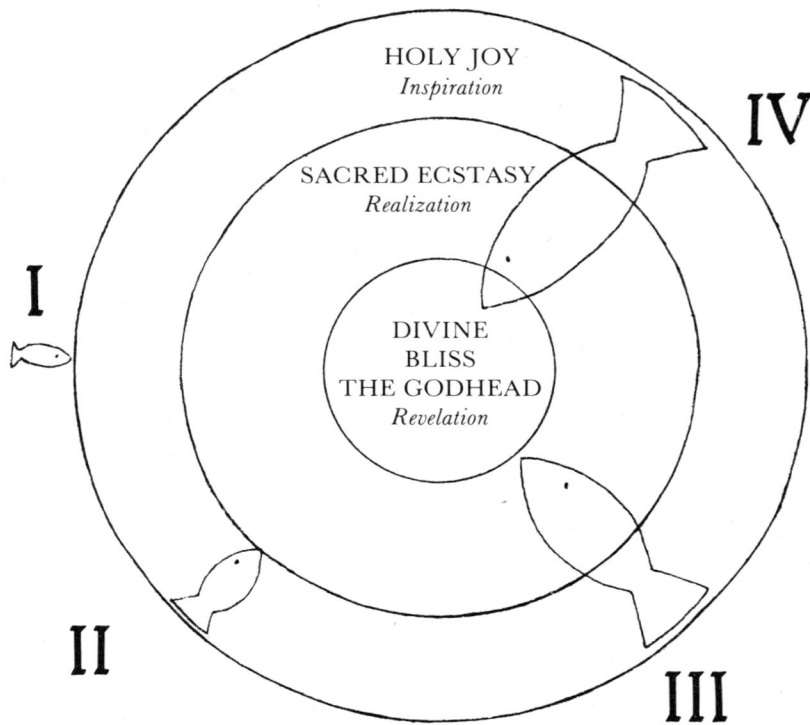

I The Fish: Symbol for the follower of Jesus. In this beginning stage, the student turns humbly toward God as a *Prodigal Son* returning to his welcoming Father.

II Through daily worship-observances and dedication to the Laws of God, the devotee becomes as a fish swimming in the Ocean of Divine Grace. The first rewards one receives on the Path of Virtue include Healings, Holy Inspirations, and other Blessings of grace manifesting through the Mercy of God.

III In this stage on the Path of Virtue, the devotee-initiate extends and expands his ranges of Holy Inspiration to the ecstasy-dimensions of Sacred Realization.

IV The Path of Virtue and Righteousness becomes the Path of Revelation and Illumination under the Grace-Mantle of the Christ. In this, one becomes a Revelator, Prophet, Healer, Teacher and Apostle *anointed, sealed* and *quickened* by the Bliss-Presence of God.

Title: *The Devotee and the Ocean of Divine Grace*

> Give me the strength lightly to bear
>   my joys and sorrows,
> Give me the strength to make my love
>   fruitful in service,
> Give me the strength to raise my mind
>   high above daily trifles,
> And give me the strength to surrender
>   my strength to Thy will with love.
> —Tagore
> 1861–1941 A.D.

O Lord, grant us to love Thee; grant that we may love those that love Thee; grant that we may do the deeds that win Thy love. Make the love of Thee to be dearer than ourselves, our families, than wealth, and even than cool weather.
—Muhammad

Beauty and the Anointing Spirit

> Pour upon us Thy Spirit of meekness and love. Annihilate selfhood in us. Be Thou all our life.
> —William Blake
> 1757–1827 A.D.

> If any man will come after me, let him deny himself, and take up his cross, and follow me.
> Jesus
> —*St. Matthew 16:24*

Every divine law, principle, ethic and virtue has its origin in the Godhead. Every element—fire, earth, air and water—has its origin in the Godhead. Every symbol, number, letter and tone has its origin in the Godhead. Every zodiacal prototype of mankind has its origin in the Godhead. When one becomes reverent toward all that *Is*, his reverence becomes the key to union with the Glory of God within all that Is; thereafter, he learns of the Beauty and Truth of God within Holiness and Righteousness.

Diverse blessings from the Godhead are transmitted to dedicated worshippers by the *Anointing Spirit* of God. The Anointing Spirit becomes an active and abiding Presence in one's life through the Virtue of Dedication and other cardinal virtues.

An enlightened Teacher prepares his students for the time when they will make full union with the multiple manifestations and versatile visitations of the Anointing Spirit of God. The Creator and His Host employ the element of *surprise* in each blessing of Anointing placed upon a dedicated devotee. The joy of surprise blessings, surprise healings and surprise inspirations is part of the many holy joys that come through union with the Love of God.

Even as God's Love is creating the Universe, so is His Joy within His Love. The joy of the masterbuilder under Christ is the joy of happy surprises and pure creations inspired by the Love within God's Anointing Spirit.

The manifold joys experienced through the Anointing Spirit of God are sweet, powerful, ever-increasing in holiness, righteousness, truth and grace. Joy-ecstasies, bliss-joys, happiness-harmonies, radiance-revelations and all other manifestations of God's Love-Presence testify to a happy marriage or union with His Anointing Spirit.

The Spirit of God opens versatility-gifts of the soul through anointings timed to the energy-processes and cycles of the Sun, the Moon and the Planets. A servant of God who proves faithful to his worship-dedications unites with the higher or pure-creation energies of the Sun, the Moon and the Planets—therefore, the anointings sealed into his heart and mind are beautiful, varied and versatile. *God is a Versatile Creator; one who unites with God becomes a versatile creator.*

The mark of God's Anointing Spirit is *Beauty:* Beauty in thoughts, beauty in feelings, beauty in actions, beauty in creations. He who lives in Beauty's Light is at one with the Anointing Spirit of God.

BEAUTY

Beauty is the gift of God. —Aristotle

Beauty is a natural superiority. —Plato

Beauty is the purgation of superfluities. —Michelangelo

Beauty is the flower of chastity. —Zeno

Beauty is part of the finished language by which goodness speaks. —George Eliot

Beauty is the mark God sets upon virtue. —Emerson

Not that which is great is beautiful, but that which is beautiful is great. —Latin Proverb

Everything has its beauty but not everyone sees it. —Confucius

He hath made everything beautiful in his time.
Solomon
—*Ecclesiastes 3:11*

Does not beauty confer a benefit upon us, even by the simple fact of being beautiful. —Victor Hugo

That Light whose smile kindles the Universe,
That Beauty in which all things work and move. —Shelley

Let the beauty of the Lord our God be upon us: and establish thou the work of our hands upon us; yea, the work of our hands establish thou it. —Psalm 90:17

Beauty is certainly a soft, smooth, slippery thing, and, therefore, of a nature which easily slips in and permeates our souls. And I further add that the good is the beautiful.
—Plato

How beautiful are the feet of them that preach the gospel of peace, and bring glad tidings of good things!
Saint Paul
—*Romans 10:15*

Grant me to be beautiful within, and all I have of outward things to be at peace with those within. —Socrates

Bliss and Revelation

In the beginning, verily, this world was non-existent. Therefore, verily, Being was produced. That made itself a Self, Therefore it is called the well-done, What that well-done is—that, verily, is the essence of existence. For truly, on obtaining that essence, one becomes blissful.
—Taittiriya Upanishad II.7

Rouse thyself! do not be idle! Follow the law of virtue! The virtuous rest in bliss in this world and in the next.
Buddha
—*The Dhammapada*

It is difficult for a man laden with riches to climb the steep path that leadeth to bliss.
—Muhammad

> The Lord thy God is a consuming fire. In truth the fire which is God consumes, to be sure, but it does not destroy. It burns sweetly. It leaves one desolate unto bliss.
>
> —Saint Bernard

Divine Bliss and Revelation are one. When one is anointed by the Bliss-Presence of God, the revelations that occur during and after each Bliss-Anointing contain the beauty of pure truth and the clear logic of inspired understanding. A Bliss-Anointing is a manifestation, visitation and *sealing* by the Spirit of God.

The reverent and sacramental use of life's energies qualify one to become anointed, sealed and quickened by the Divine Presence. The Saints in heaven and on earth prepare sincere devotees for this classic Union or Marriage with the Creator. Bliss-Anointings by the Love-Presence of God denote that a devotee's period of probation has ended and that the Divine Marriage has begun!

Before one may qualify for the Bliss-Revelation degrees of the Divine Marriage, his heart and mind must become as receptive and fertile wombs for the Anointing Spirit of God. The Saints in heaven work closely with each seeker after Truth who aspires to make pure and immaculate the wombs of his heart and mind.

The work of the Saints relates to virtues and to the soul-gifts that come through *Virtue-Illuminations*. When one begins to perceive the importance of virtues, his eyes have been opened by the gentle anointings of the Angels and the Saints. A Truth-seeker's first religious or spiritual experience occurs with his first sacred anointing. This initial anointing points him toward union with the Glory of God within the religious philosophy to which he is attracted.

The archetypal Glory of God within one's religion begins to reveal its splendor through various anointings that move a sincere devotee toward the bliss-core of certain universal truths. Gradually, through the mediative assistance of the Angels and the Ascended Saints, he becomes polarized and centered within Holy Laws and virtues. This important polarization and centering is achieved through progressive anointings that steadily increase his volume of creative productivity for God.

The closer one comes to the Glory of God within his own religion, the more he fuses or unites with the wisdom-essences of the Creator within other religions. The Saints' healing ministrations and sweet benedictions work to release him from bondage to conscious and subconscious prejudices toward the religions of others. Freedom from religious prejudice is required before one may qualify for union with the Eternal Spirit within the human spirit.

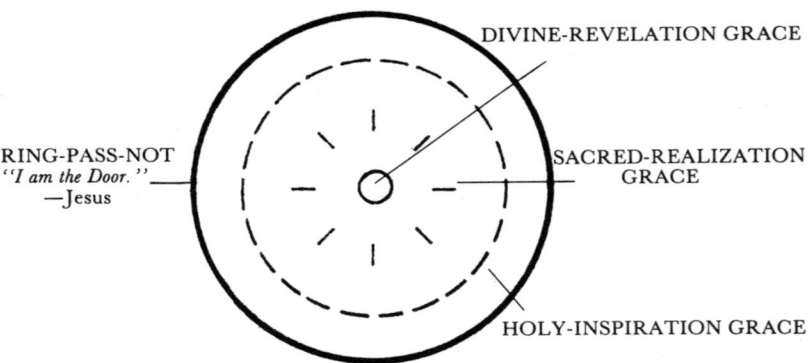

A mighty *Ring-Pass-Not* provides an invisible barrier that prevents the unrighteous, the self-deceived and the unteachable from entering the sacred waters of the Ocean of Divine Grace. Jesus, the Great Shepherd, lifts His faithful followers over this Ring-Pass-Not so that they may discover the Treasures of Illumination within the Godhead.

Joy-Anointings and Ecstasy-Anointings by the Spirit of God produce vital breakthroughs in one's understanding of the importance of Holy-Inspiration Grace and Sacred-Realization Grace as related to the Process of Illumination. Divine-Bliss Anointings by the Spirit of God enable the devotee-initiate to enter into the dimensions of Revelation Grace. All anointings received from the Spirit of God give testimony to the perfect Mediation of the Lord Jesus and the Host working with Him to unite Heaven and Earth.

A Truth-seeker who qualifies to receive Divine-Bliss Anointings becomes as a diver who is permitted by God to dive into the sacred waters of Revelation Grace. These holy waters contain treasure chests with many priceless jewels (truths). The anointed one then carries the treasure chests back with him to dry land (physical-world responsibilities), and lives each day with the beauty of the jewels—a beauty that becomes more precious with the passing of time.

In the Sermon on the Mount, Jesus stresses the importance of almsgiving, prayer, fasting and meditation. These devotional dedications observed with love for God and His Laws are the ways one earns *Spiritual Insulation.* Spiritual Insulation is a vital necessity in a devotee's quest for union with the Power of God radiating through Holiness. *God, in His Mercy, waits until a devotee is insulated by a loving obedience to His Commandments and a natural expression of virtues before He sends the more powerful charges of His Anointing Spirit into the heart and the mind.*

To earn Spiritual Insulation, one must use his physical, emotional, mental and spiritual energies with reverence and love. While working to attain Insulation, the devotee is blessed, anointed, guided, inspired and quickened by the Saints through the mighty and miraculous powers at their command.

Spiritual Insulation is the result of numerous Righteousness Initiations. As one meets and masters each Righteousness Initiation related to Laws and Virtues, his Spiritual Insulation is increasingly strengthened until it becomes a protective Virtue-Garment of Love-Insulation. The teacher of the higher life serves God by helping each earnest devotee weave the Virtue-Garment of Love-Insulation so that the Light (Electricity) of Illumination may come in increasing voltages of Inspiration, Realization and Revelation. When the Omnipresent Creator perceives that a worshipper has attained Insulation, the door opens to the multidimensional splendors of the Godhead.

> It is your Father's good pleasure to give you the kingdom.
>
> Jesus
> —*St. Luke 12:32*

> I am the door: by me if any man enter in, he shall be saved, and shall go in and out, and find pasture.
>
> Jesus
> —*St. John 10:9*

The Saints in heaven who work with sincere devotees in the religions of the earth provide protection, inspiration and guidance, gently shepherding their proteges toward a firm union with the holy light of God's Spirit. Through the work of the Saints and other Mediators, a devotee's initiations related to the Joy, Ecstasy and Bliss degrees of the Godhead move him beyond man-made religious barriers. In this, he becomes aware of the divine purposes within each religion. With awareness comes understanding, and with understanding comes Revelation.

I will come to visions and revelations of the Lord.

> Saint Paul
> —*2 Corinthians 12:1*

Spirit is known through revelation. The living man who finds Spirit, finds Truth.
> —Kena Upanishad

"Judge not, that ye be not judged." *(St. Matthew 7:1)* The judging mind and the critical mind are the exact opposite of the Virtue of Compassion. When one comes under the Saints' Mantle of blessings, he becomes increasingly compassionate in his thoughts and charitable in his giving. Compassion and charitableness in heart, mind and deed are major strides toward the receiving of the Gift of Revelation and other priceless gifts that manifest through the Anointing Spirit of God.

COMPASSION

And Jesus went forth, and saw a great multitude, and was moved with compassion toward them, and He healed their sick.
> —St. Matthew 14:14

Thus speaketh the Lord of hosts, saying, Execute true judgment, and shew mercy and compassions every man to his brother.
> —Zechariah 7:9

It is of the Lord's mercies that we are not consumed, because his compassions fail not.
> —Lamentations 3:22

Go forth . . . for the help of the many, for the well-being of the many, out of compassion for the world.
> —Buddha

> Humblest of heart, highest of reverence,
> Benign flower, crown of virtues all.
> —Chaucer

> The four duties are love, compassion, rejoicing and alms-giving.
> —Milarepa

> Though our Savior's Passion is over, His compassion is not.
> —William Penn

Union with the Omnipresent Spirit of God within the human spirit requires that a student or devotee of the higher life undergo numerous Love-Thy-Neighbor Initiations. These initiations seek to inspire him to increase his expression of love, compassion and kindness. All Love-Initiations and Virtue-Initiations are timed by the cyclic action of the Sun, the Moon and the Planets.

Certain Saints in heaven, working with the devotee's budding Gift of Revelation, open his understanding of the cycles and rhythms of the solar-system harmonics and mathematics. In this, an alert Truth-seeker begins to comprehend the creative rhythms and sacred purposes of the Sun, the Moon, the Planets and the Stars.

Reverence for the mighty creations of God in the Cosmos and on Earth unites one with the Blessing-Streams of the Saints—and with the Saints' gentle blessings and grace-anointings comes the prize of Understanding. Oneness with the Saints of the East and the West makes one receptive to an expanding spectrum of Saintly blessings.

During the Divine-Marriage Anointing, numerous seeds of truth and wisdom are implanted and quickened within the core of one's being. These seeds germinate and come to birth in his outer consciousness in perfect timing. To be anointed and sealed by the Creator is to henceforth express increasing degrees of one's true identity and spiritual-creative uniqueness. This is due to the quickening of the Image and Glory of God within his soul.

> Now he which stablisheth us with you in Christ, and hath anointed us, is God; Who hath also sealed us, and given the earnest of the Spirit in our hearts.
> Saint Paul
> —*2 Corinthians 1:21, 22*

> Labor not for the meat which perisheth, but for that meat which endureth unto everlasting life, which the Son of man shall give unto you: for him hath God the Father sealed.
> Jesus
> —*St. John 6:27*

"Behold, I will pour out my spirit unto you." (Proverbs 1:23) Certain Bliss-Anointings manifest as great waterfalls of wisdom that pour upon a receptive heart and mind. The Presence of God within His Laws and Commandments floods one's being with beautiful inspirations, prophecies and revelations.

When one is anointed by the Truth of God, the Spirit of Truth is in him. When he is anointed by the Righteousness of God, the Spirit of Righteousness is in him. When he is anointed by the Love of God, the Spirit of Love is in him.

Those upon whom the Creator places His Spirit live in the grace-state of Pure Creation. Pure creations continuously move from their hands, hearts and minds. The Anointing Spirit of God *is* Pure Creation. Therefore, one who is receptive to the Anointing Spirit of God lives in a perpetual state of Pure Creation; he has attained the cherished goal of *Fulness.*

FULNESS

We hold that to the whole of human nature the whole essence of the Godhead was united . . . He in his fulness took upon himself me in my fulness, and united whole to whole that he might in his grace bestow salvation on the whole man.
—Saint John of Damascus

And of his fulness have all we received, and grace for grace. For the law was given by Moses, but grace and truth came by Jesus Christ. —St. John 1:16, 17

. . . the fulness of Him that filleth all in all.

Saint Paul
—*Ephesians 1:23*

The yon is fulness; fulness, this. From fulness, fulness doth proceed. Withdrawing fulness's fulness off, E'en fulness then itself remains. —Upanishads

Thou wilt shew me the path of life: in Thy Presence is fulness of joy . . . —Psalm 16:11

The light of the body is the eye: if therefore thine eye be single, thy whole body shall be full of light.

Jesus
—*St. Matthew 6:22*

That Christ may dwell in your hearts by faith; that ye, being rooted and grounded in love, may be able to comprehend with all saints what is the breadth, and length, and depth, and height; and to know the love of Christ, which passeth knowledge, that ye might be filled with all the fulness of God.

Saint Paul
—Ephesians 3:17–19

Blessed are they which do hunger and thirst after righteousness: for they shall be filled.

Jesus
—St. Matthew 5:6

HOLY GHOST

And the Holy Ghost descended in a bodily shape like a dove upon him, and a voice came from heaven, which said, Thou art my beloved Son; in thee I am well pleased.
—*St. Luke 3:22*

The kingdom of God is not meat and drink; but righteousness, and peace, and joy in the Holy Ghost.
Saint Paul
—*Romans 14:17*

For the power of the Holy Ghost seizes the very highest and purest, the spark of the soul, and carries it up in the flame of love . . . The soul-spark is conveyed aloft into its source and is absorbed into God and is identified with God and is the spiritual light of God. —Meister Eckhart

Now the grace of God, pouring forth from God, is an inward thrust and urge of the Holy Ghost, driving forth our spirit from within and exciting it towards all virtues.
—John Ruysbroeck

And when they bring you unto the synagogues, and unto magistrates, and powers, take ye no thought how or what thing ye shall answer, or what ye shall say: For the Holy Ghost shall teach you in the same hour what ye ought to say.
Jesus
—*St. Luke 12:11, 12*

The love of God is shed abroad in our hearts by the Holy Ghost which is given unto us.
Saint Paul
—*Romans 5:5*

And Jesus being full of the Holy Ghost returned from Jordan, and was led by the Spirit into the wilderness.   —*St. Luke 4:1*

Conscience is a portion of the Holy Ghost in man; the more conscience, the more Holy Ghost action.   —Ann Ree Colton

6

THE HOLY GHOST

Receive ye the Holy Ghost.
Jesus
—St. John 20:22

Now the God of hope fill you with all joy and peace in believing, that ye may abound in hope, through the power of the Holy Ghost.
Saint Paul
—Romans 15:13

TEN-YEAR CYCLES

And when the day of Pentecost was fully come, they were all with one accord in one place. And suddenly there came a sound from heaven as of a rushing mighty wind, and it filled all the house where they were sitting. And there appeared unto them cloven tongues like as of fire, and it sat upon each of them. And they were all filled with the Holy Ghost.
—Acts 2:1-4

The Anointing Spirit of God works through the Quickening Light of the Christ. The Light of the Christ blesses, heals and enlightens through the Holy Ghost. The Holy Ghost manifests gifts and rewards through Solar Cycles, Seasonal Cycles, Holy Day Cycles, Lunar Cycles, Sabbath Cycles, and Daily Worship Cycles. These Sacred Cycles have interrelated meanings and purposes within the Time Cycles as created by God.

Solar Cycles pertain to the progression of each solar year. Seasonal Cycles relate to the solstices and the equinoxes; Lunar Cycles, New Moons and Full Moons; Holy Day Cycles, sacred days of profound significance; Sabbath Cycles, reverence in sanctuaries of devotion; Daily Worship Cycles, sacramental meditation and prayer.

Holy Day Cycles pertain to the annual occurrences of Christmas, Epiphany, Easter and Pentecost. On Pentecost, the flame of the Holy Ghost appeared over the disciples of Jesus after His Ascension—and they were spiritually quickened and illuminated. Each year during the Fifty-Day Cycle from Maundy Thursday to Pentecost, the flame of the Holy Ghost comes upon those who are "chosen" to enter into marriage with their Beloved Lord. The flame of the Holy Ghost *ignites* the memory-cells of truths gained through diligent study of Sacred Scriptures; *ignites* the volatile truths sealed into one's heart and mind by his living teacher; and *ignites* other truths earned through personal experiences and realizations over the days, months and years. The Holy Ghost ignition or "baptism" also presents one with spiritual gifts and illuminations earned during past lives of service to God.

> I indeed baptize you with water unto repentance: but he that cometh after me is mightier than I, whose shoes I am not worthy to bear: he shall baptize you with the Holy Ghost, and with fire.
>
> —St. Matthew 3:11

The Holy Ghost

Every devotee-initiate on the Path of Virtue must be prepared, inwardly and outwardly, for the Baptismal Anointing by the Holy Ghost. The Mantle of the teacher provides one with Spiritual Insulation until he earns his own Insulation. When a Truth-seeker attains Spiritual Insulation through love and virtue, the Creator places His *Spirit* upon him through the mediation of the Christ and the Holy Ghost.

> He who has found Spirit, is Spirit.
> —Mundaka Upanishad

> It is said everything can be got through the knowledge of Spirit. What is that knowledge?
>
> In the beginning there was Spirit. It knew itself as Spirit; from that knowledge everything sprang up. He who knows that he is Spirit, becomes Spirit, becomes everything.
> —Brihadaranyaka Upanishad

Each Ten (10) Year Cycle on the Path of Virtue is a *Holy Ghost Cycle*. Holy Ghost Cycles begin the moment a sincere aspirant dedicates his life and being to the service of God.

In the number 10, the 1 represents the Father Principle working through the masculine or yang polarity; the 0, the Divine Mother Principle working through the feminine or yin polarity. The sacramental use of Time makes of each Ten (10) Year Cycle a *Sacred Cycle* within the Yin-Yang polarity-drama of an illuminative union with God.

> I and my Father are one.
> Jesus
> —*St. John 10:30*

The Whole Armour

> Let us put on the armour of light.
>
> Saint Paul
> —*Romans 13:12*

> . . . the armour of righteousness on the right hand and on the left.
>
> Saint Paul
> —*2 Corinthians 6:7*

> He shall take holiness for an invisible shield.
>
> Wisdom of Solomon
> —*Apocrypha*

> Put on the whole armour of God.
>
> Saint Paul
> —*Ephesians 6:11*

For the pure in heart, Holy Ghost Cycles lead to the whole armour of Holy Ghost Insulation. Holy Ghost Insulation is a Mantle of Holiness and Protection placed by the Christ upon those who prove to be trustworthy guardians or stewards of the mysteries of God.

> Let a man so account of us, as of the ministers of Christ, and stewards of the mysteries of God.
>
> Saint Paul
> —*1 Corinthians 4:1*

> For a bishop must be blameless, as the steward of God; not selfwilled, not soon angry, not given to wine, no striker, not given to filthy lucre; but a lover of hospitality, a lover of good men, sober, just, holy, temperate; holding fast the faithful word as he hath been taught, that he may be able by sound doctrine both to exhort and to convince the gainsayers.
>
> Saint Paul
> —*Titus 1:7-9*

The Holy Ghost

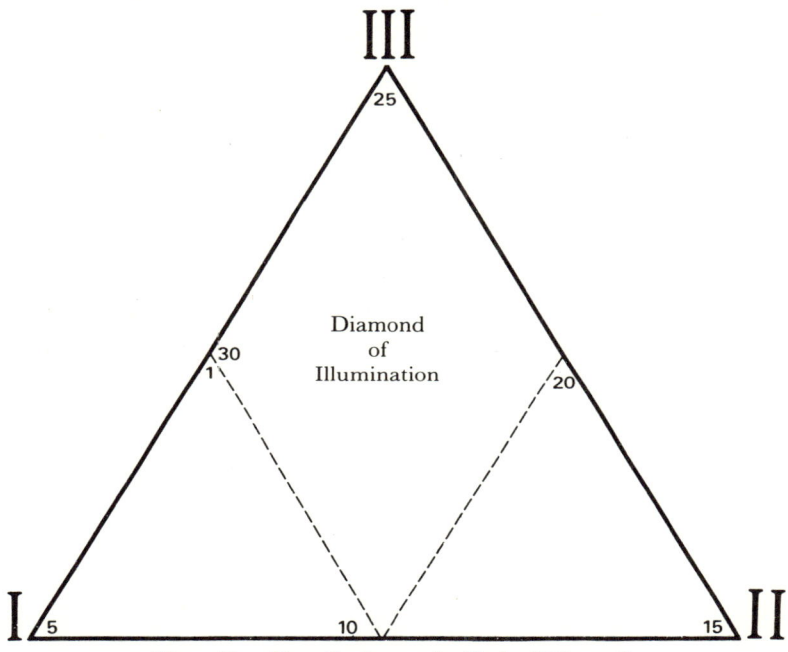

Three Ten-Year Cycles on the Path of Virtue.*

During the first ten (10) years on the Path of Virtue, a teachable student earns his first Insulation; he has begun to "put on the whole armour of God." The 1 is the number of the *will*. During the first 10 years, the will of the devotee makes its first blending with the Will of God through worship, study and service. At the end of the 10-year cycle, the 0 in the number 10 becomes as a circle or ring of insulation around the Truth-seeker. ⊕ This symbol indicates the progress being made during the probationary period.

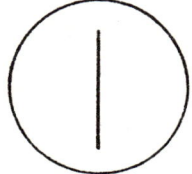

The first 10-year Cycle on the Path of Virtue.

*Chart by Ann Ree Colton and Jonathan Murro

The first 10-year cycle contains repeated tests regarding one's attitudes toward the Ten Commandments, the Holy Law of Tithing, the Commandments of Love, and daily Worship-observances. The probationer is tested each day as to his reverence, devotion, sincerity, integrity, and obedience to spiritual instruction. If one proves worthy, he comes under the blessing-streams of the Angels, the Saints and other Mediators working under the Christ.

If an aspirant earnestly desires an illuminative union with God, the Creator will place an enlightened teacher in his life. The teacher's sole task is to help the student qualify for the receiving of the Holy Ghost. The Holy Ghost, through the magnification-light of holiness, works to qualify the devotee-initiate for union with the Pure Light of the Christ.

② 20 years on the Path of Virtue: the probationary period before the Divine Marriage.

During the second 10-year cycle on the Path of Virtue, one earns his second Insulation. Twenty years of devotion to the Creator build a strong insulation so that one may receive the more powerful voltages of God's Anointing Spirit. When the flame of the Holy Ghost ignites one or more virtues, one is anointed, sealed and quickened; his conscience, logic and love are anointed, sealed and quickened. In this, the servant of God unites with the Eternal Essences in their work of Cosmos Creation.

The number 2 is the number of *devotion;* the shape of the 2 is the position of a devotee kneeling in prayer. After daily devotion to God for 20 years, one qualifies for the harvests of pure creations inspired by the Love and Grace of God. *"The harvest truly is plenteous, but the labourers are few."* (St. Matthew 9:37)

The 2 is the number of the *dual* polarities of Masculine and Feminine. *"Male and female created he them." (Genesis 1:27)* If a devotee, initiate or teacher is married, his or her relationship with wife or husband becomes part of the 1 (yang) 0 (yin) initiations that seek to bring all masculine and feminine polarities into harmony. The persons placed in his life by the Spirit of God denote polarity balances and imbalances. As polarity imbalances are rectified through love, worship and selfless service, all aspects of his life and being come into the polarity balance necessary for Spiritual Insulation and Illumination.

The closer a devotee comes to the time of receiving the Holy Ghost, the more magnified become his faults and flaws, as well as his gifts and talents. Therefore, as one moves toward the Pure Truth and Pure Righteousness within the Godhead, it is imperative that he work directly with the Creator, the Christ and His Host in order to remove all obstructions remaining between him and the harmonious flow of Soul Grace and Divine Grace.

Daily worship, study, selfless love, and a genuine Agape-spirit* during the second 10-year cycle lift one toward the Holy-Ghost radiations of light within the sacrament-degrees of the virtues. In this, the Holy-Ghost magnification action within the sacrament-degrees of the virtues increases dramatically within his heart, mind and conscience. This Gift of Magnification of Truth denotes that the Truth-seeker is drawing closer to the Godhead.

If an initiate proves worthy in the sight of God, his 20th year on the Path of Virtue is the time when he receives the Divine-Marriage Anointing. This monumental Anointing opens his eyes to the beauty of Truth and unites him with the Holiness degrees and dimensions of God's Presence.

---

*The word *Agape* means love, charity, hospitality, a holy concern for others.

Those who receive the full Baptismal Anointing by the Holy Ghost walk the earth as *Anointed* servants of God and His Word. The Anointing establishes the yin-yang polarity balance between heart and mind, soul and spirit. He who earns the Divine-Marriage Anointing attains the grace-state of *Fulness;* thereafter, he observes all dedications with effortless effort.

> The way of the sage is work without effort.
> —Lao Tzu

During the third 10-year Cycle on the Path of Virtue, one earns his third Insulation; the Holy Ghost works to make of him a skilled craftsman in the use of Christ-Mind Gifts and Graces.

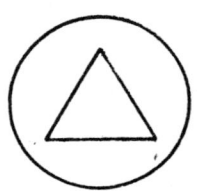

Three 10-year Cycles produce the pyramid of Christ-Mind Illuminations. Each side of the Pyramid denotes a 10-year Cycle.

The 3-sided Pyramid is an ages-old symbol of Illumination. The Illumined Jesus began his Ministry in His 30th year; the life of Jesus contains the blueprint for all who walk the Path of Virtue toward God-Realization. When a follower of the Christ proves faithful for 30 years, his Mantle of Spiritual Insulation enables him to receive the more powerful electricities of God's Anointing Spirit. In this, his understanding expands into greater ranges of Christ-Mind Gifts and Graces.

Each of the first three 10-year cycles is a period of tests, trials and challenges. All virtues are tested repeatedly; all attitudes toward Holy Laws and Commandments are weighed on the fine scales of justice and restitution; all areas of the conscience are purged; all motives and dedications are searched as to their selflessness and sincerity.

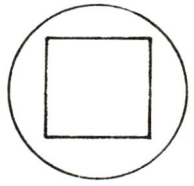

Four 10-year Cycles on the Path of Virtue make of the Anointed Teacher a Masterbuilder-Apostle under Christ.

The 4 denotes the 4-sided Square or Building Block. After 40 years on the Path of Virtue, the Anointed Teacher serves as a *Masterbuilder* insulated by the Love and Grace of God. Each side of the square represents a Ten-Year Holy-Ghost Cycle. The 40-day fasts of Moses and Jesus, Noah's 40 days in the Ark, and the Israelites' 40-years search for the Promised Land call attention to the importance of the number 40 in the Scriptures. The *Promised Land* symbolizes the Godhead; all Kingdoms of Heaven are within the Godhead.

Five 10-year Cycles of dedicated service to God.

The 5-pointed star is a symbol of the 5 senses in the state of Illumination-Grace. After 50 years on the Path of Virtue, the 5-pointed Star Insulation represents five Holy-Ghost Cycles. Each progressive Holy Ghost Cycle of increasing magnification of Truth quickens, expands and reveals new wonders within the Glory of God. Spiritual Insulation enables the Apostle-Teacher to *pass on* to others the Holy Spirit, thereby freeing persons from karmic bondages and opening them to their souls' treasures.

130   THE PATH OF VIRTUE

 Six 10-year Cycles.

After 60 years on the Path of Virtue, the *6-pointed Star* denotes the Spiritual Insulation gained during six Holy-Ghost Cycles. The 6 is the number of God's Law. He who teaches others the Laws and Commandments of God for 60 years is a venerable sage adorned with the crown of light and a mantle of righteousness.

> What? know ye not that your body is the temple of the Holy Ghost which is in you, which ye have of God, and ye are not your own?
>
> Saint Paul
> —*1 Corinthians 6:19*

NIRVANA-POINTS

> Ye are the soldiers of the Tathagata (Perfect One), while Mara, the evil one is the enemy who must be conquered. And the Tathagata will give to his soldiers the city of Nirvana, the great capital of the good law. And when the enemy is overcome, the Dharma-raja, the great king of truth, will bestow upon all his disciples the most precious crown jewel which brings perfect enlightenment, supreme wisdom, and undisturbed peace.
>
> —Buddha

Nirvana, as taught by Buddha, relates to the bliss, ecstasy and joy degrees of pure love *within* the great Laws creating Man and the Universe. Buddha speaks of

Nirvana as being "the great capital of the good law." The "great capital" of Nirvana is the heart or core of the Creator's Beauty, Wisdom and Glory within His Laws. When one is wearing a vestment of virtues, he gains entry into the *great capital of the good law*—that is, the nirvana-degrees of holiness and righteousness from which emanate the pristine energies of enlightenment and truth.

The sacrament-degrees of the virtues begin one's direct union with the Wisdom, Love and Beauty of God within His Laws and Commandments. A Truth-seeker who expresses the sacrament-light of his soul through love, reverence and selflessness is initiated in the mysteries of the *Nirvana-Points*. These beautiful experiences with Pure Truth and Divine Grace enable him to gain an enlightened understanding of the correlation between Virtues and Laws.

Every truth has a nirvana-point. A virtue, being a truth, has its nirvana-point. The nirvana-point within a virtue is one's entry into the dimensional energy-worlds of the soul and the spirit—the Kingdom of God within.

Even as a physical atom has its point of explosion, so does each spiritual atom of pure truth have its point of explosion. This point of explosion is the Nirvana-Point. Nirvana-point explosions of grace and truth are one's introduction to union with the Godhead.

The nirvana-point within a holy law, a divine virtue, a sacred principle, an ethic or any other truth may be likened to the explosions of energy occurring on the Sun's surface. Nirvana-point explosions of energy and light release powerful essences of revelation into one's heart and mind. The initiate under Christ becomes a skilled craftsman receiving and utilizing the Grace-essences and Wisdom-essences within Cosmos truths and Archetypal ideas being opened and freed by the Christ.

Each virtue has a masculine polarity and a feminine

polarity. During one's efforts to make an illuminative union with God, the masculine and the feminine polarities of each virtue experience a gradual or rapid merging and blending until a fusion or marriage is accomplished. Each virtue must achieve this marriage as part of the Divine Marriage.

In each life one lives on earth, there is the expression of either the masculine polarity of the male sex or the feminine polarity of the female sex. The soul's choice of a male or female body is based upon mathematical laws of God seeking to manifest the merging and marriage of the two polarities within each virtue.

The feminine (yin) and masculine (yang) polarities within a virtue undergo their "marriage" within the sacrament-degrees of the virtue. This marriage occurs at the nirvana-point, resulting in Truth-ecstasies. The yin-and-yang marriage within the atom-core of a virtue or any other truth produces mighty explosions of grace and understanding supervised by the Christ. Through a nirvana-point, numerous grace-explosions occur in nuclear-like action—and one moves from Christ-Realization to God-Realization.

> Grace and peace be multiplied unto you through the knowledge of God, and of Jesus our Lord.
> —2 Peter 1:2

> Enter thou into the joy of thy Lord.
> Jesus
> —*St. Matthew 25:21*

> . . . The joy of the law.
> —Buddha

Now unto him that is able to keep you from falling, and to present you faultless before the presence of his glory with exceeding joy, To the only wise God our Saviour, be glory and majesty, dominion and power, both now and ever. Amen.

Saint Jude
—*Jude 24, 25*

VIRTUE-DIAMONDS

We have the mind of Christ.

Saint Paul
—*1 Corinthians 2:16*

"And other sheep I have, which are not of this fold . . ." (St. John 10:16) All persons in the world who aspire to express the holy or higher degrees of the virtues come under the Healing, Blessing and Quickening Power of the Christ. Through His miraculous Mediation, they are participating in the great Drama of Divine Illumination through the transforming of anti-virtue energies into virtue energies.

The process through which an anti-virtue is gradually changed into a virtue may be likened to the ages-long transformation of carbon into a beautiful diamond. Each virtue evolves from a carbon-like beginning to the time when it becomes a priceless diamond with scintillating facets.

The compass of Illumination is ever pointed toward the vast resources of grace that God has sealed into the soul. The Great Teachers and Saints work with the compass needle showing the human spirit the way toward the Greater Illuminations. Each virtue—when discovered as a precious diamond—becomes a *World* of Illumination.

Great Souls come to the earth from time to time to remind mankind of the importance of love and virtues and to direct the human spirit toward the discovery and polishing of each virtue-diamond.

Dramatic virtue-births are occurring in societies, cultures, nations and families where the wisdom of the Great Teachers is revered and lived. The appearance of Jesus on earth as Messiah generated tidal waves of spiritual power that are increasing through each successive century of life on earth. The wisdom of Jesus is gradually covering the earth with a mantle of holiness and righteousness. The virtue-dramas being enacted on the stage of life are under command of the Great Shepherd.

> Jesus is honey in the mouth, music in the ear, a shout of gladness in the heart.
> —Saint Bernard

> These things have I spoken unto you, that my joy might remain in you, and that your joy might be full.
> Jesus
> —St. John 15:11

The Christ, the *Eternal* Son of God, has the power to overcome the Time Factor; thus, the virtues of His devoted and loyal followers experience *miraculous* quickenings. Even as Jesus healed the lepers and the lame in the twinkling of an eye, so does His ability to accelerate Time enable Him to move certain virtues from the carbon-stage into the diamond-stage in the twinkling of an eye. Such is the wondrous nature of the Glory of God working through His Beloved Son!

A virtue-diamond is part of a greater Diamond—the Diamond of the Soul. When a virtue-diamond is used to

The Holy Ghost

I

The birth of several Virtues may occur simultaneously or one by one. The birth of each Virtue is determined by the Wisdom of God and His mathematics of Creation.

Over the ages, a Virtue increases and expands its light.
The beginning point of a Virtue-birth in one's heart and mind.

II

After one reaches the Nirvana-Point within a Virtue, the Christ uses the Nirvana-Point to unite the devotee-initiate with the *Expanding* Grace and Truth of the Godhead.

The *Nirvana-Point* of a Virtue is attained when the Virtue reaches the *Sacrament-degrees* of righteousness and holiness.

III

The Nirvana-Point is the point of fusion or *marriage* between the masculine (yang) and feminine (yin) polarities within the Virtue. After experiencing the bliss-ecstasy of the Nirvana-Point, one begins the ascent up the pyramidal-shaped portion of the Virtue-Diamond, partaking of the Illumination-fruits on the Lord's Table. The closer one moves toward the apex of the Virtue-Diamond, the more compressed and accelerated become the energies within Time, thereby opening the Dimensional Soul-Gifts of Healing, Prophecy and Revelation.

A Virtue-Diamond with energy-radiations illuminating the heart and mind.

TITLE: *THE NIRVANA-POINT WITHIN A VIRTUE-DIAMOND*

glorify God, new facets continuously appear, thereby adding their luminosity to one's being. Virtue-diamonds reveal their soul-origin by providing the heart and the mind with supersensory energies and dimensional capabilities.

The Christ-Mind is the composite of virtue-diamonds radiating in God-given splendor. He who travels the Path of Virtue experiences Christ-Mind Illuminations according to the virtue-diamonds present within his armour of Insulation.

If one has earned one or more virtue-diamonds in past lives—but in the present life has permitted the soot of cardinal sins to temporarily cover these diamonds—his first earnest prayers of repentance and confession to God begin the immediate freeing of the light of these priceless virtues. Each sincere prayer of repentance and honest confession enables the Christ to do His perfect healing and freeing work—and the virtue-diamonds, as treasures bequeathed to oneself from past lives, return to bless his present life.

Through one's faith and love, the Christ frees the virtue-diamonds one has earned in previous lives and accelerates the process of new virtue-diamonds coming into being. The miraculous quickenings of a devotee's virtues by the Christ is dependent upon the degree of sincerity in his repentance and the degree of honesty in his confessions to God.

A seeker after Truth assists the Christ when he covenants with the Creator to make a full and honorable restitution for all sins, offenses and transgressions of the present life and former lives. With each willing act of restitution, virtue-diamonds brought to light by the Christ experience steady increases in height and breadth blessed by God's Expanding Love and Grace.

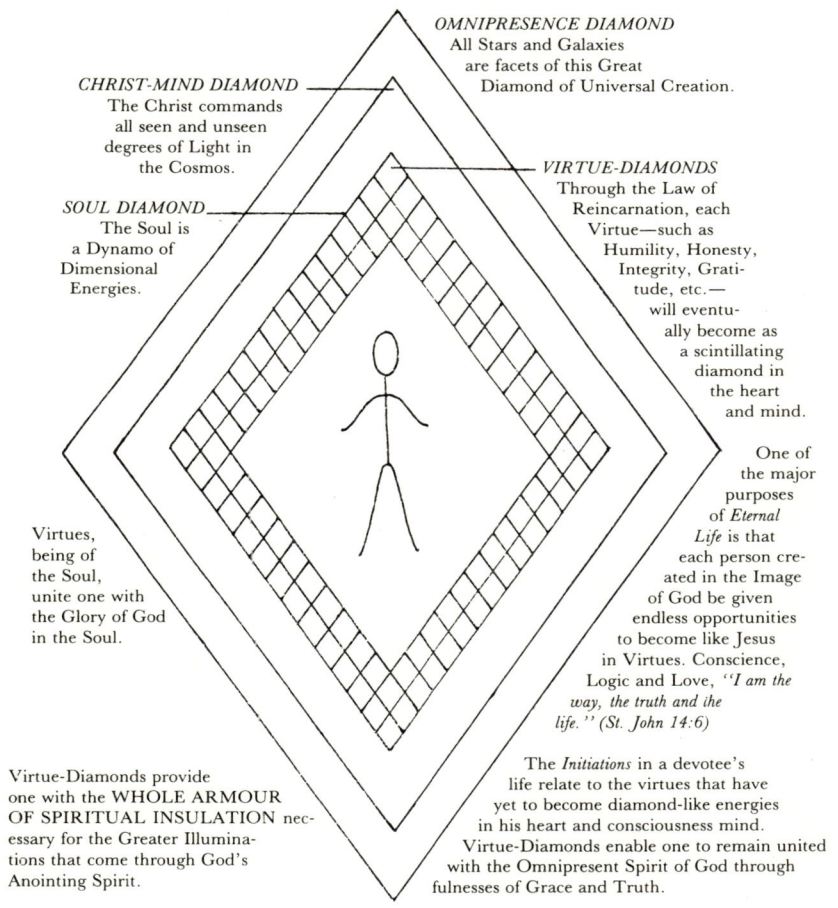

TITLE: VIRTUE-DIAMONDS AND
THE ANOINTING SPIRIT OF GOD

A virtue-diamond, as a radiant manifestation of the Diamond of the Soul, is part of the Diamond of the Christ-Mind. The Diamond of the Christ-Mind is part of the Diamond of God as *Omnipresence*.

Androgynous Virtues

> And when you make the inner as the outer, and the outer as the inner, and the upper as the lower, and when you make male and female into a single one, so that the male shall not be male and the female shall not be female, then shall you enter the Kingdom.
> —Gospel of Thomas

All virtues, in their higher or sacrament degrees, are *androgynous*. The Virtues of Jesus are Androgynous Virtues; therefore Jesus is an Androgynous Being. When man, created in the Image of God, attains and expresses Androgynous Virtues, he will be an Androgynous Being; he will be "like" Jesus as prophesied by John the Beloved: "*When He shall appear, we shall be like Him.*" (1 John 3:2)

The sacrament-degrees of the virtues are the androgynous degrees of the virtues. In their beginning stages, certain virtues have stronger Masculine Polarities while other virtues have stronger Feminine Polarities until the higher androgynous degrees of the virtues are attained. As one evolves spiritually through sacramental worship and sacrificial restitution, he reaches the time when the virtues become polarized and harmonized through pure and selfless love. In this, he begins to express the Androgynous Light of the Virtues—and in so doing, he becomes increasingly like Jesus in principles, ethics and love-compassion.

"*And I, if I be lifted up from the earth, will draw all men unto me.*" (St. John 12:32) Jesus, as Messiah, expressed the

Androgynous degrees of all Virtues. His devotees, walking the Path of Virtue, are gradually lifted up by Him until they begin to taste the sweetness and power of God's Glory within the Sacrament or Androgynous degrees of the Cardinal Virtues.

An Androgynous Love is without prejudice, without lust, without vanity. An Androgynous Love is a Pure Love, a Healing Love, a Love Transcendent and Triumphant. Androgynous Love is of the Soul's *Eternality*. The Eternal *Third Polarity* under command of the Christ merges the Feminine and the Masculine Polarities into the Divine-Marriage State of Grace. Thus, he who follows the Lord Christ to Androgynous Being reaches the time of Eternal Being. Eternal Being blessed by God is the Illuminated Radiance produced by the Sacrament-light of Androgynous Virtues.

> My sheep hear my voice, and I know them, and they follow me: And I give unto them eternal life.
>
> Jesus
—St. John 10:27, 28

MEMORY

Great is the power of memory, a fearful thing, O my God, a deep and boundless manifoldness; and this thing is the mind, and this am I myself. What am I then, O my God? What nature am I? A life various and manifold, and exceeding immense. —Saint Augustine

Memory: what wonders it performs in preserving and storing up things gone by, or rather, things that are! —Plutarch

This sort of thing cannot be taught, my son; but God, when he so wills, recalls it to our memory. —Hermes

For there is not any thing which is of greater importance with respect to science, experience and wisdom, than the ability of remembering. —Iamblichus

My Lord includeth all things in His knowledge. Will ye not then remember?
Muhammad
—*Koran VI.80*

Memory is the most wonderful glory of God given to man.
—Ann Ree Colton

They shall abundantly utter the memory of Thy great goodness, and shall sing of Thy righteousness. —Psalm 145:7

When a man dwells in his mind on the objects of sense, attachment to them is produced. From attachment springs desire and from desire comes anger. From anger arises bewilderment, from bewilderment loss of memory; and from loss of memory, the destruction of intelligence and from the destruction of intelligence he perishes.
—Bhagavad Gita II.62, 63

The memory of the just is blessed . . . —Proverbs 10:7

7

MEMORY TREASURES

> Memory is the treasury and guardian of all things.
>
> —Cicero

Energy and the Soul

> Grace and peace be multiplied unto you through the knowledge of God, and of Jesus our Lord, According as his divine power hath given unto us all things that pertain unto life and godliness, through the knowledge of him that hath called us to glory and virtue: whereby are given unto us exceeding great and precious promises: that by these ye might be partakers of the divine nature.
>
> —2 Peter 1:2-4

> The just seek his soul.
>
> Solomon
> —*Proverbs 29:10*

Each Star in the Cosmos is a dynamo of energy. The Sun, the Moon and the Planets are great dynamos of energy. The Creator of life provides each individual with a personal source of powerful energies: the Soul. The soul's cycles and energy-dynamics work in perfect harmony with the cycles and energies of the Sun, the Moon, the Planets and the Stars. The soul and all celestial bodies are fulfilling God's Will each moment of the day and the night.

The Spirit of God, through the soul, provides the energies that animate the body, the feelings and the thoughts. Whenever there is movement of the body, movement of the emotions, or movement of thoughts, the soul's energy-action is present.

The Omnipresent Spirit of God animating the soul determines each person's portion of energies in each life. This mathematical action of the Spirit of God provides the necessary energies for all mankind—from those who are lethargic, to the energetic selfish; and from the energetic selfish, to the selflessly dedicated servants of God.

Even as the Sun's light works through a gradation of energies from the Sun's atmosphere to the Earth's atmosphere, so does the soul's light work through a gradation of energies from Eternal Spirit to human spirit. Each soul created by God has a divine nature and a human nature. The divine nature of the soul is forever within the Eternal Spirit of God. The human nature of the soul pertains to the energies used during life in the physical world.

The divine nature of the soul is the eternal heritage of all persons breathing the breath of life. However, the creation of the Earth in its placement in Cosmos requires that virtue-births and virtue-illuminations occur in the *human* nature. The Spirit of God animating the soul, the solar system and life on earth determines the timing of each virtue-birth and each increase of virtue-light in the heart and mind. The Spirit of God also determines the timing of each cycle in one's life, his placement in each life, and the persons in his life.

The Omnipresent Spirit of God is a Multidimensional Spirit; therefore, the portion of the soul centered in the

Eternal Spirit is multidimensional. The divine nature of man as a soul is the dimensional nature of man as a soul. As the divine nature of the soul increasingly energizes and suffuses the heart and the mind, one unites with the soul's energy-essences that awaken him to his innate divinity and dimensionality as a son of the Living God.

Even as the Sun emits units of energy each second, so does the soul send forth units of energy each moment of the day and the night. The physical body receives energy from the soul and transforms it into actions. The emotions receive energy from the soul, and one expresses different feelings. The mind receives energy from the soul, thereby enabling one to have a thought process.

The physical body may be depleted of energies or completely immobilized; yet, the emotions and the mind may be charged with energies that permit them to function. The physical body may be expressing great quantities of energy, while the emotions and the mind may be extremely low in energy-vitality.

Each unit of energy utilized by the body, the emotions and the mind is a precious portion of the soul. When the energies of the emotions and the mind are expressed with reverence and love, their use is disciplined, wholesome and harmonious.

The physical body's energies may be undisciplined or disciplined; the emotions may be fiery or serene; the mind may be coldly intellectual or warmly spiritual. Even as the Sun's energies may be used by man for destructive or creative purposes, so may the energies provided by the soul be used for selfish interests or for noble purposes.

"A good man out of the good treasure of his heart bringeth forth that which is good; and an evil man out of the evil treasure of his heart bringeth forth that which is evil." (St. Luke 6:45) The heart is the determiner of how the energies provided by the soul are utilized. If the heart is a greedy or covetous

heart, one uses his energies for selfish purposes. If the heart is a loving heart, one uses his energies to worship God and to serve his fellow man. Jesus taught His followers to love God and to love one another, for through the heart's love the energies provided by the soul retain their original soul-essences.

Even as pure rain water is changed and darkened when it falls into a muddy pool, so are the pure energies of the soul changed and darkened when received by an impure heart. If the pure energies of the soul are received by a pure heart, they remain pure—and one thinks pure thoughts and expresses pure love-emotions. *"Follow righteousness, faith, charity, peace, with them that call on the Lord out of a pure heart."* (2 Timothy 2:22)

All energies released by the soul for use by the physical body, the emotions and the mind should be received with gratitude to God and used for His Glory. If one takes the energies of his physical body for granted or uses them irreverently, the soul slowly or quickly withdraws the energies—and the physical body suffers various afflictions, chronic fatigue, weakness of limbs, and, in certain instances, immobility. A sluggish organ or impaired bodily function due to energy-depletion is a reminder from the soul to correct one's attitudes and to purify his feelings and thoughts. As one's attitudes become more reverent, the soul quickens the energy-processes of the body—and health is restored. A happy step on the Path of Virtue signifies a body charged with a holy vitality received from the soul's benign and beneficent energy-resources.

The stewardship of procreation energies is a sacred trust. The irreverent use of these energies builds a dragonlike specter that stands between one and the door to Enlightenment. Unlawful sexual ecstasies attract physical, emotional and mental ills in one's present life and in his coming lives. When procreation energies are used with reverence and pure love, one lives within the protection and blessing of Nature's Laws and God's Providence.

The soul provides the energies for the will. Will-energies kept pure through daily prayer and meditation make of the will a disciplined instrument for union with the Will of God. The malicious use of will-energies invites strong reprovings and heavy penalties from the soul.

The soul's withdrawal of energies from the will makes one will-less, insecure, dependent on others, parasitical. The soul's withdrawal of energies from the mind causes retardation, depression, senility and other forms of mental deterioration. The soul's withdrawal of procreation energies results in impotence and frigidity. The soul's withdrawal of emotional energies makes of the heart a loveless vacuum; one dwells in self-imposed exile in the barren land of the unloved.

When all energies provided by the soul are received with reverence and gratitude to God, one is provided with an abundance of energies on all levels of physical, emotional, mental and spiritual expression. One who proves to be a wise steward of the energies of the body, heart, mind and will is graced by God with the knowledge and use of the dimensional energies of the soul and the spirit.

THE PRINCIPLE OF GRADATION

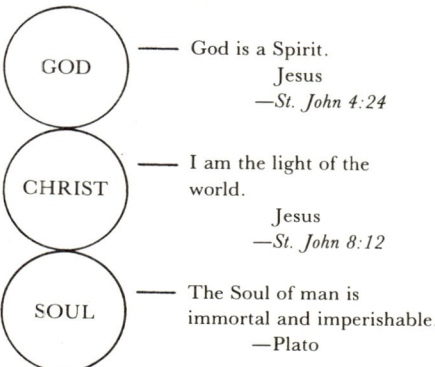

God is the *Spirit* energizing all creations in the Cosmos. The Omnipresent Spirit of God provides the energy for all energy processes: Galaxy, solar, lunar and planetary; animal, plant and man. All kingdoms of Nature; all kingdoms of God, with their Beings and Presences; and all kingdoms within the body, heart, mind and soul of man are energized by the Spirit of God. God as Spirit is Omnipresent within each atom and cell of life in all seen and unseen universes and in all souls. *In Him we live, and move, and have our being." (Acts 17:28)*

The Christ, *"the only begotten Son of God,"** is the *Light* projected from the Spirit of God. As *"the light of the world,"*** He is the *Light* within all Galaxies, Stars and Heavenly Kingdoms. Wherever there is physical light and spiritual light in the Universe, the Christ IS.

"That was the true Light, which lighteth every man that cometh into the world." (St. John 1:9) The Christ, as Light, is in command of all degrees of Consciousness-Light, Conscience-Light, Virtue-Light, Logic-Light and Soul-Light. The Christ, *"the mediator of the new covenant"**** between God and man, is present within all initiatory processes through which man is illumined and God is glorified.

The Energy-Spirit of God—present in the chaos caused by galactic energies during the creation of new solar systems—is also present in the chaos experienced by individuals during the energy-birth of virtues, conscience, logic and love. Through the perfect Mediation of the Christ and the progressive Plan of God, man is destined to understand all energy-processes within his soul and within the Cosmos.

The energies of the Sun travel from its powerful core

*St. John 3:18.
**St. John 8:12
***Hebrews 12:24.

into the far reaches of the Universe; only minute portions of the Sun's energies are received by the Earth. As these fiery solar energies move through the different atmospheres around the Earth, they decrease in heat and power until they become gentle energies that can be utilized by the various forms of life on earth. The *Principle of Gradation* through which the energies of the Sun are gradually reduced in power is also used by the soul in its energization of the body, the emotions and the mind.

Each degree of energy sent forth from the soul into the physical body, the emotions and the mind is related to a great *Learning Process*. In the Scriptures, this Learning Process is called "the Tree of Knowledge."* During each moment of the day and the night, all persons are learning what to do and what not to do; in God's Plan for man on earth, the Learning Process is one of trial and error.

The Learning Process is progressive due to an important attribute that God has sealed into the soul: *Memory*. Each atom of energy in the physical body, the emotions and the mind has the Gift of Memory. Memory is eternal, even as Life is eternal; because of *Memory,* Life on earth has meaning and purpose.

THE RECORD OF THE SOUL

> Moreover I call God for a record upon my soul.
> Saint Paul
> —*2 Corinthians 1:23*

> The soul, then, as being immortal, and having been born again many times, and having seen all things that exist, whether in this world or in the world below, has knowledge of them all; and it is no wonder that she should be able to call to remembrance all that she ever knew.
> —Plato

*Genesis 2:9

The memory of the history of Eternal Life is sealed into the soul. Each life one has ever lived since time immemorial is recorded in the soul. This imperishable treasure of memory is retained by the soul as it fulfills the Eternal Plan of God.

The miracle of Memory in all levels of one's being—from soul to thought—is a mystery yet to be solved. However, when one places his trust in God, the Creator opens the door to the soul's *memory-archives*—and priceless treasures of Memory become part of his present life.

All past-lives' memory-cells contributing to one's present life behavior as an honorable citizen in a nation, a loyal and loving mate in a marriage, and as a spiritual-creative child of God are memory-treasures received from the Creator's Glory manifesting through the soul's memory-archives and record.

Little children—prodigies in music, mathematics or other arts and sciences requiring brilliance and dedication—are blessed with past-lives' memory-resources that are producing their present-life genius. On the Path of Virtue, one's progress toward divine union is marked by timely and gentle manifestations of memory-cells that awaken in him qualities and capabilities of talent, skill or genius on spiritual levels of accomplishment. Each activation of past-lives' memory-treasures in one's present life is a testimony to the Glory of God in the memory and in the soul.

The Glory of God within the atoms of memory may be likened to the tremendous power and energy latent within physical atoms. If the Creator blesses one with magnanimous releasements of virtue memory-cells earned in past lives, the recipient of this mighty blessing is fortified, strengthened and inspired in his present life by the virtues he has earned in former lives. Through this miracle of memory made possible by God's Mercy and Love, repentant sinners are immediately transformed into proteges of the Saints; lethargic and unhappy individuals become spiritually animated, joy-filled, creative and versatile; and timid devotees are changed into bold and eloquent spokesmen for God and His Truth. Countless persons over the ages have experienced this miracle of transformation that manifests through the Glory of God in their memories!

Regardless of one's belief or nonbelief in reincarnation, the emergence of memory-treasures from the soul's record of past lives into his present life occurs to all who love, serve and worship God. However, when one knows that the Law of Reincarnation is a Holy Law of God, he can better understand the miracle that is occurring within him and through him.

>   Is virtue a thing remote? I wish to be virtuous,
>   and lo! virtue is at hand.
>   —Confucius

The *wisdom* one has earned in his search for Truth over the aeons and the eternals is part of his soul's memory-treasures. When portions of this wellspring of wisdom are released by the soul into his present life, memory cells are provided for the wise and ethical use of the energies of the physical body, the emotions and the mind. Through wisdom's light, one is drawn to study the Wisdom of the Great Teachers. This inspiring Wisdom activates new levels and dimensions of memory within his being—and he is miraculously transformed and spiritually enlightened.

>   If any of you lack wisdom, let him ask of God,
>   that giveth to all men liberally, and upbraideth
>   not; and it shall be given him.
>   —James 1:5

The Memory of God

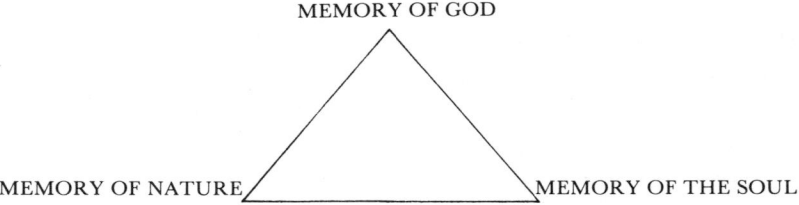

Through the memory-treasures of the soul, one learns of the *Memory of Nature*. The Memory of Nature rewards each person according to his reverence for Nature in past lives and in the present life. The Memory of Nature blesses those who tenderly care for and preserve the Beauty that is God's Gift to man through Nature. The Memory of Nature provides one with healing for the body, the heart and the mind. To those who revere life, Nature reveals numerous secrets stored within the treasures of its memory-vaults.

The *Memory of God* is Supreme, All-encompassing, Eternal. All who have ever loved, worshipped, adored and served God in previous lives are bountifully rewarded in their present lives due to the Memory of God.

The immediate answers to prayers that miraculously deliver persons from serious crises in health or free them from painful associations testify to the Memory of God. For whenever one has blessed God in a lesser or greater way—in the present life or in former lives—the Memory of God recalls his deeds, sacrifices, renunciations, or his suffering persecution or martyrdom for righteousness' sake—and the answers to urgent prayers are quick, perfect, merciful.

The Memory of God remembers *eternally* those who make sacrifices on His behalf; place tithes and offerings on His altars; worship in His sanctuaries; live according to His Commandments; and testify to His Truth. All who have ever loved and preserved the Word of God in previous lives come under the Memory-Mantle of God's Graciousness and Magnanimity. In countless ways does the Creator's Memory reveal its Treasures to those who teach and live His Word from life to life.

While the Memory of God remembers eternally all that one does in His Name and for His Glory, another important aspect of God's Memory is His ability to forget. The Memory of God instantly and completely *forgets* the sins and trespasses of contrite persons whose repentance leads to a willing rectification of former transgressions.

> For thus saith the high and lofty One that inhabiteth eternity, whose name is Holy; I dwell in the high and holy place, with him also that is of a contrite and humble spirit, to revive the spirit of the humble, and to revive the heart of the contrite ones.
> —Isaiah 57:15

> The Lord is nigh unto them that are of a broken heart; and saveth such as be of a contrite spirit.
> —Psalm 34:18

The memory-treasures of the soul are received by a penitent as he makes restitution to God for past offenses. The interrelationship between restitution and the soul's memory-treasures of past lives is *mathematical*. The more rapidly one makes restitution for the sins of the present life and former lives, the more quickly does God heal, free and enlighten him through memory-treasures and other dimensional blessings activated through His Mercy and Love.

When one has proven his love for Truth in past lives, his prayer for a teacher in his present life is quickly answered as a choice blessing from the Memory of God. If one is graced with a loving mate, good health, intelligent and obedient children, and a profession that brings joy and inner satisfaction, he has earned these treasures through union with the Memory of the Soul, the Memory of Nature and the Memory of God.

> It is a brief period of life that is granted us by nature, but the memory of a well-spent life never dies.
> —Cicero

> The angels are the keepers of memory.
> —Ann Ree Colton

Magnification

> My soul doth magnify the Lord.
> Mary
> —*St. Luke 1:46*

The beautiful memory-treasures of the soul pertain to the conscience as well as to virtues. As the priceless memory-treasures earned in past lives move into the heart and mind, one is motivated to live with increasing conscience and virtue. In this, his heart and mind are compelled to seek union with the Creator of life through worship, study and service.

Conscience memory-cells and virtue memory-cells inspire one to live according to the Laws and Commandments of God. The *number* of energy-units within one's conscience memory-cells and virtue memory-cells determines his degree of dedication to Holy Laws and to daily Worship Cycles.

The Laws of God revealed to mankind by the Great Teachers have vital meaning to one when conscience memory-cells and virtue memory-cells begin to saturate his feelings, thoughts and actions. The Parable of the Prodigal Son describes individuals who reach the time when they desire to return to the Protection, Providence and Love of the Father. This desire occurs when the heart and the mind experience the birth of conscience and virtues as memory-treasures from the soul.

The Laws of God creating and governing the solar systems in the Universe are determining the Creation of all facets of man's being: physical, emotional, mental, will, imagination, memory, conscience, virtues, logic, etc. Thus, when conscience motivates an individual to repent of wrongdoing and to live according to Holy Laws, the Laws—as manifestations of God's Love—enfold him in an embrace of tender love.

Union with God begins with one's dedication to honor, revere and fulfill each Commandment. This loving dedication prospers one's union with the soul and its infinite memory-treasures and with the Kingdom of God and its Dimensional Providence.

Holiness magnifies. All degrees of God's Holy Light are degrees of Magnification of Truth. Every earnest devotee on the Path of Virtue experiences the *magnification* of memory-cells through the Holy Light of Pure Truth. As one progresses spiritually, he becomes knowledgeable in the soul-sciences of Magnification, Amplification and Grace-Multiplication.

> But the Comforter, which is the Holy Ghost, whom the Father will send in my name, he shall teach you all things, and bring all things to your remembrance, whatsoever I have said unto you.
>
> Jesus
> —*St. John 14:26*

One of the greatest Gifts to be received on the Path of Virtue is when the Holy Ghost presents one with the memory-treasures of *Illuminations* he has earned and expressed in past lives. This monumental Gift of memory-grace enables the devotee-initiate to build his present-life dedication to God upon the solid foundation of illuminations earned in previous lives of devotion, worship and selfless service.

> Then Peter said unto them, Repent, and be baptized every one of you in the name of Jesus Christ for the remission of sins, and ye shall receive the gift of the Holy Ghost.
> —Acts 2:38

The *Gift* from the Holy Ghost may be likened to one's being given keys to numerous bank vaults containing endless treasures. When the memory-treasures of past-lives' illuminations flood the heart and mind, the Truth-seeker gains access to treasures of beauty and truth that he has earned over the Eternals.

The Gift from the Holy Ghost may also be likened to a powerful lens in one's consciousness that *magnifies* Truth millions of times more than the former lens of his mind. The magnification-light of the Holy Ghost works in the consciousness as a combination electron microscope and electron telescope. Wherever the Creator directs the consciousness-lens of His servant, the *Truth* being revealed is seen in the clear light of magnification.

Each increase of virtue and conscience in the heart increases the magnitude of magnification in the mind. The increasing magnitudes of magnification experienced on the Path of Virtue transform the lens of the consciousness into a sacred instrument of perception for union with God as Pure Truth and Omnipresent Being.

Memory-treasures that manifest as talents, skills, soul-powers and other spiritual gifts and graces should always be *returned* to God. In this, one expresses the sacrament-degrees of the Virtues of Self-Denial, Renunciation and Holy Poverty. If a devotee immediately returns to God each blessing, the blessing is taken up by the Expanding Love of God. One does not *lose* any blessing he returns to God; on the contrary, each blessing is increased, magnified and multiplied due to the Expanding Love of God within the sacrament-degrees of Self-Denial, Renunciation, Holy Poverty and the other virtues being expressed in service to Him. Those who practice this cardinal Truth remain receptive to a widening spectrum of greater blessings, gifts and memory-treasures.

> Take, O Lord, and receive my entire liberty, my memory, my understanding, and my whole will. All that I am, all that I have, Thou hast given me, and I give it back again to Thee to be disposed of according to Thy good pleasure. Give me only Thy love and Thy grace; with Thee I am rich enough, nor do I ask for aught besides.
> —Saint Ignatius Loyola

Love for God and love for one's fellow man keep active the dynamo-action of the soul and its memory-treasures. All virtues, talents, skills, aptitudes, enlightened attitudes, soul-gifts, illumination-graces and Spirit-of-God Anointings earned during one's present life become the treasures of memory he will inherit in the afterlife and in coming lives.

> Lay not up for yourselves treasures upon earth, where moth and rust doth corrupt, and where thieves break through and steal: But lay up for

yourselves treasures in heaven, where neither moth nor rust doth corrupt, and where thieves do not break through nor steal.

                    Jesus
                    —*St. Matthew 6:19, 20*

The Power of Blessing

To heal divisions, to relieve th' oppress'd,
In virtue rich; in blessing others, bless'd.
                    —Homer

He who blesses most is blest:
  And God and man shall own his worth
Who toils to leave as his bequest
  An added beauty to the earth.
                    —Whittier

The moment a seeker after Truth desires knowledge and wisdom for the purpose of blessing others, he becomes a protege of the Saints. A wholesome desire to bless, heal and instruct others opens the heart and mind to the secrets of the Saints regarding the supernatural power of Blessing, the ethical ways of Blessing, and the soul's memory-treasures that come through Blessing.

The numerous Scriptural references to Blessing are treasure chests of wisdom and truth. These priceless passages reveal the Power of Blessing to overcome the destructive havoc caused by curses; the Power of Blessing to manifest miracles; the Power of Blessing to change darkness into light, unknowing into knowing, pain into joy, vice into virtue.

But I say unto you, Love your enemies, bless them that curse you, do good to them that hate you, and pray for them which despitefully use you, and persecute you.

Jesus of Nazareth
—St. Matthew 5:44

The Lord thy God turned the curse into a blessing unto thee, because the Lord thy God loved thee.

Moses
—Deuteronomy 23:5

The Creator grants to each of His children an *elixir of holiness* to be used in the blessing of others. This elixir is used whenever one blesses his fellow men through prayer, meditation, fasting, almsgiving, selfless service and other sacramental dedications.

Each person created in the image and likeness of God has his own unique elixir of holiness that passes from him to those whom he blesses with his love, kindness, prayers and instruction. This elixir of holiness is swiftly telepathic on soul-levels of telepathy and light-waves of love, moving upon the recipients of his blessings as silent anointings of healing, joy and understanding. The Saints and all other enlightened servants of God in heaven and on earth are skilled in the telepathic sending of their elixirs of holiness.

"Bless the Lord, O my soul." (Psalm 103:1) The Divine Presence begins to reveal its wisdom and grace the moment one is moved to bless God and the human spirit. Each blessing sent forth in the spirit of pure love is as "bread upon the waters"*—for when one continually blesses the Creator and his fellow man, the bread of his blessings is recorded by the Memory of God and returned to him magnified and multiplied. Such is the nature of God and His Glory working through His Saints and through all who bless, heal, teach and create in His Name.

*"Cast thy bread upon the waters: for thou shalt find it after many days." (Ecclesiastes 11:1)

The Path of Virtue

Father in heaven, who lovest all,
  O help Thy children when they call;
That they may build from age to age,
  An undefiled heritage.

Teach us to bear Thy yoke in youth,
  With steadiness and careful truth;
That, in our time, Thy grace may give
  The Truth whereby the nations live.

Teach us to rule ourselves alway
  Controlled and cleanly, night and day,
That we may bring, if need arise,
  No maimed or worthless sacrifice.

Teach us to look in all our ends
  On Thee for judge, and not our friends,
That we, with Thee, may walk uncowed
  By fear or favor of the crowd.

Teach us the strength that cannot seek,
  By deed or thought to hurt the weak;
That under Thee, we may possess
  Thy strength, to succor man's distress.

Teach us to delight in simple things,
  And mirth that has no bitter stings;
Forgiveness free of evil done,
  And love to all men 'neath the sun.

—Rudyard Kipling
1865-1936

Memory Treasures

The Candelabra of the Soul

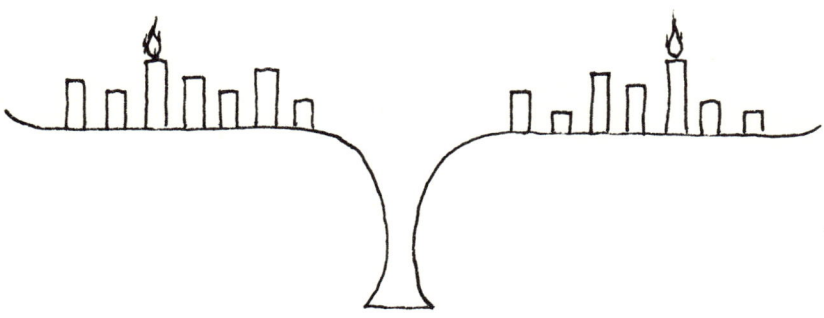

> For thou wilt light my candle: the Lord my
> God will enlighten my darkness.
> —Psalm 18:28

The soul is as a *candelabra* with many candles. Each candle is a virtue being shaped and formed by one's experiences and lessons in life. As a Truth-seeker evolves spiritually, his virtues become as tall and stately candles in the Candelabra of the Soul.

Eyes open to the beauty of the cardinal virtues perceive the luminous splendor of the Virtues of Jesus, His Apostles and all other Saints, Bodhisattvas and Great Souls. The opening of the eyes to beauty's light inspires one to work more diligently in his seeking to emulate the virtues of the illumined personages who have walked the earth.

Virtue-candles that reach the sacrament-light of the soul are anointed and ignited by the Bliss-Love of God through the Holy Ghost. Anointed virtues burn with the flame of Illumination. The many different degrees and kinds of Enlightenment and Illumination being experienced by seekers after Truth are dependent upon the virtue-candles that have earned the Creator's Blessing and Anointing.

The height, breadth and color of each virtue-candle in the Candelabra of the Soul is determined by one's wholesome attitudes toward God and His Laws. As a virtue-candle reaches toward the sacrament-light of the soul, one becomes "a new creature"* transformed, energized and enlightened by the Grace of God. The memory-treasures of past-lives' virtues contribute to each virtue-candle and its upward reaching toward the sacrament-light of the soul.

Faith in God is the *wick* in each virtue-candle. If a person with many virtues does not have faith in God, the important wick of faith is missing from his virtue-candles. Where there is no wick of faith, one is unable to experience Virtue Illuminations. These priceless Illuminations occur only when the wick of faith is ignited by the Bliss-Flame of God's Love.

If a virtue-candle is glowing with the flame of Illumination, it does not burn down; paradoxically, an illumined virtue increases and expands in height and light due to the expanding Glory of God within virtues.

All earnest aspirants who seek union with God must earn the illumination of each virtue. If only one virtue becomes illumined in a lifetime, this is a mighty occurrence in the soul's memory-record.

Illumined virtues light one's way into broader and deeper dimensions of God's Love and Grace. With each Virtue Illumination, the eyes are able to behold new vistas of beauty and wisdom within the Eternal Plan of God. In this, one's creations become more beautiful and his wisdom is increased manifold.

> But the wisdom that is from above is first pure, then peaceable, gentle, and easy to be intreated, full of mercy and good fruits, without partiality, and without hypocrisy.
>
> —James 3:17

*2 Corinthians 5:17

PROPHECY

And Moses said unto him, Enviest thou for my sake? Would God that all the Lord's people were prophets, and that the Lord would put his spirit upon them!   —Numbers 11:29

Desire spiritual gifts, but rather that ye may prophesy.
>Saint Paul
>—*1 Corinthians 14:1*

The Prophet is closer to the believers than their selves.
>Muhammad
>—*Koran 33:6*

I shall pour out teaching like prophecy and bequeath it to all generations forever.
>Apocrypha
>—*Ben Sira 24:33*

The Spirit of the Lord will come upon thee, and thou shalt prophesy with them, and shalt be turned into another man.
>—I Samuel 10:6

Jesus said unto them, A prophet is not without honour, save in his own country, and in his own house.
>—St. Matthew 13:57

Despise not prophesyings. Prove all things; hold fast that which is good.
>Saint Paul
>—*1 Thessalonians 5:20, 21*

And it shall come to pass in the last days, saith God, I will pour out of my Spirit upon all flesh: and your sons and your daughters shall prophesy and your young men shall see visions, and your old men shall dream dreams; And on my servants and on my handmaidens I will pour out in those days of my Spirit; and they shall prophesy.   —Acts 2:17, 18

8

THE ROYAL GIFT OF PROPHECY

Worship God: for the testimony of Jesus is the spirit of prophecy.

John the Beloved
—Revelation 19:10

He that receiveth a prophet in the name of a prophet shall receive a prophet's reward; and he that receiveth a righteous man in the name of a righteous man shall receive a righteous man's reward.

Jesus
—St. Matthew 10:41

The Relativity of Illumination

He who is happy within, who rejoiceth within, who is illuminated within, that Yogi, becoming the ETERNAL, goeth to the Peace of the ETERNAL.

—Bhagavad Gita

> We possess God, not in the sense that we become exactly as He, but in that we approach Him as closely as possible in a miraculous, spiritual manner, and that our innermost being is illumined and seized by His truth and His holiness.
>
> —Saint Augustine

The Tree of Knowledge is a mighty Tree whose branches reach from the planet Earth into the stars and the galaxies. A man with All-Knowledge relating to the Earth would be *illumined* regarding the Earth; however, to be illumined through All-Knowledge pertaining to all stars and galaxies is the ultimate in Illumination. Jesus, as the Messiah, came to prepare mankind for the time when the hearts and minds of men will reach the highest branches on the Tree of Knowledge. When this occurs, men will partake of the fruit that will produce Illumination regarding all stars and galaxies.

The Path of Virtue takes one through different states, stages, degrees and expansions of Illumination, for the expanding Glory of God within virtues is an expanding rainbow-spectrum of Gifts, Powers and Skills. There are illuminations of the heart and illuminations of the mind, illuminations of the soul and illuminations of the spirit. One literally swims in a Sea of Illumination after he places his trust in God and heeds the wise words of the Illumined Jesus.

Jesus was and is a Cosmos-Illumined Being. Thus, when one begins to be *filled* with the Light of the Christ, it is natural for him to think and feel on expanding wave lengths of light and love. Gradually, the Dimensional Power of the Christ within him becomes the Door to Versatility Illuminations, Cosmos Revelations and Archetypal Prophecies.

The work of the Christ is an *eternal* work, for the Image of God within each person is an eternal Image. The Image of God within every individual is that which will make possible the attaining of Illumination on Cosmos-Galactic levels. Through the work of the Christ, this Divine-Image potentiality will become one day a manifested reality!

Even as the stars are measured in magnitudes of light and power, so are there different magnitudes of Spiritual Illumination. The Great Teachers, the Saints, the Prophets and the Sages of all pure religions represent the greater magnitudes of Illumination.

"Draw nigh to God, and He will draw nigh to you." (*James 4:8*) As one draws closer to the Glory of God within virtues, he expresses steadily-increasing magnitudes of Illumination. With each increase of virtue-light within his heart and mind, he becomes more qualified to represent God as an enlightened ambassador of His Truth.

The word *Illumination* refers to a vast science of Relativity. Each aspirant on the Path of the higher life is expressing degrees of love, virtues, conscience and logic that determine his relationship to Time and Space. As one evolves spiritually, his degree of understanding increases, thereby lifting him to higher levels of light and truth. Individuals who express the greater magnitudes of Illumination are Prophets and Revelators by nature, for they are thinking, seeing and hearing on wave lengths of spiritual light in which Time functions at finer and faster dimensional frequencies.

In the present age, many different degrees of Illumination are being expressed by individuals in various physical and spiritual sciences. The nature of Illumination is one of rapid expansion and growth, for as old areas of Illumination are expanded through knowledge and experience, new areas appear. Spiritual Illumination is not a static state of heart and mind; it is an ever-expanding miracle of comprehension and coordination producing a multiplicity of versatile creations for and with God.

The Teacher's task is to qualify his students for the illuminations that come through union with the Glory of God and its multitudinous manifestations. In the higher life, the first illuminations pertain to one's attitudes. Attitude Illuminations lead to Virtue Illuminations. Virtue Illuminations lead to the next stages of Illumination. Thus, if one is graced with a living Teacher, he is being called by God to purify his attitudes so that they may become radiating vortices of love and virtue.

An attitude may be dark and self-defeating or it may be lighted and freedom-giving. A devotee on the Path of Virtue may have numerous attitudes that require transformation and cleansing. If there are dark attitudes inherited from one's ancestors, friends or the nation in which he lives, each of these attitudes must be healed, transformed and illumined. When spiritual light radiates through one's attitudes, the result is a radiant, enthusiastic, loving and enlightened individual centered in the Laws and Commandments of God.

Even as each attitude must be illumined, so must each virtue be illumined. Virtue Illuminations may occur singly or in combinations; the timing of each Virtue Illumination is determined by the Wisdom of God.

Virtue Illuminations prepare one for the next steps and stages of Illumination. Each new area of knowledge or activity opened to the dedicated devotee or initiate is determined by the Wisdom of God. If one is rewarded with gifts of the soul, these priceless gifts increase the degrees of his illuminative union with the Creator. Thus, each person on the Path of the higher life is experiencing a different degree and relativity of Illumination determined by his attitudes, virtues and soul-gifts.

The Royal Gift of Prophecy

> From understanding come virtues. From virtues come spiritual gifts. And from all of these come the miracles.
> —Ann Ree Colton

Archetypal Prophecies

> Howbeit when he, the Spirit of truth, is come, he will guide you into all truth: for he shall not speak of himself; but whatsoever he shall hear, that shall he speak: and he will shew you things to come.
> Jesus
> —*St. John 16:13*

There are many different levels and states of the Gift of Prophecy. Prophecy may be on the level of Tribes, Families, Races, Nations, Religions, Science, Art, Music, Industry, and in other fields of activity. The inspired prophet on any level is a forerunner, a way-shower, preparing the human spirit for the next stages of progress in the world. God is forever preparing His children for the future through hearts and minds receptive to His Prophetic Light.

The Hebrew word for prophet is "Nabi," which is derived from another word meaning "to boil forth as a fountain." A prophet anointed by the Spirit of God is as a fountain that provides unceasing waters of wisdom, righteousness and truth.

"Desire spiritual gifts, but rather that ye may prophesy." (1 Corinthians 14:1) This wise directive by Saint Paul attests to the importance of prophecy as a sovereign Gift of the soul, a Gift that radiates its light throughout all other spiritual gifts and soul-skills. The royal Gift of Prophecy links the heart and mind with the Glory of God within the Commandment of Everlasting Life.

The Eternal Spirit of God in the soul is beyond Time and Space; therefore, when one begins to make union with the supernal dimensions of the Godhead, he learns of degrees of God's Spirit beyond Time and Space. In this, he becomes a Prophet and a Revelator.

The sacrament-light of the soul is timeless. *Timelessness* in the realm of soul-light is a quickened state of *Knowing* and *Being* filled with the Beautiful Intelligence of God. He who unites with God's Presence within Timelessness attains Fulness, for Timelessness and Fulness are one.

Virtue-initiations prepare a devotee for union with the Glory of God in Time so that he may learn of the different soul-light relativities between heaven and earth. Through these initiations, one's understanding opens regarding the royal Gift of Prophecy—and he is able to think and to *know* on soul-light wave lengths of Time and Timelessness. Accompanying the Time-Relativity Gift of Prophecy is the birth to new areas of the Conscience and the World-Conscience. The degrees of virtue-light and pure love within one's conscience determine the nature and range of the prophecies revealed by the Creator.

The gradual states of Time's overcoming—from the Earth-level of Time to the soul-levels of Timelessness—relate to the virtues being expressed by the individual. The greater the degree of the soul's sacrament-light within one's virtues, the clearer and more extended is his prophetic seeing and knowing. The sacrament-light of the soul is the beginning of union with the Glory of God in Time and Timelessness. Therefore, when one seeks to do all things sacramentally as dedications to God, he looks upon Life and Creation through the eyes of the prophet.

If one has earned the Gift of Prophecy and other spiritual gifts in former lives, he experiences recapitulations of past-lives' virtue-initiations. If he meets with integrity each virtue-initiation recapitulation, his former-life spiritual gifts return to bless and prosper his present-life dedication to God.

All persons desirous of making an illuminative union with the Creator experience virtue-initiation recapitulations. Through these tests and trials, one rekindles the past-lives' memory-flames relating to the Laws and Commandments of God. In this, a sincere devotee returns to his rightful and hard-won placement on the Path of Virtue fortified by an innate intuition regarding the *rightness* of each Law and Commandment. Gradually, his intuition and faith prosper his union with the Wisdom of God within each of His statutes until he becomes centered in Holy Law. After one becomes centered in Holy Law, he experiences the rapid flowering of the gifts and skills of the soul and the spirit.

The knowledge of the Laws and Commandments recorded in the Old Testament, the New Testament and in other Sacred Scriptures provides the fertile soil for the soul's harvest of spiritual gifts. When the Gift of Prophecy is being quickened within one's being, the Spirit of God *anoints* his virtues, conscience and logic—and the Light of His Love manifests each Holy Gift in perfect timing and perfect harmony.

The past, present and future permeate the Laws of God. As one moves closer to the Godhead, he touches, simultaneously, the degrees of God's Laws relating to the past, present and future. In this, he experiences the *Prophetic Knowings* and *Clear Seeings* that come through union with the Glory of God within Time and Timelessness.

Through the genius of Albert Einstein, it has been proven in scientific laboratories and in space exploration that *Time* is related to the speed of physical light. As the speed of light increases, time slows down. If a clock is sent into space at the speed of light, time stands still; also, any object traveling at the speed of light completely disappears. Scientists now realize that a thirty-year-old astronaut traveling at the speed of light for one hundred years would be the same age on his return to the Earth, even though the planet would have aged one century. This scientific breakthrough in comprehending the relationship between Time and light holds the key to mankind's union with the Wisdom and Will of God creating the stars and galaxies.

Over the centuries, Saints, Sages and Adepts have utilized the Power of Appearance and Disappearance due to their knowledge of the laws of light governing spiritual quickenings. These holy personages could make themselves invisible to others; they also could travel physically to distant places through their use of divine degrees of light.

Jesus used His knowledge of spiritual light to *disappear* during times of danger while on earth. After His resurrection, He used this knowledge of light to *appear* to His Apostles. A visitation by Jesus, Mary, a Saint or any other Great Soul is made possible through their knowledge and use of the Laws of Spiritual Light.

Devotees and initiates who experience powerful quickenings of light within their beings are uniting with the Glory of God within Time and Timelessness. In time, the human spirit will become knowledgeable in the spiritual spectrum of light as well as the physical spectrum of light.

Even as a wise architect carefully prepares his drawings to the minutest details, so does God, the Great Architect of the Cosmos, establish blueprints for the creation of each solar system. These blueprints contain the design and purpose of each age and period during the life-span of a Star. The solar system containing the planet Earth is fulfilling this blueprint-design of the Great Architect during each moment of its existence. If one proves worthy in the sight of God, his eyes are opened through memory-treasures and prophetic visions—and he perceives that which the Creator would have him know and share.

Sacramental meditation enables a Truth-seeker to purify his heart and to still his mental processes so that he may become receptive to *Archetypal Prophecies.* Archetypal Prophecies pertain to the archetypes or blueprints of God for the creation of the solar system, the earth and the human spirit.

One of the primary purposes of the Gift of Prophecy is to give comfort and hope to others. Comfort, hope, guidance and good cheer come to those who hear the words of prophecy spoken by lips dedicated to the Commandments of Love.

The royal Gift of Prophecy is the natural result of union with the supernatural and prophetic light of the Lord Jesus. The Gift of Prophecy, when blessed by the Christ, defies definition or description, for it becomes one's entry into the Dimensional Worlds of Truth.

To be cognizant of the mathematical nature of the Laws and Commandments of God enables one to prophesy through *Logic.* Prophecy through logic may be likened to the knowledge of the meaning of traffic signals. Each Commandment of God is a traffic signal on the Highway of Life. Thus, when one has the knowledge of the Laws and Commandments of God, he can logically prophesy that which will occur when these statutes are fulfilled or not fulfilled. The knowledge of Holy Laws and their cycles enables one to accurately prophesy through logic the sweet blessings that come to the law-minded, the reverent, and the pure in heart.

Prophecy through logic also may be likened to one who recognizes and understands the seeds for fruit-bearing trees. If someone has never seen the seeds, he would have no idea of the nature of the trees-to-be or their fruit. However, if one *knows* each seed and its future tree, he can describe to others the tree and its fruit. So it is when an enlightened teacher prophesies through his knowledge of Holy Laws and Virtues.

Prophecy may be through logic, intuition, apprehension, dreams, symbols, inspiration, realization or revelation. If the Creator and His Angels remove certain *Timeseals* on His Laws and Commandments, one expresses the Gift of Prophecy on levels of Pure Inspiration and Divine Revelation. When God reveals the long-range purposes of each Law and Commandment, the Truth-seeker attains a high degree of Enlightenment and Illumination.

> And I saw in the right hand of him that sat on the throne a book written within and on the backside, sealed with seven seals. And I saw a strong angel proclaiming with a loud voice, Who is worthy to open the book, and to loose the seals thereof?
>
> <div align="right">Saint John
—<i>Revelation 5:1, 2</i></div>

The Gift of Prophecy is accompanied by a cross—the cross of seeing the inevitable suffering that comes when individuals or nations flagrantly disobey the Commandments of God. However, the Gift of Prophecy is also accompanied by a living hope based upon the knowledge that the Image of God within each soul will prove victorious through the action of the Time Cycles.

Mankind is in the process of learning a basic **Cosmos Truth:** *As ye sow, so shall ye reap.* The logic in this Scriptural precept eludes the selfish, the irreverent and the undisciplined. When a person begins to perceive the wisdom, justice and love of God within the Holy Law of Sowing and Reaping, he has made a major breakthrough in understanding the Plan and the Will of God.

The incessant challenges and changes in the world require a reverent dedication to spiritual values, laws and ethics. All too often, this dedication is totally absent—and the results are nightmarish catastrophes in the lives of individuals and nations.

The holiness of God's Laws fills the hearts of those who love Him, and brings compassion to the eyes as the eyes become filled with prophetic vision. The prayers of a prophet to remain centered in love, compassion and detachment keep him united with the Mercy of God—and the harsh realities of Pure Truth, when seen in prophetic light, become not a burden to him.

The Christ-Mind Gift of Archetypal Prophecy is an Apostolic Gift that comes forth in direct correlation to one's degree of Detachment. Numerous initiations related to Pure Love and the Virtue of Detachment accompany the birth of the Gifts of Archetypal Prophecy, Healing Miracles and Revelation-Illuminations.

DETACHMENT

The sage . . . is detached, thus at one with all. Through selfless action, he attains fulfillment. —Lao Tzu

He who would be serene and pure needs but one thing, detachment.

List ye, good people all: there is none happier than he who stands in uttermost detachment. —Eckhart

He, who regards well wishers, friends, foes, neutrals, mediators, the objects of hatred, relatives, the virtuous and the sinful alike, he stands supreme. —Bhagavad Gita VI.9

That thou mayest have pleasure in everything,
    seek pleasure in nothing.
That thou mayest know everything,
    seek to know nothing.
That thou mayest possess all things,
    seek to possess nothing.
That thou mayest be everything,
    seek to be nothing.

—Saint John of the Cross

Not to be cheered by praise.
Not to be grieved by blame.
But to know thoroughly one's own virtues or powers
Are the characteristics of an excellent man.

—Subhashita Ratna Nidhi

Him will I call a Brahmin who has cut all the fetters, who never trembles, who has passed beyond attachments.

Buddha
—*Dhammapada*

There is nothing in the world which I could not dispense with at a moment's notice.

—Albert Einstein

Everything in this whole round of the universe is God-made, God-protected and God-pervaded; enjoy what He gives thee, sharing it with thy fellow creatures and without attachment. For whose is all this wealth? It is God's and God's alone. Be not proud, be not greedy. —Yajur Veda

By detachment I mean that you must not worry whether the desired result follows from your action or not, so long as your motive is pure, your means correct. Really, it means that things will come right in the end if you take care of the means and leave the rest to Him. —Mohandas K. Gandhi

DEDICATED FASTING

> But thou, when thou fastest, anoint thine head, and wash thy face; That thou appear not unto men to fast, but unto thy Father which is in secret: and thy Father, which seeth in secret, shall reward thee openly.
>
> Jesus
> —*St. Matthew 6:17, 18*

> Sanctify ye a fast, call a solemn assembly, gather the elders and all the inhabitants of the land into the house of the Lord your God . . .
>
> —Joel 1:14

> For a man who is fasting his senses,
> Outwardly, the sense-objects disappear,
> Leaving the yearning behind; but when
> He has seen the Highest,
> Even the yearning disappears.
>
> —Bhagavad Gita

> I humbled my soul with fasting.
>
> —Psalm 35:13

> I wept, and chastened my soul with fasting.
>
> —Psalm 69:10

> Instead of using medicine, better fast today.
>
> —Plutarch

> He who fasts is in the hands of the inner physician.
>
> —Paracelsus

> The illness that cannot be cured by fasting, cannot be cured by anything else.
>
> —German Proverb

> Went to Church and fasted all Day.
> —George Washington
> (Entry in his diary,
> June 1, 1774)

> O ye who believe! Fasting is prescribed for you, as it was prescribed for those who preceded you —that you may be reverent.

> A man whilst fasting must abstain from bad expressions, and not even resent an injury.
> Muhammad
> —*Koran*

> All fasting, if it is a spiritual act, is an intense prayer or a preparation for it. It is a yearning of the soul to merge in the divine essence.
> —M.K. Gandhi

> It is in consequence of holiness and virtue alone that men attain to regions of blessedness and fasts and vows become efficacious.
> —The Mahabharata

Fasts observed as sacraments of worship are powerful and effective ways of communing with the Creator. A dedicated fast* one day a week or one day every two weeks establishes a *Fasting Cycle*. A fast observed on each Saturday followed by worship on Sunday makes of these two days of each week a Sacred Cycle of reverence, purification and spiritual quickening.

One who perceives the wisdom in dedicating his fasts to God unites with the virtue-light of the Saints and other Great Souls. The virtues of these enlightened Beings and

---

*One should not fast longer than one day unless the fast is supervised by a qualified physician.

Holy Presences become his life-lines to health, harmony and happiness.

If one dedicates certain fasts to the Lord Jesus, the Angels, the Saints or other Mediators of Heaven, he strengthens his union with their Wisdom and Love. Also, if one dedicates one or more fasts to a saying of the Lord Jesus or to any other Scriptural passage pertaining to a specific virtue, he will begin to draw upon a mysterious and supernatural power assisting him in the daily expression of the virtue. In asking, one receives; and in receiving, his lips sing praises to the Wonder, Power and Love of God working through the Mediation of His Saints and His Son.

> Come unto me, all ye that labour and are heavy laden, and I will give you rest.
>
> Jesus
> —*St. Matthew 11:28*

A sacramental fast observed with pure love and devotion to God may be likened to certain areas of the Cosmos where one teaspoon of matter weighs millions of tons. So is the condensed power and energy within a one-day sacramental fast used by God to manifest mighty miracles of healing and quickening in the world!

The royal Gifts of Prophecy, Healing and Revelation are prospered through sacramental fasting, for the five senses become purified and extended through the soul's virtue-light and God's Anointing Spirit. Sacramental fasts increase dramatically in power and light after one earns the Divine-Marriage Anointing; thereafter, each sacred fast lengthens his strides on the Path of Virtue.

Fasting, as a dedication to God, may be observed on the levels of student, devotee, initiate or teacher. Each level denotes a stage of progress on the Path of Virtue.

Every sacramental fast activates a direct confrontation with the dark side and the light side of the soul's record. As one progresses spiritually, the dark side of the soul's record becomes cleansed by the purifying action of each sacramental fast—and the grace-energies of the soul flow more freely into his heart, mind and life. With the increasing tide of grace-energies and essences from the soul, the royal Gifts of Prophecy, Healing and Revelation appear as jewels in the crown of consciousness.

> Fasting can help to curb animal passion, only if it is undertaken with a view to self-restraint. Some of my friends have actually found their animal passion and palate stimulated as an after-effect of fasts. That is to say, fasting is futile unless it is accompanied by an incessant longing for self-restraint.
>
> Fasting and similar discipline is, therefore, one of the means to the end of self-restraint, but it is not all, and if physical fasting is not accompanied by mental fasting, it is bound to end in hypocrisy and disaster.
> —M. K. Gandhi

> The first fruits of fasting are exposure to one's own egotism. With perseverance, the egotistical covering is removed, and a sustaining holy-virtue comes forth. When one has attained the goal of the holy-virtue, he should persevere even more in his fasting, for the spirit of fasting in the virtue-light achieves miracles.
> —Ann Ree Colton

Each sacramental fast should begin with heartfelt words of Dedication, such as, *I dedicate this Fast to whatever purposes*

God would put the spirit of this Fast. Specific dedications may be spoken before each sacramental fast and during the day of fasting. If one retains the spirit of Dedication during the hours of the fast, he will reap the greater rewards that come through reverent fasting.

"And he said unto them, This kind can come forth by nothing, but by prayer and fasting." (St. Mark 9:29) In this Scriptural passage, Jesus instructed His disciples to observe prayer and fasting in order to exorcise unclean spirits from their human victims. The Lord Jesus, as the Great Physician, is the Great Exorcisor. He uses the spirit of love within one's dedicated prayers and fastings to manifest mighty miracles in the healing of oneself, individuals, marriages, families, races, nations, religions, etc.

Obsession and possession plague many persons caught in the snares of lust, pride, hate, selfishness, greed, envy, vanity and other anti-virtues. To be mesmerized by the malicious and destructive wills of unclean, perverted and evil spirits is to be bound to sensuality, immorality and addictions that lead to sorrow, suicide or insanity. Through sacramental fasting combined with the miraculous healing power of prayer, a devotee on the Path of Virtue is exorcised of unholy and unsavory influences from the subtle worlds of unclean spirits so that he may become a dedicated healer in the Name of the Great Physician.

A *Prophet's Fast* is a three-day fast consecrated to the Christ. A Prophet's Fast may be observed for the purpose of healing an individual, a group of persons or a nation; or this special fast may be a time of personal purification and re-dedication.

Dedicated fasts observed by a religion or a nation are powerful and quick ways of communing with the Mercy and Might of God. When dozens, hundreds, thousands or millions of persons join together for a consecrated fast of gratitude to God, restitution for past sins, or for the healing of a religion or a nation, guidance comes through the prophets, sages or leaders in positions of public trust.

In the United States of America, three Presidents proclaimed days of national fasting, humiliation and prayer: John Adams, on May 9, 1798; James Madison, January 12, 1815; and Abraham Lincoln, the last Thursday in September, 1861, April 30, 1863, and the first Thursday in August, 1864.

> Whereas, the Senate of the United States, devoutly recognizing the Supreme Authority and Just Government of Almighty God, in all the affairs of men and of nations, has, by a resolution, requested the President to designate and set apart a day for National prayer and humiliation:

> And whereas, it is the duty of nations, as well as of men, to own their dependence upon the overruling power of God, to confess their sins and transgressions, in humble sorrow, yet with assured hope that genuine repentance will lead to mercy and pardon; and to recognize the sublime truth, announced in the Holy Scriptures and proven by all history, that those nations only are blessed whose God is the Lord:

> And insomuch as we know that, by His divine law, nations, like individuals, are subjected to punishments and chastisements in this world, may we not justly fear that the awful calamity of civil war, which now desolates the land, may be but a punishment inflicted upon us for our presumptuous sins, to the needful end of our national reformation as a whole People? We have been the recipients of the choicest bounties of Heaven. We have been preserved, these many years, in peace and prosperity. We have grown in numbers, wealth, and power as no other nation has ever grown. But we have forgotten God. We have forgotten the gracious hand which preserved us in peace, and multiplied and enriched and

strengthened us; and we have vainly imagined, in the deceitfulness of our hearts, that all these blessings were produced by some superior wisdom and virtue of our own. Intoxicated with unbroken success, we have become too self-sufficient to feel the necessity of redeeming and preserving grace, too proud to pray to the God that made us! It behooves us, then, to humble ourselves before the offended Power, to confess our national sins, and to pray for clemency and forgiveness.

Now, therefore, in compliance with the request, and fully concurring in the views of the Senate, I do, by this my proclamation, designate and set apart Thursday, the 30th day of April, 1863, as a day of national Humiliation, fasting and prayer. And I do hereby request all the People to abstain on that day from their ordinary secular pursuits, and to unite, at their several places of public worship and their respective homes, in keeping the day holy to the Lord, and devoted to the humble discharge of the religious duties proper to that solemn occasion.

All this being done, in sincerity and truth, let us then rest humbly in the hope authorized by the Divine teachings, that the united cry of the Nation will be heard on high, and answered with blessings, no less than the pardon of our national sins, and restoration of our now divided and suffering country, to its former happy condition of unity and peace.

In witness whereof, I have hereunto set my hand, and caused the seal of the United States to be affixed.

Done at the city of Washington this thirtieth day of March, in the year of our Lord one thousand eight hundred and sixty-three, and of the Independence of the United States the eighty-seventh.

—Abraham Lincoln

Moderation: The Golden Mean

You are holy, Lord, the only God,
and your deeds are wonderful.
You are strong.
  You are great.
  You are the Most High,
  You are almighty.
  You, Holy Father, are
  King of heaven and earth.
You are Three and One,
  Lord God, all good.
  You are Good, all Good, supreme Good,
  Lord God, living and true.
You are love,
  You are wisdom,
  You are humility,
  You are endurance.
  You are rest,
  You are peace.
  You are joy and gladness.
  You are justice and moderation.
  You are all our riches,
  And you suffice for us.
You are beauty.
  You are gentleness.
  You are our guardian and defender.
  You are courage.
  You are our haven and our hope.
You are our faith,
  Our great consolation.
  You are our eternal life,
  Great and wonderful Lord,
  God almighty,
  Merciful Saviour.

—Saint Francis of Assisi

Worship Cycles of fasting, prayer, meditation and almsgiving unite a sincere devotee with the Wisdom of God within the Virtue of Moderation. Moderation normalizes and polarizes, bringing into balance the body, heart, mind and soul. Gluttony, sexual excesses, obsessive habits, overexertions, and all other imbalances of the energy-processes within one's being are healed by the Presence of God within the Virtue of Moderation.

Moderation, as an initiating virtue, places one in the protective arms of common sense and logic so that wisdom's light may become part of the heart and mind. The royal gifts of the soul and the spirit flower forth in soil made fertile by the Love and Wisdom of God within the Virtue of Moderation.

> Let your moderation be known unto all men.
> Saint Paul
> —*Philippians 4:5*

> Moderation, the noblest gift of heaven.
> —Euripides

> Moderation: a virtue not to be despised by the most exalted among men, and prized also by the gods.
> —Tacitus

> It is the quality of a great soul to despise great things, and to prefer moderation to excess.
> —Seneca

> Fortify yourself with moderation; for this is an impregnable fortress.
> —Epictetus

The sage avoids extremes, excesses, and complacency.
>
> Lao Tzu

Virtue is a habit of the mind, consistent with nature and moderation and reason.
>
> —Cicero

Everything in excess is opposed to nature.
>
> —Hippocrates

Yes, there's a mean in morals.
Life has lines
To north and south of which all virtue pines.
>
> —Horace

Moderation is the silken string running through the pearl-chain of all virtues.
>
> —Thomas Fuller
> 1608–1661
> Quotation also attributed to:
> Joseph Hall
> Bishop of Norwich
> 1574–1656

Moderation in all things.
>
> —Terence

He in whom there is truth, virtue, pity, restraint, moderation, he who is free from impurity and is wise, he is called an elder.
>
> —Buddha

True happiness springs from moderation.
>
> —Goethe

Where there is Mercy and Prudence, there is neither Excess nor Harshness.
>
> —Saint Francis of Assisi

CONSCIENCE

The foundation of true joy is in the conscience. —Seneca

There is one thing alone that stands the brunt of life throughout its course: a quiet conscience. —Euripides

One's own actions will confront each soul after death in the form of a good or an evil conscience. —Zoroaster

The testimony of a good conscience is the glory of a good man; have a good conscience and thou shalt have gladness. A good conscience may bear right many things and rejoices among adversities. —Thomas á Kempis

There is a spectacle more grand than the sea; it is heaven: there is a spectacle more grand than heaven; it is the conscience. —Victor Hugo

Conscience is God's presence in man. —Swedenborg

The great beacon light God sets in all,
The conscience of each bosom. —Robert Browning

The conscience is eternal and will never die. —Martin Luther

Conscience is the voice of the soul, the passions are the voice of the body. —Rousseau

Labor to keep alive in your breast that little spark of celestial fire, called Conscience. —George Washington

For this is thankworthy, if a man for conscience toward God endure grief, suffering wrongfully. —1 Peter 2:19

I have lived in all good conscience before God until this day.
Saint Paul
—Acts 23:1

9

THE ANOINTED CONSCIENCE

And herein do I exercise myself, to have always a conscience void of offence toward God, and toward men.

Saint Paul
—*Acts 24:16*

VIRGINITY AND MORALITY

Saint Dionysius being bent on lauding Mary's virtues found them so inconceivable he held his tongue.

—Eckhart

Behold My heart surrounded with the thorns which ungrateful men place therein at every moment by their blasphemies and ingratitude.

—Apparition of the Virgin Mary to Lucy dos Santos

For it is fitting God should converse with an undefiled, an untouched and pure nature, with

187

> her who in very truth is *the* Virgin, in fashion very different from ours. For the congress of men for the procreation of children makes virgins women. But when God begins to associate with the soul, He brings it to pass that she who was formerly woman becomes virgin again.
> —Philo of Alexandria

The rare virtues of Mary qualified her to become the Mother of the Lord Jesus, the long-awaited Messiah. Mary expressed the virtues of a pure woman endowed with a blessed conscience. Joseph, a reverent man of character and integrity, was selected by the Hand of God to be the third member of the Holy Family.

In certain religions and ethical philosophies, high value is placed upon virginity before marriage. In other societies and cultures there is little or no value placed upon virginity. Diverse attitudes toward virginity and morality reflect the presence or absence of virtues and conscience.

A person may be born with a conscience, or the conscience may not make its appearance until adolescence, adulthood or until one is on his deathbed. Some persons live their complete lifetimes without a conscience.

An individual may go to bed in the evening without a conscience and awaken in the morning with a conscience. Even as a virtue may come to birth in a moment, so may the conscience come to birth in the twinkling of an eye.

The birth of the conscience may occur as the sun's light periodically breaking through dark clouds, or the conscience may come to birth during an explosion of Truth in the consciousness mind. The birth of the conscience may be the beginning of a new life of repentance and joy, or the appearance of the conscience may result in anguish leading to suicide.

Many men and women are born to the world with a moral conscience and with a reverent love for the beautiful and the holy. Others must learn the importance of morality from their parents or other loved ones. Some persons refuse to learn from others and must learn from Life itself through painful lessons. If lessons pertaining to the sacredness of Morality, Character and Integrity are not learned in one's present life, these necessary lessons continue to present themselves in future lives until morality, character and integrity are expressed with naturalness and love.

INTEGRITY

... till I die I will not remove mine integrity from me.
—Job 27:5

Let me be weighed in an even balance, that God may know mine integrity. —Job 31:6

The Lord shall judge the people: judge me, O Lord, according to my righteousness, and according to mine integrity that is in me. —Psalm 7:8

Let integrity and uprightness preserve me; for I wait on thee.
—Psalm 25:21

But as for me, I will walk in mine integrity: redeem me, and be merciful unto me. —Psalm 26:11

A great integrity makes us immortal. —Emerson

Follow your honest convictions and be strong. —Thackeray

The integrity of the upright shall guide them.
—Proverbs 11:3

> The just man walketh in his integrity: his children are blessed after him.
> —Proverbs 20:7

> The strength of a nation is derived from the integrity of its homes.
> —Confucius

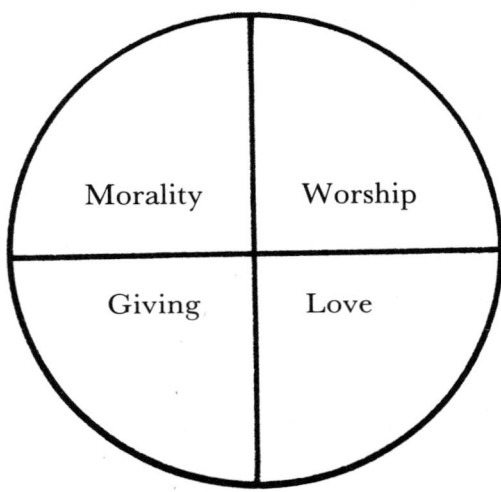

Integrity-Lens of the Conscience

Through Character and other Cardinal Virtues, the Integrity-Lens of the Conscience is shaped and formed, thereby beginning one's union with the *magnification power* of the soul and the Holy Ghost. The Integrity-Lens of the Conscience keeps one united with the Laws and Commandments of God relating to Morality, Worship, Giving and Love. Individuals who have these areas of the conscience active and magnified in the consciousness express a mature sense of morality, a deep hunger to worship God, a charitable and giving heart, and a compassionate love for their fellow man.

There are five major stages in the birth of the conscience: The birth of the conscience to man-made laws; the birth of the conscience to spiritual laws; the loyal fulfilling of spiritual laws and commandments; the anointing of the conscience by the Spirit of God through the mediation of the Christ; the anointed conscience as a Holy-Ghost lens of magnification.

"Render therefore unto Caesar the things which be Caesar's, and unto God the things which be God's." (St. Luke 20:25) Hosts of Heavenly Mediators work with each stage of conscience-birth and conscience-quickening. Many persons have yet to evolve a conscience that willingly accepts the disciplines imposed by man-made laws. After one attains a conscience that heeds the laws of the land, he is then prepared throughout numerous lifetimes for the energy-degrees of conscience that inspire him to revere and to embrace the wise disciplines related to the Laws and Commandments of God.

> Now the end of the commandment is charity out of a pure heart, and of a good conscience, and of faith unfeigned.
> Saint Paul
> —1 Timothy 1:5

Dedication, Earnestness, Sincerity, Integrity and Character form a beautiful cluster of virtues upon which God places His Anointing Spirit. As these virtues increase through worship, study and selfless service, the conscience becomes a bright and guiding light in the consciousness. The degree of one's moral conscience determines the degree of his character.

CHARACTER

Character is a man's guiding destiny.   —Heraclitus

I would rather be adorned by beauty of character than by jewels. Jewels are the gift of fortune, while character comes from within. —Plautus

A man's own manner and character is what becomes him.
—Cicero

The light of a good character surpasseth the light of the sun.
—Baha'u'llah

Without an acquaintance with the rules of propriety, it is impossible for the character to be established. —Confucius

A talent can be cultivated in tranquility; character, only in the rushing stream of life. —Goethe

Pure gold does not fear the smelter. —Chinese Proverb

Character gives splendor to youth and awe to wrinkled skin and gray hairs. —Emerson

To teach through deeds and to manifest deeds in others is the most noble character in man. —Ann Ree Colton

If there is righteousness in the heart, there will be beauty in character, there will be harmony in the home. If there is harmony in the home, there will be order in the nation. Where there is order in the nation, there will be peace in the world. —Chinese Proverb

"Walk in the Spirit, and ye shall not fulfill the lust of the flesh. Now the works of the flesh are manifest, which are these; Adultery, fornication, uncleanness, lasciviousness, idolatry, witchcraft, hatred, variance, emulations, wrath, strife, seditions, heresies, envyings, murders, drunkenness, revellings, and such like: of the which I tell you before, as I have also told you in time past, that they which do such things shall not inherit the kingdom of God. But the

THE ANOINTED CONSCIENCE 193

fruit of the Spirit is love, joy, peace, longsuffering, gentleness, goodness, faith, meekness, temperance. . ." (Galatians 5:16, 19-23) Lust, incest, rape, abortion and other foes of Morality claim many victims, and often leave in their wake painful and tortured consciences. Stealing, coveting, kidnaping, murder, adultery, perversion, masturbation, fornication, and all other crimes against the soul, the Commandments and the Image of God reveal the need for the birth of conscience or the cleansing of the conscience.

Unrighteous, irreverent and immoral persons inflict deep wounds upon themselves and their fellow men, causing grievous consequences that are reaped either in their present lives or in coming lives.

> Unto the pure all things are pure: but unto them that are defiled and unbelieving is nothing pure; but even their mind and conscience is defiled.
> Saint Paul
> —*Titus 1:15*

> It is neither safe nor prudent to do aught against conscience.
> —Martin Luther

> There is no witness so dreadful, no accuser so terrible as the conscience that dwells in the heart of every man.
> —Polybius

> A good conscience is a continual Christmas.
> —Benjamin Franklin

> With sympathy and pure faith and conscience,
> Embrace ye all beings and befree them from greed,
> That they might attain to the highest intelligence of the Tathagata (Perfect One).
> —Outlines of Mahayana Buddhism
> *Hymns of Mahayana Faith*

A woman who is sincerely repentant for having offended the sacred laws governing morality and procreation experiences a gradual *re-sanctification* of the womb. This blessing of God's forgiveness and mercy occurs while she applies herself to daily worship-cycles, the study of Scriptural truths, reverent obedience to Holy Laws, and loving service to others. In this, her womb experiences progressive stages of purification and re-sanctification correlating to the divine quickenings of her heart, mind and soul.

When a man who repents of moral and sexual offenses honors God's Laws and is faithful to daily worship-periods, there is a *re-purification* of the seed. This re-purification occurs in direct degree to the sincerity of his repentance and the cleansing of his thought process related to the procreative function. *"Ye have heard that it was said by them of old time, Thou shalt not commit adultery: But I say unto you, That whosoever looketh on a woman to lust after her hath committed adultery with her already in his heart."* (St. Matthew 5:27, 28)

Mary Magdalene was not a physical virgin when she met Jesus; however, she became a spiritual virgin through repentance. Over the centuries, countless persons who have experienced God's forgiveness of their errors and sins have become loyal and inspired followers of the Lord Jesus. *"I am not come to call the righteous, but sinners to repentance."* (St. Matthew 9:13)

> There are many religions, but there is only one morality.
> —Ruskin

> The one morality produces the perfect virtue, which produces the perfect goodness.
> —Ann Ree Colton

The Anointed Conscience

> Come now, and let us reason together, saith the Lord: though your sins be as scarlet, they shall be as white as snow; though they be red like crimson, they shall be as wool.
> —Isaiah 1:18

The Kiss of the Christ

> How much more shall the blood of Christ, who through the eternal Spirit offered himself without spot to God, purge your conscience from dead works to serve the living God?
> Saint Paul
> —*Hebrews 9:14*

It is an unalterable and eternal law of God that all who would become spiritually illumined must first purify their consciences. The Christ and His Host are the Mediators in the great drama of Consciousness-Illumination through Conscience-Purification.

Conscience is an *eternal* attribute of the soul. For many persons, the birth of conscience related to the Commandments of Morality, Worship, Giving and Love will require numerous lives, ages or solar systems. To assist and inspire those who are yet in the process of giving birth to conscience, God sends His Conscience Ones as Wayshowers. The Christ works with and through all Conscience Ones; Conscience Ones are His sheep—the sheep that hear His voice.

Wherever there is a pure conscience, there is Christ; for where there is a pure conscience, there is light. He whose consciousness is lighted by conscience is at one with his soul's light and divine grace. The purged and purified conscience ripened through love and virtue and anointed by the Creator becomes the *Anointed Conscience.* The Anointed Conscience makes of the faithful servant an Anointed Teacher of the higher life.

The conscience cleansed and purged by the Holy Fire of Pure Truth and Divine Love sits as a wise king upon the throne of consciousness—and henceforth, the consciousness is governed by the spiritual royalty of a sanctified conscience. A sanctified conscience is a conscience anointed by the Spirit of God through the Light of the Christ. An anointed conscience keeps one ever in communion with the Lord of Lords, the King of Kings.

The Spirit of God—through the mediation of the Christ, the "Bridegroom"*—*anoints, seals* and *quickens* His faithful servants with His Bliss-Presence, thereby consummating the Divine Marriage. Those who receive this powerful Anointing become revelators of Pure Truth and ambassadors of God's Mercy. The world moves forward through the inspired revelations of the Anointed.

> But the anointing which ye have received of him abideth in you, and ye need not that any man teach you: but as the same anointing teacheth you of all things, and is truth, and is no lie, and even as it hath taught you, ye shall abide in him.
> —1 John 2:27

> Now he which stablisheth us with you in Christ, and hath anointed us, is God; Who hath also sealed us, and given the earnest of the Spirit in our hearts.
> Saint Paul
> —*2 Corinthians 1:21, 22*

*St. Matthew 9:15

The Anointed Conscience

> The Spirit of the Lord is upon me, because he hath anointed me to preach the gospel to the poor; he hath sent me to heal the brokenhearted, to preach deliverance to the captives and recovering of sight to the blind, to set at liberty them that are bruised, To preach the acceptable year of the Lord.
>
> Jesus
> —*St. Luke 4:18, 19*

To be anointed by God is to be anointed by His *Cosmos-Eternal* Spirit—His Spirit of *Pure Love* creating the Universe. Therefore, after one receives this mighty Anointing, Sealing and Quickening, his heart and mind become increasingly filled with illuminations regarding *Cosmos, Eternal Life, Pure Love,* and the *Anointing Spirit.*

All who desire to unite with the Creator undergo a lengthy period of probation during which their virtues and conscience are repeatedly tested. At the beginning of the probationary period, the Light of the Christ moves upon one as a Holy Kiss. The heart and the mind receive this Kiss as the first purgings of the conscience. An aspirant's future progress on the Path of Virtue is determined by his accepting or refusing the Kiss of the Christ as the cleansing light in his conscience.

The probationary period before the Divine Marriage is an "engagement period" lasting twenty years. Upon the conclusion of this sacred cycle, a sincere devotee who proves worthy in God's sight receives the Christ-Kiss of Illumination!

Everything in the Universe is progressive, for the Spirit of God creating the Universe is an Ongoing Spirit. After progressive stages of lesser anointings, a probationer is made ready for the majestic Divine-Marriage Anointing that produces Fulnesses of Grace and Truth. This Great Anointing heralds the time when the Spirit of God becomes an Abiding Presence within one's being. The Great Anointing is followed by an acceleration of progressions, realizations and versatilities.

During the twenty-year probationary period, the devotee-initiate must prove that he loves God more than he loves any one or any thing. He must convince the Creator of his love for each Law and Commandment; he must know in his heart that, if necessary, he would willingly and happily lay down his life to preserve and protect the knowledge of God's Laws in the world. If he is required to suffer persecution for righteousness' sake, he accepts this dedication with faith and courage.

Throughout numerous testings during the probationary period, an earnest devotee must prove to God that he knows the difference between right and wrong, and that he is free from prejudice toward races, nations, religions, and the opposite sex. He must be sincerely repentant for each sin committed wittingly or unwittingly in his present life and in past lives; and he must desire to make an honorable restitution for each and every sin, offense and transgression. Also, he must prove to God that, regardless of the world's resistance to sacred truths, he will continue to fulfill and to teach the Virtues, Principles and Commandments taught by Jesus and His Holy Apostles. These "high calling*" dedications, when combined with daily worship-disciplines, prepare one for the Illumination-Feast following the Divine Marriage.

"For many are called, but few are chosen." (*St. Matthew 22:14*) Many aspirants seek to qualify for the Divine Marriage, but very few qualify for this powerful Anointing, Sealing

---

*Philippians 3:14: *"I press toward the mark for the prize of the high calling of God in Christ Jesus."*

and Quickening. God knows the heart of each of His children; He knows the purity and sincerity of the heart—and He knows if one is willing and ready to meet the increasing responsibilities that follow the Divine Marriage.

Total dedication to God is a rare virtue. The earnest desire to make a full and honorable restitution for all sin-offenses in the present life and in previous lives is a rare virtue. The willingness to be completely honest with God through a purged conscience is a rare virtue. Upon those who have these rare virtues, the Creator places His Spirit and unites with them in the Marriage Divine.

FAITHFULNESS

His lord said unto him, Well done, thou good and faithful servant: thou hast been faithful over a few things, I will make thee ruler over many things: enter thou into the joy of thy Lord.

Jesus
—St. Matthew 25:21

Moreover it is required in stewards, that a man be found faithful.

Saint Paul
—1 Corinthians 4:2

Hold faithfulness and sincerity as first principles.

—Confucius

A faithful man shall abound with blessings. —Proverbs 28:20

Be thou faithful unto death, and I will give thee a crown of life. —Revelation 2:10

The Conscience of the Cosmos

> Conscience is a working of the Law. In the Cosmos, Galaxies would collapse were it not for the Conscience Principle supporting the Universe.
>
> In the life of man, man without Law or Conscience is a collapsed individual of no use to himself and to his environment.
>
> —Ann Ree Colton

A Commandment-minded conscience acts as spiritual yeast within the consciousness. A spiritualized conscience enables one to commune with the finer frequencies of God's Mercy and Love—and he is lifted above the vibratory wave lengths of suffering. All Great Teachers, Saints and Prophets come to the world to lift the human spirit above the wave lengths of suffering. When their instruction is heeded, suffering decreases and enlightenment increases. One who reveres and applies the wise directives of the Great Souls is blessed with conscience; and, in being blessed with conscience, he works as a servant of God in the creative, holy and merciful work of lifting the world above the pain-tones of suffering into the joy-tones of soul and spirit.

Conscience is one of the pervading essences of the Universe. As one evolves spiritually, the *Expanding* Spirit of God within the heart's love and the mind's light gradually extends the range of the conscience from Individual Conscience, Family Conscience, Religious Conscience and National Conscience to the Conscience of the World. These expanding ranges of conscience-light in the consciousness prepare one for union with the Conscience of the Cosmos. All degrees of a purified conscience anointed and blessed by God signify different stages of union with His Anointing Spirit and with His Omnipresent Intelligence suffusing the Universe.

The Principle of Conscience is ever-present throughout the Cosmos; the Conscience Principle is within each Star and Galaxy. Even as the conscience of a person inspires him to remain within the purposes of God's Laws and Commandments, so does the presence of Conscience in the Universe keep all celestial bodies in perfect harmony.

In the life of an individual, the keynote of a cleansed conscience is harmony with oneself and with the Creator. The fruits of a cleansed and purified conscience are union with the Will of God creating man in His Image and union with the Wisdom of God creating the solar systems.

The conscience becomes an enemy only when man removes himself from the harmony of Holy Law. The conscience, as an attribute of the soul, is an eternal friend seeking to remind each person of his or her eternal heritage as a creation of God.

Conscience, as the Door to the Soul, is the Door to the Soul of Cosmos. The truth-songs of the Stars and the Galaxies may be heard only through the ear of the Conscience. Thus, he who prepares his conscience for the Anointing Spirit of God is working toward the time of oneness with the Wisdom and Love of God creating the Stars and Galaxies.

> Seven sins of the world:
>   Wealth without work,
>   Pleasure without conscience,
>   Knowledge without character,
>   Commerce without morality,
>   Science without humanity,
>   Worship without sacrifice,
>   And politics without principle.
>   —M. Gandhi

PART TWO

When you invite a stranger in, give him food, drink, and a place to pray.

MARRIAGE

And he (Jesus) answered and said unto them, Have ye not read, that he which made them at the beginning made them male and female, and said, For this cause shall a man leave father and mother, and shall cleave to his wife: and they twain shall be one flesh? Wherefore they are no more twain, but one flesh. What therefore God hath joined together, let not man put asunder. —*St. Matthew 19:4-6*

There is no more lovely, friendly and charming relationship, communion or company than a good marriage.
—Martin Luther

Marriage is honourable in all, and the bed undefiled.
Saint Paul
—*Hebrews 13:4*

This procreation is the union of man and woman, and is a divine thing; for conception and generation are an immortal principle in the mortal creature. —Plato

It is better to marry than to burn.
Saint Paul
—*1 Corinthians 7:9*

Let every one of you in particular so love his wife even as himself; and the wife see that she reverence her husband.
Saint Paul
—*Ephesians 5:33*

In marriage, one must desire the happiness of his or her own mate more than he desires his own happiness.
—Ann Ree Colton

But in marriage do thou be wise; prefer the person before money, virtue before beauty, the mind before the body. Then thou hast a wife, a friend, a companion, a second self; one that bears an equal share with thee in all thy toils and troubles. —William Penn

10

JOY IN MARRIAGE

The greatest happiness which a mortal man can imagine is the bond of marriage that ties together two loving hearts. But there is a greater happiness still: it is the embrace of truth. Death will separate husband and wife, but death will never separate him who has espoused the truth.

Therefore be married unto the truth and live with the truth in holy wedlock. The husband who loves his wife and desires for a union that shall be everlasting must be faithful to her so as to be like truth itself, and she will rely upon him and revere him and minister unto him. And the wife who loves her husband and desires for a union that shall be everlasting must be faithful to him so as to be like truth itself; and he will place his trust in her, he will honor her, he will provide for her. Verily, I say unto you, their wedlock will be holiness and bliss, and their children will become like unto their parents and will bear witness to their happiness.

Let no man be single, let every one be wedded in holy love to the truth. And when Mara, the destroyer, comes to separate the visible forms of your being, you will continue to live in the truth, and you will partake of the life everlasting, for the truth is immortal.

—Buddha

Dowry of Virtues: Preparation for Marriage

Blessed are you, God of our fathers, blessed is your name forever and ever. May the heavens bless you and all your creation forevermore. You made Adam, and you made Eve, his wife, to help him and sustain him. All mankind come from them. You said: It is not good for the man to be alone; let us make a helper for him. And now, Lord, you know that I am not taking this sister of mine out of lust but with a pure heart and according to your law. Have pity on us both, and let us grow old together.

Tobias
—*Apocrypha*

Who can find a virtuous woman? for her price is far above rubies. The heart of her husband doth safely trust in her, so that he shall have no need of spoil. She will do him good and no evil all the days of her life.

Solomon
—*Proverbs 31:10–12*

A devotee who can call on God while living a householder's life is a hero indeed. God thinks: "He who has renounced the world for My sake will surely pray to Me. He must serve Me. Is there anything very remarkable about it? People will cry shame on him if he fails to do so. But he is

blessed indeed who prays to Me in the midst of his worldly duties. He is trying to find Me, overcoming a great obstacle—pushing away, as it were, a huge block of stone weighing a ton. Such a man is a real hero."
—Sri Ramakrishna

The Earth is a planet of Initiation. All aspects, degrees and dimensions of human life are initiatory—from birth to death and from death to rebirth. Marriage is one of the greatest Initiations to be experienced by men and women on earth. A marriage dedicated to God becomes part of the Divine-Marriage Initiation through which comes Spiritual Illumination.

Even as a chain is as strong as its weakest link, so is a marriage only as strong as the weakest virtue of husband and wife. If beautiful virtues are present in the marital partners, their marriage is used by God to bless each other and to bless the world. The highest calling in a marriage is when both husband and wife are devoted to God and are unwaveringly true to His Commandments.

The virtues absent or present in a marriage with a physical mate are the very same virtues that are absent or present in one's quest for union with God. A person who does not have a giving heart in marriage will not have a giving heart toward God. If honesty is the missing virtue, one will be unable to be honest with his mate or with God. As one grows spiritually in his physical marriage, he grows spiritually in union with God, for one's physical marriage is a direct reflector and gauge of his placement on the Path of Virtue.

Many persons who contemplate marriage do not consider the importance of the presence of the cardinal virtues in themselves or in their prospective mates. Such persons base their future marriages solely on physical companionship, sexual gratification, or financial expediency.

Often, individuals who enter into marriage under the hypnosis of sexual passion soon discover that their mates have immature emotions, devitalizing fears and primitive prejudices.

The greatest dowry one may give to one's beloved is a dowry of virtues expressed with a true and tender love. When bride and bridegroom enter into marriage with a dowry of virtues from their souls' records, their future as husband and wife begins on the firm foundation of faith, love, conscience and wisdom.

One who has failed to evolve the cardinal virtues before marriage gives his or her mate a *negative dowry*. A negative dowry may consist of numerous anti-virtues, such as selfishness, irresponsibility, slovenliness, hates, prejudices, lust, greed, pride, angers, childishness, fears, guilts, hostilities, laziness, inflexibility, inconsiderateness, envy, jealousy, covetousness, an unforgiving nature, etc. These and other anti-virtues drain the joy from a marriage. Those who enter into marriage unencumbered by these foes of happiness are free to receive the first fruits of God's choicest blessings.

If one is responsive to the teachings of enlightened teachers, the rough edges of his or her personality will be smoothed away before entering into marriage. If a man or woman keeps delaying the overcoming of undesirable personal traits and repugnant habits, the marriage will be burdened by his or her immaturity.

A marriage based upon selflessness becomes a blessed state of happiness anointed by the Love of God. When one is married to a selfless and loving mate, there are many joys, delights and blessings that come through their love and association.

An anointed marriage must be earned. It is earned through many lives of faithfulness to marriage as a *Sacrament* authorized and hallowed by the Creator. The joys in an anointed marriage stem from the Joy of the Lord made manifest through virtues.

Anointed marriages experience the rapid strengthening and increasing of all virtues. In this, marriage contributes to the spiritual individuality and soul-grace prosperity of the husband and wife. This is the true purpose of Marriage as a part of the Divine Marriage or Union with God.

When two devotees marry and become householders for God, all aspects of their physical marriage are preparation for the Divine Marriage. If the Divine-Marriage Anointing is earned by one or both, their physical marriage becomes a projection of the grace and joys of the Divine Marriage with God. Physical marriage is strengthened by the Divine Marriage, and the Divine Marriage is prospered through the physical marriage.

The marriage state becomes part of the state-of-grace degrees of union with God through the soul's grace-cycles. If the soul's grace is free to flow through the virtues of the husband and wife, their harmonious and creative association moves them as "one flesh" into the higher precincts of Truth and spiritual fulfillment. The presence of holy virtues in a marriage assures the partners of a tranquility born of loyalty, fidelity, trust in one another, and devotion to God.

> Loyalty is the holiest good of the human heart.
> —Seneca

> Nothing is more noble, nothing more venerable than fidelity. Faithfulness and truth are the most sacred excellences and endowments of the human mind.
> —Cicero

> Fidelity is the sister of justice. —Horace

If a marriage is to become a strong alliance that prospers in grace and love, it is mandatory that the cardinal virtues be natural expressions of the husband and wife. The virtues observed and revered in each other before marriage become the virtues cherished and treasured after marriage.

The importance of virtues increases over the years as the responsibilities in marriage and family life increase. If important cardinal virtues are absent in one or both marital partners, the missing virtues will be the cause of many problems and woes.

The first flush of romantic attraction during courtship should be followed by a serious appraisal of the virtues of the person to whom one is attracted. Pre-marital sexual indulgences often make one feel obligated to the other—and marriage may be entered into prematurely with little value placed upon virtues. To be properly prepared for marriage, one should assess his own virtues and the virtues of his mate-to-be.

The first virtues to be considered are the prospective mate's attitudes toward God and His Laws. Does he or she have an innate desire to worship God and to live according to the Ten Commandments? Does he or she have faith, patience, a giving heart, a charitable mind? Is one's future mate neat and clean, have a sense of humor, a sense of responsibility? Is he or she a good steward of monies, generous, kind, forgiving, friendly, tolerant? Does he or she love to work and love to study? Are honesty, humility and gratitude natural attributes? These and many other factors contribute to a happy and joy-filled marriage.

When God is the Central One in a marriage, the marriage prospers in grace and love—and each virtue becomes an increasing strength, a source of rich blessings. An immature person places himself or herself, rather than

God, as the chief one in the marriage. If the Love-Presence of God withdraws from a marriage, the marital partners become bitter adversaries who constantly call attention to each other's weaknesses in character and other shortcomings.

When husband and wife concentrate their mental energies upon each other, these energies become as flames that irritate and burn. However, when husband and wife dedicate their marriage to God, and live according to His precepts and statutes, their energies are directed toward *Him* —and the Creator reciprocates by blessing all aspects of the marriage.

Without the Light of God in a marriage, the marriage becomes a gloomy union doomed to mediocrity. When the Light of God is present, spiritual treasures continually appear to bless the husband and wife, lifting them to higher and higher pinnacles of wisdom, understanding and joy.

A marriage passes through many different stages of testing. Virtues enable the marriage to survive all challenges.

Previous to marriage, some persons place unnecessary burdens upon their future mates by confessing their sexual sins to them rather than confessing to God. If one is merciful, all confessions of moral offenses will be directed to God rather than to his or her betrothed—and the marriage will begin as a clean white page upon which the Hand of God will write a new story of love, joy and pure creation.

A *Betrothal Sacrament* during the engagement period prepares the man and the woman for the seriousness and sanctity of the marriage bond. The Betrothal Sacrament cleanses and quickens the heart, mind and soul, thereby enabling the Wedding Ceremony to be the beginning of a new life in Christ.

The shared worship of God by husband and wife; the saying of grace at the family table; the devotion to moral values and ethical principles—these make a marriage an increasing harvest of love, virtue and fulfillment.

The more virtues in husband and wife, the more joy in the marriage, for God blesses their virtues with expanding love—and the marriage becomes a *Grace-Marriage.* A Grace-Marriage is a marriage in which husband and wife live within the wisdom and protection of the Golden Rule, and express a true and pure love for one another.

If husband and wife dedicate each day of their marriage to God, they remain under the blessings of the Almighty. These blessings increase with each sacramental meditation and prayer and with each holy tithe given to God with love. Blessings also increase after each Sabbath Day shared together in the sanctuary of the Lord. Scriptural study and spiritual instruction received in a house of worship inspire husband and wife to express the many virtues that make of marriage a holy and joyful institution.

When God perceives that husband and wife are proving true to their marriage vows—meeting and overcoming all challenges and temptations with dignity, honorableness and righteousness—He anoints them with the Greater Benedictions of Grace. Thereafter, the love between husband and wife adds to the world rare blessings of Beauty, Truth and Pure Creation.

The Virtue of Kindness is the keynote of a happy marriage. If this virtue is included in one's dowry of virtues, the marriage experiences the protection of the Angels, the blessings of the Saints, and the Providential Grace of God.

KINDNESS

Kindness is the golden chain by which society is bound together. —Goethe

A good deed is never lost; he who sows courtesy reaps friendship, and he who plants kindness gathers love. —Saint Basil

Be ye kind one to another.
Saint Paul
—*Ephesians 4:32*

What wisdom can you find that is greater than kindness?
—Rousseau

Kindness is a mark of faith, and whoever hath not kindness hath not faith. —Muhammad

In her tongue is the law of kindness. —Proverbs 31:26

Kindness is ever the begetter of kindness. —Sophocles

Kindness is produced by kindness. —Cicero

No act of kindness, no matter how small, is ever wasted.
—Aesop

Great persons are able to do great kindnesses. —Cervantes

Life is so short, and we have never too much time for gladdening the hearts of those who are traveling the dark journey with us. Oh, be swift to love, make haste to be kind.
—Amiel

Kindness is the sunshine in which virtue grows.
—R. G. Ingersoll

So many gods, so many creeds,
   So many paths that wind and wind,
     While just the art of being kind
Is all the sad world needs. —Ella Wheeler Wilcox

Recompense injury with justice, and recompense kindness with kindness. —Confucius

Nothing is so popular as kindness. —Cicero

Enough, and more than enough, has your kindness enriched me. —Horace

Persistent kindness conquers the ill-disposed. —Seneca

The heart benevolent and kind
The most resembles God. —Robert Burns

That best portion of a good man's life,
His little, nameless, unremembered acts
Of kindness and of love. —Wordsworth

Marriage-grace increases whenever a husband and wife express the virtues of loyalty, honesty, forgiveness, flexibility, a sense of humor, kindness, gentleness, generosity, humility, integrity and a sense of responsibility. These and other virtues protect the marriage and continuously add new joys to family life. This is especially true when father, mother and children are endowed with the Virtue of Cheerfulness.

CHEERFULNESS

Cheerfulness is a divine virtue. —Meher Baba

The most manifest sign of wisdom is a continual cheerfulness. —Montaigne

Mirth is like a flash of lightning, that breaks through a gloom of clouds, and glitters for a moment; cheerfulness keeps up a kind of daylight in the mind, and fills it with a steady and perpetual serenity. —Joseph Addison

Joy in Marriage

A poor man who does not flatter, and a rich man who is not proud, are passable characters; but they are not equal to the poor who yet are cheerful, and the rich who yet love the rules of propriety. —Confucius

Be of good cheer; it is I; be not afraid.
Jesus
—*St. Matthew 14:27*

The Altar in the Home

Be ye not unequally yoked together with unbelievers.
Saint Paul
—*2 Corinthians 6:14*

It matters not if you live the life of a householder, only you must fix your mind on God. Do your work with one hand and hold the feet of the Lord with the other. —Sri Ramakrishna

Train up a child in the way he should go: and when he is old, he will not depart from it.
—Proverbs 22:6

The children of godly parents are the children of many prayers. They are prayed for before and prayed for after they are born. The prayers of a godly father and a godly mother do much.
—John Bunyan
1628–1688

Marriage is holy; procreation is holy. The raising of children is a sacred responsibility. When parents are reverent in their love for God, and teach their children the importance of worship, the Grace of God blesses the parents, the children and the home.

Marriage between a reverent, spiritually-minded person and one who has unawakened virtues regarding the worship of God is often painful to both parties. In such marriages, hatreds, jealousies, rivalries and tyrannies sometimes surface.

To be unable to share the joy of worship with one's mate; or to be wed to someone who does not delight in study and learning, or who is antagonistic toward one's tithing to God—these and other differences in heart and mind are a cross that may become extremely heavy over the years. To attract such a mate indicates that in past lives one has imbalanced the Holy Laws governing Marriage, Procreation and Worship. Repentance and confession to God begin the process of healing—and prepare one for coming lives in which the perfect and holy Law of Attraction will bless the penitent with a mate who will be like-minded in religious aspirations and a kindred spirit in the love of worship, the love of study and the love of Truth.

Many persons with the *physical degrees* of the virtues make compatible mates on the materialistic levels of life. However, their limited range of virtues renders them incapable of lifting their thoughts and hearts to higher or spiritual levels of thinking and feeling. Such persons are content with the mundane—the comfortable—meeting their physical-world responsibilities with honor and living peaceably with their fellow man.

The desire to enter into marriage with God requires that one work to bring forth the *spiritual degrees* of the virtues. Each increase of spiritual-light within the cardinal virtues makes of one a more loving mate, a more responsible parent and a more qualified servant of God.

A moody mate subject each day to a kaleidoscope of moods is a reflection and projection of one's own past lives. When a man marries, he marries the subconscious of his mate as well as all other aspects of her being; when a woman marries, she marries the subconscious of her husband. A temperamental, moody, indecisive, careless, lazy and tempestuous mate signifies a subconsciousness seething with unresolved sin-debts. To be married to such a complex person is to be confronted by the many faces of one's own lower self in past lives. Marriage to a person of extremes in multi-moods offers one the opportunity to make restitution for previous lives when he, too, was unstable, unreliable—and, in some instances, unfaithful.

Marriage to a mate suffering from severe psychosis, neurosis or manic depression indicates one's own past lives in which he imbalanced the Energy Laws of the heart, mind, body and soul. Each life is an opportunity to bring the scales of God's Energy Laws into balance. All Commandments are Energy Laws. Love for God and His Commandments restores one to an equilibrium in all energy-processes in body, heart, mind and soul.

If one is graced with a mate having a spiritualized conscience, this blessing is the result of the Law of Attraction rewarding him for past lives of goodness and mercy. When two persons with conscience marry, there is *communication* between them. In marriages where one party has a spiritualized conscience and the other has a weak or vacillating conscience, there is difficulty in communicating with each other—and the marriage suffers. A husband and wife who have great differences in conscience are as two individuals speaking different languages.

A spiritualized conscience is a conscience that loves and worships God; is centered in morality; thinks of the good of others more than self; contributes to world betterment; uses Time creatively with a wisdom inspired by the Creator. A feeble conscience is unable to perceive the importance of daily worship-periods or the worship of God on the Sabbath Day; is uncertain as to morality; thinks primarily of self; contributes little or nothing to good in the world; squanders precious time.

The joys of marriage are unceasing and expanding joys when husband and wife are spiritual-law minded, virtue-inspired and conscience-anointed. The knowledge of holy laws and virtues inspires householder-devotees of the higher life to experience the happiness-joys of a marriage based on divine goals.

"A man's foes shall be they of his own household." (St. Matthew 10:36) During certain initiatory trials, a devotee on the Path of Virtue may be challenged by one or more members of his family who try to interfere with his daily worship of God. If he remains true to his Daily Worship Cycles and Sabbath-Day Worship Cycles, he will prove his love for God—and the Creator will reciprocate with His Love and Blessings.

Each married couple that expresses an innate reverence, wisdom and love for God establishes an altar in the home. This altar provides a warm and sacred atmosphere for the worship of God through daily prayer and meditation, and for other spiritual and creative dedications.

The altar in the home is an extension of the altar in the Sanctuary, Chapel or Church where husband, wife and children join others in the worship of the Creator. The altar in the home and the altar in the house of prayer lead the family members to the inner altar of the soul and the Cosmos-Altar of the Holy Spirit.

When marriage partners teach their children the importance of the Ten Commandments, the Holy Law of Tithing, and the Sermon on the Mount—and prove to be good examples to their offspring—the Love-Presence of God blesses and prospers their family life every day in every way.

The hope for the preservation of God's Word in the world, the preservation of sanctuaries of worship, and the preservation of religious and spiritual freedoms is in the hands of parents who teach their children the importance of tithing to God. The present-age freedoms are the results of the dedications and sacrifices of countless tithers over the centuries. Future centuries and ages will be the beneficiaries of tithes given to God today. Children who are taught this truth are the hope for the future—and their children and children's children who have the open ear and the giving heart will also work to preserve the healing power of God's Word and the sacredness of His Sanctuaries on earth.

GIVING

The tenth shall be holy unto the Lord.   —Leviticus 27:32

Will a man rob God? Yet ye have robbed me, But ye say, Wherein have we robbed thee? In tithes and offerings. Ye are cursed with a curse: for ye have robbed me, even this whole nation. Bring ye all the tithes into the store house, that there may be meat in mine house, and prove me now herewith, saith the Lord of hosts, if I will not open you the windows of heaven, and pour you out a blessing, that there shall not be room enough to receive it.   —Malachi 3:8-10

And Melchizedek king of Salem brought forth bread and wine: and he was the priest of the most high God. And he blessed him, and said, Blessed be Abram of the most high God, possessor of heaven and earth: And blessed be the most high God, which hath delivered thine enemies into thy hand. And he gave him tithes of all.   —Genesis 14:18-20

For this Melchisedec, king of Salem, priest of the most high God, who met Abraham returning from the slaughter of the kings, and blessed him; To whom also Abraham gave a tenth part of all; first being by interpretation King of righteousness, and after that also King of Salem, which is, King of peace; Without father, without mother, without descent, having neither beginning of days, nor end of life; but made like unto the Son of God; abideth a priest continually. Now consider how great this man was, unto whom even the patriarch Abraham gave the tenth of the spoils. And verily they that are of the sons of Levi, who receive the office of the priesthood, have a commandment to take tithes of the people according to the law.

                                          Saint Paul
                                        —Hebrews 7:1-5

Restore to God His due in tithe and time;
A tithe purloin'd cankers the whole estate.   —George Herbert

God loveth a cheerful giver.

                                          Saint Paul
                                       —2 Corinthians 9:7

Almsgiving extinguishes the wrath of God.   —Muhammad

For it is by giving that we receive.   —Saint Francis of Assisi

Giving is living.   —Anonymous

He gives twice who gives quickly.   —Publius Mimus

We make a living by what we get, but we make a life by what we give.   —Winston Churchill

Theirs was the fulness of heaven and earth; the more that they gave to others, the more they had.   —Kwang-Tze

Joy in Marriage

Give, and it shall be given unto you; good measure, pressed down, and shaken together, and running over, shall men give into your bosom. For with the same measure that ye mete withal it shall be measured to you again.

Jesus
—St. Luke 6:38

And Jesus sat over against the treasury, and beheld how the people cast money into the treasury: and many that were rich cast in much. And there came a certain poor widow, and she threw in two mites, which make a farthing. And he called unto him his disciples, and saith unto them, Verily I say unto you, That this poor widow hath cast more in, than all they which have cast into the treasury: For all they did cast in of their abundance; but she of her want did cast in all that she had, even all her living.

Jesus
—St. Mark 12:41-44

But rather give alms of such things as ye have; and, behold, all things are clean unto you.

Jesus
—St. Luke 11:41

A marriage blessed by the Creator is a *creative* marriage. The complementing virtues of the husband and wife provide an energy field through which the Creative Spirit of God inspires the minds' light and the hearts' love. In this, the marriage partners become creative individuals whose dedications to God infuse their words and their works with healing energies and holy inspirations. The marriages of spiritual-creative persons are testimonies of their love for God and their fellow man.

To retreat from God is to retreat from life, for God is Life. The recluse type of individual seeks to isolate mate and self into a shell of disassociation from others. If this occurs, the home becomes a prison; friendships are shunned; and the marriage enters into a decaying state.

When love for God is present in the hearts of the husband and wife, there is an expanding love for each other and for the human spirit. Daily worship-observances by husband and wife generate love-actions in harmony with holy law. Thus, friendships abound—for the Unitive Light of God's Love attracts to them spiritual-creative persons of virtue, conscience, integrity and character. From such harmonious associations, the causes of liberty, humanitarianism and benevolence are prospered in one's community and nation.

FRIENDSHIP

Virtue is not left to stand alone. He who practices it will have neighbors. —Confucius

A faithful friend is a strong defense,
a treasure, if he can be found.
A faithful friend is beyond price;
there is no measure of his worth.
A faithful friend is a staff of life
which he who fears God shall obtain.
He who fears God respects his friend,
and loves him as he loves himself.

Ben Sira
—*Apocrypha*

A man that hath friends must shew himself friendly: and there is a friend that sticketh closer than a brother.
—Proverbs 18:24

Thy friend has a friend and thy friend's friend has a friend; be discreet. —The Talmud

Joy in Marriage

I destroy my enemy when I make him my friend.
—Abraham Lincoln

I live in the hope that I shall be able to hug all humanity in friendly embrace. —M. Gandhi

Whenever there is friendship, there is a chance for human beings. —Alexander Pope

A friend is long sought, hardly found, and with difficulty kept.

The friendship that can cease has never been real.
—Saint Jerome

He who has a thousand friends has
  not a friend to spare.
And he who has one enemy will meet
  him everywhere.

—Ali Ibn-abu-talib
602–661 A.D.

Greater love hath no man than this, that a man lay down his life for his friends. Ye are my friends, if ye do whatsoever I command you.

Jesus
—*St. John 15:13, 14*

Dedication and the Tester

And when the tempter came to him (Jesus), he said, If thou be the Son of God, command that these stones be made bread. But he answered and said, It is written, Man shall not live by bread alone, but by every word that proceedeth out of the mouth of God.

—St. Matthew 4:3, 4

> For this cause, when I could no longer forbear, I sent to know your faith, lest by some means the tempter have tempted you, and our labour be in vain.
>
> Saint Paul
> —*1 Thessalonians 3:5*

Even as marriage to a physical mate is a continuous dedication, so is marriage or union with God a continuous dedication. Dedication in physical marriage is essential if one would experience the happiness, joys, ecstasies and bliss of marriage; dedication in union with God is of vital importance if one would experience the happiness, joys, ecstasies and bliss of the Divine Marriage.

A marriage dedicated to God brings husband and wife increasingly closer to the Creator; and, eventually, they become trustworthy stewards of sacred truths. Unfortunately, many married couples forget about God soon after the wedding ceremony; they forget about worship; they forget about preserving His Word. If this forgetfulness persists, the Love-Presence of God removes itself from the marriage. Without God's Presence in a marriage, the joy goes out of the marriage; problems mount; tensions build; desertions and divorces occur.

God's Presence increases in a marriage through a couple's devotion and dedication to Him and to His Commandments of Worship, Giving, Morality and Love. In a marriage blessed by God's Presence the husband and wife complement, supplement and support each other's efforts on the Path of Virtue and Illumination.

If one wisely dedicates to God his marriage, worship, work, etc., he will be protected and blessed by the power within the Virtue of Dedication. After one makes a dedication of any kind, he should remain true to the dedication.

He should fulfill each dedication as a *sacrament* to God, placing his efforts as offerings on His Holy Altar.

It is the tester's work to test one's integrity. Any thought of discontinuing a dedication is a thought inspired by the tester. To permit such thoughts to continue despoils the purity and sincerity within one's dedications to God. Such persons become increasingly vulnerable to the subtle voice of the tester, who seeks to steadily and methodically tear down every dedication they have made—be it the spiritual life, work, education, marriage, etc.

The tester is successful in destroying marriages when men and women who speak marriage vows are insincere and fickle. Rather than work *with God* in the healing and overcoming of their problems and differences, they permit the tester to plant seeds of dissension, dispute and disagreement. These seeds grow in the soil of insincerity, halfheartedness and fickleness—and marriage often ends in bitterness, separation or divorce. The numerous divorces today give evidence of the tester's ability to decimate a marriage due to the absence of true love, sincerity and dedication.

When one knows in his heart, mind and soul that his vows of dedication in marriage with a mate and in marriage with God are sincere vows, the tester has no way or means to complete his disruptive work—for the idea or thought of "quitting" is alien to a truly dedicated heart.

The Virtue of Dedication is a major part of one's "whole armour" of Spiritual Protection and Insulation. Quitting, after one makes a dedication to God, reveals a major flaw in the character; such persons can never become leaders of others on the Path of Virtue. The world needs spiritual leaders dedicated to God. Leaders come forth from those who prove capable of remaining true to their Dedications.

The tester's work is to test one's dedications and virtues. To be grateful for each test—and to remain courageously firm in one's dedications—is to pass the tests and to strengthen the armour of Spiritual Insulation. After each strengthening, the Virtue of Courage and correlating Virtues make one more receptive to the Joy and Love of God.

COURAGE

Courage is the best gift of all; courage stands before everything. It is what preserves our liberty, safety, life, and our homes and parents, our country and children. Courage comprises all things: a man with courage has every blessing.
—Plautus

Courage leads starward, fear toward death. —Seneca

Courage is that virtue which champions the cause of right.
—Cicero

Courage conquers all things: it even gives strength to the body. —Ovid

Wait on the Lord: be of good courage, and He shall strengthen thine heart: wait, I say, on the Lord. —Psalm 27:14

Courage, the footstool of the Virtues, upon which they stand.
—R. L. Stevenson

Jesus was sent by the Father to lift all persons and families of the Earth into the spiritual life of worship of God and devotion to moral principles. A spiritually-minded person is sent by the Father into a family to help lift his family closer to God. If he permits the non-spiritual members of the family to pull him down to their level, he will become less and less devoted to God. However, if he emulates Jesus by remaining firm in his dedications to God, he will be an example to his family—and one or more family members will be lifted up.

Each spiritually-minded person in a family is faced with this test: to fall backward or to lift others. Courage is the keynote, and patience is the way of victory.

> Be such a husband to your believing wife that she may say, "God has not only given me a husband, but such a husband as preaches to me every day the way of Christ to his Church.
> —John Bunyan

THE DIVINE MOTHER

> The true saint goes in and out amongst the people and eats and sleeps with them and buys and sells in the market and marries and takes part in social intercourse, and never forgets God for a single moment.
> —Aru Sa'id ibn Abi'l-Khayr

> A householder, endowed with knowledge like Janaka's,* can enjoy fruit both from the tree and from the ground. He can serve holy men, entertain guests, and do other things like that. I said to the Divine Mother, "Oh Mother, I don't want to be a dry sadhu."
> —Sri Ramakrishna

The body temple is sacred; therefore, all cycles related to the physical body are sacred cycles. These pertain to the

*Janaka (7th Century B.C.?), the father of Sita, was a great philosopher king similar to the prototype of Solomon.

cycle of the breath; the cycle of the blood, the heart beat; the cycles of secretions and excretions; menstrual cycles; cycles of cell reproduction; the cycles of sleep and waking, birth and death.

If husband and wife prove their love for God and His Laws—serving and worshipping Him as "one flesh"—the Divine Mother and the Heavenly Father bless and govern all cycles of their joint-dedication to God. The Divine Mother blesses and times the sexual cycles and all other cycles relating to the natural functions of the body. If there is reverent love rather than lust, husband and wife experience increasing joy in their love-making and in all other aspects of their marriage due to the sweet blessings of the Divine Mother.

In family life, the eating of meals occurs in cycles. To speak a prayer of gratitude before partaking of food makes of each mealtime a sacred cycle. Fasting, when sacramentally observed by husband and wife one day a week or one day every two weeks, also establishes a sacred cycle through which their souls may send forth rhythmic tides of Grace.

When husband and wife fulfill the giving to God of tithes and offerings as a cyclic dedication, they remain united with the Providential Grace of God. Married or single devotees who partake of the Sacrament of Communion in the rhythm of the seasons and Holy Days activate the laws of the soul through which Grace Inheritances are received from previous lives. Through Worship Cycles, Tithing Cycles and Sacrament Cycles, the Holy Eucharist becomes the *wine* of Holy-Grace Inspiration and the *bread* of Physical and Spiritual Sustenance.

The soul lavishes its treasures upon one who wisely and reverently establishes Cycles of Dedicated Creativity. A single or married devotee is at his very best in fulfilling the

Divine Image sealed into his soul whenever he dedicates to create works of beauty and truth for the Glory of God. A prayer spoken at the beginning and ending of a time of Dedicated Creativity keeps one united with the Creator's Love and Grace.

When the sexual aspect of marriage is reverently dedicated to God, a strong foundation is built for all other aspects of the marriage. Reverence in sex perpetuates the Creator's Love-Presence in a marriage. Lust and selfishness denote the absence of key virtues, thereby inviting harsh lessons and stern penalties. With the overcoming of lust and selfishness, the spirit of dedication in the marriage becomes a mighty strength solidifying the marriage and prospering the spiritual pursuits of the husband and wife.

The dedication to bring children into the world is blessed by God when acts of procreation are fulfilled with reverence and sacredness. This sacramental attitude toward the creation of new life unites one with the Grace of God working through the Laws of Attraction, Birth and Creation.

Self-honesty during meditation makes one aware of his faults so that he may begin their overcoming; a spiritual dedication in marriage also works as a revealer of faults stemming from weak or missing virtues. In this, marriage is used by God to reveal the truth about oneself in a magnified light, for an anti-virtue or non-virtue becomes increasingly apparent by the pain it brings to one's mate. The dedication to give birth to the missing virtue brings the balm of healing peace and adds new joys to the marriage.

One should avoid becoming a "policeman" over the anti-virtues of his mate, for this negative trait will add to the spirit of discord and disharmony. Through fervent prayer, pure love and reverent example, one works with the Divine Mother and the Heavenly Father—and miracles occur in the marriage.

Marriage to a selfish or lustful mate with childish behavior patterns requires great patience, much prayer, compassion and long-suffering. In time, one's mate may begin to experience the virtue-quickenings that will bring with them miraculous healings.

"God hath taken away my judgment." (Job 24:5) Adultery committed in past lives takes a terrible toll in one's present-life marriage if he left the world in an unrepentant state. Any cardinal sin for which one remains unrepentant causes the eyes to be blinded during courtship in his present life—and his judgment may be impaired in the selection of a mate. Unexpiated sin-debts of past lives present their penalties through one's present-life erroneous decisions and misdirected goals. Repentance at any moment in Time and Space begins the healing process and the transformation from suffering to joy.

> I put on righteousness, and it clothed me: my judgment was as a robe and a diadem.
> —Job 29:14

> Teach me good judgment and knowledge: for I have believed thy commandments.
> —Psalm 119:66

Pre-marital sexual indulgence and lustful attitudes after marriage become as rocks in the machinery of marriage—causing many perplexing problems. Through repentance, confession and restitution, a penitent husband and wife prove to God that they have attained the ability to perceive the difference between right and wrong. The healing of the soul's record occurs in direct relationship to the sincerity of one's repentance and his earnest desire to rectify his errors. One way of rectification is by teaching children and adults the value of Virtue and the wisdom of the Golden Rule.

Reverence in sex places a married couple under the direct blessings of the Divine Mother. As long as any shadow or remnant of lust remains in the heart of husband and wife, the spirit of discord will be permitted to intrude upon their marriage—and their hearts will become hardened toward one another. Lust is destructive; pure love is holy creation blessed by the Divine Mother.

Unresolved lust-sins committed before or after marriage are self-created curses that return in cyclic tides of negation, inharmony and incompatibility. These negative cycles, timed to the Moon's energy-influences upon the deep waters of the lower subconscious, subject a marriage to repetitive irritations, frictions and tensions.

The Moon is constantly trying to remind husband and wife of the importance of reverence and pure love in sex and in all other areas of their lives. If one is alert to the Moon's energy-cycles as they affect his family life and spiritual life, he will quickly and easily identify the lunar lessons related to unexpiated moral offenses staining the soul's record. If there is any imbalance in the soul's record, the Moon will reveal it and prayers will heal it.

Every thing and every person in one's life are the *Omnipresence* of God revealing his soul's record and his placement on the Path of Virtue. A Truth-seeker who becomes alerted to the Moon and its cycles may work more closely with the Creator in the healing and resolving of past-lives offenses and in the receiving of his soul's grace-treasures earned in former lives.

All marriages are seeking to become the ideal marriage as portrayed by Mary and Joseph. Many marriages are far from this goal; others are close to this perfection in harmony and divine purpose. The *Child* born to those emulating Mary and Joseph is that One who comes to birth in the world through all pure souls who venerate the virtues of the Saints and create holy works in God's Name.

When a man has the right kind of love for his wife, the Divine Mother opens to him many levels of beauty within his wife. A wife at one with the Divine Mother is a perfect helpmate, a strength, a fountain of unceasing love and blessings.

If the Divine Mother's Presence is in a marriage, there is joy in cooking, joy in the partaking of food, joy in work, joy in recreation, joy in worship, joy in love-making, joy in raising children, joy in creativity, and joy in serving God as one flesh. The joys inspired by the Presence of the Divine Mother are contagious joys, in that they bring joy to others. Such married couples have an anointed marriage blessed by God. Their harmony, happiness and combined virtue-light become a magnified presence for good through which God may heal, bless and create.

Celibacy in marriage should be practiced only when there is mutual consent between the marital partners. If vows of celibacy are taken out of timing, new problems will appear in the marriage. Celibacy observed as a dedication to God should be in timing to His Will and Plan. Single or married devotees who are committed to celibacy should pray to remain centered within the Virtues of Purity and Chastity so that they may remain true to their dedication.

Marriages blessed by the Divine Mother and the Joy-Presence of the Angels inspire in husband, wife and children a wholesome sense of humor. The love of God's laws invites increasing blessings from the Cherubim Angels who quicken the heart with a holy happiness. The Cherubim bless the family with cycles of joy and jubilation, and enable the family members to express a philosophical calm and sense of humor during times of stress and crisis.

Wit accompanies wisdom; these two are inseparably wed in hearts and minds devoted to God. To add joy to the world through wholesome humor renders a great healing service to one's fellow man. Joy heals; happiness is a powerful medicine in the life of the individual and the family.

WHOLESOME SENSE OF HUMOR

A merry heart doeth good like a medicine.   —Proverbs 17:22

A merry heart keeps a man alive.   —Apocrypha

God is the creator of laughter that is good.
  —Philo of Alexandria

If I did not laugh, I should die.   —Abraham Lincoln

One shows his character by what he laughs at.
  —German Proverb

One who is always laughing is a fool, and one who never laughs a knave.   —Spanish Proverb

The mind ought sometimes to be amused that it may better return to thought and itself.   —Phaedrus

Good taste in humor is exquisite creation.   —Ann Ree Colton

To laugh is proper to man.   —Francois Rabelais

A good laugh is sunshine in a house.   —Thackeray

Man is distinguished from all other creatures by the faculty of laughter.
—Joseph Addison

... a time to laugh.
—Ecclesiastes 3:4

Health is the greatest of gifts, contentedness the best riches; trust is the best of relationships, Nirvana the highest happiness.

Buddha
—*The Dhammapada*

If ye keep my commandments, ye shall abide in my love; even as I have kept my Father's commandments and abide in his love. These things have I spoken unto you, that my joy might remain in you, and that your joy might be full.

Jesus
—*St. John 15:10, 11*

He that keepeth the law, happy is he. —Proverbs 29:18

SILENCE

Silence is a great help to a seeker after Truth. In the attitude of silence the soul finds the path in a clearer light and what is elusive and deceptive resolves itself into crystal clearness. Our life is a long and arduous quest after Truth, and the soul requires inward restfulness to attain its full height.
—Mohandas K. Gandhi

Silence is the garden of meditation. —Ali

Silence is a healing for all ailments. —Babylonian Talmud

Silence is the eternal duty of man. —Carlyle

Silence is the mother of Truth. —Benjamin Disraeli

Silence is man's chief learning. —Palladas

The Lord is in His holy temple: let all the earth keep silence before Him. —Habakkuk 2:20

Be silent, O all flesh, before the Lord. —Zechariah 2:13

To the mind that is still, the universe surrenders.
—Chinese Saying

When mind is still, the Truth gets her chance to be heard in the purity of silence. —Sri Aurobindo

Stillness and tranquility set things in order in the universe.
—Lao Tzu

Signs from the Soul come silently, as silently as the sun enters the darkened world. —Tibetan Saying

One word spake the Father, which Word was His Son, and this Word He speaks ever in eternal silence, and in silence must it be heard by the soul. —Saint John of the Cross

11

MEDITATION AND THE LAW

The law was therefore given that grace might be sought; grace was given that the law might be fulfilled.

—Saint Augustine

We must so train ourselves that the mind, as it were, swims in the law of God, under the guidance of which our life must be governed.

—Saint Seraphim of Sarov

Let the truth of Braham be taught only to those who obey his law, who are devoted to him, and who are pure in heart. He who knows Braham becomes Braham.

—Upanishads

The gift of the law surpasses all gifts; the flavour of the law surpasses all flavours, the delight in the law surpasses all delights. The destruction of craving conquers all sorrows.

—Buddha

His delight is in the law of the Lord; and in his law doth he meditate day and night.

—Psalm 1:2

THE QUALITY OF SILENCE

> Any clown can tell the difference between wise talk and foolish talk; but it takes a good master to distinguish between wise silence and foolish silence.
> —Japanese Saying

> You listen and hear the Silence.
> You listen and see the Silence.
> You listen and smell the Silence.
> You listen and taste the Silence.
> You listen and feel the embrace of the Silence.
> —Seneca Indians

> Without knowledge there is no meditation,
> Without meditation there is no knowledge:
> he who has knowledge and meditation is near to Nirvana.
> Buddha
> —*The Dhammapada*

> He quickly gains meditation free from sin. These are the blessings of one whose virtue is pure.
> —Candrapradipa Sutra

> Meditation is the clarifier of a beclouded mind.
> —The Tibetan Doctrine

> My meditation of him shall be sweet.
> —Psalm 104:34

"*Study to shew thyself approved unto God.*" (2 Timothy 2:15) The daily study of Scriptural truths improves the *Quality* of Silence in one's meditations. The wisdom of the Great Teachers gained through the study of sacred writings is an integral part of the meditative stillness. Through increasing knowledge and experience, the quality of a devotee's silence during daily meditation becomes a creative state of continuous improvement and expansion.

The illuminating wisdom of the Great Teachers acts as a germinating essence within the heart and mind. This essence, permeating the consciousness and the conscience, increases from study period to study period. When the wisdom of the Great Teachers, Prophets, Saints and Sages becomes part of the devotee's life and thoughts, he experiences rapid results and rewards by steadily improving the quality of silence during his sacramental meditations.

As one walks the Path of Virtue, the quality of silence within his meditations is prospered after each increase of virtue-light and conscience-light. Meditators who evolve a purified moral conscience unite with the Wisdom of God within the great Commandments of Morality. Progress through meditation is also determined by one's conscience as related to the Sabbath-Day Commandment, the Holy Law of Tithing and the Commandments of Love. Conscience inspires one to fulfill all Holy Laws and Commandments with reverence and enthusiasm; therefore, his progression on the Path of Virtue is assured—and his meditations are blessed with peace, inspiration and realization.

As a meditator becomes increasingly dedicated to the Ten Commandments and the Sermon on the Mount, he follows the Path of Virtue on its spiraling course up the Mountain of Illumination. The four major plateaus on this Holy Mountain are: student, devotee, initiate and teacher. *A student learns the Law. A devotee applies the Law. An initiate is washed clean by the Law. And a teacher is enlightened by the Law.*

> The Commandment of the Lord is pure, enlightening the eyes.
> —Psalm 19:8

The Sacrament of Baptism received from a dedicated servant of God begins the cyclic quickenings that seek to qualify a student for the Divine-Marriage Anointing. After the Sacrament of Baptism, all aspects of a sincere student's life come under the protection and direction of the Christ; in this, he experiences the progressive stages of simplification and synchronization that transform him into a devotee and, eventually, an initiate. In time, a faithful follower of the Great Shepherd becomes an anointed teacher; thereafter, he meditates, fasts, prays and creates in the magnification-light of the Holy Ghost. *"But ye, beloved, building up yourselves on your most holy faith, praying in the Holy Ghost, keep yourselves in the love of God, looking for the mercy of our Lord Jesus Christ unto eternal life."* (Jude 20, 21)

> The first meditation is the meditation of love in which you must so adjust your heart that you long for the weal and welfare of all beings, including the happiness of your enemies.
> —Buddha

> Love your enemies.
> Jesus
> —St. Matthew 5:44

The greatest magnifier of Truth is Silence filled with Love. The love-filled Silence of sacramental meditation makes of meditation a **Cosmos Science**. The Saints in heaven—blessing all sacraments of worship and devotion—open the eyes and ears of their proteges regarding the Cosmos Sciences of Grace and Truth.

Holiness magnifies; simplicity glorifies. When one dedicates his love and virtues to God, the Holy Light of God within love and virtues adds increasing magnitudes of magnification to the consciousness. In this, a devotee gains a magnified awareness of Scriptural truths and their purposes within the Will and Plan of God.

The integrity-lens of the conscience becomes part of the consciousness through purification, dedication and sacramental meditation. The degree of magnification within the integrity-lens increases with each new addition of love and virtue in the heart and the mind. This attribute of magnification through love and virtue remains with one as long as his dedications to God and His Laws are sincere and wholehearted.

The most important element in life and in meditation is love. In Buddhistic writings, it is said that whenever Mara, the tester, sent an arrow (test) toward the meditating Buddha, the arrow, on coming close to Buddha, changed into flowers. Such is the nature and power of love during meditation: the *energy* within each test is immediately changed by the meditator's love into flowers of grace. A pure love toward all during reverent meditation enables one to remain centered in serenity, compassion and grace.

Thoughts or feelings of lust, pride, greed, vanity, judging, critical-mindedness, anger, etc. that telepathically move upon a meditator from others or from his own lower subconscious are as "arrows" testing his purity, character and integrity. If a devotee meets each test with pure love, the energy within the test is changed into *light*. The greater the love and virtue in one's heart, the more rapidly does love do its perfect work of changing dark or undesirable thoughts into the light of holy inspirations and sacred realizations.

If hate is in the heart during meditation, meditation becomes black magic. The same is true if the heart of the meditator is filled with covetousness, greed, pride, envy or jealousy. Whenever the heart is devoid of love, forgiveness and compassion, meditation becomes a black-magic art harmful to oneself and to others.

It is essential that love be part of each meditation and that the Truth-seeker be dedicated to the Ten Commandments and the wisdom-teachings of the Great Souls. In this way, a devotee on the Path of Virtue is protected from sending hate-energies to others during meditation or at any other time of the day or night. Love keeps one centered in Holy Law—and the Love-Spirit of God within Holy Law protects, quickens and enlightens.

As a seeker after Truth purifies his love, the obstacles impeding his spiritual progress are removed one by one by the Hand of God; also, he gains protection from persons antagonistic to his spiritual aspirations. If his love is pure and sincere, the Spirit of God will soften the hearts of his adversaries—and there will be healing, peace, reconciliation and joy. This miracle is experienced through the power of pure love earned through meditations based upon dedication to the Creator and His Commandments.

An alert meditator comes to the realization that the Creator is providing him with many different sources of energy. The lower subconscious, the dark side of the soul's record, is the repository of all unresolved sins of the present life and previous lives. The energy within the sins recorded in the lower subconscious is as a powerful ocean; through the truth-light of honest confession, the devotee gives the Christ the means of harnessing, healing and purifying this sin-ocean of energy. The time required for the Christ to manifest this miracle of freedom and forgiveness depends upon one's faith in God and love for His Laws.

A deep love for God and His Son during sacramental meditation is as a flame under the cauldron of the consciousness. As the cauldron begins to boil, the sediment on the bottom (lower subconscious) of the cauldron is gradually dislodged. The loosened sediment (sin-debt energies) floats to the surface of the consciousness-cauldron, where it becomes visible scum. Prayers of repentance and confession and sacrificial works of restitution remove the scum from the cauldron—and the consciousness becomes a pure vessel for the golden waters of Soul Grace and Divine Grace.

Many ages of sin-debts may be lodged in the lower subconscious. Meditation enables one to work with God and the Christ in the removal of this sediment through daily cleansings and purifications of the heart, mind and soul. With a purified consciousness comes a clear conscience; and with a clear conscience come the spiritual quickenings that prosper one's union with the Love and Grace of God.

As the dark energies within the lower subconscious are changed into pure light through the Christ and His Mediation Host, the soul's pure energies flow more freely into one's heart, mind and being. The soul's pure energies are *pure-creation energies;* therefore, the meditator at one with God is ever in the grace-state of Pure Creation.

All outer-world bondages are projections of unexpiated sin-debts lodged in the lower subconscious. As long as these debts remain unresolved, the lower-subconscious energies will continue to intrude upon one's meditations—and his physical-world relationships and responsibilities will seek to remove him from the Path of Virtue.

Love, virtue and conscience inspire one to learn important lessons *during* the silence of sacramental meditation. Lessons learned during meditation are lessons that need not be learned through painful experiences in the world of action and association. As long as a meditator is lacking in love, self-honesty and conscience, he will attract necessary virtue-lessons through negative persons, health conditions or other outer-world problems and difficulties. However, if the quality of silence during meditation is wholesome, love-filled and forgiving, one quickly perceives and corrects his faults—and, in so doing, he avoids sorrow and suffering.

As the quality of silence improves through the study of the wise words of the Great Teachers—and through a reverent and enthusiastic obedience to Sacred Statutes—holy inspirations expand into priceless realizations. Thus, one's union with the worlds of holy inspiration and realization is dependent upon the quality of silence in his dedicated meditations.

The Divine-Marriage Anointing accelerates and expands the action of all virtues in the heart and the mind. After this mighty Anointing, the quality of silence during one's meditations provides God with a clearer, broader and more receptive field through which to reveal His Plan of Creation.

The crown of meditation is Revelation. When rhythmic tides of Revelation Grace are received by the meditator, this indicates that the quality of silence in his meditations is proving worthy in the sight of God.

To be Law-minded is to become Love-centered.
To be Love-centered is to become Light-inspired.
To be Light-inspired is to become Truth-filled.
To be Truth-filled is to become Grace-illumined.

The Importance of Enthusiasm

And whatsoever ye do, do it heartily, as to the Lord, and not unto men; Knowing that of the Lord ye shall receive the reward of the inheritance: for ye serve the Lord Christ.
> Saint Paul
> —*Colossians 3:23, 24*

In order to do great things, one must be enthusiastic.

> —Saint Simon

To love the Creator with the energy and vitality of an enthusiastic love is the key to union with His Love. The word *enthusiasm* comes from the Greek word *enthusiathnos,* meaning *God within.* One must prove his love for God through an enthusiastic love for His Laws and Commandments before he may qualify for the Divine-Marriage Anointing. Numerous lesser anointings prepare an earnest aspirant for the time of this Great Anointing.

One who is dedicated to sacramental meditation progresses on the Path of Virtue according to his degree of love. He experiences God's Presence according to his degree of love. He is illuminated through the Mediation of the Christ according to his degree of love.

Love is an incinerator burning up the sin-debts of many ages. Love frees one from all bondages when his love is united with God's Love. An enthusiastic love for God increases the incinerator action of love as ages of transgressions are consumed in the twinkling of an eye. An enthusiastic love for God and His Laws hastens the day of the Divine Marriage.

The Scriptural passage "God is a consuming fire"* discloses the power of God's Love to consume or burn away all obstacles to the devotee's union with Him. This miraculous action of God's Love is dependent upon the degree of enthusiasm within the devotee's love for God and His Laws.

In marriage, if husband and wife have an enthusiastic love for one another, the marriage is one of joy, harmony and fulfillment. So it is in the Divine Marriage: if one loves God and His Laws with an enthusiastic love, the Divine Marriage is one of expanding joys and enlightenments as God answers love with love.

*Hebrews 12:29.

Love is the key to Cosmos. Love is the lifter of all veils, the dissolver of all obstacles, the healer of all divisions and separateness. Love overcomes Time and Space. Love unites one with the Glory of God in the Soul and in the Spirit.

The Law and Love of God are *one*. When one loves God's Law, he experiences God's Love—for Holy Law and Love are one. The more one loves God's Law, the more is he enfolded by His Love. The Law-Love of God is that which anoints, heals, lifts, protects, quickens and enlightens.

God's Love is within His Law, and His Law is within His Love. To the spiritually enlightened, Law and Love are one, for God, as Law and Love, is One.

> Love is the fulfilling of the Law.
> Saint Paul
> —*Romans 13:10*

Love and Simplicity

> . . . the simplicity that is in Christ.
> Saint Paul
> —*2 Corinthians 11:3*

When one loves, he comes into simplicity. Love simplifies his motives, desires and goals; love simplifies all aspects of his being. Love is the simplicity-expression of all virtues; when one loves purely, each virtue sends a healing light into the world.

Love simplifies all spiritual disciplines and worship observances. When one loves God with a simple, childlike love and humility, he fulfills all Holy Laws with naive naturalness; therefore, he unites with the Love, Wisdom and Beauty of God sealed into the heart or core of His Laws.

Love simplifies prayer and meditation; these become as one breath of love for God. Love simplifies fasting and almsgiving, making of them pure essences of devotion and reverence.

Love simplifies because it purifies. It purifies the grace-corridors of the heart so that the Grace of God may flow in abundant measures through the heart. Love purifies the grace-corridors of the mind—and Pure Grace, as holy emanations of truth and wisdom, radiates from the mind. Love purifies the grace-corridors of the Soul—and Pure Grace, as Soul-Skills and Gifts, becomes part of one's being.

Love simplifies all relationships: marriage, family, business, friendship, discipleship. Through love, all relationships become one joy-tone sounding throughout the day and the night.

Love simplifies one's sleep. The world of dreams reflects this simplicity, and one's sleep becomes more peaceful, more synchronized with the Love-simplification of the day.

Love simplifies death and dying; for when one loves, he rests peacefully in the Bosom of God in life or in death. Love for the Eternal God brings the understanding of Eternal Life. Love for the Eternal Spirit of God in man brings patience, compassion and enlightenment. Love for God and man makes one at home in heaven or on earth. Wherever he is, in whatever world he dwells, he is at home, for love is the Energy-Essence of God within His Creation of heaven and earth.

Love simplifies one's comprehension of the Christ. As the devotee simplifies his life through love, he is illuminated by the Christ. In becoming illuminated by the Christ, his simplicity is anointed by the Spirit of God, thereby becoming sacred versatilities of the heart, mind, soul and spirit.

When one's love transcends racial barriers, national barriers, religious barriers and personality barriers, he is ready to begin the process of transcending Solar-System barriers. The Christ, the Mediator and Coordinator of all Stars and Galaxies, is then free to reveal secrets and mysteries regarding the Glory of God in the Cosmos.

Love, the protector; Love, the peace-giver; Love, the simplifier; Love, the magnifier—these prosper one's meditations so that he might become a spiritual scientist in the laboratory of the soul.

SIMPLICITY

O holy simplicity!

—John Huss (1373–1415)
Last words at the stake

The more wise and powerful a master, the more directly is his work created, and the simpler it is. —Meister Eckhart

Only let me make my life simple and straight, like a flute of reed, for Thee to fill with music. —Rabindranath Tagore

In character, in manners, in style, in all things, the supreme excellence is simplicity. —Longfellow

Blissful are the simple, for they shall have much peace.
—Thomas á Kempis

The art of art, the glory of expression and the sunshine of the light of letters, is simplicity. —Walt Whitman

What is true, simple and sincere is most congenial to man's nature. —Cicero

Simplicity, simplicity, simplicity! I say, let your affairs be as two or three, and not a hundred or a thousand . . . Simplify, simplify. —H. D. Thoreau

Hail! divine lady Simplicity, child of glorious Temperance, beloved by good men. All who practice righteousness venerate thy virtue. —Crates

Simplicity, most rare in our age. —Ovid

However insignificant Simplicity seems, the whole world cannot make it submissive. If princes and kings could keep to it, all things in the world would of themselves pay homage. Heaven and earth would unite to send down sweet dew.
—Tao Te Ching

THE VIRTUE OF HONESTY

> But that on the good ground are they, which in an honest and good heart, having heard the word, keep it, and bring forth fruit with patience.
> Jesus
> —St. Luke 8:15

Meditation is a Great Polarizer. The Laws of God are Great Polarizers. When Meditation is wed to the Laws of God, one comes into Polarity Balance. Polarity Balance brings Centering in the Grace of God—and the Grace of God opens the Christ World of Illumination. This is the procedure by which Meditation leads to Illumination.

Meditation, in the Scriptural meaning of the word, is a reverent sacrament of worship. Meditation is spiritually fruitful when one is united with the beauty of law and the wisdom of love and virtue. Meditation minus law and virtue equals disappointment; meditation plus law and virtue equals enlightenment.

Meditation—when not based upon law and virtue—can be dangerous in that it may give one a false sense of well-being. Meditation—when based upon law and virtue—is freedom-giving, for all holy laws and divine virtues are part of the soul's radiant splendors and joy-freedoms.

In ancient China, teachers of meditation referred to virtues as "excellent roots." In any age or time, one must have excellent roots, or mature virtues, before meditation can become a vehicle for Illumination.

Many persons believe that the daily practice of meditation exempts them from observing the basic Commandments of God; this erroneous belief leads to dead-ends, repetitive troubles and complex problems. Meditation, when accompanied by a dedication to the Ten Commandments and the Sermon on the Mount, reveals a spiritual maturity necessary for union with God as Pure Truth.

The Ten Commandments and the Sermon on the Mount provide an earnest aspirant with guidance and direction in his outer life of action and in his inner life of meditation. The virtues expressed during one's fulfilling of these statutes and principles create a momentum that lifts him toward the higher degrees of light and truth.

"If ye love Me, keep My commandments." *(St. John 14:15)* The Commandments of God contain the keys to understanding the Cosmos, the Soul and Eternal Life. Even as the Commandments search one at the time of death, so do they search him during each life on earth. For the pure in heart, the Commandments are the wisdom-lights that produce the Greater Illuminations.

> With thoughts all stilled, the pure of heart behold Him at long last; and meditating on Him they behold Him partless and entire.
> —Mundaka Upanishad

Meditation and the Law

> Blessed are the pure in heart: for they shall see God.
>
> Jesus of Nazareth
> —*St. Matthew 5:8*

"Be still, and know that I am God." (*Psalm 46:10*) The stilling of the thoughts during sacramental meditation gives a devotee daily opportunities to know himself so that he may come to know God. Self-Realization leads to Soul-Realization; Soul-Realization, to Christ-Realization; Christ-Realization, to God-Realization.

When meditation is removed from the frame of Law and Virtue, it is no longer a devotional art and sacramental science. Modern-day meditators who fail to revere and fulfill the basic Laws and Commandments are pseudo-students rather than sincere students of the Word of God.

If a person new to the higher life resists applying one or more of God's Laws, the Creator may send periodic holy inspirations as *touches of grace* in an effort to inspire the probationer to remove his resistances to His Will. As long as an aspirant continues to remain unfaithful to a cardinal Commandment, he delays the receiving of important spiritual quickenings and anointings.

"Be not deceived; God is not mocked: for whatsoever a man soweth, that shall he also reap." (*Galatians 6:7*) Stubbornness, obstinacy, lethargy, disobedience, furtiveness and fickleness defeat one's efforts to unite with the Divine Presence. An obstinate will, hardened heart and disobedient spirit that fail to soften through years of daily meditation become part of the soul's record. These self-defeating traits determine one's course in the present life and in future lives.

An honest openness with God through a loving obedience to His cardinal Commandments makes pure the heart and mind. When this love-filled purity and obedience are accompanied by the Virtue of Honesty, one's silence during meditation provides the perfect soil for the Creator to plant His seeds of Grace and Truth.

HONESTY

An honest man's the noblest work of God. —Alexander Pope

Never too late is trod the path to honesty. —Seneca

I am looking for an honest man. —Diogenes

No legacy is so rich as honesty.

Divine Providence has granted this gift to man, that those things which are honest are also the most advantageous.
—Quintilian

Let us walk honestly, as in the day . . . —Romans 13:13

. . . ye should do that which is honest . . .
—2 Corinthians 13:7

Honesty with yourself is sweet paradise. —Ann Ree Colton

. . . that we may lead a quiet and peaceable life in all godliness and honesty. —1 Timothy 2:2

I hope I shall always possess firmness and virtue enough to maintain what I consider the most enviable of titles, the character of an "Honest Man." —George Washington

Honesty is the first chapter of the book of wisdom.
—Thomas Jefferson

Each virtue sounds a sweet tone. Each Law and Commandment sounds a beautiful tone. When one's virtue-tones come into harmony with the tones of Holy Laws, he lives in a state of harmony with the Music of God's Love creating the Universe.

In the silence of sacramental meditation, virtues sound their melodious music. The music of meditation is unheard by the ears of men; however, it is heard by God and His angels. The virtue-tones sounding during one's meditations are the tones of Honesty, Humility, Integrity, Dedication, Sincerity, Gratitude, and all other virtues. These virtue-tones are part of the Music of the Soul, the Music of the Spheres and the Music of the Universe. When a reverent meditator seeks "the Kingdom of God, and His righteousness,"* his virtue-tones are an inspired and love-harmonized symphony.

The "honest and good heart" (St. Luke 8:15) required for union with God is the heart ever receptive to the Grace of God blessing and quickening the soul and its gifts. The honest tithe given to God with love; honest confessions to God; the honest desire to make a full and honorable restitution for all past offenses, sins and transgressions—all contribute to the purity of the Tone of Honesty sounding in one's meditations. The Creator responds to this purity of Tone by blessing the devotee-initiate with the first fruits of pure-creation inspirations.

The Virtue of Honesty is as a radiant diamond with many facets. As this virtue-diamond is formed and polished through sacramental meditation, prayer, fasting and tithing, the heart and mind sound vibrant tones of pure love for God as the Absolute and Omnipresent Truth.

---

*St. Matthew 6:33 "But seek ye first the Kingdom of God, and his righteousness: and all these things shall be added unto you."

Thus, through the reverent worship of God and honest perception of His Truth, the soul's primary hunger to worship is fulfilled, and one comes into a closeness with the Creator during worship-times and during his activities in the waking world and in the world of sleep. This constant awareness of God's Omnipresence is blessed by the soul as long as honesty, love and the worship-adoration of God are foremost in the heart and mind.

> O how love I thy law! it is my meditation all the day.
> —Psalm 119:97

> Purity and stillness give the correct law to all under heaven.
> —The Texts of Taoism

Meditation-Adoration

> Every devoted thing is most holy unto the Lord.
> Moses
> —*Leviticus 27:28*

Meditation-adoration of God is a feeling, an attitude, a reverence charged with faith, a devotion filled with love, an eagerness radiant with holy expectations. Through meditation-adoration of the Creator, one is magnetically drawn into the Bosom of God's Love, and he is electrically quickened by the Grace-Spirit of His Omnipresence.

Adoration of the Omnipotent One is the central heartbeat within all sacramental sciences and devotional observances. Meditation-adoration, prayer-adoration, fasting-adoration and almsgiving-adoration build a mighty fortress of virtue-light and conscience-light. This soul-fortress provides one with an invisible wall of protection, and becomes a telepathic receiving station for holy-inspirations that lead to revelation-creations.

Meditation-adoration inspires one to remain in a state of reverence and sacred awe at all times of the day and night, for he is filled continuously with the intoxicating wonder of the vastness of Space and the perfection of God's Plan for Stars and Galaxies.

Adoration and veneration of the Most High lead to emancipation and elation. To adore the Exalted One is to become exalted through the inheritance of spiritual riches.

Adoration of the Christ Child by the Magi or Wise Men is told in story and song. Adoration is an expression of the highest wisdom; for when wisdom is accompanied by adoration, the soul is free to sing its song of Eternal Truth.

During each moment of meditation-adoration of God, one's heart should be filled with the words: *How may I better serve Thee, O Lord?* The earnest desire to become increasingly worthy to serve God draws forth immediate beneficial results and bountiful rewards. A closeness with the Creator is established—and one's life comes into order, harmony and creative fruitfulness.

The grandeur of adoration is due to the virtue-essences that swell and rise in crescendo-tones of love and devotion. These tones sound throughout Time and Space, preparing a pathway or rainbow bridge toward coming lives and future solar-system mansions in which one will live—ever adoring, worshipping and serving the One who gives him life.

In my Father's house are many mansions.
Jesus
—St. John 14:2

Meditation and the Cosmos

Omnipresence, I send my love to Thy farthest star.

In the beginning moments of sacramental meditation, it is wise and good for a worshipper to send love to the farthest star, embracing all Stars and Galaxies with the arms of his love. The Creator will reciprocate by expanding and enlightening one's concepts of Space and Time. In this, the elixir-essences of Eternal Life will become part of his being; his thoughts will be filled with the wisdom of eternality. Wisdom-thoughts, peace-patience and other fruits of love and joy manifest through meditations upon the wonder of God as Omnipresence.

"The Kingdom of God is within you." (St. Luke 17:21) The farther one reaches *outwardly* in his love for the Spirit of God energizing the Stars and Galaxies, the more he is able to reach *inwardly* into the inner Kingdom of God during sacramental meditations. This ability to steadily increase one's union with the inner Kingdom and the outer Cosmos is due to the Spirit of God working through the Principle of *Pulsation*. The Principle of Pulsation determines the life-span of each person through the heart's beat and the breath's inhalation and exhalation. The pulsating Spirit of God within each heartbeat and each breath is within all living things—from man to creature, from star to galaxy.

In uniting with God through a love for His Laws of Creation, one unites with the Principle of *Divine Expansion* as well as the Principle of Pulsation. Through the Principle of Pulsation, a devotee may live and move in harmony with the heartbeat of the Universe. Through the Principle of Divine Expansion, his thoughts, moving toward the far reaches of Space, gather a momentum that carries them farther outwardly in the outgoing pulsations of Grace and farther inwardly in the incoming pulsations of Grace.

Mysteries within the Principle of Pulsation, the Principle of Divine Expansion and other powerful Principles and Truths are revealed by Omnipresence to those who send their love to the farthest star during the beginning of sacramental meditation.

The language of God is *Paradox*. The Paradox of seeking the Kingdom of God within one's being through meditation in order to gain knowledge of Space, Time, Stars and Galaxies is one of His greatest Paradoxes. Through the reverent stillness of sacramental meditation, one learns to listen to the Voice of God revealing the Splendor and the Significance of the Cosmos. Thus, those who turn toward the inner Kingdom of Light and Righteousness through sacramental meditation become revealers and teachers of Cosmos Truths and Eternal Realities.

The speed of physical light cannot compare with the speed of spiritual love. Physical light sent to a distant star will require billions of years before it reaches its destina-

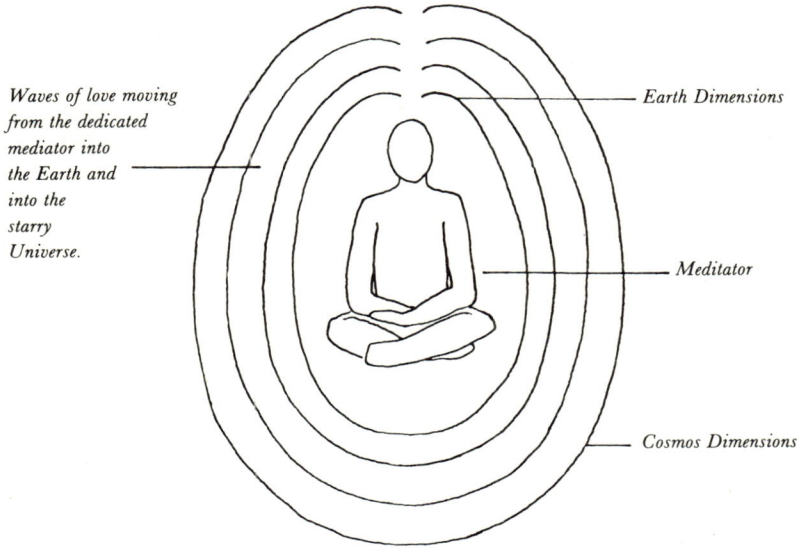

tion, even though the light is traveling 186,282 miles a second. However, if one sends his *love* to a distant star, the love is received *instantaneously* by the star, *for love is the Eternal Essence beyond Time and Space.*

"God is love." *(1 John 4:8)* God IS. Love IS. The Isness of God's Omnipresence and the Isness of Love are One. The meditator sending love to the Stars in the Cosmos is *one* with all Galaxies through love. This oneness through love is the Door to all knowledge and truth—human and Divine, terrestrial and Celestial.

Love escapes all atmospheric, gravitational and electromagnetic barriers around the Earth—and moves into the Cosmos as an energy used by God for the creation of Stars and Galaxies. Therefore, when one worships God sacramentally and with pure love, he becomes a co-creator with God in the creation of the Universe.

If one dedicates to God his Meditation-Love, his love becomes part of the Creator's Eternal Essence of Pure Love. God then uses one's love in His creating the Earth and the Human Spirit and in His creating the Stars and the Galaxies.

Countless new Suns are forever in the process of being born as the Spirit of God quickens new voids. The Creator uses the meditator's love for the *Human Spirit* by placing this love on wave lengths of spiritual light that bless, heal and quicken mankind in its birth to light. Omnipresence also utilizes the meditator's love for His *Universe* by making this love part of His Love-Spirit as it quickens new voids and creates new Stars. In this, the dedicated meditator who sends his love to the Human Spirit and into the star-filled Universe becomes a co-creator with God.

> Is it not written in your law, I said, Ye are gods?
> Jesus
> —*St. John 10:34*

Meditation and the Law

When one sends his love into the starry Cosmos during sacramental meditation, the *energy* within his love and virtue-light becomes part of God's Love-Spirit as it prepares voids in Cosmos for the births of new Suns. Some of these Solar Systems will be the future homes for the human spirit when life on earth has ended, thereby fulfilling the continuity of Creation according to the *Commandment of Life Everlasting*.

> The Father which sent me, he gave me a commandment, what I should say, and what I should speak. And I know that his commandment is life everlasting.
> Jesus
> —*St. John 12:49, 50*

The Spirit of God may use one's sacramental love and worship-adoration in different ways. While some of the energy-units of a meditator's love are utilized in the creating of distant celestial bodies, other energy-units of his love remain in that portion of Space where his love through worship was expressed. The planet Earth travels on its course around the Sun at the rate of 66,600 miles an hour—over 1000 miles a minute! The portion of one's love that *remains* where the Earth *was* at the time of his meditation-adoration of God becomes a Path of Virtue through the Cosmos. This Path is a stream of Everlasting Light which is used by God in His creating of future Stars and Galaxies. Thus, portions of one's love go forth into distant Universe creations and portions of his love remain where the Earth had been moments, days and years before; and portions of his love are used by God in the healing and quickening of the human spirit.

Love is the Eternal Essence of God creating the Universe. He who loves God and worships sacramentally is expressing the highest adoration of the Most High—and his love becomes as rays of eternal light moving in many different directions in the Cosmos. Through sacramental meditation, one's love becomes part of the Love of God creating the human spirit, the Earth, the Sun, the Stars and the Galaxies.

THE GALAXY CONSCIOUSNESS AND THE NEW COVENANT

> But now hath he obtained a more excellent ministry, by how much also he is the mediator of a better covenant, which was established upon better promises.
> Saint Paul
> —*Hebrews 8:6*

> . . . Jesus the mediator of the new covenant.
> Saint Paul
> —*Hebrews 12:24*

The *Galaxy Consciousness* is beginning to awaken in the human spirit through enlightened souls being blessed by the Christ, the Mediator of the New Covenant. The Christ Mind is the Galaxy-Consciousness Mind. The Galaxy Consciousness is the goal of each living soul into whom God is breathing life.

Those who are dedicating their lives to sacramental meditation and correlating spiritual disciplines *in the Name of the Christ* are forerunners in the great new worlds of Enlightenment opening to mankind. Through the Christ and the Mediation Host working with Him, the mind and heart become receptive to the Love and Wisdom of God creating Man in His Image through the energy-processes of the Sun, the Moon, the Planets, the Stars and the Galaxies.

The planet Earth and its Sun are but one of the 200 billion Solar Systems in the Milky Way Galaxy. Billions of other Stars in billions of other Galaxies await to reveal their secrets and purposes within the Cosmos and Eternal Plan of God. The Christ, as the Mediator of the New Covenant, is mankind's Door to the knowledge of the Glory of God in the Galaxies.

Uninitiated man has no desire to worship God or to learn about the spiritual sciences, arts and gifts of the soul. Such persons learn Life's lessons solely through the energy-processes of Nature and human association. One who desires to worship God begins the procedure through which he opens the grace-record of his soul. Through initiation, he gains access to the priceless energy-reservoirs of the soul and, eventually, the pristine energies of the Godhead.

When one becomes a dedicated and ethical craftsman in the use of the soul's energies, and utilizes Nature's energies with reverence and love, his sacramental approach to Life enables him to approach the Godhead. Gradually, the working of the Godhead is revealed through the Mediation of the Lord Christ. This may be likened to a scientist becoming skilled in the working of a nuclear power plant. The Godhead is an endless, ceaseless, eternal Power Plant or Dimensional Dynamo beyond Time and Space. The Christ, as the Mediator of the New Covenant, is the Shepherd to the Illumination-Treasures of the Godhead and the crowning Gift of the Galaxy Consciousness.

"I am the good shepherd." (St. John 10:11) The Christ is the Shepherd to the Inner Kingdoms of righteousness and holiness; these Kingdoms contain the *Knowledge* of the Outer Universe with its multitudinous Stars and Galaxies. Thus, the inner quest becomes the Door to the unveiling of the secrets and mysteries of the Cosmos.

The Godhead-Light is centered within the soul. This Omnipresent, Omniscient and Omnipotent Light—when revered and contemplated—provides the Knowledge of God sealed into the Outer or Visible Universe. Through the Light of God within the soul, one unites with the Light of God within the Soul of Cosmos.

The Godhead energy-radiations of Spirit and Truth move upon mankind from the Third Heaven to the Second Heaven to the First Heaven. Man, through devotion and love, communes with the First Heaven that he may qualify for union with the Second Heaven. The Second-Heaven Initiations and Realizations qualify him for union with the Third Heaven and its Revelations.

> I knew a man in Christ above fourteen years ago (whether in the body, I cannot tell; or whether out of the body, I cannot tell: God knoweth;) such an one caught up to the third heaven.
>
> Saint Paul
> —*2 Corinthians 12:2*

> What is needful? Righteousness, and sacred learning and teaching. Truth, and sacred learning and teaching. Meditation, and sacred learning and teaching. Self-control and sacred learning and teaching. Peace, and sacred learning and teaching. Ritual, and sacred learning and teaching. Humanity, and sacred learning and teaching.
>
> —Taittirya Upanishad I 5-6

PRAYER

Learn first to acquire the power of prayer and you will easily practice all the other virtues. —Saint Isaac of Syria

This is the business of our life: by effort and by toil, by prayer and by supplication, to advance in the grace of God, till we come to that height of perfection in which with clean hearts we may behold God. —Saint Augustine

Thou shalt make thy prayer unto Him, and He shall hear thee . . . —Job 22:27

The Lord hath heard my supplication; the Lord will receive my prayer. —Psalm 6:9

The sacrifice of the wicked is an abomination to the Lord: but the prayer of the upright is His delight. —Proverbs 15:8

The key of paradise is prayer, and the key of prayer is ablution. —Muhammad

Therefore I say unto you, What things soever ye desire, when ye pray, believe that ye receive them, and ye shall have them.
                Jesus
               —*St. Mark 11:24*

Pray without ceasing.
              Saint Paul
            —*1 Thessalonians 5:17*

But I say unto you, Love your enemies, bless them that curse you, do good to them that hate you, and pray for them which despitefully use you, and persecute you.
                Jesus
               —*St. Matthew 5:44*

Confess your faults to one another, and pray one for another, that ye may be healed. The effectual fervent prayer of a righteous man availeth much. —James 5:16

12

PRAYERS FOR THE DEDICATED HEART

> But thou, when thou prayest, enter into thy closet, and when thou hast shut thy door, pray to thy Father which is in secret; and thy Father which seeth in secret shall reward thee openly.
>
> Jesus
> —*St. Matthew 6:6*

DEDICATION OF THE DAY

O God who hast folded back the mantle of the night to clothe us in the glory of the day, chase from our hearts all gloomy thoughts, and make us glad with the brightness of hope that we may effectively aspire to unknown virtues.

—Collect from the Sixth Century

Let us meditate upon the adorable Glory of the Divine Vivifier! And may He direct our thoughts!

Hindu Morning Prayer
—*Rig Veda 3:62, 10*

> Grant us to know Thee and love Thee and rejoice in Thee. And if we cannot do these perfectly in this life, let us at least advance to higher degrees every day 'till we can come to do them to perfection.
> —Saint Augustine

The dedications of the Saints inspire all who travel the Path of Virtue. An aspirant who dedicates his days and his nights to God becomes a protege of the Saints; he places the direction of his life in God's Hands—and guidance comes. The Creator directs him to his perfect placement in life where he may study, serve and create in atmospheres conducive to his spiritual growth.

The *Word* of God is creating all living things each moment of the day. When one dedicates each day to God, the spirit of his dedication attunes his ears to the Word of God creating the Earth, the Solar System and Man. His progress on the Path is determined by his ability to perceive the Wisdom and Beauty of God inherent in all forms and degrees of Creation.

The higher life of dedication begins when the lips speak heartfelt words such as: *"God, use me."* This simple prayer, when sincerely spoken, brings forth an immediate response—and one is guided to a living teacher.

All knowledgeable teachers and ethical teachings offer instruction in the basic Laws and Commandments of God and in the cardinal virtues that qualify one for the Divine Marriage. If one heeds this instruction, his life comes into order and harmony through the daily expression of virtues.

> Vouchsafe to bestow upon us some portion of Thy heavenly Bread, day by day, that the hunger and thirst for earthly things may diminish in us continually.
> —Erasmus
> 1466–1536 A.D.

> Give us this day the daily manna, without which through this rough desert he backward goes who toils most to go on.
> —Dante
> 1265–1321 A.D.

> We are forced, O Father, to seek Thee daily, and Thou offerest Thyself daily to be found; whensoever we seek Thee we find Thee, in the house, in the fields, in the Temple, and in the highway.
> —John Norden
> 16th Century

Even as a life has a beginning, the life of each virtue has a beginning. A cardinal virtue, such as the Virtue of Dedication, may be expressed in many different ways before one turns wholeheartedly to God. For example, an individual may be *dedicated* to his tribe, race, nation, family, wife and children, or his business. One's chief concern and foremost love determine his level and degree of dedication.

Many persons are dedicated to self rather than to God. This level of dedication denotes a degree of *energy* that must yet be refined and purified. Some individuals are dedicated to irreverent activities and unlawful pursuits; such persons are on the lowest rungs of the Energy-Ladder of Dedication.

Each rung of the Energy-Ladder has its own *Learning Process*. The dedicated thief, the dedicated prostitute, and all other forms of unwholesome and unsavory dedication are on the lowest rungs of the Energy-Ladder. In the present life or in coming lives, the Learning Process gradually refines and purifies the energies within dedication until one desires to love and serve the Creator.

God does not create a thief, a prostitute, a murderer, a

kidnapper, a sadist, or a rapist. God creates a Learning Process—a Tree of Knowledge. Through *free will,* each person created in the Image of God is given the opportunity to worship or not to worship, to love or not to love, to live with virtue or to shun virtue, to live righteously or riotously.

Each virtue has a Tone, a Light, an Energy. As one purifies his love for God and his fellow man, the virtue-seeds sent forth from the soul grow rapidly into blossoms of righteousness and fruits of holiness. In this, the Learning Process becomes the Process of Illumination.

The story of Eternal Life is being written on the pages of virtue-births, virtue-quickenings and Virtue-Illuminations. Through Virtue-Illuminations, the mind becomes the illumined mind in Christ; and the heart, the illumined heart in Christ. From Antichrist to Christ—from the lowest to the highest rungs on the Ladder of Life—the Learning Process is ever present and ever active. From the mud of sin and darkness (Satan), the Lotus of Law, Love and Light (Christ) is opening broad Virtue-doors through which the human spirit may perceive the Eternal Future.

"Blessed is he that cometh in the name of the Lord." (St. Matthew 23:39) Those who come in the Name of the Lord are dedicated to the teaching of His Word and the doing of His Will. Dedication to God is the most sublime and exalted Dedication. All other dedications stem from this all-important Dedication. A devotee may be a dedicated husband, a dedicated family man, a dedicated teacher; however, in his heart he knows that his dedication to God supercedes his other dedications and prospers his other dedications.

Genuine love results in sincere dedication. Sincere dedication begins with one's first prayers and meditations observed as sacraments of worship. Dedication thereafter becomes as a radiant diamond that steadily expands in size as one proves his love for God each day.

Each virtue is a potential diamond-like energy vortex with numerous facets. When the Virtue of Dedication is reverent and wholehearted, it becomes as a diamond with numerous scintillating facets. New facets of the Diamond of Dedication are continually discovered as one walks the Path of Virtue; each new facet adds luminosity to the heart's love and the mind's light. So it is with all other virtues used in dedicated service to God: As new facets are revealed and polished, one increases in his competency, perception and understanding.

Each time one dedicates his daily prayers and meditations to God, his time of worship is *anointed* in lesser or greater degree by the Divine Presence. Each devotional period is as water into which God places the honey of His Spirit. Over the years, the many drops of honey in the water of one's daily devotions and worship ferment until they become as honey-wine. This potent wine produces spiritual ecstasies or holy intoxications.

The Hand of God presents one with the ecstasy-wine of former dedications as timely blessings to strengthen, fortify and magnify his present-day covenants. Thus, each daily dedication to worship God through prayer and meditation becomes a vial of grace that will ferment over the years and return to one as the holy wine of the soul and the spirit. When many vials of grace are opened at one time, one experiences major breakthroughs in understanding and realization accompanied by sacred joys and ecstasies.

> The Lord is my shepherd; I shall not want. He maketh me to lie down in green pastures: He leadeth me beside the still waters. He restoreth my soul: he leadeth me in the paths of righteous-

ness for his name's sake. Yea, though I walk through the valley of the shadow of death, I will fear no evil: for thou art with me; thy rod and thy staff they comfort me. Thou preparest a table before me in the presence of mine enemies: thou anointest my head with oil; my cup runneth over. Surely goodness and mercy shall follow me all the days of my life: and I will dwell in the house of the Lord forever.

David
—Psalm 23:1-6

Our Father which art in heaven, Hallowed be thy name. Thy kingdom come. Thy will be done in earth, as it is in heaven. Give us this day, our daily bread. And forgive us our debts, as we forgive our debtors. And lead us not into temptation, but deliver us from evil: For thine is the kingdom, and the power, and the glory for ever. Amen.

Jesus
—St. Matthew 6:9-13

This is the day which the Lord hath made; we will rejoice and be glad in it. (Psalm 118:24) The first thought on awakening from the night's sleep should be a thought of dedication such as: *"Father, I dedicate this day unto Thee."* This thought and feeling of reverent dedication should be repeated when one speaks his morning prayer.

A Prayer of Dedication each morning helps one to attain and to express the sacrament-degrees of the virtues. The yeast of God's Spirit is within the Virtue of Dedication. When the light of this mighty virtue permeates one's feelings, actions and thoughts, he unites with the Grace-essences of Omnipresence.

Prayers for the Dedicated Heart

The following Prayer of Dedication, spoken while kneeling, should precede morning meditation. After morning meditation, one should speak a Prayer of Confession, Praise, Petition and Gratitude, beginning with the Lord's Prayer. The Morning Prayer of Dedication is:

> *Father, I dedicate this day unto Thee: My prayers, meditations, serving, study, creation and recreation. I pray to do each thing in right timing according to Thy Will and Plan—and for Thy Glory.*
> *. . . In Jesus' Name.*
> *Amen.*

One may end the Prayer of Dedication with "Amen"— or if desired, he may add the following words of Gratitude and Blessing:

> *Thank Thee for my Teacher, and for all who come in Thy Name. May they know Thine Eternal Blessings. Blessed be all who are created in Thy Image and Likeness. Blessed be all children of Thy Spirit.*
> *. . . In Jesus' Name.*
> *Amen.*

On each Sabbath Day, one should begin the Morning Prayer of Dedication with the words:

> *Father, I dedicate this Holy Sabbath Day unto Thee. . . .*

On a day of Sacramental Fasting, the devotee should add the word "Fasting" to the Morning Prayer of Dedication:

> *Father, I dedicate this day unto Thee: My prayers, meditations, fasting, serving, study, creation and recreation . . .*

He should then speak the remainder of the Prayer. If any other words of consecration fill the heart, one should speak these as part of the dedication of his day to God. Gradually, the eyes will begin to recognize evidences that the Creator is acknowledging and answering his dedication with Miraculous "Coincidences," Timing Confirmations, Love Healings, Grace Blessings and Holy Inspirations.

After each obvious evidence of the Creator's Blessing and Anointing, one should be reverently prayerful and humbly grateful. Reverence, Humility and Gratitude keep open and expand the Blessing Streams of the Mediation Host working with the Christ, and accelerate the activity of the Anointing Spirit of God in one's life and being.

"Looking unto Jesus the author and finisher of our faith . . ." *(Hebrews 12:2)* When one dedicates each day to God in the Name of His Son, the Lord Jesus becomes the supervisor and coordinator of his days. As the devotee's spirit of dedication begins to permeate each moment of the day, he is lifted over each initiatory hurdle, that he may remain centered in God's Love and Guidance.

Each virtue is a degree of the Spirit of God. As one adds the leaven of Dedication to each day's actions, feelings and thoughts, the Spirit of God begins to pulsate through the *spirit* of his Dedication. In this, the devotee's union with the Wisdom of God prospers in increasing measures of Grace and Truth.

"What is man . . . that thou shouldst visit him every morning, and try him every moment?" *(Job 7:17, 18)* Each step of progress on the Path of Virtue is preceded by a test. As one learns to recognize this cardinal truth, he realizes that each

test, when met and mastered, produces a necessary strengthening of the fabric of his dedication.

Each meditation should be preceded by words and feelings of Dedication, such as, *I dedicate this Meditation unto Thee, O Lord.* Sacred mantras or mantrams spoken before and after meditation make each worship period a time of reverence, love and spiritual power.

The Dedication to speak a prayer of Blessing and Gratitude before each meal helps to sustain the *Tone* of the Spirit of Dedication throughout the day. The sacramental partaking of food and beverage each day strengthens one's union with the Divine Omnipresence—and his family life and spiritual life are prospered with increasing measures of Grace and Love.

As the Tone of one's dedication to God is purified through daily worship-cycles, Scriptural study and selfless service, the purity of this Virtue-Tone telepathically attunes him to the higher wave lengths or atmospheres of God's Spirit. In this, one makes union with the dimensional kingdom called the *Music of the Spheres.* The Tone of one's Dedication, when pure and love-filled, blends with other virtue-tones active in his Dedication to God—and the devotee unites with the tones of Pure Creation in the Music of the Spheres. Therefore, he becomes inspired in heart and mind, bringing forth words and works of *Pure Creation.*

When one devotes a special time or times each day for Dedicated Creativity, the Wisdom of God blesses these periods with the first fruits of Holy Inspiration. Union with God begins when one's spirit of Dedication qualifies him for the receiving of Holy-Inspiration Creations. One should begin each period of Sacramental Creativity with a Prayer of Dedication, such as,

> *Heavenly Father, I dedicate unto Thee my hands, heart and mind. May my soul's grace speak through my hands. And may I create within the Joy and Beauty of Thy Love . . . and for Thy Glory.*
> *In Jesus' Name. Amen.*

If one speaks words similar to these before each period of Dedicated Creativity, his works of Art, Music, Writing, Speaking, etc., will be blessed. The Creator will reward his loyalty and sincerity with the choicest fruits from His endless resources of Pure Creations.

Each pure-creation inspiration received by a dedicated servant of God is timed by the Wisdom of the Creator. Each holy inspiration is part of a great Mosaic Mural of Understanding in the consciousness mind—a Mural that expands with each inspiration. This Mosaic Mural, in time, is *illuminated* by the Light of the Christ—and the first stages of Illumination are experienced.

As one proves loyal to his daily worship-dedications, the flow of holy-inspirations increases, gradually adding deeper and broader dimensions of Divine Grace. A Prayer of Dedication *before* Creativity and a Prayer of Gratitude *after* each time of Creativity keep one telepathically receptive to the Dimensional Kingdoms of Grace and Truth as a dedicated masterbuilder for God.

> By their fruits ye shall know them.
> Jesus
> —*St. Matthew 7:20*

In dedicating each recreation period to God, one should remember to observe the recreation times *sacramentally*. This reverent approach toward daily periods of yoga, meditative walking or other forms of gentle recreation enable a devotee to remain receptive to God's Blessings for his physical health as well as for his spiritual well-being.

During sickness, business trips, or vacations—when one is unable to worship in his spiritual home or sanctuary on the Sabbath Day—he may fulfill this Commandment of Worship by lighting a candle; dedicating the day to God; thanking God for His Laws and Commandments; meditating and praying; and studying and reading aloud passages from the Sacred Scriptures and other inspired writings.

If one is visiting a community away from his spiritual home—and desires to worship in a sanctuary with other worshippers—he should speak a prayer for guidance.

> *Father, I pray to fulfill Thy Holy Laws and Commandments as* Thou *wouldst have me fulfill them in the present life and in all lives to come. On this Sabbath Day, guide me, I pray, to the sanctuary where I may worship Thee in spirit and in Truth.*
> *Bless all sanctuaries of worship and all servants of Thy Word.*
> *Bless all who heed and do Thy Word.*
> *And may Thy Word live and prosper in the world, and bring forth the fruits of holiness and righteousness. . . . In Jesus' Name. Amen.*

Whenever possible, one should heed these words of Jesus when worshipping God on the Sabbath Day: *"Where two or three are gathered together in my name, there am I in the midst of them." (St. Matthew 18:20)* If the Truth-seeker is not able to be with others, such as in times of sickness, he should light a candle (if possible), dedicate the day to God, study, read aloud, pray on the knees, speak mantras or mantrams and observe sacramental meditation.

It is the Teacher's task to shepherd each student to the

Glory of God within each Holy Law and Commandment. The student makes rapid progress when he:

1. Expresses Gratitude to God for His Commandments, and praises Him for His Laws, Love and Mercy.

2. (a) Expresses Gratitude to God for all persons in times past who have preserved the knowledge of Holy Laws.

(b) Special Gratitude for those who have laid down their lives so that the knowledge of the Commandments may live from generation to generation.

(c) Gratitude for those who are keeping alive the knowledge of God's Laws in the world today.

(d) Gratitude for those who will preserve this knowledge in the future.

3. Honors, reveres, and fulfills each Holy Law and Commandment with enthusiasm and joy. Gradually, the seeker after Truth will draw closer to the Glory of God within His Laws and Commandments—and he will receive confirmations, healings, refreshings and realizations. These and other sweet blessings indicate that he is making union with the Glory of God within His Laws and Commandments.

If one remains unwaveringly true to the Sabbath Day Commandment and the other Holy Laws, he will also begin to make union with the Glory of God within Virtues, for each Divine Law when fulfilled in the right spirit of love activates and quickens the *Divine* degrees of one's virtues. The Divine degrees of virtues *are* the Presence or Glory of God within Virtues.

Holy attitudes toward holy laws manifest holy miracles. The holy attitudes of contrition, repentance, confession and restitution prosper one's union with God from day to day. These inspired attitudes continuously add new insights, inspirations, realizations and revelations related to the miracle-producing manifestations of God's Glory.

One who dedicates each day to God is dedicating the day to *Pure Truth*—therefore, he should realize that the Divine Omnipresence will reveal the *Truth* each moment of the day and the night. One's ability to unite with God as Pure Truth is determined by his degree of self-honesty and selfless love.

The dedication of each day to God places one under the Magnification Light of Pure Truth. Pure Truth will *magnify* one's faults as well as his virtues, talents and gifts. Alert students will diligently apply themselves to the necessary task of overcoming their faults as their faults are revealed by the Mercy of God and the Clear Light of Truth. When an earnest devotee asks God's help in healing his faults, he receives perfect and supernatural assistances according to his degree of faith and his heartfelt desire to render a reverent service to the world.

> When God wishes well unto His servant He causes him to see the faults of his soul. —Muhammad

> Cleanse Thou me from secret faults. —Psalm 19:12

> When you have faults, do not fear to abandon them. —Confucius

> He who tells me of my faults is my teacher;
> he who tells me of my virtues does me harm. —Chinese Proverb

> Let a wise man blow off the impurities of himself, as a smith blows off the impurities of silver, one by one, little by little, and from moment to moment. . . The fault of others is easily perceived, but that of one's self is difficult to perceive; a man winnows his neighbor's faults like a chaff, but his own fault he hides, as a cheat hides an unlucky cast of the die. If a man looks after the faults of others and is always inclined to be offended, his own passions will grow. . . —Buddha

Why beholdest thou the mote that is in thy brother's eye, but considerest not the beam that is in thine own eye? Or how wilt thou say to thy brother, Let me pull out the mote out of thine eye; and, behold, a beam is in thine own eye? Thou hypocrite, first cast out the beam out of thine own eye; and then shalt thou see clearly to cast out the mote out of thy brother's eye.

Jesus
—St. Matthew 7:3–5

The greatest of faults, I should say, is to be conscious of none.

A fault confessed is half redressed.   —Thomas Carlyle

Deal with the faults of others as gently as with your own.

—Confucius

Think of your own faults the first part of the night when you are awake, and of the faults of others the latter part of the night when you are asleep.   —Chinese Proverb

It is not so much the being exempt from faults as the having overcome them that is an advantage to us.   —Alexander Pope

It is the characteristic of folly to discern the faults of others and forget its own.   —Cicero

Prayers to Overcome Faults

Father, I place my faults and flaws on Thy Holy Altar, that they may be consumed by the fire of Thy Love. May the Light of Thy Beloved Son abide in me and I in Him, that we may be as one light in Thee.

Father, I place my faults on Thy Holy Altar. I pray that they will be healed by Thy Love and Mercy, and changed into light and strength and joy. I ask this in Jesus' Name, O Lord, that I might better serve Thee. Let all victories be, Thine. Amen.

Praise

> And a voice came out of the throne, saying, Praise our God, all ye his servants, and ye that fear him, both small and great.
> —Revelation 19:5

When prayers of praise are spontaneously spoken from the heart, one draws closer to the Heart of God. To praise God for His mighty creation in the Cosmos prepares one for the gift of understanding and other gifts. The voice that praises God becomes part of the chorus of the Angels, Saints and other Holy Mediators who are proclaiming His Glory and praising His Name.

> Praised be Thy Name, not mine;
> magnified be Thy work, not mine;
> blessed be Thy Holy Name, but to me let
> no part of man's praises be given.
> —Saint Thomas á Kempis

> Lord, when I look upon mine own life it seems
> Thou hast led me so carefully, so tenderly,
> Thou canst have attended to none else; but
> when I see how wonderfully Thou hast led the world
> and art leading it, I am amazed that Thou hast
> had time to attend to such as I.
> —Saint Augustine

Thou hast quieted those which were in confusion. Praise to Thy calmness, praise to Thy reconciliation, O Lord God.
—Saint Ephrem the Syrian

Praise be to Thee, O hidden One and manifested One. Praise be to Thy Glory, to Thy Might, To Thy Power, and to Thy Great Skill.

O Allah, to Thee all greatness belongs. O Thou who possessest the Power and Beauty and Perfection. Thou art the Spirit of All.

Praise to Thee, O sovereign of all Monarchs; to Thee, O Master of all affairs; to Thee, O Controller of all things; to Thee, Ruler of all beings.

Thou art free from death, free from birth and free from all limitations. O Thou Eternal One, Thou art free from all conditions, pure from all things. O Allah, Thou art the God of Souls on earth; Thou art the Lord of Hosts in the Heavens.
—Sufi Invocation

In what blaze of Glory dost Thou rise, O Sun Righteousness, from the heart of the earth, after Thy setting!

In what resplendent Vesture, O King of Glory, dost Thou enter again the highest heaven!

At the sight of all these marvels, how can I do otherwise than cry: "All my bones shall say, Lord, who is like unto Thee?"
—Saint Bernard

Glory be to Thee, Propitiator.
Glory be to Thee, undying One.
Glory be to Thee, King of Peace.
Glory be to Thee, Who was not born.
Glory be to Thee, the Incorruptible.

Prayers for the Dedicated Heart

Glory be to Thee, King of Glory.
Glory be to Thee, the Head of the Universe.
Glory be to Thee, Holy and Perfect One.
Glory be to Thee, Thou Treasury of Glory.
Glory be to Thee, Thou true Light.
Glory be to Thee, Deliverer of the Universe.
Glory be to Thee, Thou Who art indeed the Good One.
Glory be to Thee, Alpha of the Universe.
Glory be to Thee, Life of the Universe.
O Sweet Name.
O Thou, Who art at the head of the Universe.
O Thou Beginning and End of Everything. Amen.
—Coptic Apocrypha

I will praise thee, O Lord, with my whole heart; I will shew forth all thy marvellous works. I will be glad and rejoice in thee: I will sing praise to thy name, O thou most High.
—Psalm 9:1, 2

Petition

Ask, and it shall be given unto you.
Jesus
—St. Matthew 7:7

And whatsoever we ask, we receive of him, because we keep his commandments, and do those things that are pleasing in his sight.
—1 John 3:22

O God, Who dost grant us what we ask, if only when we ask we live a better life.
—Saint Augustine

Do not punish me by granting that which I wish or ask, if it offend Thy love which would always live in me.
—Saint Teresa

Prayers containing the elements of Praise and Petition fulfill a mighty formula for spiritual freedom and progress. In prayer-words of Petition one is *asking* God; and in so doing, he is fulfilling a great Law of Illumination. Ethical asking in prayer is an integral part of divine union. As one becomes more selfless in his praying, his asking becomes more sensitively attuned to the Word and Will of God.

To pray for the healing and quickening of others is the work of the dedicated healer under Christ. Prayer-petitions in which one asks to become more worthy in the sight of God are ethical prayers. Prayer-asking for guidance and for wisdom are beautiful prayers, for the Father *desires* that each of His children come under the mantle of His perfect guidance and be filled with His perfect Wisdom. *"If any of you lack wisdom, let him ask God, that giveth to all men liberally, and upbraideth not; and it shall be given him."* (James 1:5)

>Grant me, O Lord, heavenly wisdom, that
>I may learn above all things to seek and
>to find Thee; above all things to relish and
>to love Thee; and to think of all other
>things as being what indeed they are, at
>the disposal of Thy wisdom.
>   —Saint Thomas á Kempis

>O Thou plenteous Source of every good and perfect gift, shed abroad the cheering light of Thy sevenfold grace over our hearts.
>   —Saint Anselm
>   1033–1109 A.D.

>Grant me fervently to desire, wisely to search out, and perfectly to fulfill all that is well-pleasing unto Thee.
>   —Saint Thomas Aquinas

With bended knees, with hand outstretched, I pray to Thee, my Lord, O Invisible Benevolent Spirit! Vouchsafe to me in this hour of joy, all righteousness of action, all wisdom of the good mind, that I may thereby bring joy to the Soul of Creation.
—Zoroaster

Teach us, good Lord, to serve Thee as Thou deservest; to give and not to count the cost; to fight and not to heed the wounds; to toil and not to seek for rest; to labour and not to ask for any reward, save that of knowing that we do Thy Will.
—Saint Ignatius Loyola
1491–1556 A.D.

GRATITUDE

Thanks be to Thee, O God, for everything.
—Saint John Chrysostom

We give Thee thanks—yea, more than thanks—O Lord our God, for all Thy goodness at all times and in all places.
—Liturgy of Saint Mark

Daily prayers of praise and thanksgiving unite one with the Glory of God within the sacrament-degrees of the Virtue of Gratitude. Through gratitude-prayers, gratitude-fasts and gratitude-offerings, one learns of the Gratitude of God. To those who are adding light, truth and beauty to the world in His Name, the Creator reveals *His* Gratitude through many rewards and gifts.

Special one-day *gratitude-fasts* are part of one's thankfulness to God for the blessings received through His Mercy and Love. Gratitude fasts may be observed also as expressions of one's appreciation for the Lord Jesus, Mary, one or more Saints, the Angels, or one's teacher, religion, etc. Such fasts are powerful ways of making a stronger union with the Mediation Host of Heaven. In time, the Virtue of Gratitude becomes as a multifaceted diamond that reflects the Holy Light and Grace of God.

As one progresses on the Path of Virtue, he becomes grateful for each painful test and trial as well as for the joyful blessings, for he perceives that each pain or affliction has been necessary in his giving birth to virtues and conscience.

> Many are the afflictions of the righteous: but the Lord delivereth him out of them all.
> —Psalm 34:19

> Before I was afflicted I went astray: but now have I kept thy word . . . I will keep thy precepts with my whole heart . . . I delight in thy law. It is good for me that I have been afflicted; that I might learn thy statutes.
>
> The law of thy mouth is better unto me than thousands of gold and silver.
> —Psalm 119:67, 69–72

> For whom the Lord loveth he chasteneth, and scourgeth every son whom he receiveth.
> Saint Paul
> —*Hebrews 12:6*

Each major trial and test on the Path of Virtue helps to bring the soul's record into balance with the Laws of Love. At the ending of a difficult initiatory period, one should speak a Prayer of Gratitude such as:

Father, thank Thee for Thy Lifting-Light.

If a worshipper speaks words of gratitude to God for His Mediation Host each day during morning prayer, he strengthens his love-union with all Great Souls, Beings and Presences in Heaven and on earth.

> *Almighty God, thank Thee for the Holy Angels, Devas, Saints, Illuminati, Great Immortals, Comforter, Spirit of Truth, Holy Ghost, Mary, Apostles of Jesus, Lord Jesus, Divine Mother, Heavenly Father, Hierarchs, Archangels, Lord Christ, and Thine Omnipresent Spirit.*
>
> *
>
> *Father, thank Thee for Thy Fulness, Thy Wholeness, Thy Oneness.*
>
> *
>
> *Thank Thee, Father, for all Teachers of Truth in Heaven and Earth; all Teachers, past, present and future. Thank Thee for all doers of Thy Word, all children of Thy Spirit.*
>
> *
>
> *Thank Thee, Father, for the Lord Jesus and for the Miracle-Essences of His Virtue-Light.*
>
> *
>
> *Thank Thee, Father, for Thy Stars and Galaxies. Thank Thee for Thy Holy Harmony.*

Gratitude to God expressed through prayer, fasting and almsgiving keeps open and *expands* the Blessing Streams of the Angels, the Saints and other Ambassadors of God's Grace, Love and Truth. Gratitude-offerings placed on holy altars; prayers of humility and gratitude following each healing and each holy inspiration—these and all other expressions of one's sincere and heartfelt appreciation lift one into the exalted atmospheres of the sacrament-degrees of the Virtue of Gratitude, wherein abides the fulness of God's Mercy, Wisdom and Love.

GRATITUDE

Enter into His gates with thanksgiving, and into His courts with praise: be thankful unto Him, and bless His name.
—Psalm 100:4

For all things are for your sakes, that the abundant grace might through the thanksgiving of many redound to the glory of God.
Saint Paul
—*2 Corinthians 4:15*

Be forgetful of favor given; be mindful of blessings received.
—Chinese Proverb

Gratitude is like diamonds and jewels ignited by thousands of stars. The angels use your gratitude to widen the portals of your consciousness. —Ann Ree Colton

This glory and honor wherewith man is crowned ought to affect every person that is grateful, with celestial joy: and so much the rather because it is every man's proper and sole inheritance. —Thomas Traherne

Gratitude is not only the greatest of virtues, but the parent of all others. —Cicero

He who is not thankful to men, is not thankful to God.
—Muhammad

Gratitude is the sign of noble souls.   *—Aesop's Fables*

In every thing give thanks: for this is the will of God in Christ Jesus concerning you.
>Saint Paul
>*—1 Thessalonians 5:18*

Guidance

>Into Thy guidance and care, O Lord, Thou Lover of Man, we entrust all our life and hope.
>—Saint Chrysostom
>347?–409 A.D.

>Guide me, O Lord, in all the changes and varieties of the world; that in all things that shall happen, I may have an evenness and tranquillity of spirit; that my soul may be wholly resigned to Thy divinest will and pleasure, never murmuring at Thy gentle chastisements and fatherly correction.
>—Jeremy Taylor
>1613–1667 A.D.

>May the Strength of God pilot us. May the Power of God preserve us. May the Wisdom of God instruct us. May the Way of God direct us.
>—Saint Patrick

Daily prayers of dedication, praise and gratitude bring daily guidance. Each Law and Commandment of God is pure guidance. Each Virtue known to mankind is also a direct and perfect guidance from God. Each Scriptural Law and Commandment provides essential guidance in the use of time and in one's attitudes and conduct. The virtues expressed during one's obedience to the Holy Laws and Commandments provide immediate guidance and open the eyes and ears to other forms of guidance.

"*He shall send His angel before thee.*" (*Genesis 24:7*) Before embarking on a short or long journey, one should ask God for the guidance and help of His Holy Angels. The Angels are perfect in their mediation and intercession; they delight in assisting, guiding and blessing all who love, worship and serve God.

> *May the Angels go before me and light my way.*
>
> *
>
> *Guardian, I ask thy blessing and protection . . . in the Name of the Christ.*

Many accidents, sicknesses, afflictions and other causes of pain and unhappiness are due to one's being out of timing with God's Will for him. Prayers in which he asks to come into timing with God's Will help him to attain the higher grace-states of oneness with the sacred cycles of the soul and with the Time Cycles creating the Solar System.

A prayer to do each thing in *right timing* according to the Father's Love, Plan and Image is a mighty prayer, for the Father's timing is Perfect and Beautiful. To do all things in the Creator's timing is to come into Effortless Effort blessed by the Christ.

> *Father, I pray to do each thing in right timing according to Thy Love, Plan and Image for me as a child of Thy Spirit. In Jesus' Name. Amen.*
>
> *
>
> *Order my days, O Lord, that I may become like Thy Beloved Son.*

Punctuality

> The law of the Lord is perfect.
>
> —Psalm 19:7

The Virtue of Punctuality is an aspect of Timing. A Truth-seeker must attain the Virtue of Punctuality before he can begin to comprehend the Perfect Timing of God, the mathematical Precision of His Laws, and the flawless and flowing Harmony of His Creation of the Universe.

Students of the higher life who are chronically unpunctual should pray to overcome this fault. To persist in unpunctuality reveals a disregard for others and an inability to relate to the Golden Rule. Such irresponsible persons, regardless of their intellectual brilliance or the number of their talents, will miss key timings of their souls' grace and Divine Grace.

Promptness and punctuality reveal a consideration for others and keep one in timing with the progressive grace-processes of the higher life. Through the Virtue of Punctuality, one may work to attain an equanimity born of alertness, obedience, diligence and love.

The Virtue of Punctuality relates to all aspects of Time and Timing. When one reveres Time as a sacred Gift of God, he strives to be punctual at work, at worship, and at all other times and occasions.

To be unpunctual is to be careless. God rewards not carelessness; His clock is an exact clock always in timing to His Will and Plan. He who moves in timing with the Cosmos Clock of the Creator becomes a trustworthy steward of His mysteries.

> *Father, I pray to do all things in perfect timing according to Thy Holy Will. Time is sacred. And he who reveres Time is revering Thee and Thy Plan.*

> *May I unite with Thy Glory within Time and Timing, that I may become more worthy within Thy Sight. In Jesus' Name. Amen.*

Obedience and Diligence

> I receive, in proportion to my obedience, truth from God; I put myself aside and let Him be.
> —Emerson

> I was not disobedient unto the heavenly vision.
> Saint Paul
> —*Acts 26:19*

> And he went a little further, and fell on his face, and prayed, saying, O my Father, if it be possible, let this cup pass from me: nevertheless not as I will, but as thou wilt.
> Jesus
> —*St. Matthew 26:39*

> Lady Holy Love, God keep you, with your sister, holy Obedience.
> —Saint Francis of Assisi

Students who pay little or no attention to their Teacher's instruction or assignments have yet to manifest the essential Virtues of Obedience and Diligence. If these Virtues are present in an aspirant's heart and mind, he moves rapidly on the path toward God-Realization.

Devotees who were obedient to their instructors during their years in academic study are sometimes the least diligent when presented with spiritual instruction from a Teacher of the higher life. In school, they worked for a degree, a diploma, a graduation certificate—something tangible and helpful to their careers in the physical world.

However, their progress on the Path of Virtue is hindered by their inability to hear and obey Scriptural truths presented by a Teacher of the spiritual life.

Whenever a student of the higher life is diligent to his Teacher's instruction, he is being diligent to the Holy Ghost, who is blessing him *through* the Teacher's instruction. The Holy Ghost blesses the devotee through his Teacher until the probationer is able to receive *directly* from the Holy Ghost. Obedience and Diligence are among the major virtues that qualify alert devotees for the receiving of the Gifts of the Holy Ghost and the Christ-Mind Illuminations.

The Creator selects but few devotees to *anoint* with His Spirit, for so very few in modern times have attained the Virtues of Obedience and Diligence. When these key Virtues are present in the heart and mind, all other virtues come into harmonious accord with God's Will and Timing.

Truth-seekers who express the Virtues of Obedience, Diligence and Punctuality remain in timing with the Grace-Tides of God. Omnipresence reveals to them secrets within Time and also quickens the Gifts that come only to the obedient, the diligent, the punctual, the precise, the prepared, and the pure in heart.

DILIGENCE

The substance of a diligent man is precious. —Proverbs 12:27

Thou hast commanded us to keep thy precepts diligently.
—Psalm 119:4

And they that are far off shall come and build in the temple of the Lord, and ye shall know that the Lord of hosts hath sent me unto you. And this shall come to pass, if ye will diligently obey the voice of the Lord your God.
—Zechariah 6:15

Ye shall diligently keep the commandments of the Lord your God, and his testimonies, and his statutes, which he hath commanded thee. —Deuteronomy 6:17

Say unto the men of the world, "Be ye diligent that ye may receive the mysteries of Light, and enter into the height of the Kingdom of Light. —The Pistis Sophia

But without faith it is impossible to please him: for he that cometh to God must believe that he is, and that he is a rewarder of them that diligently seek him.
Saint Paul
—Hebrews 11:6

Diligence is the mother of good fortune. —Cervantes

Therefore as ye abound in everything, in faith, and utterance, and knowledge, and in all diligence, and in your love to us, see that ye abound in this grace also.
Saint Paul
—2 Corinthians 8:7

And beside this, giving all diligence, add to your faith virtue; and to virtue knowledge . . . —2 Peter 1:5

Wherefore, beloved, seeing that ye look for such things, be diligent that ye may be found of him in peace, without spot, and blameless. —2 Peter 3:14

Give me, O Lord, a steadfast heart, which no unworthy affection may drag downwards; give me an unconquered heart, which no tribulation can wear out; give me an upright heart, which no unworthy purpose may tempt aside.

Bestow upon me also, O Lord, my God, understanding to know Thee, diligence to seek Thee, wisdom to find Thee, and a faithfulness that may finally embrace Thee.
—Saint Thomas Aquinas

Teaching the Word of God in Public

> Almighty God, make me a worthy and aware vessel of Thy Power. And if it is Thy Will, may the Archangels unveil the Archetypes so that men may be instructed in Thy forthcoming Will for them.
>
> —Ann Ree Colton

If one is called upon to speak in public on the Sabbath Day or during any other meeting offering spiritual instruction, he should prepare himself by entering into the spirit of humility through prayer. This preparation will enable him to teach the Word of God with reverence, love and inspiration.

> *Father, may Thy Love within Thy Word be free in me, that I may give a perfect testimony of Thy Perfect Love.*
>
> *Who can be worthy enough to speak Thy Word, O Lord? Only* Thou *art worthy enough to speak Thy Word!*
>
> *Let Thy Word be spoken.*
> *Let Thy Word be heard.*
> *And let Thy Word be glorified!*

After one proves his love for God and his Laws, the Gifts and inspirations of his soul come forth. One of these Gifts is the Gift of *Logos*—the inspired speaking of God's Word. Whenever a devotee, initiate or teacher receives praise or compliments for any Gift he shares in public—be it speaking, writing, teaching, healing, music, art, etc.—he should always remember to remain centered in humility and gratitude—and immediately and silently send the compliment or words of praise to the Giver of all Gifts—the Heavenly Father.

Every good gift and every perfect gift is from above, and cometh down from the Father of lights, with whom is no variableness, neither shadow of turning.

—James 1:17

SELF-MASTERY

One man may conquer in battle a thousand times a thousand men; but if another conquer himself, he is the greatest of conquerors. —Buddha

He is strong who conquers others; he who conquers himself is mighty. —Lao Tzu

The most excellent Jihar (Holy War) is that for the conquest of self. —Muhammad

I count him braver who overcomes his desires than him who conquers his enemies; for the hardest victory is the victory over self. —Aristotle

He is most powerful who has power over himself. —Seneca

No man is free who cannot command himself. —Pythagoras

He that is slow to anger is better than the mighty; and he that ruleth his spirit than he that taketh a city. —Proverbs 16:32

Prosperity never resides in one who suffers himself to be tortured by grief, who is addicted to evil ways, who denies Godhead, who is idle, who hath not his senses under control, and who is divested of exertion. —The Mahabharata

The Supreme Spirit is firmly established in the knowledge of the self-controlled man whose mind is perfectly calm in the midst of pairs of opposites such as cold and heat, joy and sorrow, and honor and shame. —Bhagavad Gita VI.7

Who has a harder fight than he who is striving to overcome himself? —Thomas á Kempis

Self-reverence, self-knowledge, self-control, These three alone lead life to sovereign power. —Tennyson

13

THE IMAGE OF GOD

So God created man in His own image, in the image of God created He him; male and female created He them.

> Moses
> —*Genesis 1:27*

For God created man incorruptible, and to the image of His own likeness He made him.

> Apocrypha
> —*Wisdom 2, 23*

But we all, with open face beholding as in a glass the Glory of the Lord, are changed into the same Image from Glory to Glory, even as by the Spirit of the Lord.

> Saint Paul
> —*2 Corinthians 3:18*

QUICKENINGS

I give thee charge in the sight of God, who quickeneth all things.

> Saint Paul
> —*1 Timothy 6:13*

> It is the Spirit that quickeneth; the flesh profiteth nothing.
> > Jesus
> > —*St. John 6:63*

> Quicken me, O Lord, according to Thy lovingkindness.
> > —Psalm 119:159

The Image of God within each living soul is centered in the sanctified sea of Holy Bliss within the Godhead. Every individual born in the physical world experiences *Image-of-God Quickenings*. The different timings in which all persons are being quickened make of the earth a world of great diversity in evolvement: from the unenlightened to the enlightened, from the unloving to the pure in heart. Even as the Galaxies in the Cosmos testify to the different creation-stages of solar systems, so do the diverse degrees of human life testify to the different degrees of Image-of-God quickenings.

If a person is without virtue and without conscience, he may be likened to a solar system in its initial or nebular stages of creation before the formation of a central sun and correlating planets. When an individual is filled with virtue-light and conscience-light, he is as a solar system with all planets moving in rhythmic harmony around a central sun.

The earth is approximately four and one-half billion years old. The physical body, with its glandular system and five senses, has evolved over the ages to its present state of quickening. The physical aspects of man's being have responded to the Laws of Nature, which, in turn, have responded to the Cosmos Laws governing the Sun, the Moon, the Planets and the Stars. The spiritual aspects of man's being also have evolved according to the energy-influences of the Sun, the Moon, the Planets, and the Constellations. *"Canst thou bind the sweet influences of the Pleiades, or loose the bands of Orion?" (Job 38:31)*

Over the ages, mankind has experienced life in tribes, races, nations, religions and families during the progressive stages of Image-of-God quickenings. Tribal Virtues and Tribal Conscience, Race Virtues and Race Conscience, National Virtues and National Conscience, Family Virtues and Family Conscience—all denote different stages of Image-of-God quickenings. Since the coming of Jesus, the *Individual* is coming to spiritual birth beyond tribe, race, nation or family.

> He that loveth father or mother more than me is not worthy of me.
>
> Jesus
> —*St. Matthew 10:37*

> Who is my mother? and who are my brethren? . . . whosoever shall do the will of my Father which is in heaven, the same is my brother, and sister and mother.
>
> Jesus
> —*St. Matthew 12:48, 50*

Presently, all tribal, racial, national, religious, family and individuality levels of the human spirit are experiencing an *acceleration* of Image-of-God quickenings. In this increase of quickenings, the rapid tempo of life is pressing mankind toward future eras in which the Image of God will manifest its perfect Glory in and through the human spirit.

> And so it is written, The first man Adam was made a living soul; the last Adam was made a quickening spirit.
>
> Saint Paul
> —*1 Corinthians 15:45*

The Ten Commandments and the Sermon on the Mount

> Thou shalt therefore keep the commandments, and the statutes, and the judgments, which I command thee this day, to do them.
>
> —Deuteronomy 7:11

> And seeing the multitudes, he went up into a mountain: and when he was set, his disciples came unto him: And he opened his mouth, and taught them.
>
> —St. Matthew 5:1, 2

The Image of God for man is an indwelling and an overdwelling Image. The overdwelling Image of God for man permeates the Solar System; it is in the air men breathe and in the atoms of food taken into their bodies. The Sun, the Moon, the Planets and the Stars that correlate to the Sun direct their energy-processes toward the creation of man in the Image and Likeness of God. As one progresses on the Path of Virtue, secrets and mysteries related to the Image of God are revealed in rhythmic tides moving from the Godhead. When this occurs, one has begun to unite with the Wisdom and Will of God in the Outer Universe and in the Inner Kingdom, thereby linking the Image of God within his being with the Image of God suffusing the Solar System and the Universe.

As one draws closer to the Godhead, the Image of God within his being—pulsating with the breath of Eternal Life

The Image of God

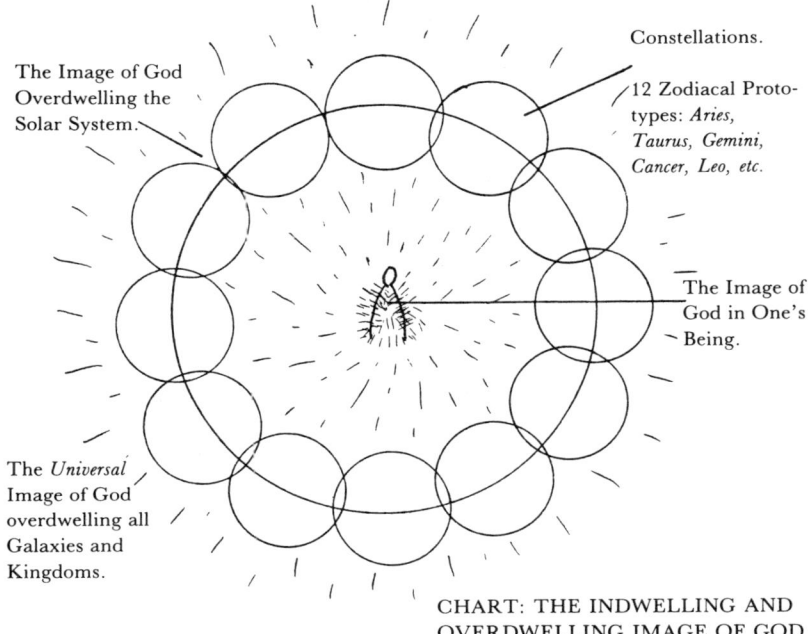

CHART: THE INDWELLING AND OVERDWELLING IMAGE OF GOD

—opens his eyes to the beauty and the holiness of the Creator's Plan. In this, one becomes vividly aware of the preciousness of the soul, the sacredness of life, and the innate divinity within all persons being created in the Image of God.

In His Wisdom, the Creator sends to the earth enlightened personages who exemplify the noble degrees of the Image-of-God quickenings: the Great Teachers, the Sages, the Seers, the Prophets and the Saints. Jesus, expressing Messianic Virtues, represents the highest degrees of Image-of-God quickening attainable by man in this Solar System.

> And we know that all things work together for good to them that love God, to them who are the

> called according to His purpose. For whom He did foreknow, He also did predestinate to be conformed to the image of His Son, that He might be the firstborn among many brethren.
>
> Saint Paul
> —*Romans 8:28, 29*

The Image of the Christ, the Son of God, was revealed to mankind through the perfected Virtues of the Lord Jesus. These miracle-producing Virtues of the Messiah were mankind's first glimpse of the Great and Eternal Image of God.

The Image of God in man contains the seeds of the virtues. In the Great Teachers of the past, these beautiful virtue-seeds blossomed into a glorious fulness and spiritual ripeness. When one seeks to emulate the virtues of the Enlightened Teachers of the East and the West—especially the virtues of the Lord Jesus—he has discovered the key to union with the Creator's Glory within the Godhead.

Even as seeds planted in the ground are steadily quickened until they grow into fruit-bearing trees, so are Image-of-God virtue-seeds coming to birth in mankind. Persons experiencing the early stages of Image-of-God Quickening are totally unaware of the importance of virtues and conscience, for they are as babes yet in the womb, or as new seeds under the ground with no awareness of the sun's light. Over a period that may extend for many lives, ages or solar systems, the Image-of-God Quickenings produce in such persons the first stirrings of virtues and conscience.

Through the Image-of-God Quickenings, one evolves from Prodigal-Son states of heart and mind to the higher states of enlightenment and spiritual-creative individuality. The Creator, through His Quickening Spirit, is seeking to inspire each of His children to become "like" Jesus in

The Image of God

virtue, conscience and consciousness. This mighty Quickening for each individual is the work of the ages and the eternals.

> Behold, what manner of love the Father hath bestowed upon us, that we should be called the sons of God; therefore the world knoweth us not, because it knew Him not.
>
> Beloved, now are we the sons of God, and it doth not yet appear what we shall be: but we know that, when He shall appear, we shall be like Him; for we shall see Him as He is.
>
> And every man that hath this hope in him purifieth himself, even as he is pure.
> —1 John 3:1-3

"Having eyes, see ye not? and having ears, hear ye not?" (St. Mark 8:18) In the first stages of Image-of-God Quickenings —when persons are as seeds under the ground—their eyes are unable to perceive the wisdom and beauty of God within the Ten Commandments. The Ten Commandments, as Ten Fingers, are molding and sculpturing man in the Image and Likeness of God.

In the second stages of Image-of-God Quickening, persons live according to the Ten Commandments, the Holy Law of Tithing, and the Commandments of Love for God and Neighbor. Their hearts and minds, receptive to the energy-dynamics of the soul, are experiencing the first degrees of Spiritual Illumination.

In the third stages of Image-of-God Quickening, individuals earnestly apply the principles, ethics, virtues and worship-disciplines taught by Jesus in the Sermon on the Mount. The Ten Commandments, when fulfilled with

The Path of Virtue

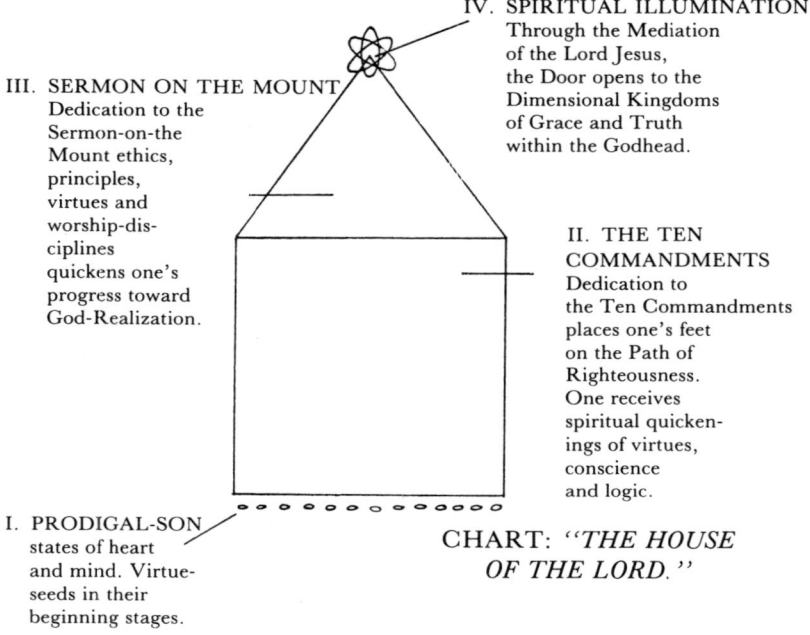

III. SERMON ON THE MOUNT
Dedication to the Sermon-on-the Mount ethics, principles, virtues and worship-disciplines quickens one's progress toward God-Realization.

IV. SPIRITUAL ILLUMINATION
Through the Mediation of the Lord Jesus, the Door opens to the Dimensional Kingdoms of Grace and Truth within the Godhead.

II. THE TEN COMMANDMENTS
Dedication to the Ten Commandments places one's feet on the Path of Righteousness. One receives spiritual quickenings of virtues, conscience and logic.

I. PRODIGAL-SON states of heart and mind. Virtue-seeds in their beginning stages.

CHART: *"THE HOUSE OF THE LORD."*

loyalty and love, prepare one for union with the righteousness and holiness of God's Wisdom within the Sermon on the Mount. The Sermon on the Mount, a masterpiece of logic and truth, provides essential virtue-knowledge for receiving the Greater Anointings of God.

The Ten Commandments contain the essence of wisdom, morality and spiritual law inherited from all former ages. The Sermon on the Mount contains the quintessence of knowledge relating to all pure teachings of virtue and truth. The marriage between the Ten Commandments and the Sermon on the Mount must occur in one's heart and mind before he may qualify for marriage or union with the Divine Presence.

In the fourth stages of Image-of-God Quickening, one becomes an anointed servant of God graced with Christ-Mind Gifts and Skills. To know the Anointing Spirit of

God as an Abiding Presence, is to remain in a continuous state of expanding Grace and Truth.

God is a versatile Creator; therefore, as a Truth-seeker experiences Image-of-God Quickenings, his spiritual dedications manifest versatile creations. Image-of-God Quickenings make of a devotee, initiate or teacher a versatile craftsman inspired in the fields of music, art, writing, speaking and other forms of creative expression.

> You will never have a greater or lesser dominion than that over yourself. The height of a man's success is gauged by his self-mastery.
> —Leonardo da Vinci

> The seeds of God, 'tis true are few, but vast and fair, and good-virtue and self-control, devotion. Devotion is God-gnosis; and he who knoweth God, being filled with all good things thinks godly thoughts.
> —Thrice-Greatest Hermes
> Corpus Hermeticum IX (X)
> *On Thought and Sense, Vol. II*

Divine-Image Electricities

> Test everything. Lay hold upon that which is good. Similarly, do not treat with contempt the image of God. Moreover, keep diligently thy youth with all care, in order that thou mayest be able to keep diligently thine old age with all care, lest thou be put to shame.
> —Coptic Apocrypha

The quickening action of the Image of God within the soul may be likened to the opening of a lotus. The petals around this Eternal Image are **Virtue-Petals.** The birth or opening of a virtue-petal may require many lives, ages or solar systems. The timing of the opening of each virtue-petal and its energization of the heart and mind is determined by the wisdom-mathematics of the Creator.

When a wayward person experiences a dramatic change of heart, this is due to the sudden opening of beautiful virtue-petals. This miraculous occurrence inspires one to repent of former ways of unrighteousness and to embrace the moral principles and ethical precepts of one or more Great Teachers. During this transition period, one may also be graced by God with guidance to a living teacher who will be the "midwife" in his birth to virtues and conscience.

Time is an everlasting ocean moving endlessly against the virtue-petals surrounding the Jewel of God's Image within the core of one's being. During certain stages of evolvement, a person may wilfully resist the opening of virtue-petals for many ages; in such instances, the virtues seeking to come to birth are subject to the persistent waves within the ocean of Time. Over the millennia, all resistances are slowly and steadily worn away by the unceasing waves of Time's ocean until each virtue becomes a luminous light in the heart and mind.

The Christ works with and through one's living teacher to inspire an earnest devotee to express with naturalness the sacrament-degrees of the virtues. Whenever this state of virtue-energization is attained, the Christ may open one's understanding of the electricities of the soul and the spirit.

Communion with the Wisdom of God pervading the Universe occurs through *Divine-Image Electricities*. Reverence for the Image of God in each living soul activates Divine-Image degrees of electricity that unite the heart and mind with the Intelligence of God within the Stars and Galaxies.

In future centuries, mankind will learn of the Divine-Image Electricities. Holy men and sages in past eras used the Divine-Image Electricities during sacramental meditation and other devotional observances. Through these powerful electricities of the soul and the spirit, oneness with the God of Cosmos is attained.

Even as the advent of television has enabled the human spirit to utilize physical-light degrees of electricity to link the eastern and western hemispheres of the planet Earth and to witness the work of astronauts on the Moon's surface, so will the knowledge and use of Divine-Image degrees of electricity be mankind's link with brother and sister Stars and Galaxies in the Cosmos. The Christ is the Quickener, Coordinator and Director of the Divine-Image Electricities.

> The Son quickeneth whom he will.
> Jesus
> —*St. John 5:21*

> The Christ Spirit is Relentless Electricity.
> —Ann Ree Colton

Kundalini, Chakras and Virtues

> The whole world of our consciousness is only a seed of the future. And when you succeed in the awakening of Kundalini, so that she moves out of her mere potentiality, you necessarily start a world which is totally different from our world; it is a world of eternity.
> —Carl G. Jung

Modern-day astronomers and radio-astronomers have made numerous discoveries pertaining to the mathematics, chemistry, physics and sounds of the Cosmos. As man becomes more spiritually-minded, he will begin to comprehend the roles of Conscience, Virtues, Logic and Love in the *Universal* Plan of God.

The Creator's Spirit of Pure Love is uniting His multitudinous Stars and Galaxies with the threads of Righteousness and Truth. Man lives in a Morality Universe based upon Laws of Righteousness. All Laws introduced to the human spirit by the Great Teachers are Laws of Righteousness. The Love-Laws of God's Righteousness are present in all Solar Systems.

"Seek ye first the kingdom of God, and His righteousness." (St. Matthew 6:33) When one seeks the kingdom of God and His righteousness, as directed by Jesus in the Sermon on the Mount, he has begun his communication with the Cosmos. For the Laws of Righteousness are everywhere present in the Universe.

The Image of God being quickened in man consists of energy-vortices called *chakras*. The chakras being opened through Image-of-God Quickenings contain the budding promise of man's becoming an illumined son of God.

The Eastern word *kundalini* refers to the progressive rise of love, virtue-light, conscience-light and logic-light from the base of the spine to the crown of the head. This ascending light of love, virtue, conscience and logic determines one's degree of union with the Love, Truth and Righteousness of God.

Man, in the first stages of chakra and kundalini development, is bestial, animal-like, devoid of virtue, conscience and logic. Over the ages, the energy-vortices of the chakras become increasingly active in one's being. This action produces major changes in one's motives and goals in life.

The Image of God

The kundalini's upward rise relates to unbridled sexual fires being purified and transformed into reverent procreation-light and, eventually, holy illumination-light. The kundalini's fiery energy-action at the base of the spine is changed into pure and holy light through the virtues quickened and expanded during sacramental meditation, prayer, fasting and almsgiving.

The kundalini's ascending energy-action is centered in the spine. The chakras, as energy-vortices, proceed from the kundalini and penetrate and permeate the glands, the muscles, the nerves and the bones. Each atom in man's physical, emotional, mental and spiritual being is part of the energy-drama related to the creation of man through his kundalini and chakras.

The purification of love-energies in the heart enables the heart chakra to become a powerful virtue-vortex. The pure conscience resulting from heart-initiations moves upward from the loins to the higher chakras en route to the thousand-petaled-lotus chakra over the crown of the head. This atom-energy area of God's Righteousness in man links the righteousness-light and conscience-light of one's being with the powerful energies of God's Righteousness and Love—and one experiences increasing magnitudes of Spiritual Illumination relating to the Cosmos.

The cardinal virtues correlating to the chakras and the kundalini are:

Chakra Location	Sanskrit Name	Virtue-Vortex	Anti-Virtue Energy Action
1. Base of Spine *Sacral Plexus*	Muladhara	Goodness	Lust
2. Pelvic area *Prostatic plexus*	Svadhishthana	Discrimination	Hate

Chakra Location	Sanskrit Name	Virtue-Vortex	Anti-Virtue Energy Action
3. Solar Plexus *Epigastric plexus*	Manipura	Giving, Magnanimity, Healing Magnetism, Detachment	Greed, Sloth, Egotism, Manipulating, Taking
4. Heart *Cardiac plexus*	Anahata	Love, Fidelity, Loyalty	Separateness
5. Throat *Pharyngeal plexus*	Vishuddha	Steadfastness to Truth	Envy
6. Between the Brows *Third Eye*	Ajni	Mindfulness	Mental Pride
7. Crown of the Head *Thousand-petaled Lotus*	Sahasrara	Selflessness	Atheism. Sin against the Holy Ghost.

The seventh chakra is the dwelling place of the Godhead Light seated within the center of the soul's medallion.

When the chakras are asleep, they are in the *potential* virtue state. When they are partially awake, they are active reminders of the conscience. When they are awake, they are then in their whole and true virtue-state; they are jewel virtue-vortices for the soul.

—Ann Ree Colton

"He shall give his angels charge over thee, to keep thee in all thy ways." (*Psalm 91:11*) The work of the Angels includes the energy-purifications and transformations occurring through the kundalini and the chakras. The moment one

begins to think of God's Image, Love and Laws—and worships Him in spirit and in truth—the Angels and the Saints bless him with their mediative assistance. The Angels and the Saints, working with the Harmony-Laws of Righteousness, bring the kundalini and chakra energies into harmony with the Righteousness-Threads of God weaving each Star and Galaxy into a perfect tapestry of Love-Creation.

The soul's energies flow through the kundalini and the chakras as virtue-energies, conscience-energies and logic-energies. Love expressed through prayer, meditation, fasting and almsgiving activates and accelerates the soul's energies throughout one's being. The Angels and the Saints use one's love and virtues as a weaver uses threads to weave a beautiful garment. The garment woven by the Angels and the Saints for the devotee-initiate is the Garment of Spiritual Insulation—the "whole armour of God."* With the weaving of this Garment, the Anointing Spirit of God increases the voltages of His Righteousness-Light through the soul's record and into the kundalini and chakras and their correlating points in the brain, heart, glands, nerves, muscles and blood. In this, one gains the *Divine Centering* that comes through union with the Righteousness, Love and Truth of God.

The *aura* of each person is an electromagnetic energy-field of processed chakra-energies and unprocessed chakra-energies. Processed energies are disciplined energies; unprocessed energies are undisciplined energies. All unprocessed chakra-energies provided by the Quickening Spirit of God require processing until they become disciplined and purified energies utilized by the body, heart,

---

*Ephesians 6:11. *"Put on the whole armour of God, that ye may be able to stand against the wiles of the devil."*

mind and soul. Love and Humility are the greatest discipliners and purifiers of all chakra-energies released into one's life and being by the Image of God.

Each new surge of chakra-energies may be likened to handfuls of clay being added to a sculptured form. Through the rhythmic Time Cycles of the Sun and the Moon, the Hand of God is shaping each person in His Image and Likeness—and new clay (energies) is constantly being added to the heart's love and the mind's light. In this shaping, molding and forming, each new addition of chakra-energies enables a Truth-seeker to continuously grow in spiritual stature and to expand the range of his love.

A love-filled aura expands in pulsating tides of grace and truth—moving ever-upward, outward and inward. In time, the love-energies within one's aura reach out and embrace all the peoples of the earth and all Stars and Galaxies.

The addition of *soul-grace* through the chakras is a time of inspiration, joy and happiness. However, the *sins* of one's ancestors or his own sins of past lives may move upon him as dark or crude energies. The receiving of these dark energies is a time of challenge and struggle until the energies are purified through love, repentance, confession and restitution. After each victory over dark energies within oneself and within mankind, one is blessed with a greater range of chakra virtue-energies with which to heal and to serve others. All who are called and chosen to serve the Living God work through chakra virtue-light to heal the woes, ills and sins of the world.

> Go ye therefore, and teach all nations, baptizing them in the name of the Father, and of the Son, and of the Holy Ghost.
> Jesus
> —*St. Matthew 28:19*

The Image of God

A *tamas* person moves more slowly through his life-cycles due to lethargy, inertia and procrastination. The aura of such a person is a turgid sea of heavy energies waiting to be processed through love, worship and self-discipline.

A *rajas* individual has an abundance of energies that become an inner and outer fire if not harnessed and expressed through love, compassion and dedicated creativity. The undisciplined and selfish rajasic person is as a sea of fiery emotional, mental and physical energies. When these unprocessed chakra-energies are finally mastered through love, worship and self-control, one becomes a tireless worker in the vineyard of the Christ.

Persons who attain the *sattva* state utilize all chakra-energies with love and understanding. Such persons are the peacemakers, the polarized, the harmonized, the enlightened.

> Blessed are the peacemakers: for they shall be called the children of God.
> Jesus
> —St. Matthew 5:9

Ancestral Armageddon

> I the Lord thy God am a jealous God, visiting the iniquity of the fathers upon the children unto the third and fourth generation of them that hate me, and shewing mercy unto thousands of them that love me and keep my commandments.
> —Deuteronomy 5:9, 10

A Holy War occurs within each person who is born to life on earth: the virtues of his ancestors enter into battle with the vices of his ancestors. In this Ancestral Armageddon within the heart and mind, the virtues of one's ancestors form one energy mass and the anti-virtues of his ancestors form another energy mass. A devotee of the higher life is caught in the middle of the Holy War between his ancestors' virtues and anti-virtues. These conflicting energy masses pull him one way and then the other until he dedicates to worship and serve God according to His Laws and Commandments. When this time of dedication is reached, he becomes increasingly aware of the importance of spiritual insulation and divine protection necessary for him to overcome and to transcend the negative traits and reflexes inherited from his ancestors.

The Ancestral Armageddon continues until one makes peace between the warring armies within his genes and within his subconscious mind. Many afflictions and sorrows are due to ancestral sins that victimize generations of children, grandchildren and great-grandchildren. These unresolved sins of one's ancestors, when combined with the unexpiated sins of his own past lives, may cause major defects at birth or chronic ailments during other periods of life. *"Master, who did sin, this man, or his parents, that he was born blind?"* (St. John 9:2)

The Ancestral Armageddon involves all persons: from the unrighteous to the righteous. Each individual is subject to the gene-memories of his ancestors in everything he feels, thinks and does. If his ancestors were atheistic or agnostic, he will be inclined to be atheistic and agnostic. If his ancestors were fearful, prejudiced, unforgiving, revengeful, covetous, these traits will seek to render him captive. If his ancestors expressed faith in God; worshipped the Almighty; valued freedom; were kind, sacrificing, loving, forgiving—these powerful assets will be his fortifications and strengths in the Ancestral Armageddon.

Ancestral sins, if free to corrupt one's moral values, become as a fire that burns, a wave that engulfs. These sins of gross sensuality and selfishness wreak havoc on the physical body, the emotions and the mind.

The sins of one's ancestors and his own sins are as a roaring dragon that dwells in the lower subconscious. The battle fought between Saint George and the dragon is the same battle that must be fought by all who seek Spiritual Liberation and Illumination. If the fiery energies from the dragon are able to saturate one's feelings and thoughts with negativity, depression, lust for power and hordes of other dark energies, the dragon is successfully expanding its range of influence from the lower subconscious into the physical world—and one becomes an adversary to Righteousness, an enemy of Holiness, and a destroyer of Beauty and Truth.

The wisdom of the Great Teachers enables one to become less and less subservient to the action of the dragon-like negative ancestral compulsions, reflexes and memories. In this, a sincere seeker after truth and righteousness steadily increases in a wisdom and freedom blessed by God.

> Grant us grace to rest from all sinful deeds and thoughts, to surrender ourselves wholly unto Thee, and keep our souls still before Thee like a still lake, so that the beams of Thy grace may be mirrored therein, and may kindle in our hearts the glow of faith and love and prayer.
> —Collection from the 18th Century

> Even a sinful person, if he worships Me with unswerving devotion, must be regarded as righteous, for he has formed the right resolution. He soon becomes righteous and attains eternal peace. —Bhagavad Gita

> The sorest judgment on evil-doing is that a man grows like those who already are evil. —Plato

Violent attachment to self is the constant source of misdeeds in every one of us. —Plato

In the march towards Truth, anger, selfishness, hatred, etc., naturally give way, for otherwise Truth would be impossible to attain. A man who is swayed by passions may have good enough intentions, may be truthful in word, but he will never find the Truth. —Mohandas K. Gandhi

Pleasant is virtue lasting to old age;
Pleasant is a faith firmly rooted;
Pleasant is attainment of intelligence;
Pleasant is avoiding of sins.

Buddha
—*The Dhammapada*

After the same fashion, sin, done with a sinful heart, produces a large crop of misery. —The Mahabharata

Supreme joy is for this Yogi whose mind is peaceful, whose passion-nature is calmed, who is sinless and of the nature of the Eternal. —The Bhagavad Gita

Sin is an obstruction in the heart; an inability to feel and comprehend all that is noble, true and great, and to take part in the good. If man is to be freed from sin, his mind and heart must be opened to the influence of enlightenment.
—The Talmud

A sin is anything that offends the purity of the soul.
—Ann Ree Colton

Sin is the fuel for virtue's fire. —Hazrat Inayat Khan

Go, and sin no more.

Jesus
—*St. John 5:14*

The victims of the Ancestral Armageddon are strewn all over the earth. Hospitals, mental institutions, emotional and mental retardations, nervous-system disorders, poverty, afflictions, distresses, terrors, tribulations, guilts, incest, hostilities, wars, rapes and robberies—all testify to the powerful armies of negativity devastating the earth with pain, sorrow and suffering.

The negative ancestral forces within one's genes and memory-cells use the power of hypnosis to mesmerize, devitalize and destroy. The reflexes motivating one to be lustful in actions, feelings and thoughts try to pull him into the encampment of the vice-brigades of his ancestors. Here, he becomes a robot-like automaton devoted to lust, greed, envy, pride, jealousy, hatred, retaliation, cruelty, secrecy, sullenness and sensuality. Even as the sin-natures of his fathers and forefathers seek to compel one to follow the path of selfishness and vice, so will his own sins seek to compel his children and his children's children to live with lust, greed, pride, prejudice and other anti-virtues.

The compounding sin-debts mushrooming from generation to generation create the abnormal in sex: the homosexual, the lesbian, the lover of self. Wherever the stench of perversion pollutes the air, hordes of casualties are added to the number of victims in the Ancestral Armageddon.

Homosexuality is a desecration of the Image of God. All irreverent and abnormal sexual practices place their mesmerized victims under bondage to lustful reflexes inherited from immoral ancestors and vice-ridden past lives.

The Sacrament of Procreative Love is a Holy Sacrament blessed by God. Homosexuals enter not into sexual relationships for the purpose of procreation; thus, their sins continually add burdens to the lower subconscious—burdens inherited in coming lives.

Homosexuals desirous of becoming religious leaders invite the reproving action of the soul. The Spirit of Truth is a powerful light that exposes all imbalances within one's body, heart and soul. These imbalances must be changed to polarity-balance through contrition, repentance, confession and restitution before any aspirant can begin to qualify for the Divine-Marriage Anointing.

If a homosexual believes that his sexual desires are "normal"—and he dies in an unrepentant state—he faces future lives in which the masculine and feminine polarities must become painfully restored to a balanced harmony. The Image of God may require many lives and ages before this necessary polarization occurs. A sincere repentance before the time of death avoids many lives of suffering, sorrow and humiliation—and enables the Angels and Saints to begin their healing work before one leaves the world.

> Homosexual practices are always an injury done to the Creator, whether or not any offence is at the same time committed against one's neighbor, since they violate His creative intent for human behavior and destroy the beauty of His work.
> —Saint Thomas Aquinas

> The intercourse of men with men, or of women with women is contrary to nature, and the bold attempt was originally due to unbridled lust. How can we take precautions against the unnatural loves of either sex, from which innumerable evils have come upon individuals and cities? How shall we devise a remedy and a way of escape out of so great a danger? We must abolish altogether the connection of men with men . . . Who would ever think of establishing such a practice by law? Certainly no one who had in his mind the true image of law.
> Plato
> —*The Laws*

... morbid abnormality. —Aristotle

Those shameful acts against nature, such as were committed in Sodom, ought everywhere and always to be detested and punished. If all nations were to do such things, they would equally be guilty of the same crime by the law of God, which has not so made men that they should use one another in this way.

Saint Augustine
—*Confessions*

Know ye not that the unrighteous shall not inherit the kingdom of God? Be not deceived: neither fornicators, nor idolaters, nor adulterers, nor effeminate, nor abusers of themselves with mankind, nor thieves, nor covetous, nor drunkards, nor revilers, nor extortioners, shall inherit the kingdom of God. And such were some of you: but ye are washed, but ye are sanctified, but ye are justified in the name of the Lord Jesus, and by the Spirit of our God.

Saint Paul
—*1 Corinthians 6:9-11*

The sins of former lives mathematically attract one to birth through ancestral lines committing the same type or nature of sins. At birth, the ancestral gene-memories of each person correlate to the actions, feelings, thoughts and motives of his own previous lives. In the higher life, one must work *with God* to overcome all tendencies toward immoral and abnormal behavior; also, he must strive through spiritual practices to bring to balance and harmony the Heavenly-Father Polarity and the Divine-Mother Polarity within his being.

Even as the sins of the fathers are visited upon their children unto the third and fourth generations, so are the virtues of the fathers visited upon their children unto the third and fourth generations. One who becomes centered on the Path of Virtue unites with his ancestors' virtue-grace. The grace earned by one's ancestors is a vast and unending reservoir of grace that blesses the body, heart, mind and soul.

As long as one loves God with all of his heart, mind, soul and strength, he remains united with ancestral-grace blessed by the Christ. In this, the Dimensional Healing Power of the Christ within his heart and mind changes the crude or dark energies of unresolved ancestral sin-debts into the light of enlightenment. However, if one does not love God, he fails to earn the protection of the Christ; thus, he remains vulnerable to the disturbing and distracting energies of ancestral transgressions.

If one's parents are not giving, charitable or compassionate—and he has a naturally giving and loving heart—he has *transcended* ancestral sins. Persons who inherit their parents' non-giving natures and unloving attitudes are caught in the quicksand of ancestral trespasses and uncharitableness. The giving heart is the way of escape and freedom.

If one has the courage, vision and forthrightness to express the virtues his ancestors or parents failed to express, his present life will bless his future lives—and he will reincarnate through more compassionate and spiritual lines of ancestors and more reverent and charitable parents. If one is graced with spiritually-evolved parents in his present life, their virtues will add to his own natural virtues—and he will be doubly and triply blessed.

Individuals who lose their footing on the Path of Virtue have fallen victim to negative ancestral compulsions feeding and stimulating their pride, vanity, selfishness, lust, covetousness and fears. The Christ, as the Good Shepherd, is ever seeking to retrieve each sheep that has strayed from the Path of Virtue.

Each time a seeker after Truth fails to fulfill a holy Law and Commandment, he is yielding to the pressures of negative ancestral influences headquartered in the lower subconscious. Each time a Holy Law and Commandment is revered and honored with gratitude, enthusiasm and joy, the Christ uses the *spirit* of one's gratitude and dedication to heal, protect and enlighten him.

The Christ increases His healing and transforming action in the lower subconscious through one's daily worship of God. Prayers of repentance and confession accompanied by acts of restitution enable the Great Exorcisor to cleanse and heal the lower subconscious, thereby enabling one to come into an undisturbed peace, calm and serenity. The peace of the Christ is charged with the grace-essences of holy inspiration and pure creation. *"My peace I give unto you: not as the world giveth, give I unto you."* (St. John 14:27)

The Christ is the Door to all degrees, dimensions, realms and kingdoms of *Grace: Ancestral Grace, Past Lives Grace, Race Grace, Nation Grace, Family Grace, Marriage Grace, Soul Grace, Apostolic Grace, Galaxy Grace, etc.* Devotees and initiates who work with God and the Christ through daily prayer and meditation gradually become free from ancestral sin-inclinations and unite with the virtues and grace of their ancestors.

Each time an aspirant makes a stand for Purity and Truth, he opens the door to his receiving fortification, strength and inspiration from his *ancestral grace*. The Christ assists the devotee through the releasement of ancestral-grace blessings into his heart, mind and life. In this, the devotee meets with equanimity and understanding the *cyclic* challenges from negative ancestral-thrusts; and, through the Mediation of the Christ, the *energy* within the ancestral sins and vices is transformed into the energy of enlightenment and virtue.

If one is aware of the power and importance of contrition, repentance, confession and restitution, and calls upon these weapons during the intense Ancestral Armageddon battles, *he gives the Christ the ways of reaching into his lower subconscious with His laser-like Light, that He may heal the roots of all sin-reflexes inherited from ancestors.* Each sincere devotee seeks to emulate the virtues of Jesus so that he may purify and transcend ancestral sins and past-lives sins.

There may be many heated battles and repeated skirmishes before the Christ Light is able to penetrate and dissolve the crystallized ancestral energies and past-lives energies causing lust, greed, envy, pride, anger and other anti-virtues to motivate or govern one's thoughts, feelings and actions. However, with persistence—and dedication to the right and the light—the tide of the battles will turn as the Christ Light begins to "abide" in one's being and to take command of the powerful energy-processes in the lower subconscious.

> Abide in me, and I in you. As the branch cannot bear fruit of itself, except it abide in the vine; no more can ye, except ye abide in me. I am the vine, ye are the branches: He that abideth in me, and I in him, the same bringeth forth much fruit: for without me ye can do nothing.
>
> Jesus
> —St. John 15:4, 5

> A man is a *faithful and prudent servant* (Matthew 24:45) when he is quick to atone for all his offences, interiorly by contrition, exteriorly by confessing them and making reparation.
> —Saint Francis of Assisi

MERCY

God, who is rich in mercy, for his great love wherewith he loved us, Even when we were dead in sins, hath quickened us together with Christ . . . that in ages to come he might shew the exceeding riches of his grace in his kindness toward us through Christ Jesus.

Saint Paul
—Ephesians 2:4, 5, 7

Allah forgiveth the entirety of sins. Lo! He is the Forgiving, the Merciful. Praise be to Allah, the Lord of creation, the merciful, the compassionate Ruler of the Day of Judgment. Help us, lead us in the path.

Muhammad
—Koran

The mercy of the Lord is from everlasting to everlasting upon them that fear him. —Psalm 103:17

Keep yourselves in the love of God, looking for the mercy of our Lord Jesus Christ unto eternal life. —Jude 21

And they lifted up their voices, and said, Jesus, Master, have mercy on us.

Lepers healed by Jesus
—St. Luke 17:13

Lord Christ Jesus, Son of God, have mercy on us.

—Early Christian Prayer

The corn that makes the holy bread
By which the soul of man is fed
The holy bread, the food unpriced,
Thy everlasting mercy, Christ. —Masefield

God hath two wings, which He doth ever move,
The one is Mercy, and the next is Love:
Under the first the sinners ever trust;
And with the last He still directs the Just. —Robert Herrick

14

THE MERCY OF GOD

Blessed are the merciful: for they shall obtain mercy.

Jesus
—*St. Matthew 5:7*

For thy mercy is great above the heavens: and thy truth reacheth unto the clouds.

—Psalm 108:4

Let the wicked forsake his way, and let the unrighteous man his thoughts: and let him return unto the Lord, and he will have mercy upon him; and to our God, for he will abundantly pardon.

—Isaiah 55:7

Repentance

He who repents his sins is well-nigh innocent.

—Seneca

Repent: for the kingdom of heaven is at hand.

Jesus
—*St. Matthew 4:17*

> And the times of this ignorance God winked at; but now commandeth all men everywhere to repent . . .
>
> <div style="text-align:right">Saint Paul
—<i>Acts 17:30</i></div>

> Forgiveness is only incumbent on Allah toward those who do evil in ignorance, and then turn quickly in repentance. These are they toward whom Allah turneth.
>
> —Muhammad

> All that I ought to have thought and have
>   not thought;
> All that I ought to have said and have
>   not said;
> All that I ought to have done and have
>   not done;
> All that I ought not to have thought and yet
>   have thought;
> All that I ought not to have spoken and yet
>   have spoken;
> All that I ought not to have done and yet
>   have done;
> For thoughts, words and works, pray I for forgiveness, and repent of with penance.
>
> —Zoroaster

Repentance opens the door to the vast world of God's Mercy. The Mercy of God is bliss-filled in its core; ecstasy-charged in its vibratory light and love; and joy-radiating, in its miracle-producing manifestations.

The desire to repent and to walk the Path of Virtue is as a magnet that attracts one to a teacher of the higher life. To be guided by the Creator to an enlightened teacher is to learn of the laws and virtues through which divine union is accomplished.

Many individuals in the world have fallen into the quicksand of frustration, confusion or affliction. If one prays to God for help, he will be guided to a teacher. The teacher will extend to him a branch and seek to pull him out of the quicksand of his problems. The branch handed to one by the teacher is the Law of God; the Law is a strong branch from the Tree of God's Mercy, ·Love and Grace. Repentance, when combined with the dedication to honor Holy Laws, enables the penitent to reach the branch and to be lifted to the dry ground of God's Mercy and Love. An insincere repentance or a halfhearted dedication keeps one from reaching the branch—and he continues to be pulled downward by the quicksand, often pulling others in with him.

The Path of Virtue is a constant testing of one's sincerity. The tests regarding sincerity begin from the time of his first prayer of repentance to his final breath of life on earth.

SINCERITY

Sincerity is the foundation of the spiritual life.
—Albert Schweitzer

Sincerely understand divine truth. —Socrates

Now therefore fear the Lord, and serve Him in sincerity and in truth. —Joshua 24:14

As newborn babes, desire the sincere milk of the word, that ye may grow thereby. —1 Peter 2:2

. . . the unleavened bread of sincerity and truth.
Saint Paul
—*1 Corinthians 5:8*

For our rejoicing is this, the testimony of our conscience, that in simplicity and godly sincerity, not with fleshly wisdom, but by the grace of God, we have had our conversation in the world, and more abundantly to you-ward.
—2 Corinthians 1:12

. . . the sincerity of your love. —2 Corinthians 8:8

In all things shewing thyself a pattern of good works: in doctrine shewing uncorruptness, gravity, sincerity. —Titus 2:7

Profound sincerity is the only basis of talent as of character.
—Emerson

Enthusiasm is the genius of sincerity, and truth accomplishes no victories without it. —Bulwer-Lytton

Therefore let us keep the feast, not with old leaven, neither with the leaven of malice and wickedness; but with the unleavened bread of sincerity and truth.
Saint Paul
—*1 Corinthians 5:8*

For we are not as many, which corrupt the word of God: but as of sincerity, but as of God, in the sight of God speak we in Christ.
Saint Paul
—*2 Corinthians 2:17*

Repentance may be likened to digging an oil well. When one's repentance is deep and sincere, it strikes the oil of God's Mercy and Love. As long as repentance remains deep and sincere, it produces a continuous flow of blessings; if repentance relaxes or ceases, the flow of blessings decreases accordingly. The same parable applies to each spiritual Law, Principle and Virtue: a depth of sincerity enables one to tap the oil of God's Glory within the

Law, the Principle, the Virtue. If one is wholeheartedly dedicated to *all* Holy Laws, Principles, Ethics, Virtues and Worship-disciplines, each of these becomes as a productive oil well uniting him with the oil of God's Mercy, Love and Joy. *"I say unto you, there is joy in the presence of the angels of God over one sinner that repenteth."* (St. Luke 15:10)

Every seeker after Truth must convince God of his sincerity. If he has been morally unclean, his repentance must be followed by daily obedience to the Commandments of Morality. If he has been negligent in his Sabbath Day worship-trysts, the sincerity of his repentance must be proven by his wholehearted love for God's Commandment of Worship. If the penitent has failed to honor the Holy Laws of Giving, his union with his soul's memory-treasures and with God's Grace is determined by the sincerity of his dedication to henceforth fulfill these sacred mandates.

A sincere repentance requires that one convince God of his obedience to the Commandments of Love regarding his fellow man. This proving of one's love for the human spirit is thoroughly tested under all manners of conditions and associations. A devotee who remains faithful to the Commandments of Love receives surprising blessings from God and priceless memory-treasures from his soul. Until one makes his peace with each Commandment of God and with each person in his life, he continues to attract painful lessons regarding the importance of love for Holy Laws, love for mankind, and love for God.

> Bow down and worship where others kneel, for where so many have been paying the tribute of adoration the kind Lord must manifest Himself, for He is all mercy.
> —Sri Ramakrishna

The forgiveness of others is mandatory before one may experience the freedom-anointings and miracle-blessings that come through the Merciful and Forgiving Love of God. To remain unforgiving toward any individual, living or dead, hinders one's progress on the Path of Virtue and exposes him to reprovings from the soul.

Forgiveness of others is a vital virtue in the armour of Spiritual Insulation. The cleansing of the conscience reveals and heals each conscious and subconscious prejudice and each unforgiving feeling and thought. He who forgives others with a sincere and compassionate love is forgiven, thereby uniting with the Mercy of God and with the Dimensional Healing Power of the Christ.

FORGIVENESS

For if ye forgive men their trespasses, your heavenly Father will also forgive you: but if ye forgive not men their trespasses, neither will your Father forgive your trespasses.
Jesus
—*St. Matthew 6:14, 15*

Forgiveness is better than revenge; for forgiveness is the sign of a gentle nature, but revenge the sign of a savage nature.
—Epictetus

To forgive is beautiful. —Publilius Syrus

Forgive that you may be forgiven. —Seneca

To be wronged is nothing, unless you continue to remember it. —Confucius

Know all and you will pardon all. —Thomas á Kempis

Blessed is he whose transgression is forgiven, whose sin is covered. —Psalm 32:1

To the Lord our God belong mercies and forgivenesses, though we have rebelled against him; Neither have we obeyed the voice of the Lord our God, to walk in His laws, which he set before us by his servants the prophets.
—Daniel 9:9, 10

A kind speech and forgiveness is better than alms followed by injury. God is Rich, Clement.
Muhammad
—*The Koran*

Forgiveness is holiness; and by forgiveness is it that the universe is held together.
    Forgiveness is the might of the mighty; forgiveness is sacrifice; forgiveness is quiet of mind.
    Forgiveness and gentleness are the qualities of the self-possessed. They represent eternal virtue. —The Mahabharata

He who is free from malice towards all beings, who is friendly as well as compassionate, who has no feeling of meum and is free from egoism, to whom pleasure and pain are alike and who is forgiving by nature, who is ever content and mentally united to Me, who has subdued his body, mind and senses and has a firm resolve, who has surrendered his mind and intellect to Me, that devotee of Mine is dear to Me.
—Bhagavad Gita

And the prayer of faith shall save the sick, and the Lord shall raise him up; and if he have committed sins, they shall be forgiven him. —James 5:15

Many persons graced with God's forgiveness use their new-found freedom to manipulate, dominate, harm, harass, judge or criticize others. Jesus offers wise counsel* regarding the importance of remaining forgiving, merciful and loving toward others in order for one to continue in the Father's Forgiveness, Mercy and Love.

"Again the kingdom of heaven is like unto a merchant man seeking goodly pearls: Who when he had found one pearl of great price, went and sold all that he had, and bought it." (St. Matthew 13:45, 46) The higher life begins in earnest when a Truth-seeker knows in his heart and mind that all he has or is belongs to God. During certain major tests of one's sincerity regarding his repentance and dedication to the Truth, he will be required to sell all for the pearl of great price: God-Realization.

If a devotee retains any feeling that some one or some thing *belongs* to him and not to God, he becomes involved in a tug-of-war with a Cardinal Truth: *Every aspect of his life and being is the Creator's to give or to take away.* The moment one experiences this necessary realization, he has made his first linking with God as the *Truth*.

Great numbers of individuals who consider themselves to be "good" believe that the worship of God is unnecessary. Often, their understanding of the word *good* falls far short of the high standards of good required in the fulfilling of the basic Laws and Commandments. These self-deceived persons fail to experience the Worlds of Enlightenment that open only through a repentance accompanied by the daily worship of God.

In the modern era, numerous persons desiring spiritual liberation are unable to remain faithful to any form of daily worship-observance or discipline. Through love of discipline and love of worship, one learns of the Grace of God that constantly expands his concepts of the word

---

*St. Matthew 18:23–35

"good." If one proves faithful to daily worship-cycles through sacramental meditation and prayer, the Worlds of Divine Grace become as multifaceted diamonds shedding upon him the light of Enlightenment.

Enlightenment increases as one experiences realizations regarding the importance of the Virtue of Humility. Humility has a powerful effect on all virtues' and their increasing energization of the heart and mind. Through these important realizations, one comes to understand something of the *exalted* humility of the Lord Jesus when He said *"Why callest thou me good? There is none good but one, that is God: but if thou wilt enter into life, keep the commandments."* (St. Matthew 19:17)

Through sacramental meditation and prayer, a dedicated worshipper comes to know that God is the *only* Source of Good, Virtue, Light. This humility-realization protects one from the pitfalls of egotism and pride and keeps him receptive to the grace and joy of true Enlightenment.

HUMILITY

God resisteth the proud, but giveth grace unto the humble.
—James 4:6

And whosoever shall exalt himself shall be abased; and he that shall humble himself shall be exalted.
Jesus
—St. Matthew 23:12

Humble yourselves in the sight of the Lord, and He shall lift you up. —James 4:10

He hath shewed thee, O man, what is good; and what doeth the Lord require of thee, but to do justly, and to love mercy, and to walk humbly with thy God? —Micah 6:8

Humility is the solid foundation of all the virtues.
—Confucius

The seeker after Truth should be humbler than the dust. The world crushes the dust under its feet, but the seeker after truth should so humble himself that even the dust could crush him. Only then, and not till then, will he have a glimpse of truth. —Mohandas K. Gandhi

By humility and the fear of the Lord are riches, and honor, and life. —Proverbs 22:4

Thus should a man tread with humility along the path trod by the good. —The Mahabharata

Humility, Humility, Humility.
—Saint Teresa
of Avila

Any one thing in the creation is sufficient to demonstrate a Providence to a humble and grateful mind. —Epictetus

Humility, a sense of reverence before the sons of heaven—of all the prizes that a mortal man might win, these, I say are wisest; these are best. —Euripides

Humility, that low, sweet root from which all heavenly virtues shoot. —Thomas More

Humble yourselves in all things. —Thomas á Kempis

The highest virtue, mother of them all. —Tennyson

Remember your sins and forget your virtues.
—Eastern Saying

The Path of Virtue is the Humility Path. —Ann Ree Colton

Wisdom is ofttimes nearer when we stoop than when we soar.
—Wordsworth

In peace there's nothing so becomes a man
As modest stillness and humility. —Shakespeare

Humble because of knowledge, mighty by sacrifice.
—Rudyard Kipling

I can of mine own self do nothing . . . The Father that dwelleth in me, he doeth the works.
Jesus
—St. John 5:30, 14:10

Dedicated teachers of the higher life are graced with the Love and Protection of God as long as they express the Virtue of Humility. Each new spiritual gift coming to birth from the soul's treasure chest is as a babe that thrives and grows when fed the milk of humility.

"If any man serve me, him will my Father honour" (St. John 12:26) As the gifts of the soul become part of one's being, he receives continuous rewards from God and numerous compliments from his contemporaries. Each time one receives a verbal or written compliment for his spiritual-creative words and works, he should immediately give credit to the Father in Heaven—the *Source* of his inspiration and creations.

Each compliment received from others should be sent to the Father through a silent love-telepathy filled with gratitude for His Mercy and Grace. In the humility-practice of quickly turning all compliments toward the Father, rather than accepting them for oneself, the servant of God becomes as a nimble-footed matador who avoids being gored by the bull of pride. Also, when one turns the compliments from others to the Father, those who are speaking the words of appreciation and praise are richly blessed by Him for their gratitude.

> Father, if there is any good in me,
>   it is Thee.
> If there is any virtue in me,
>   it is Thee.
> If there is any light in me,
>   it is Thee.

The Virtue of Discernment

> The more grievous a man's sins seem to him, the readier God is to forgive them, to enter the soul and drive them out; for everyone is most diligent in getting rid of what is most disagreeable to him. The more in number a man's sins are, the greater they are, the more immeasurably glad God is to forgive them. The more they irk him, the quicker he is about it. The sooner divine repentance reaches up to God, the sooner the sins are swallowed up in the abyss of God—as quickly as I can shut my eyes. They are annihilated as if they had never happened, if only the repentance be whole.
> —Meister Eckhart

Repentance may be likened to a Ladder. The different rungs on the Ladder of Repentance relate to the various levels of progress on the Path of Virtue. Prodigal persons have yet to begin the climb. Students of the higher life are on the first rungs; devotees are on higher rungs; initiates have an even higher over-look and perspective. Anointed teachers are on the God-Realization rungs of the Ladder of Repentance.

THE MERCY OF GOD

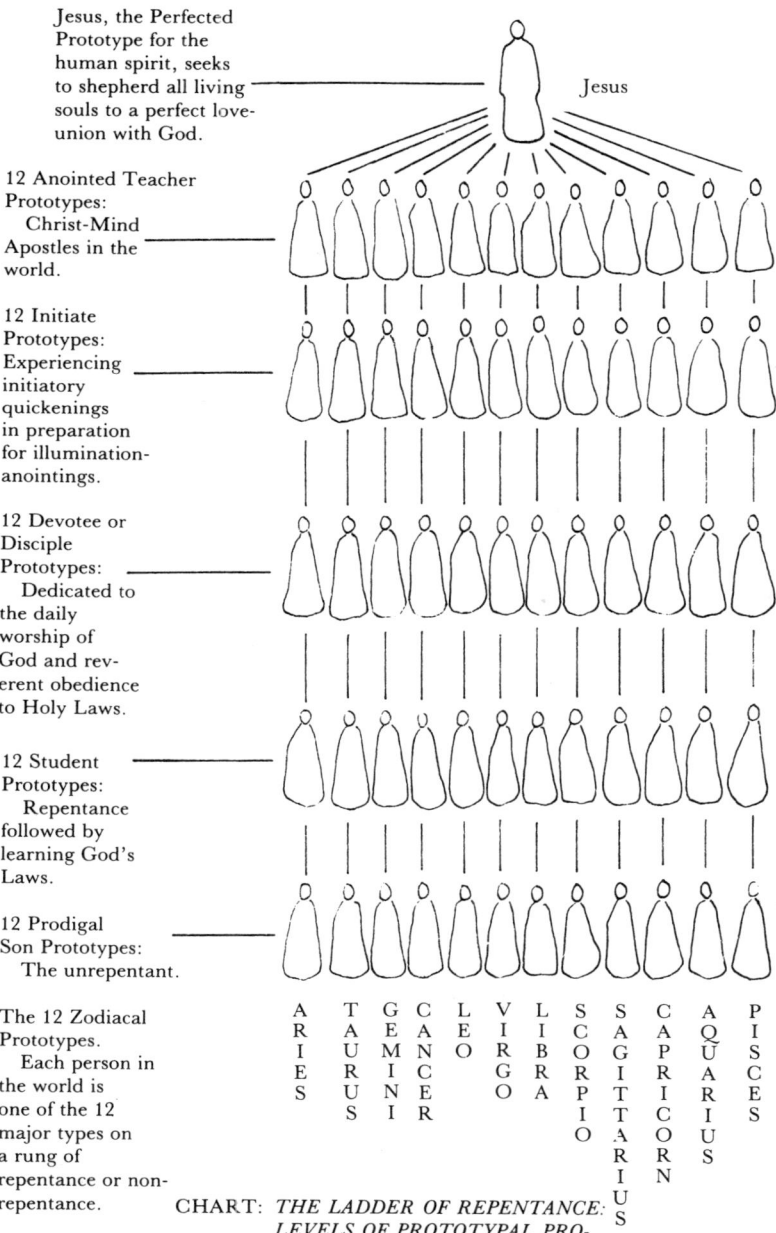

Jesus, the Perfected Prototype for the human spirit, seeks to shepherd all living souls to a perfect love-union with God.

12 Anointed Teacher Prototypes:
Christ-Mind Apostles in the world.

12 Initiate Prototypes:
Experiencing initiatory quickenings in preparation for illumination-anointings.

12 Devotee or Disciple Prototypes:
Dedicated to the daily worship of God and reverent obedience to Holy Laws.

12 Student Prototypes:
Repentance followed by learning God's Laws.

12 Prodigal Son Prototypes:
The unrepentant.

The 12 Zodiacal Prototypes.
Each person in the world is one of the 12 major types on a rung of repentance or non-repentance.

ARIES   TAURUS   GEMINI   CANCER   LEO   VIRGO   LIBRA   SCORPIO   SAGITTARIUS   CAPRICORN   AQUARIUS   PISCES

CHART: *THE LADDER OF REPENTANCE: LEVELS OF PROTOTYPAL PROGRESSION ON THE PATH OF VIRTUE.*

Sincere repentance accompanied by the dedication to revere, honor and fulfill each Holy Law and Commandment keeps one firmly united with the Miraculous Mercy of God working through the Lord Jesus and His Apostles in heaven and on earth. He who places his heart's love on God's Holy Altar dies to his Prodigal-Son self and turns his face toward the blazing light of Truth, Righteousness and Holiness.

The desire to repent stems from one's past lives in which he has known God and experienced His forgiving Love. Many prodigal persons who have no desire to repent of their sins feel they have never done any wrong and can do no wrong. Some individuals do not accept the reality of sin and believe that each person is a law unto himself.

Sin short-circuits the electricity-like energies between the soul, the conscience and the consciousness. Repentance is a healing balm that restores the harmonious flow of these lighted energies.

If a penitent earnestly desires to give birth to all virtues, he embraces each Law and Commandment of God as a drowning person holding on to a life-preserver. With this degree of determination and dedication, one moves upward on the Ladder of Repentance—and his conscience gradually becomes a fine tuning-fork for Truth, Prophecy and Revelation.

The conscience is the connecting link between the soul and the consciousness. The degree of soul-light and conscience-light in the consciousness determines the degree of one's Enlightenment.

A formidable obstacle to union with the Mercy, Love and Wisdom of God is when the consciousness remains uncertain as to right and wrong. God patiently waits until

The Mercy of God

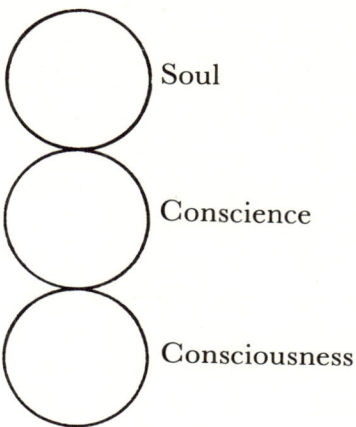

the lessons in life enable one to clearly discern the difference between right and wrong, good and evil. As long as a student of the higher life remains uncertain about the difference between right and wrong, the sincerity of his repentance is tested continuously until he proves his love for righteousness and truth. When the Virtue of Discernment of the Difference between Right and Wrong comes to birth, one is ready for rapid progress on the Path leading to Spiritual Illumination.

If the conscience remains clouded due to a halfhearted or insincere repentance, the soul withholds its gifts and memory-treasures from the consciousness. Crisis-lessons in life are the Mercy of God in disguise, for they seek to cleanse the conscience through humility and a whole repentance. The rays of sincere repentance pierce the dark sin-clouds between the consciousness and the conscience, and the grace-energies of the soul are free to bless one's heart, mind and life. The daily worship of God through sacramental meditation and through prayers of repentance, confession, gratitude and praise keeps clear the conscience so that the soul-light electricities of memory and grace may fill the heart and enlighten the mind.

In the present era, many persons have yet to give birth to the Virtue of Discernment of the Difference between Right and Wrong. Until this important virtue is present in the heart and mind, one remains conscienceless regarding certain Laws and Commandments. This inability to relate to one or more cardinal Laws of God may be likened to a music student who stubbornly refuses to play a certain note or notes in an octave. Each Law and Commandment of God is a note in the keyboard of Illumination. When an aspirant learns to play all notes with skill—that is, he lives all Laws with love and dedication—his ability to discern the difference between right and wrong prospers his union with the Mercy and Love of God.

DISCERNMENT

Give therefore thy servant an understanding heart to judge thy people, that I may discern between good and bad.
Solomon
—1 Kings 3:9

Then shall ye return, and discern between the righteous and the wicked, between him that serveth God and him that serveth him not. *—Malachi 3:18*

But the natural man receiveth not the things of the Spirit of God: for they are foolishness unto him: neither can he know them, because they are spiritually discerned.
Saint Paul
—1 Corinthians 2:14

Whoso keepeth the commandment shall feel no evil thing: and a wise man's heart discerneth both time and judgment.
Solomon
—Ecclesiastes 8:5

But the manifestation of the Spirit is given to every man to profit withal. For to one is given by the Spirit the word of wisdom; to another the word of knowledge by the same Spirit; To another faith by the same Spirit; to another the gifts of healing by the same Spirit; To another the working of miracles; to another prophecy; to another discerning of spirits.
Saint Paul
—1 Corinthians 12:7-10

Confession

And I prayed unto the Lord my God, and made my confession.
—Daniel 9:4

He that covereth his sins shall not prosper: but whoso confesseth and forsaketh them shall have mercy.
—Proverbs 28:13

Why is there no man who confesses his vices? It is because he has not yet laid them aside. It is a waking man only who can tell his dreams.
—Seneca

If we say we have no sin, we deceive ourselves, and the truth is not in us. If we confess our sins, he is faithful and just to forgive our sins, and to cleanse us from all unrighteousness.
—1 John 1:8, 9

> For it is written, As I live, saith the Lord, every knee shall bow to me, and every tongue shall confess to God.
> Saint Paul
—Romans 14:11

The Love of God creating the Universe is Pure Joy. When one proves his love for God, he is healed by the Joy-Essences within the merciful Love of God—and his conscience comes to peace. The conscience makes its peace with God through the freeing, healing and rejuvenating action of Confession.

"With the mouth confession is made unto salvation." (Romans 10:10) To confess to God all of one's sins, faults and flaws is to be born anew. It is the birth to the Spirit—the Spirit creating the wonders and the beauties of the Universe.

In the Buddhist philosophy, confession is called "disburdenment." Confession frees one from the burdens of many bondages. The freedom born of confession enables one to enter into sacramental meditation with peace and tranquility.

When one is seeking to attain a continuous union with God, he must be prepared to *immediately* confess to Him each judging, prideful, lustful, fearful thought—or any other negative thought, feeling or action. In this, the Truth-seeker becomes a Truth-teller, thereby keeping the honesty-artery continuously open to the Creator.

There are two sides to the coin of Confession: the confession to God of one's sins and faults, and the confession of the greatness and goodness of God and His Son.

> Whosoever therefore shall confess me before men, him will I confess also before my Father which is in heaven.
> Jesus
—St. Matthew 10:32

The Mercy of God

> Whosoever shall confess that Jesus is the Son of God, God dwelleth in him, and he in God.
> <div align="right">Saint John the Beloved
—<i>1 John 4:15</i></div>

> Wherefore God also hath highly exalted him, and given him a name which is above every name: That at the name of Jesus every knee should bow, of things in heaven, and things in earth, and things under the earth; And that every tongue should confess that Jesus Christ is Lord, to the glory of God the Father.
> <div align="right">Saint Paul
—<i>Philippians 2:9-11</i></div>

After one begins the daily practice of Confession, he walks the Path of Virtue with more confidence and serenity, for he is supported and strengthened by the dimensional healing-energies of the Christ and the Love-Mercy of God. Those who would attain an uninterrupted union with God must *become* Confession. One *becomes* Confession through the Virtues of Honesty and Humility. The combined action of Honesty and Humility keeps a servant of God ever receptive to the blessings of the soul, the Christ and the Creator.

The Snowflake and the Six

> All snowflakes are six-pointed. This natural phenomenon has intrigued and fascinated philosophers and scientists over the centuries.

The six-pointed star ✡ is a sacred key to the mysteries concerning the Laws and Commandments of God. These Divine Statutes, Ordinances, Fiats, Mandates and Decrees

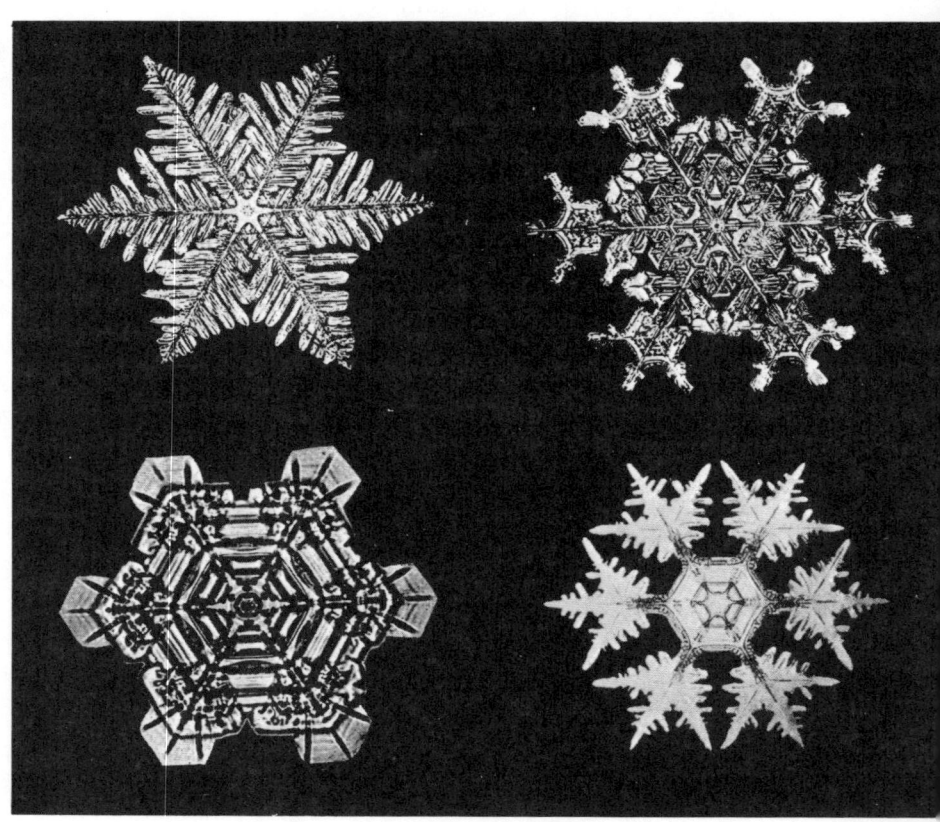

Photographs* of snowflakes. All snowflakes are six-sided, yet each snowflake reveals a unique geometrical beauty.

---

*Courtesy of Dover Publications of New York, New York, publishers in 1962 of the book *Snow Crystals* by W. A. Bentley and W. J. Humphreys.

permeate the atmosphere of the Earth with their Creation-Essences. Each raindrop that becomes an exquisitely formed *six-pointed* snowflake is fulfilling the geometry of God's Laws within the atmosphere.

Tears of repentance and prayers of confession are taken up by the Mercy of God within His Laws and changed by the supernatural Light of the Christ into snowflakes of grace. These beauteous snowflakes of grace fall into one's heart, mind and life as gentle flurries of Holy Inspiration, Healing and other Sacred Blessings.

If sin-debts recorded in the soul's record suddenly appear as a dark cloud in one's life, prayers of repentance and confession break up the *energy-cloud* into identifiable portions of past-lives offenses and present-life transgressions. Through repentance and confession, the heavy or gross energy-crystallizations of sin-debts within the dark cloud become as individual raindrops that begin to fall in the atmosphere of God's Mercy and Love. Here, the Healing and Forgiving Power of the Christ miraculously changes the individual raindrops of confessed sins into snowflakes of grace.

A devotee dedicated to Truth-prayers and Truth-meditations becomes increasingly aware of the Dimensional Healing Power of the Christ. This mighty Power is freed in his life through sincere repentance, honest confession, humility dedications, and selfless creations. The dark energies of sin-debts recorded in the soul's record are released during necessary Expiation Cycles. During these initiatory trials, one who is devoted to the Christ—the Truth—should speak words of Truth-confessions; in this, the dark energies quickly become snowflakes of grace that manifest as miraculous healings, holy inspirations, sacred realizations, divine revelations and other blessings of grace and truth.

As one becomes knowledgeable in the Dimensional

Healing Power of the Christ working through prayers of repentance and confession, he gains freedom from his own burdens so that he may serve the human spirit as a healing mediator in the world. The more one becomes cogently aware of the speed with which the Christ works through humility, repentance and confession, the more he is healed, quickened and inspired—and the more he is able to help others through his sacramental prayers, meditations and fastings. Proteges of the Saints and initiates under Christ who become skilled in the changing of dark-energies into Light-energies remain united with the higher degrees of Soul Grace and Divine Grace.

The Glory of God within the number *Six* is a mighty Glory. The Book of Genesis describes the creation of the earth in six Great Days. The Hebrews of old understood many of the powerful secrets related to the Glory of God within the 6; the Star of David and Solomon's Seal are representations of the six-pointed star. The Star of David pertains to the masculine (yang) and feminine (yin) polarity-balance, heaven and earth, heart and mind, and other symbolic nuances. The interlinked triangles of Solomon's Seal relate to the manifest and the unmanifest, the dark and the light. The triangle of light symbolizes the pure energies of the soul and the spirit. The darker triangle denotes those energies that the heavenly Father is requiring of mankind to change into the energies of pure love, virtue and intelligence. During the future ages of the earth, all energies involving the human spirit will contribute to the illumination of the heart and the mind and to the illumination of the planet Earth.

> Our Father which art in heaven, Hallowed be thy name. Thy kingdom come. Thy will be done in earth, as it is in heaven.
> Jesus
> —*St. Matthew 6:9*

The Mercy of God

The number of the Law of God is 6. The very atmosphere is permeated by the energy-essences of the Laws and Commandments. These mighty energies are creating the human spirit in the Image and Likeness of God.

Man is moved here and there by the Laws of God. He lives and dies according to the Laws of God. He is reproved, quickened and enlightened by the Laws of God. The Spirit of God within His Laws is the Glory of God within His Laws. The six-pointed snowflake and the six-pointed star speak of this Omnipresent Spirit and this Omnipresent Glory.

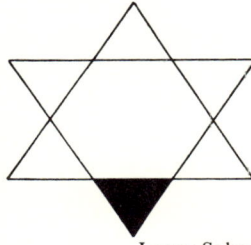

Lower Subconscious

Before repentance, the lower subconscious contains heavy concentrations of dark sin-energies. These gross energies cause numerous problems, addictions, depressions, sorrows and afflictions.

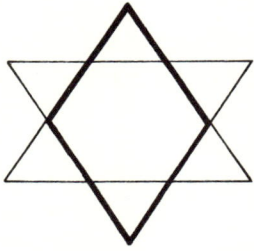

Through repentance, confession, and restitution, one experiences God's Mercy and Love. Daily worship-cycles, Scriptural study and selfless service gradually cleanse the lower subconscious. In time, an earnest Truth-seeker becomes spiritually centered, quickened and illumined; he dwells within the scintillating light of the Diamond of Illumination within the Six-Pointed Star of the Law.

For thousands of years, the Hindu sages have used the 6-pointed star as the symbol for the heart chakra. As kundalini's energies are purified through love for the Creator and His Creation, these purified love-energies become pure motives and selfless desires. Daily love-service to God and the human spirit keeps kundalini's energies flowing heart-ward, where they are polarized and purified, becoming the *marriage* of the masculine and feminine polarities within one's being. This polarization and purification through reverent love releases the Christ-Mind energy processes of Truth and Grace. In this, one lives in a state of Truth-revelations and Grace-creations blessed by the Creator and His Son.

The 6 is the number of the kundalini's action. When the kundalini's energies are moving downward ↓6, one becomes earthbound in his thinking and feeling; he is lustful, sensual, covetous and materialistic. Through love for God and the human spirit, the energy currents within the kundalini are reversed and raised toward the heart chakra and the other higher chakras ↑6. In this, the senses become illumined senses whose combined actions work as a *sixth sense*.

I. In this state of consciousness, one believes himself to be a law unto himself. He is outside the protection of the Laws of God, and therefore is exposed to repetitive tribulations in the present life and in coming lives.

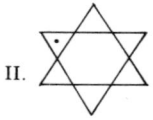

II. In this state of consciousness, one is beginning to think in terms of Law; he is awakening to Conscience, Virtue and Logic.

In this state of consciousness, one is a devotee of the higher life, moving ever closer to the Point of Centering within the Laws and Commandments of God.

III.

When one reaches the Point of Centering within Holy Law, he experiences the Divine Marriage Anointing. Thereafter, he serves God as an Apostle-Teacher anointed and illumined by His Spirit.

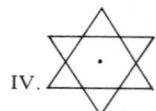

IV.

Cardinal-Virtue Energies and the Commandments

FIRST COMMANDMENT

Thou shalt have no other gods before Me.

○ When the Cardinal Virtues are *steady lights* in the heart and the consciousness mind, one has a wholehearted love for God, a strong and unwavering faith, and observes daily worship through prayer and meditation.

◐ If the Cardinal Virtues are *unsteady lights* in the heart and mind, one is subject to periods of wavering in his faith, and is unable to observe the worship of God as a daily dedication.

● The absence of certain Cardinal-Virtue energies causes the heart and mind to be atheistic, agnostic or hypocritical.

SECOND COMMANDMENT

Thou shalt not make unto thee any graven image.

○ The presence of Cardinal Virtues in the consciousness enables one to discern the difference between the Real and the False. To love any thing or possession more than God invites strong reprovings from the soul until one places all values in their proper perspective, beginning with the Image of God as the Sovereign Image.

◐ When Cardinal Virtues are wavering or unsteady lights in the consciousness, one is easily diverted from spiritual precepts, principles and practices.

● If the Cardinal-Virtue energies relating to this Commandment are absent from the heart and mind, one is narcissistic, loving self and self-pleasures. He follows selfish goals, and seeks to make everyone into the image of himself or what he thinks a person should be. When such persons meditate, they can see no further than the mirror-like reflection of their own countenances.

THIRD COMMANDMENT

Thou shalt not take the name of the Lord thy God in vain.

○ Cardinal Virtues present in the consciousness produce in one the dedication for pure and harmless speaking; prayers of praise and thanksgiving; the gift of Logos or inspired speech.
◐ The wavering light of Cardinal Virtues causes careless speaking, the double tongue, broken promises or vows.
● The absence of Cardinal Virtues pollutes the earth with sounds and words of vulgarity, profanity and insincerity.

FOURTH COMMANDMENT

Remember the Sabbath Day, to keep it holy.

○ The presence of Cardinal Virtues related to this mighty Commandment inspires one to make a firm dedication to worship God on fifty-two Sabbath Days each year. The Sabbath, the *sign* of the Covenant between God and man, is a powerful activator of *Grace* from the Soul and from the Creator, blessing one's present life and future lives.

◑ Wavering or unsteady Cardinal-Virtue energies in the heart and mind produce halfheartedness and fickleness. Such persons experience intermittent or sporadic desires to worship God in His sanctuaries.

● If the Cardinal Virtues related to Worship are missing from the consciousness, there is no desire to worship God on the Sabbath Day or at any other time.

FIFTH COMMANDMENT

Honour thy father and thy mother.

○ Cardinal Virtues enable one to love his parents with a pure love; also, one expresses an abiding gratitude for their helps, shelter, clothing, food and education provided during his early years. The greatest way one may honor his parents is by living a life dedicated to the service of God and man.

◑ Wavering Cardinal-Virtues energies cause one to be ambivalent toward his parents. If his parents have treated him unkindly, he harbors lasting resentments. Resentful persons are incapable of understanding the just Law of Attraction. To attract unkind or brutal parents is to have been such a parent in past lives. To attract unspiritual or anti-religious parents is to have been such a parent. One sows what he reaps—and all present-life relationships and associations testify to this cardinal truth.

● The absence of certain Cardinal-Virtue energies in the consciousness causes one to hate his parents with a passion. He is totally unforgiving and therefore in bondage to bitterness. Painful estrangements between persons and their parents often produce mental depressions, emotional imbalances and physical ailments.

> Follow peace with all men, and holiness, without which no man shall see the Lord: Looking diligently lest any man fail of the grace of God; lest any root of bitterness springing up trouble you, and thereby many be defiled.
>
> <div align="right">Saint Paul
—<i>Hebrews 12:14, 15</i></div>

SIXTH COMMANDMENT

Thou shalt not kill.

○ The Virtue of Ahimsa or Harmlessness is an energy-presence blessing the heart and mind with a pure compassion and a clear conscience.

◐ If the Cardinal-Virtue energies are weak or wavering, one alternates between war-like attitudes and pangs of conscience.

● The absence of Cardinal Virtues in the consciousness makes of one a conscienceless killer or heartless murderer.

SEVENTH COMMANDMENT

Thou shalt not commit adultery.

○ The Cardinal Virtues related to Morality, Fidelity and Faithfulness keep the thoughts chaste, the motives pure and the hands clean.

◐ A wavering or unsteady light of the Cardinal Virtues in the consciousness invites impure and lustful thoughts and causes one to stain the soul's record with the cardinal sin of adultery. Such stains may require many lives of unhappy marriages with unfaithful mates before they are cleansed from the soul's record.

● There are lawful sexual ecstasies and unlawful sexual ecstasies. Through *reincarnation-cycles,* one learns to distinguish between the lawful and the unlawful, the righteous and the unrighteous, the reverent and the irreverent, the pure and the impure.

If the light of the major Virtues is missing from the heart and mind, one has no sense of wrongdoing or guilt for sexual offenses. He is irreverent and immoral in his attitudes toward the sacred act of procreation. If a married man or woman commits adultery with a member of the same sex, as in homosexuality or lesbianism, the sin-debt is compounded, sending dark shadows into future lives.

EIGHTH COMMANDMENT

Thou shalt not steal.

○ When the Cardinal Virtues related to this Commandment are energizing the heart and mind, one is honorable and ethical in all relationships. He gives honest tithes to God as required by Holy Law, that the Word of God may be preserved and prospered in the world. He is careful to not steal ideas or opportunities from others, and is honest and honorable in his handling of funds and in the meeting of responsibilities.

◐ If the light of the Cardinal Virtues is unsteady, one is tempted to take from others. His conscience is as a sun darting behind clouds. On some days the sun of his conscience shines brightly, and on other days, he acquiesces to the desire to steal, take, or to borrow without thought of repayment.

● If the Cardinal Virtues are not in the consciousness, one has no conscience regarding the stealing of money, things, ideas, opportunities, or in stealing another person's mate. If such persons are in religions, they have no desire to give tithes to God; they are takers and parasites, stealing from the Creator the tenth required by His Law. Such persons invite severe penalties in future lives. In the present era, two-thirds of the earth's population is experiencing abject poverty. To steal from God or man attracts one to poverty conditions and environments until he learns that the key to receiving from God is in giving to God. *"Will a man rob God? Yet ye have robbed Me. But ye say, Wherein have we robbed Thee? In tithes and offerings." (Malachi 3:8)*

NINTH COMMANDMENT

Thou shalt not bear false witness against thy neighbor.

○ When the Cardinal Virtues relating to this Commandment are present in the heart and mind, one is faithful to the Truth in all circumstances. His love for the Truth and his love for his neighbor inspire in him a courage to speak the Truth with conscience and conviction.

◐ If the Cardinal Virtues are as weak or wavering lights in the consciousness, one feels no sense of loyalty to God as Pure Truth. Such persons offend the gift of speech through innuendos, gossip and half-truths.

● The absence of the Cardinal Virtues makes of one a malicious slanderer. He does not hesitate to lie in order to protect himself or to harm others.

TENTH COMMANDMENT

Thou shalt not covet thy neighbor's house, thou shalt not covet thy neighbor's wife, nor his manservant, nor his maidservant, nor his ox, nor his ass, nor any thing that is thy neighbor's.

◐ The Cardinal Virtues inspire one to keep his thoughts free from all forms of covetousness. The Virtues of Detachment and Reverence provide protection from the sin of covetousness and its complex and self-defeating involvements. When a nation covets a neighboring nation, there are hatreds and animosities that may erupt into wars. To live peaceably with one's neighbor—whether the neighbor be a nation or a person—is the beginning of peace on earth and good will toward men.

◑ If the Cardinal Virtues are as unsteady lights in the heart and mind, one experiences fluctuating moods regarding his neighbor. He fails to see *all* living souls as his neighbors—and therefore is unable to make union with God as *Omnipresence*.

● As long as the energies of the Cardinal Virtues are missing from one's consciousness, his thoughts and acts are inspired by covetousness, greed and envy.

> From covetousness proceeds sin . . . This covetousness is the spring of also all the cunning and hypocrisy in the world . . . From covetousness proceeds wrath; from covetousness flows lust; and it is from covetousness that loss of judgment, deception, pride, arrogance, and malice, as also vindictiveness, shamelessness, loss of prosperity, loss of virtue, anxiety, and infamy, spring.
> —The Mahabharata

COMMANDMENT

Thou shalt love thy neighbor as thyself.

○ The Cardinal Virtues inspire one to look upon all living souls as his neighbors; his concept of the word *neighbors* expands in direct proportion to the expanding energies of love within the Cardinal Virtues.

◐ If the Cardinal Virtues are weak or unsteady, one has periods when he feels superior to those less fortunate than himself. He looks upon others as potential enemies; he is quick to judge and slow to forgive.

● If the Cardinal Virtues are absent, one entertains strong prejudices toward other races, nations and religions. In many instances, these prejudices also extend toward the opposite sex.

COMMANDMENT

This is my commandment, That ye love one another, as I have loved you.

○ A love based upon sacrifice, sincerity and selflessness prospers all Cardinal Virtues. As a devotee unites with the Love-Presence of God, his love increases for his fellow man, who is made in "the similitude of God." (James 3:9)

◐ Weak or wavering virtues cause one to be ambivalent toward others; he has few friends, and rarely is hospitable. Devotees of the higher life who have yet to evolve a pure and true love for their fellow men desire to retreat from human associations rather than involve themselves in service to God by ministering to the lost, the spiritually ignorant, the sick, the dejected and the downtrodden.

● The absence of love, virtue, conscience and logic makes of one a willing instrument for the spirit of hate, jealousy and violence. Numerous reincarnation-cycles may be required of one before the gross energies within hate are purified and transformed into a pure, selfless and sacrificial love.

> Hatred will never cease by hatred at any time.
> Hatred ceases only through love. This is an eternal law.
> —Buddha

The Mercy of God

> Repay hatred with virtue.
>
> —Lao Tzu

> If ye keep my commandments, ye shall abide in my love; even as I have kept my Father's commandments and abide in his love.
>
> Jesus
> —St. John 15:10

As long as Cardinal Virtues, the Conscience and the Great Logics remain unawakened in the hearts and minds of vast numbers of persons, the reincarnation-cycles will seek to awaken these necessary attributes of the soul. Atheistic nations, immoral nations, greedy nations and impoverished nations are used by the Law of Attraction to test and sift masses of persons until they begin to respond to the soul's call and to God's Image.

Religions, providing multitudes with the knowledge of the Commandments of God, play prominent roles in the drama of the reincarnation-cycles. Each religion is a vortex of virtue-births, conscience-births and logic-births. Each religion dedicated to Truth is an ambassador of God and a door to eternal life.

The reincarnation-cycles, placing great numbers of persons in various nations and religions, are gradually drawing the human spirit toward a Golden Age when the knowledge and expression of Virtues, Conscience and Logic will be mankind's entry into a new era of Cosmos Exploration and Galaxy-Consciousness Illuminations.

> Because of evil karma, accumulated by you in past lives,
> The moment ye are of your mother born, ye delight in sinning;
> The doing of the good and merit-bringing deeds ye like not;
> E'en till ye are grown old, your nature is perverse:

Thus surely must ye garner the results of evil actions.
If ye wonder whether evil karma can be neutralized or not,
Then know that it is neutralized by desire for goodness.
But they who knowingly do evil deeds,
Exchange a mouthful of food for infamy.
They who knowing not whither they themselves are bound,
Yet presume to pose as guides for others,
Do injury both to themselves and others.
If pain and sorrow ye desire sincerely to avoid,
Avoid, then, doing harm to others.
Repenting and confessing of all previous sins,
At the feet of the Guru and the Deities,
And vowing never more in future to commit a wrong,
Are the shortest path to rapid expiation of all evils done.
The greater part of sinners are sharp-witted;
(Of mind) unstable and unfixed, they delight in various
    distractions;
And unendowed are they with love of the religious life:
This, in itself, doth signify that they are sin-obscured,
And need repentance and confession o'er and o'er.
Do ye each give yourselves, with zeal,
To expiating sins and winning merit;
If thus ye do, not only shall ye see
The Dharma-loving deities celestial,
But the holiest and highest of all gods.
The Dharma-Kaya of your own mind ye shall also see;
And seeing That, ye shall have seen the All,
The Vision Infinite, the Sangsara and Nirvana.
Then shall your karmic actions cease.

—Milarepa
c. 1100–1135. Tibet

CHARITY

Charity shall cover the multitude of sins.   —1 Peter 4:8

He is truly great who hath a great charity.
—Saint Thomas á Kempis

Charity is, indeed, a great thing, and a gift of God, and when it is rightly ordered, likens us to God himself, as far as that is possible; for it is charity which makes the man.
—Saint John Chrysostom

Charity itself fulfills the law,
And who can sever love from charity.   —Shakespeare

With malice toward none; with charity for all.
—Abraham Lincoln

Every good act is charity. A man's true wealth hereafter is the good that he does in this world to his fellows.
—Muhammad

As water quells a blazing fire so charity atones for sin.
Ben Sira
—Apocrypha

Though I speak with the tongues of men and of angels, and have not charity, I am become as a sounding brass, or a tinkling cymbal, And though I have the gift of prophecy, and understand all mysteries, and all knowledge; and though I have all faith, so that I could remove mountains, and have not charity, I am nothing. And though I bestow all my goods to feed the poor, and though I give my body to be burned, and have not charity, it profiteth me nothing. Charity suffereth long, and is kind; charity envieth not; charity vaunteth not itself, is not puffed up . . .

And now abideth faith, hope, charity, these three; but the greatest of these is charity.
Saint Paul
—1 Corinthians 13:1-4, 13

15

RESTITUTION AND MIRACLES

A death-bed repentance seldom reaches to restitution.
—Junius

The best of you is he who is the best at repaying.
—Muhammad

A man who has committed a mistake and does not correct it is committing another mistake. —Confucius

Confession without rectification is hypocrisy.
—Ann Ree Colton

The man whose heart is without holiness, suffers torture only by undergoing penances in ignorance of their meaning.
—The Mahabharata

What is past is past. There is a future left to all men, who have the virtue to repent and the energy to atone.
—Bulwer-Lytton

Repent ye therefore, and be converted, that your sins may be blotted out, when the times of refreshing shall come from the presence of the Lord; and he shall send Jesus Christ, which before was preached unto you: Whom the heaven must receive until the times of restitution of all things, which God hath spoken by the mouth of all his holy prophets since the world began.

Saint Paul
—*Acts 3:19–21*

Each aspirant on the Path of Virtue must prove himself to be honorable in the sight of God. This is accomplished when his prayers of repentance and confession are followed by charitable acts of restitution. With repentance come the joys; with confession come the freedoms; and with restitution come the miracles!

"Wherefore we receiving a kingdom which cannot be moved, let us have grace, whereby we may serve God acceptably with reverence." (Hebrews 12:28) When reverent repentance leads to reverent restitution, one becomes a participant in the drama of Miracles, for each honorable act of restitution is rewarded by the Creator with miraculous blessings, confirmations and inspirations.

Restitution may be likened to building a bridge. When the heavenly Father sees that one of His children is desirous of making a full restitution for all physical, emotional, mental and spiritual offenses, He mercifully and graciously provides all that is necessary to build the Bridge of Restitution. In this, one learns of the beauty and bountifulness of the Father's Mercy and Forgiving Love. The Bridge of Restitution takes one over the abyss of sin and links him with the Divine Presence.

The desire to be honorable in all physical and spiritual relationships with one's fellow man and with God is a sacred desire born of many lives of righteousness and love on the Path of Virtue. An honorable individual is a rare soul in any age and time.

HONORABLENESS

The works of the Lord are great . . . His work is honourable and glorious: and His righteousness endureth forever.
—Psalm 111:2, 3

Since thou wast precious in My sight, thou hast been honourable, and I have loved thee. —Isaiah 43:4

Marriage is honourable in all, and the bed undefiled: but whoremongers and adulterers God will judge.
Saint Paul
—Hebrews 13:4

Virtue is the desire to things honorable and the power of attaining them.
—Author, unknown,
lived during the
time of Socrates

"Seek ye first the kingdom of God, and His righteousness; and all these things shall be added unto you." (St. Matthew 6:33) The more one unites with the Righteousness of God, the more he becomes aware of the importance of Restitution. Honorableness, Character, Integrity and other cardinal virtues expressed during times of willing restitution draw one closer to the time of the Divine Marriage.

Restitution begins with one's first prayers of blessing and healing for others. Thereafter, the Righteousness of God will inspire and guide him as to how each restitution should be made.

One who desires to prove honorable in the sight of God receives timely confirmations that reveal his progress toward making a full and total restitution. The Creator discloses in many ways—in dreams and in waking consciousness—the soul's record of resolved and unresolved debts. As one proves to be an honorable steward of God's forgiving love and merciful loving-kindness toward him, the Door to the freedom-portals of grace and truth open wider and wider.

All manner of unresolved sin-debts press themselves forth for payment while one walks the Path of Virtue in service to God. With each honorable payment, a probationer progresses spiritually; if he proves less than honorable, he delays his union with the Divine Presence.

In the higher life, restitution occurs through the Virtue of Sacrifice; one makes willing sacrifices inspired by a pure love for God and his fellow man. The Forgiveness and Mercy of God are experienced in many different ways after each gracious sacrifice made in the spirit of restitution and pure love.

The love of sacrifice is the mark of the Saint and the true protege of the Saints. The love of sacrifice is an art, a science, a philosophy, a way of life. The mother and father who sacrifice because they love their child; the devotee and the Saint who sacrifice because they love God and their fellow man—all come under the blessing of God's Grace through the Virtue of Sacrifice.

Many offenses against Holy Laws are rectified and resolved in one charitable act of sacrifice based upon pure love with no thought of reward. As the scales of Divine Law come into balance through thousands of willing and loving sacrifices, the spirit of Restitution becomes a joyful spirit as the burdens one has accumulated over many lives and ages miraculously disappear.

> A holy restitution compels a man to give of himself without thought of reward or name or fame.

Restitution and Miracles

This is the result of illumined knowledge, which is superior to the restitution of returning deed for deed or act for act.

The magnificent restitution is *Teaching*.

From the restitution compulsion comes a willingness to serve God and one's fellow man.
—Ann Ree Colton

Remission of Sins

For this is my blood of the new testament, which is shed for many for the remission of sins.
Jesus
—*St. Matthew 26:28*

Thus it is written, and thus it behoved Christ to suffer, and to rise from the dead the third day: and that repentance and remission of sins should be preached in his name among all nations.
—*St. Luke 24:46, 47*

And when he had said this, he breathed on them, and saith unto them, Receive ye the Holy Ghost: Whose soever sins ye remit, they are remitted unto them; and whose soever sins ye retain, they are retained.
—*St. John 20:22, 23*

Then Peter said unto them, Repent, and be baptized every one of you in the name of Jesus Christ for the remission of sins, and ye shall receive the gift of the Holy Ghost.
—*Acts 2:38*

A beautiful Gift bestowed by the Christ upon His Anointed Apostles is the Gift of the Remission of Sins. This spiritual Gift enables one to activate and to witness many healing miracles in the lives of others.

If a person seeks healing from an enlightened Apostle-Teacher, he may qualify for the immediate healings that come through the Apostolic Gift of Remission of Sins. In this, the burdens of his sins are quickly lifted from his shoulders.

The remission of sins may be *temporary* or *permanent*—depending upon one's attitudes toward the Laws and Commandments of God. If the one who desires healing fails to honor one or more Holy Laws and Commandments, the remission of sins is but a temporary blessing, for his nonfulfillment of Holy Laws causes the weight or burden of his sins to return once again to his shoulders.

To experience more than a temporary remission of sins, one must prove sincere in his repentance, reverently obedient to all Holy Laws and Commandments, and dedicated to the daily worship of God. Through these efforts and virtues, the burdens of one's sin-debts remain above his shoulders and no longer press upon him. Each sacrificial act of restitution fulfilled with love blesses the penitent with greater freedom; for, through repentance combined with restitution, the sin-debt energies are gradually transformed by the Christ into the light of enlightenment! This miracle of God's Forgiveness and Love enables a sincere devotee to experience the *absolution* of his sins and the joys of a new life under the guidance and protection of the Christ and His Host.

Through honorable restitution comes total absolution. The remission of sins becomes the complete forgiveness and absolution of sins only when one makes payment for his transgressions through acts of restitution. While one is eating the sweet fruits of God's forgiveness, he is given numerous opportunities to make restitution for present-life sins and *past-lives* offenses. In many instances, an alert devotee will know how to make restitution to God and to persons; in other instances, he will need to pray for guidance in the ways restitution should be made.

Some of the ways Restitution is made are: Kindness, benevolence; charitable acts and humane deeds; holy hospitality through the Agape or Love-spirit of selfless service; partaking of the Sacrament of Communion; inspiring others to worship God; daily prayers for the good of others, especially one's foes; the speaking of healing mantrams for persons in need and holding them in the light of sacramental meditation; restitution-fasts, gratitude-fasts and other consecrated fasts of service and healing; gratitude-offerings and restitution-offerings; teaching adults and children the Laws and Commandments of God, the Cardinal Virtues and the Golden Rule; willing sacrifices in the Name of the Christ; the giving of tithes and offerings toward the preservation and prospering of God's Word; the payment of all tithes not given previous to one's entering the Path of Virtue; restitution for all moral debts; and restitution for all Sabbath Days not observed in the present lifetime and in previous lives.

> If thou . . . call the sabbath a delight, the holy of the Lord, honourable; and shalt honour Him, not doing thine own ways, nor finding thine own pleasure, nor speaking thine own words: Then shalt thou delight thyself in the Lord; and I will cause thee to ride upon the high places of the earth.
>
> —Isaiah 58:13, 14

Each Commandment of God not fulfilled previous to one's dedication to walk the Path of Virtue must be brought into balance. Thus, as a devotee observes each

Law and Commandment in his present placement on the Path, he must also exert the daily effort to make an honorable restitution for the Law or Laws that he failed to revere and fulfill in previous years and lives. The Righteousness-light of God will reveal each indebtedness to Holy Law as one is able to receive it and to make rectification.

"But be ye doers of the word, and not hearers only, deceiving your own selves." (James 1:22) If a student of the higher life remains immoral or amoral in thought, word, feeling or action; if he does not place honest tithes on God's Holy Altar; if he fails to keep the Sabbath Day Commandment; and if he is unforgiving and unloving toward others—he remains vulnerable to the penalties of karma and unrighteousness rather than qualifying for the freedoms and rewards of righteousness and holiness.

> For whosoever shall keep the whole law, and yet offend in one point, he is guilty of all.
> —James 2:10

> Owe no man any thing, but to love one another; for he that loveth another hath fulfilled the law.
> Saint Paul
> *—Romans 13:8*

THE DIMENSIONAL HEALING POWER OF THE CHRIST

> All power is given unto me in heaven and in earth.
> Jesus
> *—St. Matthew 28:18*

The harmony in the Universe is one of speed and precision. After a Truth-seeker comes into polarity balance through repentance, confession and restitution, he makes rapid progress on the Path leading to Spiritual Illumination. The still small Voice of God is heard through the *amplification* of a cleansed conscience in harmony with the Ten Commandments and the Sermon on the Mount.

To be centered within the Ten Commandments and the Sermon on the Mount is that moment in Time and Space toward which the soul has been working. Through many life-cycles of birth and death, the soul has finally fulfilled its destined task of bringing to birth the cardinal virtues, the hemispheres of the conscience, and the great logics. Henceforth, the heart and the consciousness mind become as receptive chalices for the Anointing Spirit of God.

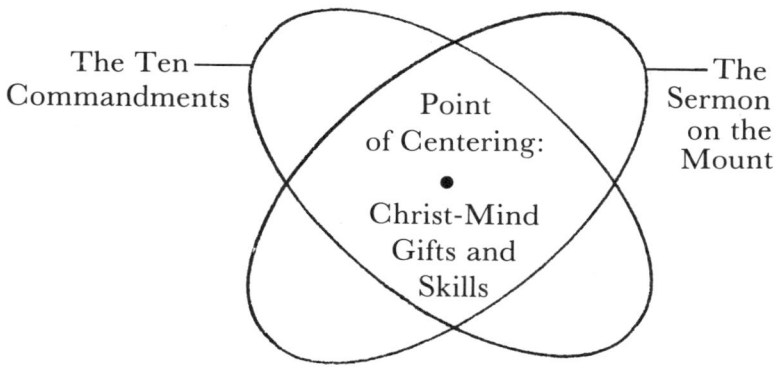

Title: ATOM ENERGY-FIELD
OF ILLUMINATION

As a devotee fulfills the Ten Commandments in their cyclic continuity, an energy-field of Insulation surrounds and protects him; in this, the Old-Testament Wisdom becomes part of his being. Daily efforts to live according to the Sermon on the Mount build another energy field of

Insulation and Inspiration. The *Marriage* between the Ten Commandments (the Old Covenant) and the Sermon on the Mount (the New Covenant) within one's heart and mind becomes a powerful atom energy-field of Insulation and Illumination. The seeker after Truth becomes centered in the Wisdom, Harmony and Timing of God's Cycles within the Ten Commandments and the Sermon on the Mount, thereby attaining the Divine-Marriage *Point of Centering*. Thereafter, the Christ, working through the Holy Ghost, makes of him an articulate spokesman for the Power and Glory of God creating mankind through the Ten Commandments and the Sermon on the Mount.

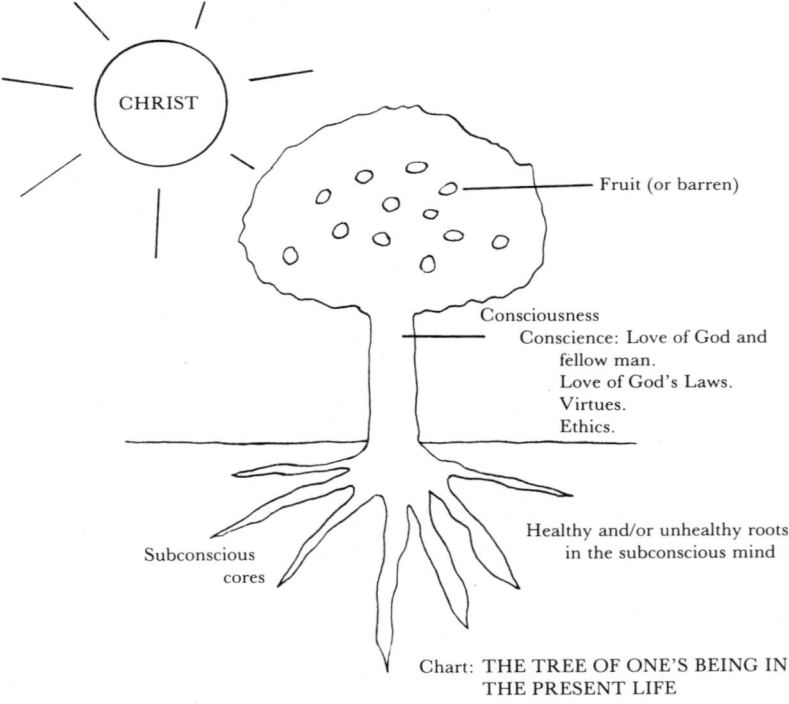

Chart: THE TREE OF ONE'S BEING IN THE PRESENT LIFE

*Ann Ree Colton: "The sacred atom is in the tap root. From the tap root project the senses. The Christ makes the senses into super-senses or super-conscious vehicles."

Healthy roots in the subconscious produce mature virtues and wholesome attitudes toward the worship of God, the acceptance of spiritual disciplines, and moral values. Healthy roots inspire one to live a life of service based upon the love of God and His Laws. If there are unhealthy roots in the subconscious mind, one's attitudes and reflexes in the present life are selfish, irreverent or non-reverent. Through dedication to the Ten Commandments and the Sermon on the Mount, the *core* of each unhealthy root is healed, thereby freeing one to become a spiritual-creative craftsman for God and His Son.

> I am the vine, ye are the branches: he that abideth in me, and I in him, the same bringeth forth much fruit.
>
> Jesus
> —*St. John 15:5*

Repentance, confession and restitution lead one to union with the supernatural powers of the Saints and the Lord Jesus. In this, a devotee-initiate learns of Their ability to manifest miracles, signs and wonders.

The desire to be forgiven of all past-lives offenses as well as present-life sins denotes that one has begun to unite with a powerful truth regarding the Miraculous Mercy of God and the Dimensional Healing Power of the Christ. This climactic and illuminative moment of realization on the Path of Virtue is accompanied by an innate knowing that one must hold fast to the directive of Jesus: *"Go, and sin no more." (St. John 8:11)*

When one asks for and receives the forgiveness of his past-lives sins and present-life transgressions, he has been shepherded by Jesus to the heart of God's Love and Grace. This high degree of divine union inspires him to desire with all his heart, mind and soul to fulfill the Ten

Commandments and the Sermon on the Mount *in all coming lives*. This noble desire builds a bridge of virtue toward the remainder of his present life, his coming life, and his future lives. It also enables him to be shepherded by the Lord Jesus toward the Bliss-Dimensions of Revelation within the Godhead.

If a seeker after Truth repents of present-life sins—and is forgiven—he should realize that *past-lives offenses* will rise periodically from the lower subconscious and try to discolor the sincerity of his repentance. Until one learns the importance of confessing the sins of previous lives, these offenses may move at any time from the sea of the lower subconscious as powerful tidal waves and seek to engulf him. Many unwary persons are drowning in the sea of past-lives transgressions. Past-lives sins recorded in the lower subconscious are the cause of many health problems, unhappy associations and negative conditions in one's present life.

Through the Dimensional Healing Power of the Christ, the dark energies of past-lives sins are changed into energies that produce healing, harmony and happiness. This miraculous power of the Christ works through one's sincerity in repentance, honesty in confession, and honorableness in making restitution.

The cyclic occurrence of a New Moon, a Full Moon, a Lunar Eclipse or a Solar Eclipse works directly with the soul's record of sin-debts and grace-treasures. During these cyclic energy-tides of the Moon and the Sun, the Christ Light is able to reach more deeply into the lower subconscious during prayers of repentance and confession. *Especially during the time of an Eclipse is the Christ able to penetrate the lower subconscious with His healing, freeing and quickening Light. Humility prayers of repentance and confession spoken on the day of an Eclipse act as a conduit of faith for the Christ and His Miracle-producing Light.*

> Miracles are not contrary to nature but only contrary to what we know about nature.
> —Saint Augustine

The lower subconscious is the repository for the memories of all sin-debts of the present life and past lives. One's *faith* in the power of the Christ to forgive and to heal all manner of sin-debts enables His laser-like Light to penetrate to the depths of the lower subconscious and to explode the heavy energy-crystallizations of dark memories accumulated over the ages. Miracles and freedoms result after the Christ Light begins its healing work in the deepest and darkest layers of the lower subconscious.

After the crystallized energies of sin-debts in the lower subconscious are exploded by the Christ, they float to the surface of the consciousness in cyclic tides, presenting themselves to the penitent for expiation through prayers of repentance and confession and through willing acts of restitution. Faith in the Mercy of God and the Power of the Christ to forgive and to heal all sins of the present life and former lives holds the key to one's future freedom and progress on the Path of Virtue and Illumination.

FAITH

> According to your faith be it unto you.
> Jesus
> —*St. Matthew 9:29*

> Reason is our soul's left hand, Faith her right,
> By these we reach divinity. —John Donne

> Much knowledge of things divine escapes us through want of faith. —Heraclitus

Faith without works is dead.   —James 2:20

Nothing in life is more wonderful than faith, the one great moving force.   —Sir William Osler

Our faith triumphant o'er our fears.   —Longfellow

Guided by faith and matchless fortitude.   —Milton

Faith is the healing panacea for all ailments.
                                          —Ann Ree Colton

Faith is the substance of things hoped for, the evidence of things not seen.
                                                Saint Paul
                                                —*Hebrews 11:1*

The shield of faith.   —Ephesians 6:16

I have fought a good fight, I have finished my course, I have kept the faith.   —2 Timothy 4:7

Faith is the force of life.   —Leo Tolstoy

The just shall live by his faith.   —Habakkuk 2:4

You will not enter paradise until you have faith; and you will not complete your faith till you love one another.
                                                —Muhammad

Strong Son of God, immortal Love,
    Whom we, that have not seen Thy face,
    By faith, and faith alone, embrace,
Believing where we cannot prove.   —Tennyson

RESTITUTION AND MIRACLES

> A man full of faith, if endowed with virtue and glory, is respected, whatever place he may choose.
>
> Buddha
> —*The Dhammapada*

> If ye have faith as a grain of mustard seed, ye shall say unto this mountain, Remove hence to yonder place; and it shall remove; and nothing shall be impossible unto you.
>
> Jesus
> —*St. Matthew 17:20*

One's *faith* acts as a cable through which the Holy Electricity or Light of the Christ may travel. When one has faith in the Christ to heal all past-lives sins as well as his present-life transgressions, the Christ may work more closely and efficaciously with the devotee in his efforts to taste the freedom-fruits of divine union.

> And if the Son therefore shall make you free, ye shall be free indeed.
>
> Jesus
> —*St. John 8:36*

Through the blessings, healings and freedoms that follow sincere repentance, honest confession and honorable restitution, one comes to the vivid realization that the Christ has the power to heal the sins of any age, time or life. Freedom from many different kinds of bondages enables one to follow the Great Shepherd to the Kingdoms of Dimensional Grace within the Godhead.

The Christ is working eternally with God in the creating of *Galaxies*. Dimensional Grace is Godhead Grace; Godhead Grace is Galaxy Grace. Therefore, when one turns to the Christ as the Son of God, his faith begins the process of his being forgiven all past offenses in former lives, Solar Systems and Galaxies. This awesome power of forgiveness of sins is but one of the Gifts of God through the Mediation of His Mighty Son.

> That ye, being rooted and grounded in love, may be able to comprehend with all saints what is the breadth, and length, and depth, and height; and to know the love of Christ, which passeth all knowledge.
>
> Saint Paul
> —*Ephesians 3:17-19*

As long as one who requests forgiveness of *all* his sins remains "grounded in love" and centered in Law, the Gift of his being forgiven extends into other marvels and miracles of Grace. Gradually, a sincere penitent recognizes that the increasing Gifts and Blessings being received by him are manifestations of God's Tender Love and Sweet Mercy manifesting through the Dimensional Healing Power of the Christ. *"For by grace are ye saved through faith; and that not of yourselves; it is the gift of God."* (Ephesians 2:8)

PRAYER OF REPENTANCE: THE DESIRE TO MAKE RESTITUTION

Almighty God, Creator of heaven and earth, I could never repay Thee for Thy Mercy. Thank Thee for guiding me to my spiritual home, where I may learn of Thee and Thy Plan for Thy children of the earth.

I desire with all my heart and being to make restitution for all past offenses against Thee, Thy Laws and Commandments, and against my fellow man.

I have foolishly listened to the voices of the unenlightened in the world rather than to the voices of the Great Teachers. I pray to henceforth build upon Their wisdom and love.

Heavenly Father, I have sinned against Thy Holy Laws and Sacred Prototypes. Please forgive me—and bless those whom I have offended in the present life and in past lives. May they know Thy Love and Healing-Good.

I pray to honor and fulfill with honesty and integrity—and with Thy help—Thy Holy Law of Tithing. Help me to make an honorable restitution for the times past in which I have failed to revere and fulfill with love this wise and mighty Law preserving and prospering Thy Word in the world.

May I be counted among the givers in the world rather than the takers, the sheep rather than the goats. And may I inspire others to see the wisdom in tithing to Thee so that Thy Word —with its Wisdom-truths, Healing-essences and Grace-manifestations—may bless the world in this generation and in all generations to come.

Help me, O Omnipresent One, to reverently fulfill Thy Ten Commandments with love, honor and integrity. Thank Thee for these priceless statutes and for the protection, guidance and enlightenment they provide. Show me, O Lord, how I may make restitution for all of my offenses regarding Thy Commandments of Morality, Thy Commandment to worship Thee each Sabbath Day, and Thy Commandments of Love.

And may I revere and fulfill each Commandment *as Thou wouldst have me fulfill it*—for the remainder of this life and in all lives to come.

Help me to make restitution for all manner of debts incurred in past lives and in the present life, that I may serve Thee and love Thee with a whole heart, mind and soul, and serve and love my fellow man as taught by Thy Beloved Son.

I ask these things in Jesus' Name, trusting in Thy Mercy, Wisdom and Love for me as a child of Thine Eternal Spirit. Amen.

Equanimity and the Moon

The precious things put forth by the moon.
—Deuteronomy 33:14

. . . Being an instrument of the armies on high, shining gloriously in the firmament of heaven.
Apocrypha
—Ecclesiasticus XLIII. 9

. . . The light of the moon shall be as the light of the sun.
—Isaiah 30:26

There is one glory of the sun, and another glory of the moon.
Saint Paul
—1 Corinthians 15:41

The moon, like a flower,
In heaven's high bower
With silent delight
Sits and smiles on the night.   —William Blake

The man who has seen the rising moon break out of the clouds at midnight, has been present like an archangel at the creation of light and of the world.
—Emerson

What is there in thee, Moon! that thou should'st move
My heart so potently?   —Keats

The Moon,
Rising in clouded majesty, at length,
Apparent Queen, unveil'd her peerless light,
And o'er the dark her silver mantle threw. —Milton

All praise be yours, my Lord, through Sister Moon and Stars. —Saint Francis of Assisi

This verily, is the door of the heavenly world—that is, the moon. Whoever answers it, him it lets go further.
—Upanishads

The Moon is the first spokesman for the Sun, the Planets and the Stars. Therefore, O devotee, thy communication with the God of Cosmos should begin by thy becoming conversant with the Intelligence of God moving the Moon.

Even as the Moon's energies determine the action of the tides of the ocean, so do the lunar energies govern the tides or cycles of the soul. As one begins to identify the cycles of the Moon and their effects upon and through his soul's record of the present life and past lives, he becomes as the captain of a ship who carefully guides his craft safely through all types of weather.

A ship's captain may navigate his ship by observing the celestial bodies. An alert devotee charts his course on the Path of Virtue through his perceptive observation of the Moon's energy-influences in his life. The energy-language of the Moon pertains to each Day of the Week, each Virtue, each Commandment of God, and each Prototype within the human spirit.

Every moment of the Day and the Night contains a message from the Moon—a message of enlightenment through Truth. As one becomes knowledgeable in the basic Laws and Commandments, the Cardinal Virtues, and the twelve Zodiacal Prototypes, he begins to comprehend the Word of God speaking through the cyclic energy-tides of the Moon.

The Virtue of Equanimity comes to birth when one begins to make his peace with his soul's record regarding each Commandment of God and each Prototype of the human spirit. When one dedicates to live according to the Commandments of Love for God and Love for his fellow man, he becomes aware of the strength of will, alertness of mind and gentleness of spirit necessary for the expression of a true and pure love. If one's love is insincere or tinged with prejudice, the cyclic action of the Moon will seek to reveal these and all other faults that need correction. Self-love and impure motives stain the beauty of love—and require the cleansing action of the lunar energies to wash repeatedly against each stain until it is removed.

When love becomes a sincere dedication of service to God and the human spirit, one becomes aware of the Moon's energy-tides as activators of the memory-treasures and grace-essences of the soul. The Moon's light illuminates the way to union with the Glory of God within the Soul and within Time.

Service to God in the world of action requires of one a high degree of the Virtue of Equanimity. To attain the Virtue of Equanimity, a seeker after Truth must be self-disciplined and emotionally stable; for he must remain poised during any and all circumstances, crises and trials. The poise gained through the Virtue of Equanimity protects the devotee, initiate or teacher from being drawn into the negative life-currents of the spiritually immature, the emotionally unstable and the mentally self-deceived. This important Virtue enables one to serve God and the human spirit with steadfastness, loyalty and love.

The Virtue of Equanimity inspires a devotee-initiate to remain true to the Laws of God throughout each initiatory challenge or trial. Thus, he is able to serve with patience and love the twelve Zodiacal Prototypes within the human spirit.

To attain the Virtue of Equanimity, one must overcome anger, critical-mindedness, and the judging of others. These and other negative traits cause the muddy waters of anti-virtues to enter into the heart and mind, thereby short-circuiting the electricity-like flow of Soul Grace and Divine Grace. The victims of this self-caused tragedy experience prolonged periods of darkness which may manifest as mental depression, self-condemnation, or open hatred of others.

Temper tantrums, spells of depression, or easily-triggered anger reveal the need for healing through spiritual exercises, prayer and meditation. Acts of violence causing grievous harm to others place one farther away from the treasures of the soul and the Image of God. When one begins to earnestly desire peace, harmony and equanimity, he is responding to his soul's light and to Divine Grace.

The energies of the Sun and the Moon are degrees of the Light of the Christ. Through the Solar Cycles and Lunar Cycles, the Son of God seeks to reveal and to heal the sin-shadows in the lower subconscious—the dark side of the soul's record. As long as one dwells in the darkness of the lower-subconscious shadows, he delights in sinning, and he takes great joy in criticizing and judging others. An initiate under Christ experiences pangs of conscience whenever he is critical-minded, judging or prideful. Each conscience-pang is a protective warning from his soul reminding him of the importance of love, compassion, forgiveness and humility.

A complete Lunar Cycle involves different stages or

phases of the Moon's light, from New to Full and from Full to New. Each New Moon and Full Moon is a period of heightened sensitivity during which the soul's record of debts and grace is magnified.

During each Lunar Cycle of 29.5 days, the Moon passes through the twelve signs of the zodiac. The zodiacal position of the Moon each day and night is an accurate indicator of the balances and imbalances within the soul's record. The soul's record pertains to one's attitudes, associations, health, degree of divine union, and all other aspects of his life.

As one learns to discern the cyclic energy-influences of the Moon in his own life, he can begin to observe these powerful energies and their effects upon individuals, races, nations and religions in the world. When one makes his peace with the Moon's energies, he experiences the peace "that passeth understanding,"* for he has begun to unite with the Glory of God in the Moon.

The many component parts of a record-player make possible the playing of a phonograph record. The Sun, Planets, Stars and Galaxies may be likened to the component parts of a record-player; the Moon is as the needle. As the needle (Moon) touches the soul's record of virtue or vice, it produces either harmony or discord in one's present life. Through the purification of the soul's record, the causes of inharmony and unhappiness are healed—and the Moon's energies are experienced as the sweet and melodious tones of pure creation.

The Virtue of Equanimity is as a steady light that shines in the consciousness mind. When the light of this Virtue is combined with the light of other key virtues, one is ready to render service to God as an ambassador of His Word.

*Philippians 4:7.

The birth of the Virtue of Equanimity requires daily care and watchfulness, prayer and selflessness. In time, the majesty of this royal virtue, working in concert with the Moon's cycles and creation-energies, enables one to create works of beauty and truth that glorify God and prosper His Plan.

EQUANIMITY

Concentration being preceded by absolute equanimity brings about the peaceful state of action and established harmony between the object and its surroundings. —Patanjali

The superior man is satisfied and composed; the mean man is always full of distress. —Confucius

Whatever sacrifice may be made in the service of the Lord, know that it is the equanimity of your soul that is the best and fittest offering. Equanimity is sweet to taste and has the supernatural power of transforming everything to ambrosia.

Equanimity expands the soul and gladdens the mind, as the sunlight fills the vault of heaven, and it is considered to be the highest devotion. —Yoga-Vasishtha

We must learn, in our pursuit of wisdom, to listen with equanimity to the reproaches of the foolish, and to despise contempt itself. —Seneca

Truly wise is he who is unstirred by praise or blame, by love or hatred. He is not moved by the opposites of life. Verily does he delight in the blissful Self. —Srimad Bhagavatam

Once upon a time a lover of secret lore came to an anchorite and asked to be admitted as a pupil. Then he said to him:

My son, your purpose is admirable, but do you possess equanimity or not? He replied: Indeed, I feel satisfaction at praise and pain at insult, but I am not revengeful and I bear no grudge. Then the master said to him: My son, go back to your home, for as long as you have no equanimity and can still feel the sting of insult, you have not attained to the state where you can connect your thoughts with God.
—Isaac of Acre

Remember that there is nothing stable in human affairs; therefore, avoid undue elation in prosperity or undue depression in adversity. —Socrates

Hence for the mind to be free from sorrow and pleasure is the perfection of virtue; to be of one mind that does not change is the perfection of quietude. —Kwang-tze

He whose mind is free from anxiety amid pains, indifferent amid pleasures, loosed from passion, fear and anger, he is called a sage of stable mind.

For wise men endowed with equanimity, renouncing the fruit of actions and freed from the shackles of birth, attain the blissful superstate. —The Bhagavad Gita

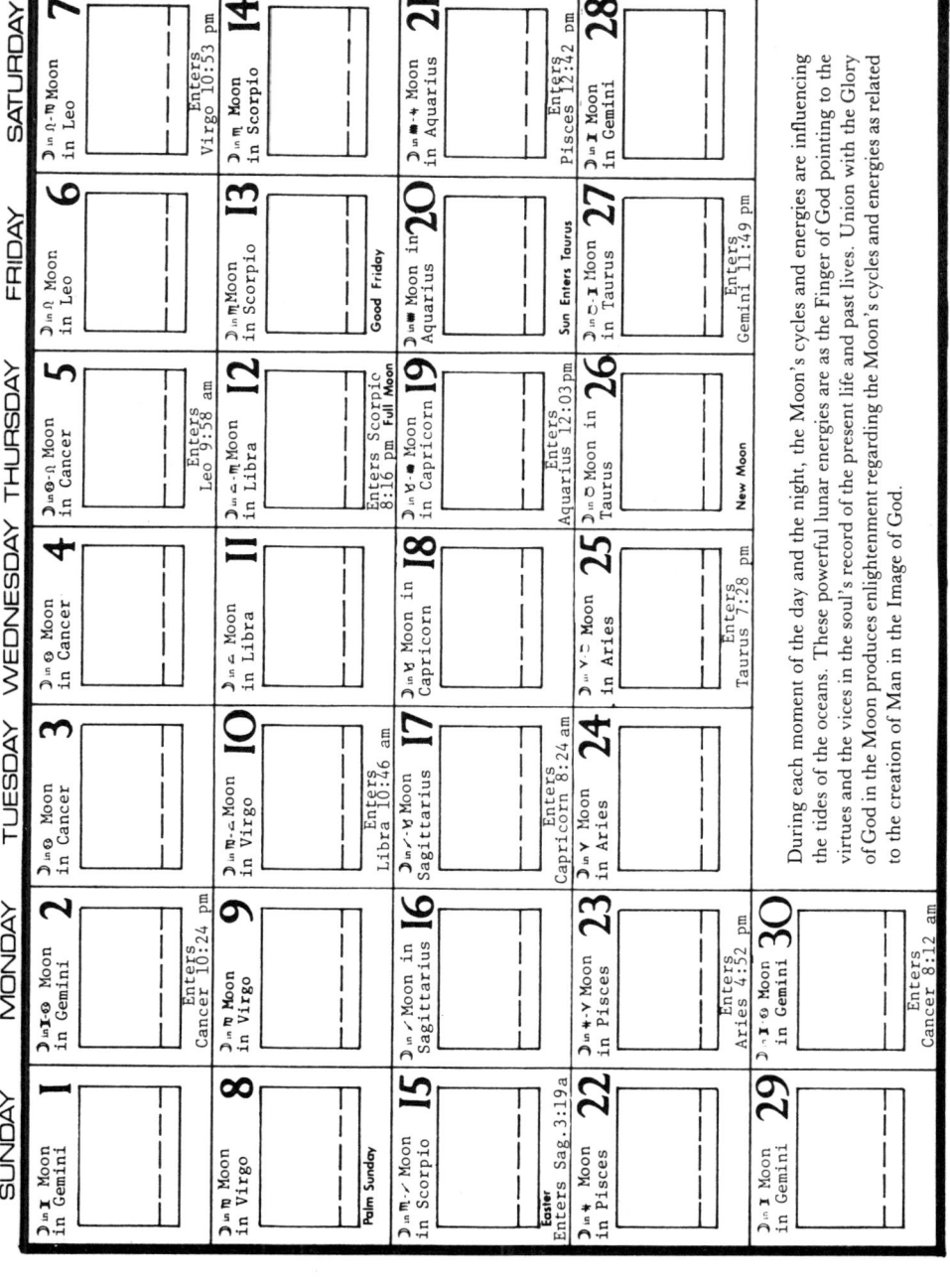

THE SUN

Praise to thee, my Lord, for all thy creatures,
Above all Brother Sun
Who brings us the day and lends us his light.
—Saint Francis of Assisi

Truly the light is sweet, and a pleasant thing it is for the eye to behold the sun.
Solomon
—*Ecclesiastes 11:7*

If the radiance of a thousand suns were to burst forth at once in the sky, that would be like the splendor of the Mighty One. —Bhagavad Gita

Dear Sun, You feed us all, every garden grows by your light. I bow to the Eastern Mountain where you rise, I bow to the Sunset Hill in the West where you go down. You unfold the flowers of day. You are bright and beautiful. If there are clouds you are always behind them. Your heart is wide, it is immeasurably wide. Take my song and give me light.
—Valmiki (Ramayana)

Man is a sun and a moon and a heaven filled with stars.
—Paracelsus

Understand that thou art a second world in miniature, and that the sun and the moon are within thee, and also the stars.
—Origen

And among his signs are the night, and the day, and the sun, and the moon. Bend not in adoration to the sun or the moon, but bend in adoration before God who created them both, if ye would serve Him.
Muhammad
—*The Koran*

The day is Thine, the night also is Thine: Thou hast prepared the light and the sun. —Psalm 74:16

16

PURE LOVE AND THE PROTOTYPES

Thou shalt love the Lord thy God with all thy heart, and with all thy soul, and with all thy mind. This is the first and great commandment. And the second is like unto it, Thou shalt love thy neighbor as thyself. On these two commandments hang all the law and the prophets.

      Jesus
      —*St. Matthew 22:37-40*

. . . the Divine furnace of purifying love.
      —Saint Catherine of Genoa

THE COUNTENANCES OF GOD

The Lord bless thee, and keep thee: The Lord make his face shine upon thee, and be gracious unto thee: The Lord lift up his countenance upon thee, and give thee peace.

      Moses
      —*Numbers 6:24-26*

Thou hast made known to me the ways of life; thou shalt make me full of joy with Thy countenance.

      Saint Paul
      —*Acts 2:28*

The energy-dynamics of the Sun, the Moon and the Planets are purposed toward one objective: The creation of Man in the Image of God; the creation of Man as a being of Love, Law and Virtue. When one becomes knowledgeable in the Laws and Commandments of God and in the Virtues proceeding from the Image of God, he may begin to comprehend the ordained purposes, cycles and energy-influences of the celestial bodies within the Solar System.

All initiations related to the receiving of the Miracle Gifts of the Soul are *Pure-Love Initiations*. Every devotee on the Path of Virtue experiences these repetitive tests of his motives and virtues, for he must prove to God that he loves purely and wholeheartedly all individual and collective manifestations of the human spirit: persons, families, races, nations, religions. He must know with all certainty in his heart and mind that all living souls are the Omnipresence of God in action.

In the present era, billions of persons live in the physical world; however, the Creator simplifies the Pure-Love Initiations into *twelve* specific categories of human life called *Prototypes*. The twelve prototypes within the human spirit are: Aries, Taurus, Gemini, Cancer, Leo, Virgo, Libra, Scorpio, Sagittarius, Capricorn, Aquarius, Pisces. Each of the twelve Zodiacal Prototypes is a *Countenance* of God. When one looks on the face of any living soul, he is looking on a human being in the process of being created in the Image of God—and the Omnipresent Spirit of God is looking at him through the eyes of the twelve Prototypes.

A devotee who is called and chosen by the Creator to become a Teacher of the higher life undergoes continuous Pure-Love Initiations regarding the Twelve Zodiacal Prototypes. As he draws closer to the Godhead, he gradually unites with the Glory of God's Countenance within each

Pure Love and the Prototypes

Prototype. Union with the Glory of God within each of the twelve Zodiacal Prototypes results in *Prototypal Illuminations*. In this, one serves with love and impartiality all whom God sends to him for instruction, healing and enlightenment.

"Thou shalt love thy neighbor as thyself." *(St. Matthew 19:19)* The Commandment to love one's neighbor relates to a pure love for the twelve Zodiacal Prototypes; for in the Cosmos starry mathematics, each Prototype is a *neighbor* to the eleven other Zodiacal Prototypes.

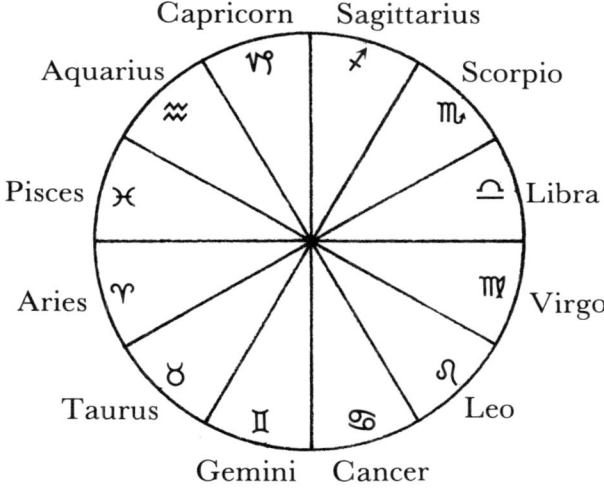

Each virtue has electromagnetic properties. As one ascends the Virtue-Ladder of Illumination, the Spirit of God attracts to his virtue-light new friends and spiritual associates who will love, assist and bless him. In this, the *Countenance* or Glory of God will be revealing itself to him through the faces of reverent friends and loving spiritual companions.

Virtues are the hem of God's Glory. Progress toward Prototypal Illuminations occurs as one learns to identify the virtues that prosper his union with the multifaceted splendor of the Creator's Glory.

Each Zodiacal Prototype being projected from the Divine Image contains the Glory of God within it. This Glory manifests in the world of action as and through key or outstanding virtues. Through cycles of reincarnation, each person expresses the twelve Zodiacal Prototypes and is given numerous opportunities to master the virtue-energies represented by each Sun Sign.

The Path of Virtue is the Path of the Saints. Each perfected Saint expressed the perfected virtues of the Zodiacal Prototype through which he or she came to birth on earth. When one becomes a protege of the Saints, he begins the process of perfecting the virtues of his Zodiacal or Sun Sign. The Saints assist him in this necessary dedication and preparation for Spiritual Illumination.

While each alert devotee is cognizant of the cardinal virtues related to his Sun Sign—and works to attain the sacrament-degrees of the virtues—his initiations with persons of all twelve Zodiacal Prototypes assist him in the birth and quickening of all other cardinal virtues. The paramount initiations pertain to the virtues correlating to his own Birth Sign.

The Omnipresent Spirit of God is revealing the soul's record each moment of the day and the night. This revealing is occurring through every person and condition—pleasant or unpleasant, happy or unhappy, joyful or sorrowful. Union with God as the Omnipresent Truth begins with one's understanding the daily drama of the twelve Zodiacal Prototypes as they move in and out of his life. Pure-Love Initiations occur regarding each co-worker or fellow seeker on the Path; each business associate; each marital and family relationship; and every other person one meets, serves or thinks about.

Zodiacal Prototype	Parts of Body	Integrity-Cores	Low-Notes
1. Aries	Head	Paternal Love Leadership with God-like Pioneering	Insensitivity Hatred Impulsiveness Impatience Heated Mentality Militant
2. Taurus	Throat Cerebellum Back	Stewardship of Possessions Loving Speech	Coveting Dishonesty Stubbornness Hardness of Heart

3. Gemini	Nervous
	  System
	Lungs
	Hands
	Arms
	Shoulders
		Mental Honesty
		Charity Towards Races
		Sibling Happiness
			Fantasy
			Division
			Resisting Mind
			Demoting Self-Confidence
			  in Others
			Mental Pride

4. Cancer	Stomach Solar Plexus Breasts	Spiritual Empathy Selective Palate Mother Love	Possessivism Retreatism Dominating
5. Leo	Heart Spine	Cosmos Love Giving Forgivingness	Unforgiveness Self-Pity Pride Arrogance Lack of Confidence
6. Virgo	Intestinal Tract Tissue	Honor Realistic	Parasitism Vagueness Wrong Use of Conversation Critical Mind
7. Libra	Kidneys Lower Back	Divine Law Non-Judging Comprehension of Karma	Lawlessness Retaliation Manipulation Procrastination

8. Scorpio	The
	  Generative
	  System
		Chastity
		Charitable Honesty
		Sincerity
		Constancy
		Illuminative Telepathy
			Lustfulness
			Revenge
			Suspicion
			Rigidity
			Secrecy

9. Sagittarius	Hips Thighs Flesh	The Keeping of Vows Dedicated to the Afflicted Giving in the Small	Untruthfulness Evasiveness Psychic Trickery
10. Capricorn	Knees Bones Skin	Reverence Character Releasing Service	Self-Ambition Inclusiveness Resisting Mind Materialistic
11. Aquarius	Ankles Circulation	Right Use of Power Altruistic Detachment	Misuse of Power Ruthlessness Manipulation Psychic Electricity
12. Pisces	Feet	Charity Agape Asceticism Thoroughness	Miserliness Evasiveness Psychic Euphoria Fantasy

—Chart by Ann Ree Colton

During Pure-Love Initiations, it is imperative and mandatory that a devotee or initiate express a *pure love* for each of God's Laws and Commandments as well as His Twelve Countenances or Prototypes. Pure-Love Initiations continue throughout one's lifetime, for only through pure love may one remain united with the purity of God's Love, the fulness of His Grace, and the power of His Righteousness and Truth.

PURITY

Blessed are the pure in heart: for they shall see God.
Jesus
—St. Matthew 5:8

Unto the pure all things are pure.
Saint Paul
—Titus 1:15

Every man that hath this hope in Him purifieth himself, even as He is pure. —1 John 3:3

Make thy own self pure, O righteous man! Any one in the world here below can win purity for his own self, namely, when he cleanses his own self with good thoughts, words and deeds. —Zoroaster

Surely God loves those who turn towards Him, and He loves the pure. —Muhammad

Physical cleanliness leads to spiritual purity.
—Hebrew Saying

Who shall ascend into the hill of the Lord? or who shall stand in his holy place? He that hath clean hands, and a pure heart. —Psalm 24:3, 4

Pure Love and the Prototypes

During intense initiatory-cycles, the energy-influences of the Sun, the Moon and the Planets increase their action upon certain key virtues. The Omnipresent Spirit of God places these initiatory dramas in one's life in perfect timing according to his need to grow in spiritual stature. In time, the cyclic repetition of these initiations is observed as involving one with the *same* Sun Signs of the Zodiacal Prototypes in his life and with the Moon's rhythmic return to the *same* positions in its travels through the heavens each lunar month.

Even as each person is called to perfect the predominant virtues related to his Sun Sign, so is he required to overcome certain negative or crude energies also correlating to his Zodiacal Prototype. This dual action is interrelated. As one perceives the importance of purification, he begins to recognize each cyclic test or lesson regarding the virtues and anti-virtues in his nature and temperament. With the key of purification in his hand, one comes closer and closer to the Saints' helps and assistances; and, in so doing, he begins to unite with the Glory of God within Holy Laws, within Virtues and within the Zodiacal Prototypes. This period of divine union is a major breakthrough in one's understanding the Image of God as it relates to the work of the Sun, the Moon and the Planets.

> He maketh His sun to rise on the evil and on the good, and sendeth rain on the just and on the unjust.
> Jesus
> —*St. Matthew 5:45*

Prototypal Illuminations

> The inward lover of God, who possesses God in fruitive love, and himself in adhering and active love, and his whole life in virtues according to

righteousness; through these three things, and by the mysterious revelation of God, such an inward man enters into the God-seeing life.
—John Ruysbroeck

He that is joined unto the Lord is one spirit.
Saint Paul
—*1 Corinthians 6:17*

The Sun and the Moon, in their travels through the twelve signs of the zodiac, are revealing the dark and the light within the soul's record of the present life and past lives. If one desires to work with and for God, the Creator communicates with him through the solar and lunar energies and their revealing of the soul's record of dark and light. *Prototypal Karma* pertains to the dark side of the soul's record; *Prototypal Grace,* to the light of the soul earned through love and virtue. If a devotee is closely associated with a person bringing him both sorrow and joy, the soul is revealing his own former-lives' ambivalence toward God and his fellow men.

Prototypal Grace is earned through pure love in lives past and in one's present life. If a Truth-seeker perceives the wisdom in contrition, repentance, confession and restitution, the Hand of God mercifully lifts each burden; healings and freedoms come—and Prototypal Grace is earned. In this, one's dedication to pure love gradually unites him with the Glory of God within each of the twelve Zodiacal Prototypes or Sun Signs.

Unhappy marriages, afflictions and other painful conditions and associations in life are disclosing the dark side of the soul's record. If the Spirit of God *hardens* the heart of any person toward a devotee, the Creator is revealing Prototypal Karma in the soul-record. Whenever the Spirit of God opens the heart's love of others toward one, He is revealing Prototypal Grace. Pure-Love Initiations prepare one for the time when he will live in the state of Prototypal Grace, harmoniously united with the Spirit of God within the human spirit.

The joys that come through restitution accompanied by Pure-Love Initiations are the joys of Healing Miracles, Archetypal Prophecies, Prototypal Illuminations and Revelation-Creations. These beautiful manifestations of Divine Grace manifest through union with the Glory of God within His twelve Zodiacal Prototypes.

The "five hindrances"* of lust, malice, sloth, pride and doubt—and all other anti-virtues—contest each earnest aspirant on the Path of Virtue. The sin-debts one is working to overcome within himself through restitution are the same sins he will see in the persons that God places in his life through His mathematical Laws of Attraction. When one lovingly serves others and sincerely prays for them to overcome their problems and faults, his sacrificial works and prayers gradually bring his soul's record into balance, harmony and peace through the healing power of restitution.

The antagonistic or hostile persons in a devotee's life are golden opportunities for him to apply the Christ-principles of pure love, prayer, fasting, forgiveness, turning the other cheek, and offering them "a cup of cold water"** in Jesus' Name. Each Christ-principle is filled with a perfect wisdom through which restitution may be accomplished.

A cardinal sin committed when the Sun is in a Zodiacal Sign has far-reaching consequences in one's present life—and, if he leaves the world unrepentant, the unresolved

---

*Buddha
**St. Matthew 10:42.

sin-debt, as a stain on the dark side of the soul's record, will present itself for expiation in a future life on earth. Any sin for which one remains unrepentant will attract painful associations with a person or persons born in the Zodiacal Sign when the sin occurred. This is true of each Zodiacal Sign in which the scales of law, love and virtue have become imbalanced.

The position of the Moon at the time of each cardinal sin also is inscribed upon the dark-side of the soul's record. These sins present themselves for payment in one's present life or in a coming life.

The *Sun Signs* of the persons involved with one in sinning become as time-bombs that will explode in a timing determined by the soul. Reprovings from the soul manifest through various degrees of suffering, afflictions or unhappiness either in one's present life or in some future life or lives.

A cardinal sin is a complex matter. This is due to the *position* of the Sun and the Moon at the time of one's sins of omission and commission, and also because of the Zodiacal Prototypes of the person's own Sun Sign and the Sun Signs of the victims and the conspirators. Each of these imbalances must be rectified at some moment in Time and Space. *"Till heaven and earth pass, one jot or one tittle shall in no wise pass from the law, till all be fulfilled."* (St. Matthew 5:18)

If a thief steals from a family, the theft is recorded by the action of the Sun and the Moon in the soul's record, and a debt is owed to the persons from whom he steals. The same is true of any other cardinal sin, such as adultery, coveting, murder, etc. To offend any Holy Law is to be entangled in a web of one's own making. A contrite and repentant heart begins the process of becoming extricated from this self-made imprisonment. Confession and restitution bring balance to the scales, and restore one to an equilibrium and soul-health conducive to peace, harmony and well-being.

Even as one's sins are recorded by the zodiacal positions of the Sun and the Moon, so are his charitable acts, worship observances, tithes to God, sacramental fasts and other deeds of faith and virtue recorded in his soul's record by the Sun and the Moon. For example, if a devotee tithes to God and observes the Sabbath Day Commandment when the Sun is in the sign of Aquarius and the Moon is in Cancer, he has earned *Aquarius Grace* and *Cancer Grace*. This earning of Prototypal Grace pertains to all spiritual practices, observances and dedications. As one observes each rhythmic cycle of daily worship and Sabbath worship, Prototypal Grace gradually replaces Prototypal Karma—and one comes closer to a firm union with the Glory of God within the twelve Zodiacal Prototypes.

If one is called by God to minister to others and to instruct them as to His Laws, Commandments, Principles and Ethics, he serves the twelve Prototypes—and thus earns Prototypal Grace regarding each sign of the zodiac. All sacramental services rendered in the Name of the Christ accelerate the overcoming of Prototypal Karma so that one may become centered in Prototypal Grace.

Prototypal Grace regarding the twelve types of persons within the human spirit leads to Prototypal Illuminations. Prototypal Illuminations produce Image-of-God Revelations. Image-of-God Revelations manifest Soul-Gifts through which one may serve the twelve Zodiacal Prototypes with pure love, ethics and Christ-Mind versatilities.

During certain periods of Pure-Love Initiations, an initiate under Christ is exposed to the weak or vulnerable places in his armour of insulation. If painful lessons are coming to him through a Gemini person or persons, this indicates that he must be more pure in his love toward *all* Geminis. In time, through numerous Pure-Love Initiations with *each* of the twelve Zodiacal Prototypes, the initiate evolves a pure and true love for all types or prototypes. This high attainment on the Path of Virtue signifies one's readiness to represent God in the world as an Ambassador of His Word and Truth.

If one has offended or sinned against an Aries Prototype in his present life or in past lives, the Law of Attraction will continue to involve him in painful or difficult situations with Aries persons until the offense is resolved through love and restitution. When the sin-debt is forgiven and healed, one gains freedom from *Aries Karma* and begins to unite with the Glory of God within the Aries Prototype. This victory through pure love and restitution unites one with *Aries Grace.* Each devotee on the Path of Virtue experiences repeated trials and challenges from the twelve Zodiacal Prototypes until he becomes centered in Prototypal Grace, thereby revealing a soul-record cleansed and healed through Pure-Love Initiations and the miraculous action of Restitution.

The Gift of Healing

> And the whole multitude sought to touch Him: for there went virtue out of Him, and healed them all.
> —St. Luke 6:19

Apostolic Virtues and Bodhisattva Virtues are attained through sacrificial works of restitution accompanied by Pure-Love Initiations. In Sanskrit, the word *Bodhi* means Wisdom; the word *Sattva* means purity, virtue, goodness, harmony and rhythm. A Bodhisattva is a holy seer who has attained these attributes. The *Bodhisattva Vow* is taken by illumined personages who dedicate to return to the earth "as long as one blade of grass remains unenlightened."

Yogic Virtues are virtues earned through self-discipline, love, spiritual principles, and devotion to God. In Eastern philosophies teaching Yogic Virtues, *Yama* pertains to truth; honesty; chastity; non-covetousness; and the practice of Ahimsa or non-injury either by acts, speech or thoughts to any sentient being, and compassion for all creatures. *Niyama* relates to purification; contentment; perfection of the senses through the removal of impurity; study of Sacred Scriptures; the repeated speaking of holy words or *mantrams;* and a persevering devotion to God.

> The mantram becomes one's staff of life, and carries one through every ordeal. It is repeated not for the sake of repetition, but for the sake of purification, as an aid to effort . . . It is no empty repetition. For each repetition has a new meaning, carrying you nearer and nearer to God.
> —Mohandas K. Gandhi

An enlightened Initiate under Christ synthesizes and utilizes the wisdom-teachings of both East and West, for the power of love gained through Pure-Love Initiations unites him with the Omnipresent Spirit of God within the twelve Zodiacal Prototypes throughout the world.

The Gift of Healing occurs in direct degree to one's pure love for the human spirit. Pure love expressed through Sacramental Meditation, Prayer, Fasting and Almsgiving enables one to become a healer in the Name of the Great Physician, the Lord Jesus. When Jesus walked the earth, His pure love and virtues enabled Him to heal multitudes of people in one moment of time. All who heal in Jesus' Name and for God's Glory become part of His network of Holy Mediators lifting the world from darkness to light, from misery to happiness, from hatred to love.

> Beloved, believe not every spirit, but try the spirits whether they are of God . . . Hereby know ye the Spirit of God: Every spirit that confesseth that Jesus Christ is come in the flesh is of God: And every spirit that confesseth not that Jesus Christ is come in the flesh is not of God: and this is that spirit of antichrist, whereof ye have heard that it should come; and even now already is it in the world.
> —1 John 4:1-3

The miraculous healing power of the Lord Jesus to exorcise "evil spirits" (St. Luke 7:21) and "unclean spirits" (St. Mark 5:13) provides many persons with healing and freedom. This healing power works through all dedicated hearts who have been initiated through the fires of Pure-Love Initiations.

Anger, jealousy, lust and other anti-virtues reveal a soul-record in need of cleansing and purifying. If one continues to *add* to the sin-debt record of his soul, he eventually suffers *obsession* with some selfish, sinful or addictive way of life; if he continues in this course of action for many years and many lives, he becomes *possessed* by an unclean spirit, an evil spirit or a "foul spirit." (St. Mark 9:25) Persons in bondage to dark spirits behave in erratic manners subject to uncontrollable angers and urges.

Obsession, if unrestrained, leads to the abnormalities that work through an unclean or evil spirit; however, if one is blessed with conscience and strength of will, he will move from the darkness of obsession into the light of hope and freedom. Daily prayers of repentance and confession begin the process through which one is liberated from varying degrees of obsession and possession.

The cyclic action of the Moon is forever revealing the *Truth* related to the soul's record of virtues and antivirtues, Holy Laws fulfilled and Holy Laws offended, Zodiacal Prototypes loved or Zodiacal Prototypes sinned against. He who confesses his sins—as his conscience is able to identify them through self-honesty—comes to spiritual birth through union with God as the Omnipresent Truth, the Omniscient Mercy and the Omnipotent Love.

> And Jesus answering said, O faithless and perverse generation, how long shall I be with you, and suffer you? Bring thy son hither. And as he was yet a coming, the devil threw him down, and tare him. And Jesus rebuked the unclean spirit, and healed the child, and delivered him again to his father.
> —St. Luke 9:41, 42

The numerous Biblical references to possession by unholy and unclean spirits are a constant reminder to the dangers inherent in all forms of wilful deviation from the protection of God's holy ordinances.

The Lord Jesus came to free man from all addictions, bondages, obsessions, and possessions by unclean spirits. He came to release the gifts of the soul so that each person might express the Image Divine sealed into him by the Creator. *"If the Son therefore shall make you free, ye shall be free indeed."* (St. John 8:36)

Addiction to drugs, alcohol or tobacco; addiction to immorality or perversion; addiction to angers, hates and prejudices—these and other forms of addiction in one's present life are due to the seeds of unrighteousness sown in many previous lives. Numerous cycles of difficult incarnations may be required of obsessed and possessed persons until a polarity balance is restored between body, heart, mind and soul. If one becomes the hapless victim of a possessing entity, the *exorcism* may be long and tedious throughout many years, lives or ages.

Through *specific* prayers of Confession combined with restitution through love-actions and sincere forgiveness of others, one moves from sadness and unhappiness into joy and gladness as the Spirit of God gradually brings the scales of His Holy Laws into balance within the soul's record.

The Virtue of Honesty enables one to recognize the Prototypal Drama occurring in, to, through and around him. The Virtue of Humility, as expressed through prayers of Confession, enables him to experience and witness the Merciful Love of God and the Healing Power of the Lord Jesus as real and abiding Presences in all aspects and areas of his life of dedication and service.

The dedicated heart establishes a *Truth-rapport* with God during the Confession portion of his prayers.

> *Father, please forgive me, for I am a sinner. I have offended Thy Laws and Commandments in this life and in past lives.*
>
> *I have sinned against Thy Sacred Prototypes, Holy Laws and Divine Image.*
>
> *Bless those whom I have offended in this life and in past lives. May they know Thy good for them and Thy Love for them.*

Pure Love and the Prototypes

And henceforth may I fulfill Thy Laws as Thou wouldst have me fulfill them in this life and in all lives to come.

I pray to love as Thou wouldst have me love, and to serve as Thou wouldst have me serve.
In Jesus' Name.
Amen.

During Pure-Love Initiations, one's lessons come through *specific* Prototypes; for example, an *Aries* wife or husband, a *Sagittarius* child, a *Capricorn* business associate, etc. In such instances, one should speak prayers of Confession regarding the *specific* Prototype.

Father, please forgive me, for I have sinned against Thy sacred (Sun Sign) Prototype. I ask Thy good for them, Thy blessings upon them . . . In Jesus' Name. Amen.

Prayers of Confession regarding the twelve Zodiacal Prototypes lead to union with the Glory of God within the human spirit; in this, a Truth-seeker experiences increasing degrees of Prototypal Illuminations. Through the progressive stages of Pure-Love Initiations, a dedicated servant of God evolves a Pure Love for all souls created in the Image of God. Utilizing the Power of Pure Love and Modesty, he becomes a Healing Mediator for God and an enlightened Apostle of the Lord Jesus.

MODESTY

Modesty is the citadel of beauty and of virtue. —Demades

> The firm, the enduring, the simple, and the modest are near to virtue.

> He who speaks without modesty will find it difficult to make his words good. —Confucius

> An egotist will always speak of himself, either in praise or in censure; but a modest man ever shuns making himself the subject of his conversation. —Bruyère

> Courage plus self-modesty are two of the most valued attributes of the spiritual initiate. —Ann Ree Colton

Proteges of the Saints, Proteges of the Hierarchs

> Behold, the Lord cometh with ten thousands of His saints.
> —Jude 14

A devotee who turns to God with a heart of love and a mind receptive to truth becomes a protege of the Saints. Proteges of the Saints desire with all their hearts to heal, serve and instruct their fellow man; to feed the hungry; to minister to the sick, the widowed, the fatherless; to pray for miracles; to comfort the grieving; to energize the lethargic; to bring peace to the fearful; to inspire the weary; to give direction to the lost; to quicken the soul-skills of others; and to give constant testimony to the purity and wisdom of the Great Teachers and to the Mercy and Love of God.

Each ascended Saint expressed numerous virtues while living on earth; however, one virtue stands out as being the Saint's most important contribution to the world. A Saint's work in Heaven is centered around his outstanding virtue; this holy virtue is at the heart of his blessings sent from heaven to earth.

Each sincere devotee on the Path of Virtue is a protege of an ascended Saint. The devotee's key virtue is the same as the key virtue of the Saint to whom he correlates in dedication and service. When the devotee dies, his faithfulness to God in the world enables the Blessing-Stream of the Saint to widen and quicken its action upon the earth. In this, heaven and earth draw closer—and the devotee's co-disciples living in the physical world are profoundly blessed and prospered in their works for God.

After the death of a Saint's protege, the Blessing-Stream of the Saint expands and extends its healing and freeing work for the Christ. He who serves God as devotee or initiate renders a priceless service on earth through his virtue-light; and on leaving the body, he blesses his teacher, co-disciples and the human spirit in miraculous ways. This is due to his union with the virtue-light of the Saint under whom he serves as protege.

The *rainbow* is a symbol for the Saints, for each color and hue of the rainbow-light of the Soul correlates to a cardinal virtue. Even as white light contains a rainbow spectrum of beautiful colors, so are virtues the rainbow-spectrum colors within the white light of love.

> O Lord, the sense of Thy love well-nigh overwhelms me. If it be Thy will, bestow these many tokens of Thy loving kindness on those who know Thee not, to draw them to Thy service.
>
> —Brother Lawrence
> 1666–1691 A.D.

> O Lord, Thou knowest what is the better Way, let this or that be done, as Thou shalt please. Give what Thou wilt, and how much Thou wilt, and when Thou wilt. Deal with me as Thou knowest, and as best pleaseth Thee, and is most for Thy honour. Set me where Thou wilt, and deal with me in all things just as Thou wilt. I am in Thy hand; turn me round

and turn me back again, even as a wheel. Behold I am Thy servant, prepared for all things; for I desire not to live unto myself, but unto Thee; and oh that I could do it worthy and perfectly.

—Saint Thomas á Kempis
1380–1471 A.D.

Steer Thou the vessel of our life towards Thyself, Thou tranquill Haven of all storm-tossed souls. Show us the course wherein we should go.

—Saint Basil
Martyr, 316 A.D.

In the Cosmos, hosts of Great Beings and Presences work between the Godhead and each Galaxy and between each Solar System. In the Solar System with the planet Earth, hosts of Mediators work between the Godhead and man. These Mediators include the Angels, the Archangels, the Saints, Mary, the Great Immortals, the Holy Ghost, the Apostles of Jesus, the Lord Jesus, and the Hierarchs.

The Hierarchs are Constellation Beings. As Great Mediators of Cosmos, the Hierarchs work with the Christ through Constellation Energies. The Mediation of the Saints is preparing mankind to comprehend the Mediation of the Hierarchs.

> Let us make man in our image, after our likeness.
>
> —Genesis 1:26

> We created man: and we know what his soul whispereth to him, and we are closer to him than his neck-vein.
>
> —The Koran

Pure Love and the Prototypes

In the Book of Genesis, the Hierarchs are referred to in the plural words *us* and *our*. *"And God said, let us make man in our image, after our likeness."* The Hierarchs are opening the minds of men to the Wisdom and Plan of God for the Galaxies. They work for and with the Christ in the creation of Star Clusters and Galaxy Clusters.

To contemplate the Christ is to learn of Cosmos with its sister and brother Galaxies. The Mediation Host of the Christ, inclusive of the Hierarchs, is working toward the time when the human spirit will comprehend the Christ-Mind as a Galaxy-Consciousness Mind.

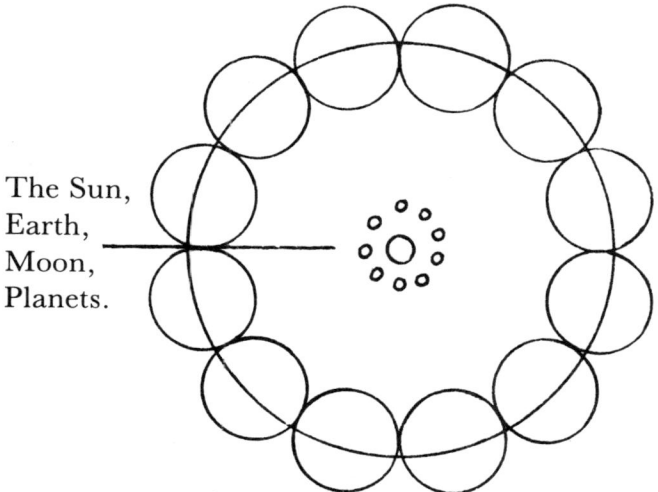

The Sun, Earth, Moon, Planets.

Constellations of Stars.

The Hierarchs work through the Constellation energies and their influences upon the twelve Zodiacal Prototypes within the human spirit.

Canst thou bind the sweet influences of Pleiades, or loose the bands of Orion? —*Job 38:31*

All Galaxies and their starry systems within the Universe are interrelated. The Hierarchs work with each grouping of Stars in Constellation action and formation. In time, the minds of men will become increasingly receptive to knowledge transmitted to the Earth by the Hierarchs.

The Divine Image, or Image of God, within each living soul is the point of contact between the Hierarch Intelligence and the Human-Spirit Intelligence. The Divine Image responds to the Cosmos-Eternal wave lengths of telepathy uniting all creations in all Stars and Galaxies.

The Divinity of man, as proclaimed by all Scriptures, is a Cardinal Cosmos Truth. The Hierarchs as Divine Beings work with Cosmos Truths and with the Image of God within the soul of man and within the Soul of Cosmos. Therefore, to become a protege of the Hierarchs is to know a closeness with Cosmos and to experience spiritual quickenings of the Divine Image. The Lord Christ, the Cosmos Son of the Living God, is the One who unites all Hierarchs in all Constellations seen and unseen. Thus, proteges of the Hierarchs are Christ-quickened souls at one with the Omnipresent Spirit of God creating all Universes and Kingdoms.

To dedicate oneself to walk the Path of Virtue is to become a protege of the Saints; to dedicate oneself to work with the Christ and His Mediation-Host is to become a protege of the Hierarchs. The Saints assist a devotee to unite with the Glory of God within Virtues; the Hierarchs work to unite him with the Glory of God within the Starry Constellations and Galaxy Creations. Virtue-knowledge opens the door to Constellation-knowledge; Constellation-knowledge prepares one for union with Christ as the Cosmos Son of the Living God.

The lessons one learns in each life are lessons related to the ethical and creative use of physical, emotional, mental and spiritual energies. Through the Mediation of the Saints and the Hierarchs, a seeker after Truth experiences the initiations that lead to an understanding of the soul and its energies.

Grace is the most mysterious and powerful of all energies. The miraculous transformation experienced by a sinner who becomes a Saint testifies to the awesome nature of Grace. Grace flows from the Love of God sealed into every soul. Learning, in its many different aspects and degrees, is grace. As one learns, he increases his capacity to receive grace and to express grace. Grace heals and transforms in the twinkling of an eye. Grace releases soul-treasures in the twinkling of an eye. Grace opens one's understanding and brings enlightenment in the twinkling of an eye.

When one becomes a protege of the Saints, he learns of the soul and its grace-energies; he learns of virtues as being arteries through which grace-energies flow from the soul into one's heart, mind and life. When one becomes a protege of the Hierarchs, he learns of the solar system and its grace-energies and creation-essences. He begins to work *with* God and *for* God as an ambassador of His Grace and Truth. The Christ, the Sovereign over all Hierarchs and all Saints, becomes his Initiator-Illuminator—and he lives and serves in the Omnipresent Spirit of Almighty God.

Proteges under the Hierarchs see the Earth and its solar system as a Cosmos-creation of God and all souls as energy-universes in different stages of creation—from energy-processes within the anti-virtues to the energy-processes within virtues.

Proteges under the Saints receive virtue-quickenings that reward their dedications and disciplines with increasing tides of Soul Grace and Divine Grace. The conscience purified through virtue-quickenings enables them to become proteges under the Hierarchs, that they may work hand-in-hand with the Christ in His lifting, quickening and illuminating the human spirit.

Proteges under the Hierarchs prepare themselves through sacramental meditation and prayer to become revelators inspired by the Christ. By serving "the only begotten Son of God," they are quickened by increasing voltages of Divine-Image electricities until they are qualified to represent the Christ as revelator-prophets.

Proteges under the Hierarchs are no longer earthbound in their thoughts; their thoughts soar with the tones of the Symphony of Cosmos Creation. To contemplate Cosmos is to contemplate the Hierarchs' work; to unite with the Christ is to become a facet of His Diamond of Illumination—a Diamond lighting all Stars and Galaxies.

The Hierarchs work as Masterbuilders of solar systems. Thus, when one becomes a protege of the Hierarchs, he becomes a masterbuilder working with the archetypal blueprints of God for the Earth's creation. He works toward goals ages away; he works toward victories eternities away.

> According to the grace of God which is given unto me, as a wise masterbuilder, I have laid the foundation, and another buildeth thereon. But let every man take heed how he buildeth thereupon.
>
> Saint Paul
> —*1 Corinthians 3:10*

> Is it not written in your law, I said, Ye are gods?
> —St. John 10:34

REINCARNATION

Master, who did sin, this man, or his parents, that he was born blind? —St. John 9:2

For all the prophets and the law prophesied until John. And if ye will receive it, this is Elias, which was for to come. He that hath ears to hear, let him hear.
> Jesus
> —*St. Matthew 11:13-15*

The soul is immortal, and is clothed successively in many bodies. —Plato

Our souls are deathless, and even when they have left their former seat, do they live in new abodes and dwell in the bodies that have received them. —Ovid

Worn-out garments are shed by the body: Worn-out bodies are shed by the dweller within . . . New bodies are donned by the dweller, like garments. —Bhagavad Gita

God generates beings, and hence they return over and over again, until they return to Him.
> Muhammad
> —*Koran*

And I was a witty child, and had received a good soul. And whereas I was more good, I came to a body undefiled.
> Wisdom VIII:19-20
> —*Apocrypha*

Him I call a Brahmana who knows his former lives, who knows heaven and hell, who has reached the end of births, who is a sage of perfect knowledge and who has accomplished all that has to be accomplished.
> Buddha
> —*The Dhammapada*

17

SOUL-COVENANTS AND REINCARNATION-CYCLES

O sweetest Love of God, too little known; he who has found Thee is at rest.

Everywhere with Thee, O my God, O my Love, all for Thee, nothing for me.

O my God, how sweet to me Thy presence. Who art the sovereign good. O Lord, I beseech Thee, leave me not for a moment, because I know not the value of my soul.

—Saint John of the Cross
1542-1591 A.D.

Ananda, such things as The Buddha, or The Law, or The Order of Brethren, through countless hundred thousand cycles of time have never been heard of by these beings. Therefore they cannot listen to this Law. In this round of births and deaths, whose beginning is incalculable, these beings have come to birth hearing only the talk of divers animals. They spend their time in song and dance, in places where men drink and gamble and the like. Thus they cannot listen to the Law. —Buddha

After I depart, I cast no look behind
Still wed to life, I still am free from care.
Since life and death in cycles come and go,
Of little moment are the days to spare.
Thus strong in faith I wait, and long to be
One with the pulsings of eternity.
—Po Chu-I
800 A.D.

Learning and the Universe

And Jesus answered and said unto them, Elias truly shall first come, and restore all things. But I say unto you, That Elias is come already, and they knew him not, but have done unto him whatsoever they listed. Likewise shall also the Son of man suffer of them. Then the disciples understood that he spake unto them of John the Baptist.
—St. Matthew 17:11-13

Approximately six thousand of the 200 billion stars in the Milky Way Galaxy are visible to the unaided eye. In 1609, Galileo's telescope increased the number of visible stars to 50,000. A century later philosophers began to theorize the existence of "island universes" of stars. The first photographs proving the reality of galaxies were taken in the early 1900's. In recent years, extraordinary photographs of clusters of stars and clusters of galaxies have provided mankind with a realistic and expanded comprehension of the Cosmos.

The period of rotation of the Milky Way Galaxy is about 280 million years. This Galaxy Cycle determines the various ages being experienced by the human spirit in its birth to virtues, conscience, logic, love, soul and spirit.

Soul-Covenants and Reincarnation-Cycles

The energy-mathematics of the Milky Way Galaxy, in conjunction with brother and sister galaxies, work with each soul assigned by the Creator to live on the planet Earth. Whenever a person reincarnates in the physical world, he is fulfilling great Galaxy Laws working through the Divine Image within his being. The Divine Image, in turn, determines each stage of progression through the learning process in the world of action and association.

The reincarnations one experiences during a 280 million-year Galaxy Cycle are providing him with invaluable lessons. Each lesson is the direct result of a *Soul-Covenant* with God. Upon the conclusion of the Earth as a planet, the souls of men will move toward new learning experiences in the Cosmos where different Galaxy Cycles will direct their potent energies upon the Divine Image and its ordained manifestations.

The perfection of the heart and the mind is the work of the soul in its Covenant with God; this perfection is occurring through *Reincarnation-Cycles*. The soul, endowed with the Gift of Eternal Life, is working day and night, life after life, to fulfill this necessary goal in God's Plan for man.

The light of learning experienced through the four races in the physical world is transforming the earth-energies into finer degrees of energy. These finer degrees of energy earned through learning become immortal and integral lights in the soul. Thus, through life after life in age after age, the soul is in a continuous (eternal) state of adding light unto itself.

The expanding light of the soul is part of the perfect mathematical harmony of God's Expanding Universe. The soul, an eternal portion of the Expanding Universe, is in a perpetual state of expansion. As the mind learns, the soul expands its love.

Even as the Earth turns in cycles, so does the learning process occur in cycles. From one's first breath to his last breath in each life, he is in a continuous state of Learning.

The Tree of Knowledge, planted in the soil of Eternal Life, is an *Eternal Tree*. As Man learns on Earth, branches of the Tree of Knowledge lead him to the Sun, the Moon, the Planets—and on and on to the Stars. Each new Star is then known to be a fruit on the Tree of Knowledge. Each Galaxy is a cluster of ripe fruit ready to be discovered and digested as part of the learning process. Man, in learning of the solar system in which he dwells, is being prepared by the Creator to learn of adjacent solar systems, and, eventually, the more distant starry bodies.

The vastness of the Universe and the multitudes of Stars and Galaxies make of man an eternal learner. To learn all that God would have him know, one moves from life to life in cycles of reincarnation, gathering the knowledge needed for his progress and evolvement. The Wisdom of God in the soul determines the lessons one learns during each lifetime. Major lessons become ingrained into one's feeling and thinking processes through a repetition in learning gained through the cycles of reincarnation as supervised by the soul and the mathematics of Creation.

The reincarnation-cycles of the individual are determined by his attitudes toward the Laws and Commandments of God. His attitudes are dependent upon his virtues. If one's virtues inspire harmonious and law-minded attitudes, his reincarnation-cycles move him ever-upward on the Mountain of Illumination. However, if one remains *prodigal* toward one or more Holy Laws and Commandments, his reincarnation-cycles seek to remove him from the prodigal state and to place his feet on the Path of Virtue.

As long as one says "No" to any Law or Commandment of God, his soul will continue to reincarnate him in circumstances and situations that will gradually impress upon him the importance and seriousness of the Law or Laws upon which he is failing to build his life. Numerous lives may be required before the "No" becomes a "Yes" toward each Law and Commandment of God.

When the heart and mind are in complete accord with the Creator's mandates, one becomes a *probationer* on the Path of Virtue. During the probationary state, the memory-treasures of past lives related to virtues, conscience and logic are increasingly quickened within his being.

In the reincarnation-cycles—from prodigal to probationer—one moves through races, nations, religions and families that hold the exact lessons needed for his progress. These lessons may be bitter, sweet or bitter-sweet. The soul gradually places a holy mantle of virtues upon the shoulders—and one attains the crown of Enlightenment.

Each virtue, in its illumined state, opens new worlds of understanding regarding the Holy Law of Reincarnation. Each illumined virtue is as a vast university with endless libraries.

The Laws and Commandments of God are as a garden in which virtues grow, flower, and produce the fruits of righteousness. Anointed teachers present the Word of God regarding His statutes and also introduce prophecies and revelations related to the *new way* for man. The Mantle of the anointed teacher is a sacred responsibility; the earning of this Mantle represents many reincarnation-cycles of devotion and dedication to God.

When Jesus, the World Teacher, walked among men, He was a judgment upon all who crossed His path. Those who recognized His pure love and wisdom—and followed Him—began a quickened activity of reincarnation-cycles blessed by God. Those who rejected Jesus' words also began new series of reincarnation-cycles designed to overcome their resistances to the eternal truths and principles taught by Jesus.

When a teacher anointed by the Spirit of God is living in the world in any age and time, he becomes a judgment on all who cross his path. Those who reject or mock the teacher begin new reincarnation-cycles affecting many lives. Students who fail to apply the Scriptural decrees and disciplines taught by an anointed teacher miss a rare opportunity in the Eternals—an opportunity that may not be presented again for many lives.

When one becomes the student of an enlightened teacher, this may be the first time in his present life that he has been taught spiritual truths and worship-disciplines. The instruction offered by the teacher will be his entry into the Truth-portals of God through prayer and meditation—blessing his present life and future reincarnation-cycles.

The birth of a virtue may be likened to the four cyclic stages in the birth of a butterfly: the egg; the caterpillar; the chrysalis; and the butterfly. In its earliest form of energy, a virtue is as an egg. After one reincarnates in many different eras, cultures, societies and civilizations, the egg stage of the virtue becomes the caterpillar stage of the same virtue. In the caterpillar stage of a virtue, one is *earthbound* in his feelings, thoughts and actions; he thinks only of the mundane and the temporal rather than the spiritual and the eternal. Through the Holy Law of Reincarnation, the Quickening Spirit of God gradually increases one's capacity to extend his thoughts farther than the self and self-pleasures; in this, his dedication to materiality slowly changes to the dedication to spirituality.

After the caterpillar stage of a virtue, one experiences the chrysalis stage of the same virtue. The Quickening Spirit of God concentrates its energy-action upon the cardinal virtue coming to *spiritual birth*—and one experiences many reincarnation-sojourns on earth during which the divine or sacrament-degrees of the virtue seek to come to birth. After intensive virtue-initiations experienced during the chrysalis stage, the virtue, as a butterfly, emerges from its cocoon as a winged creation of beauty and freedom.

Each virtue within the Image of God for man undergoes these four major stages of transition from egg to butterfly. A person may have a number of virtues in the egg stage; many other virtues in the caterpillar state; several virtues in the chrysalis state; and one or more in the butterfly state. Numerous lives previous to his present existence have accomplished his current state of being. The remainder of his reincarnation-cycles in this solar system will see new energies added to each virtue as the Quickening Spirit of God seeks to bring all virtues into the butterfly state.

> And as you, Life, I reckon you are the leavings of many deaths. (No doubt I have died myself ten thousand times before.)
> —Walt Whitman

> For sure is the death of him that is born, and sure the birth of him that is dead; therefore over the inevitable thou shouldst not grieve.
> —Bhagavad Gita

> Him that overcometh will I make a pillar in the temple of my God, and he shall go no more out.
> —Revelation 3:12

> Did I not live in another body, or somewhere else, before entering my mother's womb?
> Saint Augustine
> —*Confessions*

> It is absolutely necessary that the soul should be healed and purified, and if this does not take place during its life on earth, it must be accomplished in future lives.
> —Saint Gregory of Nyssa

Pre-Solar-System Covenant

> Father, I will that they also, whom thou hast given me, be with me where I am; that they may behold my glory, which thou hast given me: for thou lovedst me before the foundation of the world.
>
> Jesus
> —St. John 17:24

"In my Father's house are many mansions." (St. John 14:2) The soul, being eternal, has dwelt in "many mansions" or solar systems within the Cosmos. The soul, before moving into the Plan of God for a new solar system, enters into a *Covenant* with the Creator. This Covenant relates to the types of lessons one will learn in the energy-processes of the new solar system.

The Spirit of God sets new goals for the soul in each solar system to which it is assigned. This assignment or Covenant *seals* into the soul the cycles through which new facets of the Image of God will come forth through experience, learning and creating.

The *Pre-Solar-System Covenant* between God and the soul is based upon pure mathematics related to energy-units of truth, love, virtues, conscience, logic, grace and other necessary attainments. The Plan of God is being fulfilled each moment of the day and the night throughout the Life-Span of the solar system to which the soul has covenanted to come.

The soul, through its Covenant with God, *knows* what must be accomplished in its solar-system home. All lives a person lives fulfill this long-range goal involving billions of years and numerous incarnations.

The soul utilizes a gyroscopic action that keeps one ever a part of God's Eternal Plan. The gyroscope of the soul seeks to draw each person to a perfect centering on the Path of Virtue. If one continually resists the gyroscopic action of his soul, he invites stern penalties and strong reprovings throughout many lifetimes. However, if he gratefully accepts the blessing of the gyroscope of the soul, the *creative* energies within Nature, the Sun, the Moon, the Stars and the Galaxies work to qualify him for the Holy Anointings that produce the Greater Illuminations.

The gyroscope of the soul may be likened to a gyroscope that keeps a space capsule on perfect course. If one veers away from the course of the Divine Image, the gyroscope of the soul returns him to this ordained course. The farther one strays from the soul's course, the more painful is the return toward the covenanted goal. For example, if one fails to live with humility, the soul uses the devices of Nature to humble him. One who willingly accepts the way of humility as God's Plan remains on his soul's course.

The gyroscopic action of the soul is one of God's greatest blessings. This truth becomes increasingly apparent after one begins to be graced with spiritual gifts and soul-skills, for the gyroscopic action of the soul keeps him centered in the bosom of God's Love and Grace.

If a space capsule traveling thousands of miles an hour is a fraction of an inch off course, it would miss its destination by millions of miles. The gyroscope of the space capsule assures the reaching of the desired destination. So does the gyroscope of the soul enable a devotee to move ever closer to the central point within the Heart of God. When one earns the Mantle of the Anointed Apostle under Christ, the gyroscopic action of his soul enables him to remain centered in the Laws, Ethics and Principles that govern and prosper the Gifts of Prophecy, Revelation, Healing and other Apostolic Gifts.

The soul's gyroscopic action may remain quiescent for many lives while one squanders the precious energies of life; however, when the time comes for him to learn of the sacredness of life's energies, the gyroscope of the soul becomes active—and the course of one's wastefulness and callousness is abruptly changed through crises, afflictions, sorrows and suffering. The greatest casualties occur when the gyroscope of the soul becomes active in the lives of those who delight in evil-doing, sensuality and irreverence. When one abides in the safety and protection of the Laws of God, the gyroscope of the soul is able to unerringly guide him to the royal Gifts of the Soul, the priceless Anointings by the Holy Ghost, the "unsearchable riches" of the Christ, and the Illumination-Treasures of the Godhead.

> Unto me, who am less than the least of all saints, is this grace given, that I should preach among the Gentiles the unsearchable riches of Christ.
>
> Saint Paul
> —*Ephesians 3:8*

Pre-Birth Covenant

> Govern all by Thy wisdom, O Lord, so that my soul may always be serving Thee as Thou dost will and not as I may choose. Let me die to myself, so that I may serve Thee; let me live in Thee, who in Thyself art the true life.
>
> —Saint Teresa
> 1515–1582 A.D.

Soul-Covenants and Reincarnation-Cycles   423

Before each new life on the planet Earth, the soul enters into a *Pre-Birth Covenant* with God related to the challenges and purposes of the life to be lived. In this Pre-Birth Covenant between the Creator and the soul, all energies to be used in one's life are determined; physical-body energies, love-energies, will-energies, virtue-energies, conscience-energies, logic-energies, and all other energies necessary for one to fulfill the Covenant.

During each life one lives on Earth, his apportionments of energy are periodically released or withdrawn according to the soul's Pre-Birth Covenant. The Wisdom of God, working through the soul's record of past lives, determines each cyclic releasement of energies; also, when the soul is preparing to leave the world of action, energies decrease—and death occurs.

In each life, learning is the goal; new knowledge is gained and sealed into the soul's memory-treasures. If one has lived a selfish life, the after-death retrospection and introspection afford him the opportunity to view his misused energies and to be corrected and instructed during various stages of the afterlife.

The Spirit of God in the soul is *constantly* teaching. In life and in death, one is learning what to do and what not to do. Gradually, over numerous lives and deaths, one begins to respond to the patient and persistent teaching by the Spirit of God through the soul and its record.

Learning is eternal, even as life is eternal. Life is for learning; eternal life is for eternal learning.

In the Pre-Birth Covenant with the soul, each person selects the nation into which he will be born, the parents who will give him birth, the ancestral lines that will provide certain gene-traits. He also chooses the *energies* of one or more anti-virtues upon which he will work and, hopefully, change into the light of virtues.

Anti-virtue energies may be likened to coal, uranium, plutonium or other substances that are potential sources of *light*. Before each life, one determines the exact amount of anti-virtue energy he will seek to change into virtue-light. During a specific number of lives, he may elect to be born with great quantities of lust-energies, greed-energies, pride-energies, etc. As the glandular system begins to assert itself during puberty and adolescence, these energies present themselves for purification. Thereafter, in seven-year cycles throughout one's present life, the soul provides *new* increases of various kinds of energies for him to transpose into light through love. If love is absent or lacking, he will become involved in many difficult problems. These problems will continue to appear from year to year until he learns that *Love* is the miraculous catalyst that changes all energies into virtue-energy in the twinkling of an eye!

Saints and other Great Souls who have overcome and purified their own anti-virtue degrees of energy work with the world and with individuals who are yet in bondage to anti-virtue energies.

The Soul-Covenant of Jesus fulfilled Scriptural prophecies regarding the Messiah's birth, life and death. The martyrdom of Jesus overcame ages of sins of mankind and enabled them to begin a new spiral of learning. Through the Soul-Covenant of Jesus, all persons on earth are being given the opportunity to experience a personal union with the Creator.

In certain instances, Saints and other holy personages enter into a Pre-Birth Covenant with God that places upon them the robe of martyrdom. Whenever a Saint makes a Soul-Covenant to suffer persecution, an affliction or martyrdom, his life becomes a restitution-offering to God as an atonement for the sins of the spiritually ignorant and the morally unclean.

Soul-Covenants and Reincarnation-Cycles

Who can understand the love of a Saint who willingly takes upon himself suffering in order to lift the burdens of his fellow man? Such is the nature of a Great Soul dedicated to the principles of love, sacrifice and restitution for the sins of his brothers and sisters who are yet caught in the hypnotic coil of anti-virtues.

In this solar system, the *Adversary Principle* is part of the creation of Man in the Image of God. The adversary or tester works through the dark side of the soul's record as part of the learning process related to trial and error, right and wrong, good and evil. All Great Teachers show the way to wisdom and truth through which the human spirit may avoid the snares of the tester and become centered in the grace-side of the soul's record.

> The swans go on the path of the sun, they go through the sky by means of their miraculous power. The wise are led out of this world, having conquered Mara (the tempter) and his hosts.
> Buddha
> —*Dhammapada*

Even as beauty in face and form is rarely accompanied by the cardinal virtues, so is brilliance of intellect rarely accompanied by the cardinal virtues. Beauty in face and form, without the cardinal virtues, entraps one in the pitfalls of pride, vanity and licentious behavior. Brilliance of intellect, without the cardinal virtues, is as a ship without a compass, and one is in danger of drowning in intellectual pride, egotism and self-love.

Individuals who attain high positions of leadership in religions are ever in danger of taking pride in their authority, prominence and power; and, if prejudiced, their prejudices influence many persons under their charge. As long as any vestige of pride or prejudice is present in the heart of a religious leader, he will attract reincarnation-cycles specifically designed by the soul for him to overcome these obstacles to a pure union with the Love of God.

Before the cardinal virtues come to birth in the heart and mind, persons may willingly and gleefully lend themselves to works of evil, wickedness, maliciousness, unrighteousness, and the corruption of the young. These wilful offenses against the sacred energies of life attract one to reincarnation-cycles in which he will become the victim rather than the perpetrator of these deliberate acts against good and God.

The Creator is mercifully patient with each of His children; however, if one persists in evil-doing or wrongdoing throughout many incarnations, he invites stern reprovings in the form of *limitations*. In this, he experiences reincarnation-cycles in which he will be deprived of the use of *energy:* physical-body energy, emotional energy, mental energy, or will-energy, thereby rendering him incapable of harming or violating others. When the slightest glimmer of a change toward the good occurs in the heart and mind, one immediately changes the currents of the reincarnation-cycles—and the long climb begins once more toward the beginning stages of the birth of the cardinal virtues.

While the attaining of the physical degrees of the cardinal virtues may require numerous reincarnation-cycles throughout the ages, so may the birth of the spiritual degrees of these key virtues require many cycles of reincarnation under varied conditions in different nations, races, religions and families.

One's future reincarnation-cycles are determined by his being repentant or unrepentant at the time of death. If he has proved sincere in his repentance during the years previous to his passing, he can look forward to reincarnation-cycles blessed by God. And if he has served and followed the Christ with dignity, honorableness and ethic, the Christ will be his Shepherd throughout all future reincarnation-cycles remaining for him to experience during the creation of the earth.

> Lo, I am with you alway, even unto the end of the world.
> Jesus
> —*St. Matthew 28:20*

To reincarnate as a male or a female is established during the Pre-Birth Covenant with the soul. Whether one is born as a male or a female is determined by the virtues being developed throughout various reincarnation-cycles. While certain cardinal virtues (honesty, humility, integrity, etc.) are the same for both sexes, there are other virtues being specifically required of the male, such as gentleness, tenderness, compassion, mercy; and the female is adding to her nature those virtues related to learning, wisdom, and involvement in the world outside the family. Through the reincarnation-cycles, the aggressive, warlike spirit of the male is seeking to be softened; and the female, for ages filling the roles of wife and mother, is moving into the mainstream of life, where she may contribute to the worlds of science, religion, the creative arts and other fields of activity and productivity.

In each new age or era, the reincarnation-cycles are fulfilling the perfect Will of God through the soul and through the virtues coming forth within the human spirit.

The soul, through reincarnation-cycles, is moving each individual closer to the day when men and women will desire to emulate the virtues of the Lord Jesus. This sacred desire, when present in the heart and mind, enables the soul to transmit to one the higher or spiritual-creative energies of the Sun, the Moon and the Planets. The goal of all aspirants on the Path of Virtue is to become creative craftsmen for God, spiritually receptive to the pure and beautiful love-energies of the solar system and the Cosmos.

> Nothing is sweeter than Love, nothing more courageous, nothing higher, nothing wider, nothing more pleasant, nothing fuller nor better in Heaven and earth; because Love is born of God, and cannot rest but in God, above all created things. He that loveth flyeth, runneth, and rejoiceth; he is free, and cannot be held in. He giveth all for all, and hath all in all; because he resteth in One Highest above all things, from whom all that is good flows and proceeds. He respecteth not the gifts, but turneth himself above all goods unto the Giver.
> —Saint Thomas á Kempis

> He who knows his real Self as one with the universal Spirit, who sees his very Self enfolding all beings, whom can he hate? His heart accepts the whole universe as his own. He continually performs service to all beings. He can hate no one, and is equal to friend and foe alike.
> —Upanishads

During a cycle of several or more lives, the soul concentrates on the birth, quickening or illuminating of one or more key virtues. If one responds to his soul, he moves to higher plateaus of love and understanding. Each higher plateau of cardinal virtues lifts one farther away from the Law of Suffering. The Law of Suffering—with its harsh lessons through afflictions, trials and tribulations—is constantly teaching its lessons regarding the importance of virtues and conscience in God's Plan for man.

Soul-Covenants and Reincarnation-Cycles

Virtues gained through suffering become imperishable memory-treasures. In the learning process for the planet Earth, each man, woman and child is given the sacred opportunity to learn either through the joy of light or the fire of pain. When learning and love become one, one is in a state of grace.

Each soul covenanting with God to live in a Solar System in which suffering is part of the Learning Process earns great compensations. These become invaluable assets in the soul's eternal record.

All Prodigal-Son states of existence are related to anti-virtues and their painful lessons. As one begins to be receptive to his soul and its virtue-treasures, his reincarnation-cycles move him into areas of life and expression where the environments are conducive to his learning about and expressing the higher degrees of the cardinal virtues. In this, he becomes a devotee of the Lord—and places his prodigal past forever behind him. The bitter lessons learned through selfishness become an ingrained warning system alerting him to the dangers of disobedience to Holy Laws.

Many lives may be lived as a *student* of the higher life before one qualifies for the soul-quickenings that make of him a *devotee* dedicated to the daily worship of God. Many other reincarnation-cycles may be required before he becomes an *initiate*—and, eventually, an anointed teacher.

A person may make a pre-birth covenant with his soul to be born in a certain religion through which he will gain important knowledge and learn vital lessons. The religion to which one is born or drawn will emphasize various disciplines, virtues and truths. These disciplines, virtues and truths will provide him with the knowledge, experiences and associations necessary for his spiritual progression.

Some religions teach the importance of meditation as

the means of union with God; other religions stress the power of prayer. If one needs to learn of the discipline of meditation, he will be attracted to this form of worship; if he requires the knowledge of prayer and its miraculous benefits, his soul will inspire him to follow a religion that emphasizes prayer. In some instances, one will learn from his religious mentors the importance of utilizing both prayer and meditation in his quest for Truth. So it is with each worship-discipline, divine virtue and cardinal truth: the pre-birth covenant with the soul places one in the right placement during each moment of each life on earth.

When an individual chooses to be cut adrift from the company of the faithful, he exposes himself to much-needed lessons. If he is not fortified by a moral conscience, he will fall into traps and pitfalls; these negative occurrences will hold the key to future opportunities in lives to come, for lessons learned will make coming covenants with the soul more harmonious and fortuitous.

In sin-offenses leading to venereal disease, abortion and other transgressions against the Commandments and the Divine Image, one's prayers of repentance begin the process of healing. To remain unrepentant for sins resulting in a venereal disease is to inflict suffering upon oneself and others. If one is healed medically—and fails to repent spiritually—the venereal disease remains active in the invisible energy-body (etheric body) and in the soul's record. The tragic results of the disease will manifest later in one's life or in coming lives. The same is true of any sin-caused afflictions healed by medicine that are not accompanied by sincere repentance, confession and restitution.

"Who did sin, this man, or his parents, that he was born blind?" (St. John 9:2) If a person leaves the world sin-laden and unrepentant, he faces coming lives in which he will be

SOUL-COVENANTS AND REINCARNATION-CYCLES 431

required to make an *unwilling* restitution for past offenses. Many tragic defects at birth and other major afflictions during childhood and later in life signify that one has covenanted with his soul to make rectification through some form of restraint, disability or suffering. Many past lives of unrestrained sinning may be overcome in one life of pain and sorrow caused by major physical, emotional or mental problems. The soul is perfect in its meting of justice in regard to each Law and Commandment of God. *"With what measure ye mete, it shall be measured to you again."* (St. Matthew 7:2)

If one is born with a sense of responsibility and a desire to live life honorably with integrity and ethic, he will desire to make a *willing* restitution for any and all imbalances recorded on the scales of divine justice. In this, he comes under the beneficent Love and Mercy of God, and begins the process of making an honorable restitution for all transgressions recorded in the soul's record.

> In thy samskaras thou wilt continue to live and thou wilt reap in future existences the harvest sown now and in the past.
> —Buddha

Sincere repentance overcomes a multitude of potentially devastating sin-caused imbalances in the energy-processes of the body, heart and mind. These negative seeds (samskaras) die one by one in the healthy soil of contrition, repentance and restitution.

Abortions, for which one fails to be repentant before death, will compound his problems in coming lives. The Laws governing Procreation are powerful Laws that teach their lessons in life after life. To blend with the immutable

Laws of God brings joy; to resist the wisdom and purpose of Divine Laws is to come under the rod of judgment.

If a man and woman conspire to abort a fetus or embryo seeking to come to birth in a timing determined through a soul-covenant, they add complex problems to their coming lives. Repentance and restitution bring the scales of divine justice into balance—and one is blessed in the timing of his or her future births and in the timing of giving birth. Timing, when blessed by God, is the key to all joys in the present life and in all lives to come. The wise tamper not with the birth-timings and soul-covenants of babes in the womb, for they revere the sacred laws of birth and life.

Positions of prominence, leadership in national governments, mass charismatic appeal—all require a dedication to upright behavior, morality and integrity—for one's decisions, words and works will affect numerous generations. To climb to the pinnacle of popularity and to fall ignominiously through pride, greed, conceit, or vanity—is to assure oneself future reincarnation-cycles in which the basic virtues will seek to be taught and re-taught until one earns once again a high placement in the halls of decision affecting the multitudes.

> He who exercises government by means of his virtue may be compared to the north polar star which keeps its place and all the stars turn towards it.
> —Confucius

"All they that take the sword shall perish with the sword." *(St. Matthew 26:52)* To live for the love of war; to desire to

dominate, control and rule by force; to mete unfair measures to the poor, the helpless and the downtrodden—is to attract to oneself coming lives in which he will die as he has given death to others; he will be maimed as he has maimed others; he will suffer as he has caused others to suffer. The pre-birth covenant with the soul is exact, precise, perfect.

Prejudice is as a magnet. The powerful energies within prejudice place entire races, nations and religions in bondage. Prejudice toward a race will attract one to birth in that race. Prejudice toward a religion will attract one to birth in that religion. The soul-covenant places a prejudiced person in the arena where the beasts of intolerance harass him until he recognizes the values of compassion and love.

Prejudice toward the opposite sex invites incarnations in situations and positions where one is the victim of prejudice because of his or her sex. The soul-covenant may require a prejudiced male to live a series of lives as a female; this is especially true of religious leaders whose prejudice toward women blinds their eyes to the sacred work of the Image of God through both male and female.

Each sex created by God is precious in the sight of God. When compassion and love replace prejudice and hate, the soul rejoices, for Great Lessons have been learned and Mighty Energies have been transposed into the light of Eternal Virtue.

> Father, grant that my soul may merge into the light, and be no more thrust back into the illusion of earth.
> —Synesius
> Student of Hypatia

> But if he shall have sinned once, twice, or thrice, they shall reject that soul sending it back again into the world according to the sin that it may have committed.
>
> —*Pistis Sophia**

PRE-DAY COVENANT

> In a dream, in a vision of the night, when deep sleep falleth upon men, in slumberings upon the bed; Then He (God) openeth the ears of men, and sealeth their instruction.
>
> —Job 33:15, 16

In the night during sleep, God seals His instruction into the Soul as a Covenant for the coming day. This *Pre-Day Covenant* occurs each night and is fulfilled during the daytime actions and associations. A Truth-seeker who realizes that a Soul-Covenant is being fulfilled each day of his life can begin to understand the soul and its record; he can also begin to comprehend the cycles and mathematics through which God is creating him in His Image.

The soul is speaking the language of law and virtue while one is awake and asleep. Thus, he who learns of divine laws and virtues becomes knowledgeable in the language of the soul.

The dreams recalled upon awakening in the morning contain the symbols of one's placement and progress on the Path of Virtue. The more a devotee comes into Self-Realization and Soul-Realization, the more clearly can his soul communicate directly with his heart and mind during dreams and during the waking state.

The Laws and Commandments of God revealed by the

---

*A book claiming to set forth the teachings of Jesus as communicated to Mary Magdalene.

Great Teachers are *Laws of the Soul.* Therefore, as one fulfills these sacred statutes, he comes into timing with his soul and its Covenants with God. *"I will put my law in their inward parts, and write it in their hearts."* *(Jeremiah 31:33)*

One who *dedicates* each new day to God by speaking a Prayer of Dedication works hand in hand with the Creator —and the Soul-Covenants become as Cornucopias filled with God's choicest blessings. If an aspirant on the Path continues to neglect or ignore the basic Commandments, he moves out of timing with God's Good for him; consequently, he attracts reprovings in the form of painful lessons. Each of these lessons is part of the soul's covenant for him to learn the difference between right and wrong, the difference between God's Will and self-will, and the difference between dedication and wastefulness.

The dedication of each day unites one with the purpose and intent of the soul in its Pre-Day Covenant with God. When this important dedication is spoken each morning, a closeness is established with the Creator—and His Love, Wisdom and Joy increasingly permeate the minutes and hours of the day. In this, a devotee begins his direct union with God; and the Spirit of God, teaching and revealing during each moment of the day and the night, becomes his Omnipresent Instructor, Guide, Counselor, Beloved; the Source and Power of All-Good.

GOOD

Beloved, follow not that which is evil, but that which is good. He that doeth good is of God: but he that doeth evil hath not seen God. —3 John 11

He that is really Good can never be unhappy. He that is really wise can never be perplexed. He that is really brave is never afraid.

The Good man does not grieve that other people do not recognize his merits. His only anxiety is lest he should fail to recognize theirs. —Confucius

To do good to others is a meritorious act, to hurt others is a sin. —Mahabharata

Good deeds are trophies erected in the hearts of men.
—Zenophon

What is thy art? To be good. —Marcus Aurelius

The scent of flowers does not travel against the wind, nor that of sandalwood, or of Tagara and Mallika flowers, but the odor of good people travels even against the wind; a good man pervades every place.

The splendid chariots of kings wear away; the body also comes to old age but the virtue of the good never ages, thus the good teach to each other.

Buddha
—*Dhammapada*

Depart from evil, and do good; seek peace, and pursue it.
—Psalm 34:14

The steps of a good man are ordered by the Lord: and he delighteth in his way. —Psalm 37:23

A good man out of the good treasure of the heart bringeth forth good things: and an evil man out of the evil treasure bringeth forth evil things.

Jesus
—*St. Matthew 12:35*

ETERNAL AND EVERLASTING

From everlasting to everlasting, thou art God. —Psalm 90:2

Give thanks to the Creator of all things: his love is everlasting. —Apocrypha

The eternal God is thy refuge, and underneath are the everlasting arms.
Moses
—Deuteronomy 33:27

The Lord hath appeared of old unto me, saying, Yea, I have loved thee with an everlasting love: therefore with lovingkindness have I drawn thee. —Jeremiah 31:3

There is, O monks, an Unborn, Unoriginated, Uncreated, Unformed. Were there not, O monks, This Unborn, Unoriginated, Uncreated, Unformed, there would be no escape from the world of the born, originated, created, formed.
Buddha
—Udana 80-81

The only security for happiness is to have a mind filled with the love of the infinite and the eternal. —Spinoza

The renown which riches or beauty confer is fleeting and frail; virtue remains bright and eternal. —Sallust

Only virtue wins eternal Fame. —Petrarch

The gift of God is eternal life.
Saint Paul
—Romans 6:23

My sheep hear my voice, and I know them, and they follow me: And I give unto them eternal life.
Jesus
—St. John 10:27, 28

18

THE REALITY OF ETERNALITY

Lord, make me an instrument of your peace; where there is hatred, let me sow love; where there is injury, pardon; where there is doubt, faith; where there is despair, hope; where there is darkness, light; and where there is sadness, joy.

O Divine Master, grant that I may not so much seek to be consoled as to console; to be understood as to understand; to be loved as to love; for it is in giving that we receive, it is in pardoning that we are pardoned, and it is in dying that we are born to eternal life. Amen.
—Saint Francis of Assisi

And the ransomed of the Lord shall return, and come to Zion with songs and everlasting joy upon their heads: they shall obtain joy and gladness, and sorrow and sighing shall flee away.
—Isaiah 35:10

Constants in the Cosmos

For I am the Lord, I change not.
—Malachi 3:6

> Fight the good fight of faith, lay hold on eternal life.
>
> Saint Paul
> —*1 Timothy 6:12*

In recent decades, the discovery of the speed of light has enabled scientists and astronomers to accurately measure the distances between the Earth and the Sun, the Earth and the Planets, the Sun and the Planets, the Sun and other Stars; the distances between Stars; and the distances between Galaxies. The measurable speed of light is a dependable, unvarying truth throughout the Universe; it is an eternal *constant*. With the discovery of the exact speed of light, mankind embarked on a new adventure in the realm of Cosmos Truths.

The *spiritual light* within the Laws and Commandments revealed by Moses and Jesus is also a universal and eternal constant. The spiritual light within each Law and Commandment *is* the Intelligence of God creating all Stars and Galaxies. These mathematical and cyclic Laws have infinite degrees and dimensions of spiritual light; however, they are the same building blocks throughout the Cosmos.

Man is close to the discovery of mighty secrets of the Cosmos that will enable him to decipher the Energy Language of the Stars and Galaxies. The *Numbers* and *Symbols* associated with the Laws and Commandments and their Cycles contain clues to the unveiling of the mysteries of God. He who reveres all Numbers, Symbols, Laws and Commandments—and knows them to be holy—will receive the Revelation Power of the Holy Ghost, the Magnifier of all living truths.

Moses and Jesus opened the Door to Cosmos. Moses began its opening and Jesus is completing its opening.

Rays and Tones of Cosmos Light are flooding the Earth

The Reality of Eternality

through the Laws and Commandments of God. If one follows the Path of Righteousness, the Path becomes a Path of Laws and Virtues that leads him on a journey into the wonder and majesty of Galaxy Creations.

The Intelligence of God within spiritual light suffuses the Universe. Virtues, as the spectrum of rainbow colors within spiritual light, are part of the constant of spiritual light in the Cosmos. God's Love and Virtues within His Eternal Spirit make of Man an eternal creation of love and virtues. Thus, love and virtues are ever-present energies within the Universal constant of spiritual light. Due to the love-virtues constant in the Cosmos, all Stars and Galaxies are united by the same principles of creation and working toward the same goals.

"I will praise thee; for I am fearfully and wonderfully made." (Psalm 139:14) Man, created in the Image of God, is a "wonderfully made" creation beyond Time and Space; the Divine Image within his soul is an eternal portion of the Omnipresent I Am. Through the Divine Image, the human spirit will commune with the Intelligence of God within the Universe.

Man has not yet begun to realize how wonderfully he is made. The Divine Image is gradually manifesting its holy antennas of virtues through which human beings will become Divine Beings at one with all levels and degrees of life within the Cosmos.

> The end of life is to be like God, and the soul following God will be like him.
> —Socrates

> O Thou, Who art the everlasting Essence of things beyond space and time and yet within them; Thou Who transcendest yet pervadest all

things; manifest Thyself to us, feeling after Thee, seeking Thee in the shades of ignorance, yet seeking nothing beside Thee.
—John Scotus Erigena
875 A.D.

O Eternal Light, shine into our hearts. O Eternal Goodness, deliver us from evil. O Eternal Power, be Thou our support. Eternal Wisdom, scatter the darkness of our ignorance. Eternal Pity, have mercy upon us.
—Alcuin
735–804 A.D.

Surely God would not have created such a being as man, with an ability to grasp the infinite, to exist only for a day! No, no, man was made for immortality.
—Abraham Lincoln

Life is the childhood of our immortality.
—Goethe

What a man does for others, not what they do for him, gives him immortality.
—Daniel Webster

This corruptible must put on incorruption, and this mortal must put on immortality.
Saint Paul
—*1 Corinthians 15:53*

THE GREAT LOGICS

Those who seek fame are under delusion. They forget that everything is ordained by the Great Disposer of all things—the Supreme Being, and

that all is due to the Lord and to no one else. It is the wise who say always, "It is thou, It is thou, O Lord," but the ignorant and the deluded say, "It is I, It is I."
— Buddha

"Where is the locality of truth?" "In the heart," said he; "for by the heart man knows truth; the heart therefore is the locality of truth."
— Brihad Aranyaka Upanishad

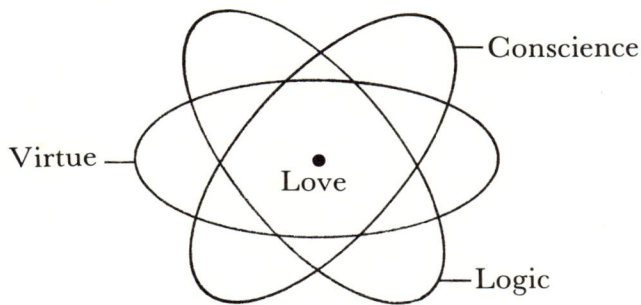

The Love of God is in the core of each atom providing energy for the body, heart, mind and soul. As one reaches toward God and His Love, the Creator reciprocates by rewarding him with atoms of energy for his physical body, the love-expression of his heart, the illumination of the mind, and the gifts of the soul.

Each atom in an enlightened consciousness is an energy-field consisting of Conscience, Virtue and Logic. Thus, when a devotee-initiate is anointed by the Love-Spirit of God, he experiences an expanding consciousness blessed with ever-increasing measures of Conscience, Virtue and Logic.

Even as each person on earth has an Intelligence Quotient (I.Q.), so does he have a Conscience Quotient, Virtue Quotient and Logic Quotient. The energy-quotient within Conscience, Virtue and Logic is determined by his attitudes toward each Law and Commandment of God.

The Glory or Presence of God within the soul gradually increases one's ability to understand the meaning and purpose of life on earth. As a devotee or initiate increases his degrees of virtue, conscience, logic and love, his *capacity* to receive prophecies and revelations from God is extended and expanded. Even as a small vessel has a limited capacity to hold liquid, so must the chalice of the consciousness be widened in its circumference before it has the capacity to comprehend the creation of the Earth and its purpose in the Universal Plan of God. In time, as the minds and hearts of men are spiritually quickened by the Creator, they will evolve the capacity to understand all that is occurring in the Cosmos. This ultimate in knowledge will manifest slowly over the ages as the human spirit increasingly dedicates to the Laws and Commandments of God.

The soul works through the reincarnation-cycles to bring forth within the heart and mind pure love, conscience, the virtues and logic. The *Great Logics* coming to birth through the cycles of birth and rebirth relate to God and His Plan. The first Great Logic pertains to the reality of God. If this logic is absent in the consciousness, the soul must work over the ages to make this paramount truth part of one's being. Through the Holy Law of Reincarnation, the soul continues to place one in atmospheres and environments where he may attain the Logic related to the reality of God as the Supreme and Eternal Spirit within all Creation.

Other Great Logics coming to birth through the reincarnation-cycles are: the Logic of the reality of the Soul and its eternality; the Logic of Reincarnation as a Holy Law through which man is being created in the Image of God; the Logic of the Afterlife; and the Logic that each individual is responsible for his thoughts, feelings and actions. If one or more Great Logics are missing from the consciousness, one attracts series of reincarnation-cycles specifically designed by the soul to awaken these cardinal truths.

After each virtue, hemisphere of conscience and great logic is active in the consciousness, the soul prepares the heart and mind for the spiritual quickenings that come through the Anointing Spirit of God. As the Anointing Spirit of God moves increasingly upon each virtue, conscience-hemisphere and logic, a devotee earns the "wedding garment" that qualifies him for marriage with his Lord.

The Laws and Commandments of God quicken, inspire and guide the conscience-hemispheres within the consciousness. After one has all hemispheres of the conscience active in the consciousness, he builds his life upon the strong foundation of Logic based upon the Commandments of Morality, Worship, Giving and Love. In this, the reincarnation-cycles have rewarded him with a Moral Conscience, a Sabbath Conscience, a Tithing Conscience and a Conscience inspiring him to fulfill the Commandments of Love.

If one should fall into the traps of lethargy, complacency and procrastination, the soul may use drastic measures to extricate him so that virtue-births, conscience-births and logic-births may occur in his being. Through reincarnation-cycles, the soul works to heal and purify all crystallized sin-energies within the heart and mind.

Persons born with beautiful talents from past lives are tested by the soul to see if they will use these talents for self-glory or for the glory of God. If one uses his talents for self-glory, he will experience reincarnation-cycles that will impress upon him the importance of the Virtue of Humility and the Logic of the Love-Commandments.

The Laws of God governing the soul and creating the individual into a *Being* of Illumined Virtues, Conscience and Logic are the same Laws governing the Sun, the Moon and the Planets; they are the same Laws revealed by the Great Teachers. If the consciousness has yet to identify the Logic within a Holy Law or Commandment, one will continue to experience reincarnation-cycles related to the attaining of this identification. For example, if the consciousness cannot identify with the logic within a Commandment of Morality, one will experience life after life until identification is made, thereby qualifying him for the next stages of logic within the reincarnation-cycles. The same is true of uniting with the Logic within the Commandment of Sabbath-Day Worship, the Holy Law of Tithing, the Commandment of Love, the Law of Karma, and the Law of Reincarnation. Gradually, through numerous cycles of rebirth on earth, the consciousness mind and heart make the necessary identifications.

Each Law and Commandment of God may be likened to the car of a train. If one or more cars of the train are not securely on the track, the train cannot travel forward to its destination. So it is with each Holy Law and Commandment: when each Law and Commandment is loved and lived as a logical and beautiful part of God's Plan, one is then free to move forward toward the goal of the Godhead.

A consciousness-identification with a Holy Law or Commandment may require ages of time involving numerous reincarnation-cycles. The Patience of God, working through the eternality of the soul, provides one with countless opportunities to make the essential consciousness-identifications. Each consciousness-identification with the *Logic* of a Holy Law is a mighty victory indelibly inscribed upon the record of the soul.

Patience is a holy virtue filled with the Love and Wisdom of God. He who serves and teaches with patience and love assists his fellow man to perceive the wisdom inherent within each Great Logic.

PATIENCE

Patience is the companion of wisdom. —Saint Augustine

Adopt the pace of nature; her secret is patience. —Emerson

Patience is a necessary ingredient of genius. —Disraeli

Patience and diligence, like faith, remove mountains.
—William Penn

Patience is one of the greatest forms of giving.
—Ann Ree Colton

He that has patience may compass anything.
—Francois Rabelais

He who has learned to suffer with patience will be purified and will be the chosen instrument for the alleviation of suffering. —Buddha

Nothing can be done at once hastily and prudently. It takes a long time to bring excellence to maturity. —Publilius Syrus

Genius is eternal patience. —Michelangelo

In your patience possess ye your souls.

> Jesus
> —*St. Luke 21:19*

The Virtue of Holy Poverty

> Blessed are the poor in spirit: for theirs is the kingdom of heaven.
>
> Jesus
> —*Saint Matthew 5:3*

> As God comprises all things, so a man who is pure and poor comprises all virtue in a love that is simple and single, and in this love he performs all virtuous acts, and all the virtues are within him and exist side by side with poverty. For only he is poor in the right way to whom virtues have become as his own nature.
>
> —From the *Book of the Poor in Spirit*

> The Saints invariably say that nothing whatever can disturb the fixity they have in God. Real sin is any disobedience to the law of divine love, any departure from the life of Jesus Christ. He is the form and essence of all things. What, then, is real virtue? Anything wrought in the soul by divine love alone, for that effects naught but its like.
>
> Such is the doctrine of spiritual poverty. Into this true poverty lead us, O superful goodness of God. Amen.
>
> —Meister Eckhart

In the Divine Marriage, God's Dowry is His Universe; the devotee's dowry is his love and virtues. The devotee gives his dowry to God; the Creator gives the devotee His

Dowry—the Universe. Thus, in the Divine Marriage, one rests serenely secure in the Love of God, and his understanding of the Universe opens wider each day as the Divine Marriage progresses.

Holy poverty builds a bond of trust between the devotee and his Beloved. Through the Virtue of Holy Poverty, one remains centered and polarized within the Love-Presence and Providential Grace of God who provides all his needs in perfect timing.

The Paradox of Holy Poverty is that one does not become "poor" in the sense of not having. By giving all to God, and God giving all to him in the Divine Marriage, each gains what the other has: the Creator gains the devotee's love and trust, and the devotee gains access to the secrets and mysteries of the Universe.

In physical marriage, when bride and bridegroom truly love one another, they literally live these words: "Beloved one, all I have is yours." Therefore, when husband and wife are made one flesh through holy matrimony, whatever they give to each other remains for the two to share; it is not lost, for it is given to the mate with whom one is united. So it is in the Divine Marriage with God: the devotee does not lose anything if he truly loves God and releases all to Him. As long as one knows in his heart that all he has given to God belongs to God, he remains in the Divine Marriage through Holy Poverty. The moment one feels that anything belongs to him, he soils the purity of his union with God.

The Paradox of Holy Poverty as the key to Universal Bountifulness is told in these words of Jesus: *"All things that the Father hath are mine."* *(St. John 16:15)* This state of Divine Union is attained and sustained through the Virtue of Holy Poverty as exemplified and taught by the Lord Jesus and His Saints.

The Divine Marriage begins in the heart, takes place in

the heart, and is sanctified in the heart. The love in the heart sends light into the mind and into the world. As one increases his love for God each day, the Love of God reciprocates, thereby magnifying and multiplying the heart's love and the mind's light. In this way, the Greater Illuminations come as the natural results of union with the Creator of the Universe.

In modern times, dedicated servants of God are often called upon to live in the world as householders active in family and community activities and responsibilities, as well as spiritual dedications. In such instances, Holy Poverty is a state of heart and mind in which one *knows* that God is governing his life and providing for each need.

All servants of God are *stewards* entrusted with the Word of God and the physical means of preserving, prospering and glorifying the Word. Holy Poverty is to know in every atom of one's being that he is but a steward and not a possessor. A devotee who is possessive of any one or any thing invites reprovings. Holy Poverty keeps the heart free from covetousness and open to Grace and Truth.

In a marriage based upon true and pure love, any amount of indebtedness accumulated by one previous to the marriage is happily paid in full by the mate who is financially able; thereafter, the marriage may proceed with joy rather than worry, fear and guilt. So it is in the *Marriage* between the Creator and His servant who gives all to his Lord in the spirit of Restitution and Holy Poverty: The Creator rewards wholehearted love by paying in full all manner of soul-debts accumulated by one over the ages and the eternities. This awesome Anointing of Love from God blesses His faithful servant with a cleansed soul-record, thereby freeing him to greater ranges of serving, understanding and creating.

> Lady Holy Poverty, God keep you, with your sister Holy Humility.   —Saint Francis of Assisi

There is that maketh himself rich, yet hath nothing; there is that maketh himself poor, yet hath great riches.

Solomon
—*Proverbs 13:7*

Charge them that are rich in this world, that they be not highminded, nor trust in uncertain riches, but in the living God, who giveth us richly all things to enjoy.

Saint Paul
—*1 Timothy 6:17*

The Nature of God

For I have not spoken of myself; but the Father which sent me, he gave me a commandment, what I should say, and what I should speak. And I know that his commandment is life everlasting: whatsoever I speak therefore, even as the Father said unto me, so I speak.

Jesus
—*St. John 12:49, 50*

In the world today, persons in inspired states of heart and mind create beautiful songs, poems and parables; in future ages, the Galaxy Consciousness will enable illumined individuals to draw upon energies of inspiration unknown in the present era. *"For the Father loveth the Son, and sheweth him all things that himself doeth: and he will shew him greater works than these, that ye may marvel."* (St. John 5:20)

The equal blending between the scientific, philosophical, spiritual and creative capabilities within the human spirit will make of man a Being of Cosmos Light in prototypal resemblance to the Lord Jesus. The more one becomes like

Jesus, the more he will have the Galaxy Consciousness—and the more he will contribute to the Creation of the Universe.

The Virtues of Jesus are *Eternal* and *Cosmos Virtues*. Those who seek to emulate the Virtues of the Lord Jesus are the meek of the earth and the children of the Resurrection. As children of the Resurrection, their hearts and minds become as chalices to receive the Anointing Spirit of God.

> When the Son of man shall come in his glory, and all the holy angels with him, then shall he sit upon the throne of his glory: and before him shall be gathered all nations: and he shall separate them one from another, as a shepherd divideth his sheep from the goats: and he shall set the sheep on his right hand, but the goats on the left. Then shall the King say unto them on his right hand, Come, ye blessed of my Father, inherit the kingdom prepared for you from the foundation of the world.
>
> Jesus
> —*St. Matthew 25:31-34*

The prophecy of Jesus pertaining to the separation of "the sheep" from "the goats" relates to the sheep, or meek, who will work *knowingly* with God in the Creation of new Solar Systems. Since the coming of Jesus, mankind has been experiencing increasing divisions between the sheep and the goats. The sheep, as little children, trust in their Father's Wisdom and Love. The goats are those who continually resist walking the Way or Path of Virtue.

As the Earth reaches toward its last days, the "sheep" will be persons who are cognizant of Love, Virtues, Conscience and Logic as Eternal aspects of God's Glory. The "goats" will be those who fail to understand the eternality of Love and Virtue. In the Plan of Everlasting Life, all laggard individuals are given endless opportunities in countless galaxies to make the necessary identification of the eternality of Love, Virtues, Conscience and Logic. Gradually, over the milleniums in numerous solar systems, the goats will begin to fulfill the *higher* design of the Image of God within them. When this occurs, they will become the sheep or meek from whom will come future Saviours in solar systems yet to be.

It is the nature of God to create as many stars and galaxies as is necessary for each one of His children to learn of the importance of Love, Virtues, Conscience and Logic. It is the nature of God to reincarnate one of His children over and over in countless lives and innumerable solar systems until he becomes law-minded, love-motivated and worship-enlightened.

When one gains a glimpse of the reality of eternity, he may witness life on earth and recognize its various stages as part of an Eternal Drama. Goats are sheep in the making. Sheep are meek in the making. The meek are Saviours in the making—Saviours of future solar systems. This is the reality of eternity: the long climb up the Mountain of Illumination to become like Jesus in Love, Virtue, Conscience and Logic. The Image of God in each person is the Perfect Design, and the Universe is the Perfect Setting for the fulfillment of this Design.

The Commandment of Everlasting Life, as taught by Jesus, began for man a new scientific-spiritual comprehension of the reality of eternity. As one ascends the Mountain of Illumination, he begins to experience the Glory of God within spiritual gifts. These dimensional graces or gifts are his means of communion with the Glory of God within the Commandment of Everlasting Life.

God is Eternal. Man, created in the Image of God, is Eternal. The Laws creating Man in the Image of God are Eternal. The Gifts and Graces quickened through the sanctification of virtues are Eternal.

A person may live and work in hundreds or thousands of lives before he adds one atom of conscience to his consciousness or one atom of love to his heart. This is the nature of God; this is the reality of eternality—for that one atom of conscience or atom of love is of the *Soul,* and will henceforth become an eternal part of one's being.

As one adds atoms of love, virtues, conscience and logic over the ages and the eternals, he eventually reaches the time when he will know himself to be created in the Image of God. He will delight in this knowledge; he will rejoice in this knowledge. And he will willingly accept the Eternal Way as God's Way; the Eternal Image, as God's Image.

Spiritual birth is a work of the ages and the eternals. Spiritual illumination is a work of the solar systems and the galaxies. Blessed is he who accepts his placement in the Eternal Plan of God; for through acceptance comes quickening, and through quickening comes enlightenment.

> The Day of Resurrection! Earth tell it out abroad! The Passover of Gladness, the Passover of God! From death to Life Eternal, from this world to the sky, our Christ has brought us over with hymns of victory.
> —Saint John of Damascus

Each living soul created in the Image of God is a potential Jesus. After one attains Sainthood, he is closer to the time of his becoming like Jesus. As the Light of the Christ fills his being, he will comprehend Cosmos and the Will of God; he will work with God in the Creation of Solar Systems.

When one becomes "like"* Jesus in Love, Virtue, Conscience and Logic, he will become the Saviour of a Solar System. The *sacred name* of every living soul is written on a star-yet-to-be at a future moment in Time and Space. When one becomes the Saviour of the Solar System sounding his sacred name, he will have attained his true Sonship in God; he will become a Being of Light living within the Wisdom and Love of the Divine Image.

"I am the Way, the Truth and the Life." (St. John 14:6) Jesus is the Way to perfection; He is the Blueprint for all human-spirit souls and all human-spirit solar systems. The Image of God within the soul of each person will manifest the perfect Jesus-likeness at some time in the eternals. It will require countless Galaxy homes before the children of men become the Sons of God emulating Jesus in Love, Virtue, Conscience and Logic.

Union with the Glory of God within one Solar System provides great Illuminations; however, union with the Glory of God within the Galaxies produces the Divine-Image Illuminations whereby one becomes a Saviour Soul. The perfected Saints and other enlightened personages are close to attaining the Image-of-God Quickenings that will make of them Saviour Souls.

Before one becomes a Saviour Soul in one of God's innumerable Solar Systems, he must walk the *Galaxy Treadmill*. Eventually, the least virtuous person on Earth will reach the spiritual heights due to his walking the Galaxy Treadmill. This Truth is written in every soul, for Man is created in the Image of the Eternal God.

The heart and mind of man are working toward the time when they will understand the purpose of *every* star and galaxy in the Universe. Such is the nature of Eternal

---

*1 John 3:1–3

Life. And such is the nature of the Image of God within Man.

The physical Universe is Eternal Time; the spiritual Universe is Eternal Timelessness. What is not accomplished by Man in one solar system is accomplished by him in another solar system. There is no end to the multiplying of stars and galaxies. For each galaxy known to man, there are countless other galaxies yet to be discovered.

Space is without end, infinite. One dimension leads to another dimension; one infinitude leads to another infinitude. Who can comprehend the magnitude, the infinity, the eternality of God? The Christ, the Son Beloved of God, is the One who comprehends the Magnificence and Illuminescence of God. And the Christ, as the Door to All-Knowledge and All-Truth, is revealing to receptive hearts and minds portion after portion of the Puzzle, the Riddle, the Goal.

No hand can withstay the Eternal Way. No heart can halt the pulse beat of the Universe. No mind can resist the Perfection that is to manifest. For the Christ has come. His work with the Solar Systems has always been, is, and will ever be. Man has *begun* to know the Christ through the Miracles of Jesus. Man, in emulating Jesus, will come to know the Christ; and the "greater works than these shall ye do," as prophesied by Jesus, shall become a way of life.

The soul is man's vehicle from solar system to solar system. The virtues of the soul earned in past solar systems are expressed in the present solar system. The virtues not earned in past solar systems press forth in the present solar system. Thus, the great in soul become greater in soul, and the less in soul become more in soul.

The soul, as taught by the wise of all ages, contains a *Divine Spark*. This Divine Spark is the Image of God. This Spark is the Igniter, the Illuminator, the Flame, the Torch, the Truth.

THE REALITY OF ETERNALITY

The Spark Divine is as small as the smallest atom and as broad and wide as all heavens and all starry galaxies. This Spark manifests the lesser and the greater Miracles, the lesser and the greater Anointings, the lesser and the greater Illuminations.

Life ends, but the light of a life never ends. The light of each life lives eternally in the soul and in the Cosmos. The light of each life becomes a thread in the Mantle of God encompassing all Creation, enfolding all Universes seen and unseen.

When one dedicates the light of each life to God, the light of each life becomes aglow with the radiance of Pure Truth and Pure Love. God as Truth becomes an Abiding Presence in the light of each life through the dedication of this light to Him. When one places the light of his life on God's Holy Altar, he has in his hand the key to all Doors, all Kingdoms, all Dimensions.

Dedication is the Bride of Illumination. Dedication to God is the Path, the Straight Way. All who walk this Path are the blessed, the meek, the way-showers, the prophetically-quickened, the God-Realized, the Revelator-Apostles of the Lord Christ.

God is Perfect. His Love is Perfect. His Law is Perfect. His Plan is Perfect. In seeking to attain Perfection, one increasingly unites with the Perfection of God. Through Perfect Love and Virtues, one renders a Perfect Service for God.

The harmony of the Universe is perfect, even as all other aspects of the Creator are perfect. As one seeks to perfect his virtues, he blends with the harmony of Universal Creation. When one begins to feel a oneness with all celestial bodies, he has made a significant breakthrough in understanding the purpose of his own existence and his future in the Cosmos as a creation of God imaged in His likeness.

The multitudinous ills that plague mankind are loud voices seeking to turn hearts and minds to the Laws governing the harmony of Universal Creation. One by one, prodigal sons and daughters are beginning to return to the protection and providence of their Heavenly Father.

While the canvas of each day is being splattered and stained by the thoughtless and selfish actions of the uninitiated, there are areas in the canvas that contain the rainbow hues of charity, charitableness, mercy, compassion and love. Until the uninitiated become initiated into the Wisdom, Love and Grace of God, the Creator will continue to send Teachers to tell of the Beauty of His Laws and the Perfection of His Plan.

All problems besetting the human spirit will gradually be solved and resolved when reverent national leaders come forth to lead their people onto the Path of Virtue. When the spirit that moved Gandhi moves the hearts of leaders in the governments of the nations, mankind will change its direction toward the Golden Age envisioned and prophesied by all Great Souls. When the spirit of Saint Francis fills the hearts of all servants of God, the religions of the earth will reach the pinnacle of their service to humankind. And when the spirit of the Lord Jesus fills the hearts and minds of all souls, the Sun, the Moon, the Planets, the Stars and the Galaxies will reveal their mighty purposes within the Eternal Plan of God.

> The most incomprehensible thing about the universe is that it is comprehensible.
> —Albert Einstein

> The perfecting of one's self is the fundamental base of all progress and all moral development.
> —Confucius

The Reality of Eternality

Among thousands of men, one perchance strives for perfection, even among those successful strivers, one perchance knows Me in essence.
—Bhagavad Gita

Be ye therefore perfect, even as your Father which is in heaven is perfect.

Jesus
—*St. Matthew 5:48*

BIBLIOGRAPHY

Babcock, Merton C. (Editor), *Wisdom of the Koran,* Peter Pauper Press, New York, 1966.

Ballou, Robert O., in collaboration with Friedrich Spiegelberg, *The Bible of the World,* Kegan Paul, Trench Trubner and Company, Ltd., London, 1939.

Barborka, Geoffrey A., *A Glossary of Sanskrit Terms,* Point Loma Publications, Inc., San Diego, California 1972.

Barnett, Lincoln, *The Universe and Dr. Einstein* (Revised Edition), William Morrow and Company, New York, 1950.

Bartlett, John, *Familiar Quotations,* Little, Brown and Company, Boston, 1968.

Blackman, Everett, *Astrology: Worlds Visible and Invisible (Periodical),* American Federation of Astrologers, Inc.

Bryant, Anita and Green, Bob, *At Any Cost,* Fleming H. Revell Company, Old Tappan, New Jersey, 1978.

Butler, Alban, *Lives of the Saints,* Benziger Brothers, Inc., New York, 1955.

Cairns, Huntington and Hamilton, Edith (Editors), *Plato: The Collected Dialogues,* Princeton University Press, New Jersey, 1961.

Carus, Paul, *Gospel of Buddha,* Omen Press, Tucson, Arizona, 1922.

Cihlar, Fr. Many (Compiled by), *Mystics at Prayer,* Rosicrucian Press, San Jose, California.

Collin, Rodney, *The Theory of Celestial Influence,* Samuel Weiser, New York, 1975.

Colton, Ann Ree, *Islands of Light,* ARC Publishing Company, Glendale, California, 1953.
Colton, Ann Ree, *Kundalini West,* ARC Publishing Company, Glendale, California, 1978.
Cott, Allan, with Jerome Agel and Eugene Boe, *Fasting, The Ultimate Diet,* Bantam Books, Inc., New York, 1975.
Coulson, John (Editor), *The Saints,* Hawthorn Books, Inc., New York, 1960.
de Lange, Nicholas, *Apocrypha: Jewish Literature of the Hellenistic Age,* The Viking Press, New York, 1978.
Easwaren, Eknath, *Gandhi the Man,* Nilgiri Press, Petaluma, California, 1978.
Edwards, Tryon, *Dictionary of Thoughts,* Standard Book Company, New York, 1952.
Einstein, Albert, *Out of My Later Years,* Littlefield, Adams and Company, Totowa, New Jersey, 1967.
Encyclopedia Britannica
Fahy, Benen (Translator), Introduction and notes by Hermann Placid, *The Writings of St. Francis of Assisi,* Franciscan Herald Press, Chicago, Illinois, 1963.
Feng, Gia-Fu and Jane English (Translators), *Tao Te Ching,* Random House, Inc., New York, 1972.
Fox, John, *Fox's Book of Martyrs,* Zondervan Publishing House, Grand Rapids, Michigan, 1967.
Fozdar, Jamshed D., *The God of Buddha,* Asia Publishing House, New York, 1973.
Friedman, Herbert, *The Amazing Universe,* The National Geographic Society, Washington, D.C., 1975.
Gandhi, M. K., *The Story of My Experiments with Truth,* Navajivan Publishing House, Ahmedabad, India, 1927.
Gersh, Harry, *The Sacred Books of the Jews,* Stein and Day, New York, 1968.
Great Religions of the World, National Geographic Society, Washington, D.C., 1971, 1978.
Hall, Manly P., *Reincarnation: The Cycle of Necessity,* The Philosopher's Press, Los Angeles, California, 1941.
Happold, F. C., *Mysticism: A Study and an Anthology,* Penguin Books, Baltimore, Maryland, 1975.

Hauser, Ernest O., *Inside the Bible's "Hidden Books,"* Reader's Digest, October, 1978, New York.
Head, Joseph and S. L. Cranston (Compiled and Edited by), *Reincarnation: An East-West Anthology,* The Julian Press Inc., New York, 1961.
Holy Bible. King James Version.
Hume, Robert E., *The World's Living Religions,* Charles Scribner's Sons, New York, 1959.
Humphreys, Christmas (Editor), *The Wisdom of Buddhism,* Random House, New York, 1961.
Jowett, Benjamin (Translator), *The Dialogues of Plato,* Great Books of the Western World, Encyclopedia Britannica, Inc., Chicago, Illinois, 1952.
Koran.
Lieber, Arnold L., M.D., *The Lunar Effect,* Anchor Press/Doubleday, Garden City, New York, 1978.
Montapert, Alfred Armand (Compiled and Edited by), *Distilled Wisdom,* Prentice-Hall, Inc., Englewood Cliffs, N.J., 1964.
Perry, Whitall, N., *A Treasury of Traditional Wisdom,* Simon and Schuster, New York, 1971.
Prince, Derek, *Shaping History Through Prayer and Fasting,* Fleming H. Revell Company, New Jersey, in Association with Derek Prince Publications, Florida, 1973.
Reinhold, H. A. (Editor), *The Soul Afire,* Image Books/Doubleday and Company, Inc., Garden City, New York, 1973.
Riley, Frank L., M.D., *The Bible of Bibles,* J. F. Rowny Press, Santa Barbara, California, 1928.
Runes, Dagobert D., *Pictorial History of Philosophy,* Bramhall House, New York, 1969.
Satprakashananda, Swami, *Hinduism and Christianity,* Vedanta Society of St. Louis, Missouri, 1975.
Schweitzer, Albert, *Out of My Life and Thought,* Henry Holt and Company, Inc., New York, 1949.
Smith, J. Harold, *Fast Your Way to Health,* Thomas Nelson Publishers, New York, 1979.
Spring 1975, *An Annual of Archetypal Psychology and Jungian Thought,* Spring Publications, New York City, New York, 1975.

Stevenson, Burton, *The Home Book of Quotations,* Dodd, Mead and Company, New York, 1967.
Strong, Mary (Editor), *Letters of the Scattered Brotherhood,* Harper and Row, Publishers, New York, 1948.
Sukul, Sri Deva Ram, *Yoga and Self-Culture,* Yoga Institute of America, New York, 1947.
Syed, Dr. M. Hafiz (Compiler), *Thus Spake Prophet Muhammad,* Sri Ramakrishna Math Publication Department, Madras, India, 1972.
The Spiritual Instructions of Saint Seraphim of Sarov, The Dawn Horse Press, Los Angeles, California, 1973.
Underhill, Evelyn, *Mysticism,* E. P. Dutton and Company, Inc., New York, 1961.
Wagner, Norton, *Unveiling the Universe,* Research Publishers, Scranton, Pennsylvania, 1936.
Willard, J. H., *Once in Seven Years,* Harry Altemus Company, Philadelphia, Pennsylvania, 1906.
Wilson, Epiphanius (with critical and biographical sketches by), *Sacred Books of the East,* The Colonial Press, London, New York, 1900.
Woods, Ralph L. (Editor), *Behold the Man,* The MacMillan Company, New York, 1944.
Woods, Ralph L., (Editor), *The Sun,* The World Publishing Company, New York, 1971.

INDEX
Inclusive of Quotation References

Abelard, Peter (1079-1142) 63
Abortion(s) 193, 430, 431
Abraham 42
Absolution 366
Adams, John 180
Addiction(s) 144, 400-402
Addison, Joseph (1672-1719) 214, 234
Adepts 170
Adoration 254, 255, 259, 260, 329
Adultery 12, 61, 192-194, 230, 352, 363
Adversary Principle 425
Aesop (fl. 620-560 B.C.) 213, 287
Afterlife 155, 423, 445
Agape Spirit 127, 367
Agnosticism 56, 62, 63, 314, 349
Ahimsa (See Harmlessness)
Air 107
á Kempis, Thomas, Saint (1380-1471) 27, 85, 186, 248, 279, 282, 292, 330, 334, 360, 406, 428
Alcohol 401
Alcuin (735-804) 442
Ali (43 B.C.-17 A.D.) 236

Ali, Ibu-Abu-Taleb (602-661) 223
Almsgiving 82, 86, 113, 157, 183, 220, 221, 247, 254, 309, 311, 399
Altar(s) 215-219, 285, 338, 368, 457
Amiel, Henri Frederic (1821-1881) 213
Ancestor(s) 166, 312-322, 423
Ancestral Armageddon 313-322
Androgynous Virtues 138, 139
Angel(s) 53, 62, 84, 111, 112, 126, 152, 172, 177, 212, 232, 253, 279, 284-286, 288, 310, 311, 318, 329, 360, 406, 452
Anger 241, 322, 381, 400, 401
Animal(s) 52, 78, 92, 146
Anointed 159
  Apostles 366, 421
  Conscience 191, 196-201, 218
  Marriage 208, 209, 232
  Teachers 417, 418, 429

Anointing(s)   42, 62, 106, 111
    -113, 116, 117, 126, 157,
    159, 196-198, 212, 245-
    247, 251, 272, 304, 330,
    421, 422, 450, 457
  Baptismal   123, 128
  Divine-Marriage   116, 177,
    197, 209, 240, 244, 245,
    318, 348
  Spirit of God   105, 107-
    109, 111, 113, 115, 117,
    118, 121, 126, 128, 137,
    155, 177, 191, 197, 201,
    272, 291, 304, 305, 311,
    369, 443, 445, 452
Antichrist   85, 268
Anti-virtues   85, 86, 88-90,
    133, 179, 229, 314, 322,
    393, 395, 400, 401, 409,
    423-425
Apocrypha   12, 13, 30, 46,
    124, 162, 206, 222, 233,
    297, 360, 378, 412, 438
Apostle(s) of Jesus   67, 68,
    159, 170, 198, 403, 406,
    457
Apostolic Grace   321
  Gift(s)   173, 366, 422
  Virtues   398
Archangel(s)   26, 406
Archetype   131
Archetypal Prophecies   164,
    167-173, 395
Aristotle (384-322 B.C.)   3, 21,
    30, 39, 109, 296, 319
Art   167, 274, 293, 305, 427
Asking   282
Astronomers   34, 307, 439,
    440
Atheism   56, 62, 63, 310, 314,
    349, 357
Atom(s)   131, 132, 146, 148,
    309, 369, 370, 443, 454,
    457

Atonement   (See Restitution)
Attitude(s)   128, 144, 155,
    160, 166, 188, 210, 230,
    254, 276, 287, 352, 353,
    371, 382, 416
Augustine, Saint (354-430
    A.D.)   3, 25, 82, 95, 140,
    164, 237, 264, 266, 279,
    281, 319, 373, 419, 447
Aura   311-313
Aurelius, Marcus (121-180
    A.D.)   38, 436
Aurobindo, Sri (1872-1950)
    236
Bach, Johann Sebastian   78
Baha'u'llah (1817-1892)   192
Baptism   122, 123, 128, 240
Beatitudes   23, 24
Beauty   53, 57, 78, 107-110,
    127, 131, 154, 159, 160,
    182, 192, 212, 229, 232,
    274, 288, 315, 345, 425,
    458
  of God   247, 266, 283, 301,
    303, 383
Beecher, Henry Ward (1813-
    1887)   64
Beethoven, Ludwig van (1770-
    1827)   100
Benevolence   93, 222, 367
Bernard, Saint (1091-1153)
    90, 111, 134, 280
Betrothal Sacrament   211
Bhagavad Gita   8, 9, 39, 50,
    57, 75, 77, 140, 163, 173,
    175, 296, 315, 316, 331,
    384, 386, 412, 419, 459
Birth   52, 54, 55, 207, 228,
    229, 232, 319, 369, 390,
    431, 432
Blake, William (1757-1827)
    107, 378
Blessing(s)   81, 84, 106, 108,
    115, 116, 126, 133, 151,

INDEX 467

155–157, 159, 199, 208, 210, 212, 218, 226, 228, 232, 253, 271–273, 283–285, 329, 343, 345, 363, 375, 376, 404, 405, 435
Bliss   99, 108, 110–114, 130, 135, 159, 196, 205, 224, 248, 298, 326, 372, 383, 384
   Anointing(s)   111, 113, 117
   Core   83, 99, 112
   Fire   98, 102, 160
   Glory of God   102
   Presence of God   106, 111
Bodhisattva(s)   159, 398, 399
Boehme, Jacob (1575–1624)   53
Browning, Elizabeth Barrett (1806–1861)   40
Browning, Robert (1812–1889)   186
Bruyere, Jean de la (1645–1696)   404
Buddha (563–483 B.C.)   2, 14, 15, 30, 38, 40, 42, 46, 60, 74, 79, 92, 102, 110, 115, 130, 132, 174, 184, 205, 206, 234, 237, 238, 240, 241, 278, 296, 316, 342, 356, 375, 412, 413, 425, 431, 436, 438, 443, 447
Bulwer-Lytton, Edward George (1803–1873)   328, 361
Bunyan, John (1628–1688)   215, 227
Burns, Robert (1759–1796)   214

Candelabra of the Soul   159, 160
Carlyle, Thomas (1795–1881)   57, 236, 278
Cause and Effect, Law of   60
Celibacy   232

Centering   112, 311, 348, 369, 370
Cervantes, Miguel de Saavedra (1547–1616)   213, 292
Chakra(s)   99, 307–313, 347, 348
Character   56, 188–192, 201, 211, 222, 233; 241, 248, 328, 363
Charitable(ness)   57, 76, 93, 115, 190, 210, 320, 362, 364, 367, 397, 458
Charity   127, 360
Chastity   109, 232, 399, 458
Chaucer, Geoffrey (1340?–1400)   116
Cheerfulness   171, 214, 215
Chemistry   308
Cherubim   232
Children   51–53, 148, 190, 205, 214, 215, 218, 219, 226, 229, 231, 232, 267, 317, 319, 431
China   17, 250
Christ   22, 43, 68, 80–82, 84, 85, 90, 101, 106, 118, 119, 121, 123, 124, 126, 127, 132–136, 139, 145, 146, 164, 165, 171, 191, 195, 196, 240, 242–249, 255, 260, 261, 268, 272, 282, 302, 306, 307, 313, 320–322, 328, 330, 343, 345, 346, 366, 368–376, 397, 399, 405, 407, 408, 410, 421, 422, 427, 456, 457
   Dimensional Healing Power   320, 330, 345, 346, 368–376
   Mind   128, 136–138, 173, 304, 348, 369, 397, 407
   Principle   395
   Realization   132, 251
Christian(s)   61, 64, 69, 70

Christmas 122
Churchill, Winston (1874–1965) 220
Cicero (106–43 B.C.) 3, 22, 38, 74, 152, 184, 192, 209, 213, 214, 226, 248, 278
Colton, Ann Ree (1898–) 64, 71, 77, 96, 120, 140, 152, 167, 178, 192, 194, 200, 204, 233, 252, 286, 293, 307, 316, 334, 361, 365, 370, 374, 391, 404, 447
Coming Lives 61, 66, 144, 155, 193, 216, 251, 255, 267, 317, 320, 348, 350, 353, 354, 372, 377, 396, 430–433
Commandment of Everlasting Life 167, 259, 451, 453
Commandment(s) 22, 37, 41, 42, 47, 56, 60–62, 86, 104, 105, 113, 117, 128, 130, 150, 152, 210, 218, 250, 251, 275, 276, 287, 288, 303, 314, 321, 332, 338, 340, 343, 347, 349–357, 366, 416, 417, 434, 435
Commandments, Love 126, 239, 303, 329, 377, 380, 445, 446
 Sabbath Day 59–64, 126, 329, 397, 446
 Ten (See Ten Commandments)
Communion, Sacrament of 80–82, 228, 367
Compassion 57, 86, 115, 116, 138, 173, 190, 230, 241, 247, 313, 320, 330, 381, 427, 433, 458
Confession 136, 211, 216, 230, 242, 243, 253, 271, 276, 312, 318, 321, 322, 340–347, 358, 361, 362, 369, 371–373, 375, 394, 396, 401–403, 430
Confucius (556–479 B.C.) 18, 19, 30, 32, 42, 53, 85, 109, 149, 190, 192, 199, 214, 222, 277, 278, 330, 344, 361, 383, 404, 432, 436, 458
Conscience 40, 42, 44, 52, 55, 58, 66, 67, 120, 126, 129, 137, 146, 152–154, 165, 168, 169, 186–201, 208, 217, 222, 239, 243, 255, 284, 298, 299, 302, 303, 306, 308, 309, 311, 328, 330, 338–340, 342, 348, 352–357, 369, 370, 381, 400, 401, 409, 414, 417, 420, 423, 428, 443–446, 452–455
 Anointed 191, 196–201, 218
 Family 200
 Integrity Lens of 241
 Moral 56, 445
 National 200
 of the Cosmos 200
 Religious 200
 Sabbath 445
 Tithing 445
 World 67, 168, 200
Constants 439–441
Constellations 299, 406–408
Contrition 151, 276, 318, 321, 394, 431
Copernicus 22, 43
Cosmos 33–48, 54, 86, 94, 95, 116, 141, 142, 164, 165, 172, 200, 201, 248, 256–262, 298–301, 357, 406–410, 440–444, 451
Countenances of God 387–392
Courage 29, 182, 198, 226,

INDEX

227, 320, 404, 428
Covenant   350, 370, 420–435
  New   260, 261
  Pre-Birth   422
  Pre-Day   434, 435
  Pre-Solar-System   420–422
  Soul   413–435
Covetous(ness)   143, 208, 241, 314, 320, 354, 355
Crates of Mallus (2nd Century B.C.)   249
Creation(s), Pure   57, 76, 86, 117, 118, 126, 211, 212, 243, 253, 273, 274, 382
Creativity   57, 82, 112, 232, 273, 274, 313
Crucifixion   67, 72
Curse(s)   156, 157, 231
Cycle(s)   41, 47, 60, 86, 116, 122, 142, 176, 197, 227, 228, 231, 233, 313, 321, 369, 370, 372, 373, 379, 388, 393, 416, 420, 423, 428, 434
  Commandment   41
  Dedicated Creativity   228, 229
  Dedication   41
  Expiation   345, 373
  Fasting   176
  Fifty-Day   122
  Five-Hundred Year   42, 43
  Galaxy   40, 41, 414, 415
  Holy Day   122
  Holy Ghost   41, 121–130
  Initiatory   393
  Life   42, 369
  Lunar   122, 142, 231, 379–385, 401
  of Sleep   53
  Reincarnation   353, 356, 357, 390, 402, 413–435, 445, 446
  Sabbath   41, 59–64, 122, 218, 397
  Sacrament   41, 228
  Sacred   59
  Seasonal   122
  Seven-Year   424
  Sexual   228
  Solar   41, 122, 142, 381
  Soul   41, 141, 142, 209, 379
  Ten-Year   121–130
  Time   39–48, 59, 62, 63, 122, 172, 288, 312
  Tithing   228
  Truth   47
  Worship   41, 53, 59, 60, 122–152, 183, 194, 218, 228, 273, 333, 347, 397

Daniel (7th Century B.C.)   103
Dante, Alighieri (1265–1321)   28, 38, 95, 267
Da Vinci, Leonardo (1452–1519)   43, 305
Days of the Week   60, 61, 379
Death   186, 188, 199, 205, 207, 228, 247, 318, 369, 405, 423, 426
Dedication(s)   43, 54–56, 62, 78, 82, 101, 104, 106, 108, 113, 128, 129, 148, 157, 168, 169, 173, 176–179, 191, 198, 199, 218, 219, 223–226, 229, 232, 241, 250, 253, 266–275, 277, 287, 321, 322, 327, 329, 332, 338, 340, 345, 397, 399, 402, 405, 417, 418, 429, 432, 435, 457
  Prayer of   435
Demades (fl. 350 B.C.)   403
Depression   145, 381
Descarte, Rene (1596–1650)   95
Detachment   173, 174, 355

Devotion 42, 54, 55, 67, 104, 126, 154, 209, 212, 224, 226, 247, 254, 255, 305, 307, 383, 399, 417
Dhammapada (See Buddha)
Dharma 15, 358
Dignity 212, 427
Diligence 159, 289, 290–292, 336
Diogenes 252
Discernment 336–341
Discipline 143, 145
Disraeli, Benjamin (1804–1881) 236, 447
Divine Grace 53, 56, 59, 63, 86, 99, 101, 106, 112, 127, 131, 195, 242, 243, 274, 289, 333, 346, 350, 381, 395, 409
  Ocean of 99, 101, 106, 112
Divine-Image (See Image of God)
  Electricities 305–307, 410
  Illuminations 135
Divine Marriage 111, 122, 126, 132, 139, 196–199, 207, 209, 224, 245, 266, 363, 370, 445, 448–450
  Anointing 116, 127, 128, 177, 197, 199, 209, 240, 244, 245, 318, 348
Divine Mother 123, 227–233, 319
Divine Presence 75, 82, 104, 105, 111, 157, 269, 304, 362, 364
Divorce(s) 224, 225
Donne, John (1573–1631) 373
Dreams 53, 172, 247, 364, 434
Drugs 105, 401
Dryden, John (1631–1700) 6

Earnestness 191
Easter 122
Eckhart, Meister (1260–1327) 27, 32, 96, 120, 173, 187, 248, 448
Eclipse, Lunar 372
  Solar 372
Ecstasy(ies) 25, 77, 99, 106, 108, 114, 130, 131, 135, 144, 224, 269, 326, 353
Egotism 331, 333
Egypt 9, 10, 68
Eightfold Path 15
Einstein, Albert (1879–1955) 34, 92, 169, 174, 458
Electricity(ies) 128, 306, 307, 340
  Divine Image 305–307, 410
  of Christ 307, 375
  of Illumination 114
  of Soul 381
  psychic 391
Eliot, George (1819–1880) 109
Emerson, Ralph Waldo (1803–1882) 2, 38, 48, 59, 63, 95, 109, 189, 192, 290, 328, 378, 447
Enlightenment 41, 104, 105, 130, 131, 159, 172, 200, 246, 247, 260, 302, 316, 320, 321, 332, 333, 338, 366, 377, 379, 389, 409, 417, 454
Enthusiasm 239, 244–246, 321, 328
Envy 317, 322, 355
Epictetus (1st–2nd Century B.C.) 183, 330, 334
Epiphany 122
Equanimity 289, 321, 378–384

Index

Erasmus, Desiderius (1466-1536) 266
Erigena, John Scotus (875 A.D.) 442
Eternal Life 35, 94, 139, 148, 182, 240, 247, 250, 256, 268, 324, 357, 416, 438-458
Eternal Spirit 112, 142, 143, 195
Ethic(s) 22, 37, 43, 51, 52, 99, 107, 131, 138, 156, 173, 212, 261, 266, 282, 304, 306, 329, 370, 397, 408, 421, 427, 431
Eucharist 228
Euripides (485-406 B.C.) 3, 32, 102, 183, 186, 334
Everlasting Life 95, 99
  Commandment of 167, 259, 451, 453
Exorcism 400, 402
Expansion, Principle of 256, 257

Faith 27, 29, 41, 43, 54, 55, 104, 136, 160, 169, 193, 198, 208, 210, 213, 254, 277, 314, 316, 331, 349, 360, 373-375, 397
Faithfulness 199, 205, 208, 209, 341, 352, 405
Family(ies) 57, 58, 61, 62, 167, 179, 200, 214, 218, 226-228, 231, 233, 247, 267, 268, 273, 299, 321, 388, 390, 417, 426, 427
Fasting 26, 82, 86, 113, 157, 175-181, 183, 228, 240, 247, 253, 254, 271, 283, 309, 311, 346, 367, 395, 397, 399

Cycle 176
National 179, 180
Father, Heavenly 228, 230
Father Principle 123
Fault(s) 127, 229, 277-279, 289, 342, 395
Feminine 127, 427, 433
  Polarity 127, 135, 138, 139, 318, 346, 348
Fidelity 209, 310, 352
Fire 107, 111, 316, 429
Flexibility 214
Food 82
Forgiveness 158, 194, 214, 326, 330-332, 338, 341, 345, 362, 364, 366, 371, 373, 376, 381, 395, 402
Former Lives (See Past Lives)
Forthrightness 320
Francis of Assisi, Saint (1182-1226) 2, 27, 72, 79, 91, 182, 184, 220, 290, 322, 379, 386, 439, 450, 458
Franklin, Benjamin (1706-1790) 29, 193
Freedom(s) 61, 66, 82, 112, 219, 362, 364, 366, 368, 373, 375, 394, 401, 419
  of Worship 58, 61
Friendship 222, 223, 247
Full Moon 59, 122, 382
Fuller, Thomas (1608-1661) 184
Fulness 76, 78, 82, 100, 118, 119, 128, 168, 198, 220, 302, 392
Future Lives (See Coming Lives)

Gabriel, Archangel 26
Galilei, Galileo (1564-1642) 39, 414

Gandhi, Mohandes K. (1869-1948) 2, 30, 79, 174, 176, 178, 201, 223, 236, 316, 334, 399, 458
Galaxy(ies) 34-41, 44, 47, 54, 82, 98, 137, 146, 164, 165, 170, 200, 201, 248, 255-257, 260, 261, 285, 298, 306-308, 311, 312, 321, 376, 382, 406-408, 410, 414-416, 421, 440, 441, 453-458
  Consciousness 43, 44, 260-262, 357, 407, 451, 452
  Cycle(s) 40, 41, 414, 415
  Laws 415
Gemara 13, 14
Gene(s) 314, 317, 319
Generosity 214
Genius 148
Gentleness 27, 43, 182, 193, 214, 331, 380, 427
Gift(s) 22, 115, 177, 178
  of Healing 83, 135, 177, 178, 398-403
  of Prophecy 83
  of Speech 99
  of Revelation 115, 116, 178
  Soul 40, 108, 111, 135, 166-173
  Spiritual 40, 80, 104, 122, 154, 167, 169, 335, 453
Gita (See Bhagavad Gita)
Giving 86, 190, 195, 207, 210, 219-221, 224, 310, 320, 329, 445, 447
God (see Anointing Spirit, Image, Kingdom, Memory, Mercy, Spirit, Word)
Godhead 83, 96-108, 112-114, 118, 127, 129, 131, 135, 168, 169, 261, 262, 298, 300, 302, 304, 310, 372, 375, 388, 406, 422

God-Realization 5, 128, 132, 251, 290, 304, 332, 336, 457
Golden Age 44, 357, 458
Golden Rule 30, 31, 212, 231, 289, 367
Good 76, 232, 332, 333, 336, 339, 367, 377, 403, 426, 435, 436
  Goodness 193, 194, 217, 309, 358, 398
Grace 59, 61, 76, 78, 81-84, 98, 100, 102, 104, 106, 112, 113, 116, 132, 237, 321, 375-377, 409, 420, 429
  Divine (See Divine Grace)
  Marriage 212
  Prototypal 394, 395, 397, 398
  Soul (See Soul Grace)
  Touches of 100, 251
Graciousness 151
Gradation, Principle of 142, 145-147
Gratitude 46, 56, 58, 81, 144, 180, 210, 253, 271, 272-274, 276, 283-287, 293, 321, 336, 340, 367
  Prayer of 228
Great Architect 170
Great Logics 357, 369, 442-447
Great Shepherd 44, 240, 261, 320
Great Souls 134, 159, 170, 176, 242, 285, 424, 425, 458
Great Teachers 4, 5, 33-37, 41, 47, 54, 55, 85, 93-95, 133, 134, 149, 152, 165, 200, 238, 239, 244, 301, 302, 306, 308, 315, 377, 404, 425, 435, 446

Goethe, Johann Wolfgang Von (1749-1832) 184, 192, 212, 442
Greed 86, 143, 179, 208, 241, 310, 317, 322, 355, 424, 432
Guidance 114, 171, 180, 189, 191, 250, 266, 272, 275, 282, 287, 288, 306, 366, 367, 377

Habakkuk 33, 236, 374
Hale, Sir Matthew (1609-1676) 64
Hall, Joseph (1574-1656) 184
Hand of God 58, 188, 269, 312, 394
Happiness 177, 205, 208, 218, 224, 232-234, 240, 312, 372, 400, 438
Harmlessness 79, 80, 352, 399
Harmony 34, 37, 41, 47, 127, 138, 142, 169, 177, 192, 201, 222, 232, 253, 255, 256, 266, 285, 289, 291, 298, 311, 318, 368, 369, 370, 372, 381-383, 395, 397, 398, 457
Hate 86, 179, 208, 216, 241, 242, 309, 317, 356, 357, 381, 400, 401, 428
Healing(s) 34, 56, 76, 103, 106, 108, 112, 133, 134, 136, 139, 150, 156, 157, 173, 179, 180, 216, 225, 229, 230, 231, 242, 246, 272, 277, 282, 286, 293, 318, 320-322, 330, 338, 341-343, 345, 346, 363, 366-377, 381, 389, 394, 395, 400, 402-404, 409, 422, 430

Gift of 83, 177, 178, 398-403
Heaven 69, 73, 75, 81, 84, 111, 114, 116, 177, 220, 247, 262, 284, 285, 325, 332
Heavenly Father 228, 230, 319, 335
Hebrews 61, 346
Heraclitus (500 B.C.) 42, 181, 373
Herbert, George (1593-1633) 220
Hermes 74, 140
Herrick, Robert (1591-1674) 324
Hierarchs 404-410
Higher Self 102-104
Hillel, Rabbi (1st Century) 31
Hindrances, Five 395
Hindus 6, 347
Hippocrates (C. 460-377 B.C.) 184
Holiness 41, 57, 66, 76, 77, 93, 98, 104, 105, 108, 113, 124, 126, 127, 131, 134, 135, 153, 157, 173, 176, 205, 261, 268, 275, 301, 304, 315, 331, 338, 368
Holy Day(s) 122, 228
Holy Fire 102, 196
Holy Ghost 83, 120-130, 153, 154, 159, 190, 191, 240, 291, 312, 365, 370, 406, 422, 440
  Cycles 41, 121-130
  Insulation 124-130
Holy Inspiration(s) 77, 99, 100, 106, 112, 113, 221, 228, 244
Holy Poverty 91, 155, 448-451
Holy Spirit 129, 218
Homer (C. 850 or earlier) 157

Homosexuality 179, 193, 317–319, 353
Honesty 56, 86, 136, 199, 207, 210, 214, 229, 243, 249–254, 277, 342, 343, 375, 399, 401
Honorableness 199, 204, 212, 362–364, 367, 368, 372, 375, 377, 402, 427, 431
Hope 34, 121, 171, 182, 360, 401
Horace (65-8 B.C.) 3, 95, 184, 209, 214
Hospitality 127, 356, 367
Householder(s) 206, 209, 215, 218
Hugo, Victor (1802–1885) 2, 109, 186
Humaneness 93
Humility 13, 56, 58, 77, 78, 85, 91, 175, 182, 210, 214, 253, 272, 285, 293, 312, 333–336, 339, 343, 345, 346, 372, 381, 402, 446
Humor, Sense of 210, 214, 232–234
Huss, John (1373–1415) 248

Iamblichus (2nd Century A.D.) 140
Ikhnaton (1385–1358 B.C.) 9, 10, 79
Illumination(s) 41, 53, 56, 60, 61, 66, 77, 81, 86, 98, 102, 105, 106, 112–114, 122, 123, 127–129, 133, 135, 137, 139, 146, 154, 155, 159, 160, 164–166, 172, 195, 197, 198, 207, 224, 245, 247, 249, 250, 261, 268, 274, 303, 308, 309, 315, 339, 340, 346, 347, 357, 369, 370, 373, 390, 410, 421, 422, 443, 454, 455, 457
Illumination(s)
 Attitude 166
 Christ-Mind 128, 136, 291
 Mountain of 4, 239, 416, 453
 Prototypal 389, 393–398, 403
 Relativity of 163–166
 Versatility 164
 Virtue 83, 166, 268
 Virtue, Ladder of 83, 389
Illumined Virtues 55, 417
Image of Christ 302
Image of God 40, 47, 56, 83, 92, 117, 157, 165, 172, 193, 201, 229, 260, 268, 271, 288, 297–322, 347, 349, 357, 381, 385, 388, 390, 393, 397, 401, 403, 406–408, 415, 419, 421, 425, 430, 433, 434, 441, 453–456
 Quickenings 297–305, 308, '455
Imagination 153
Immortals, Great 406
Incest 193, 317
India 16, 25, 42, 67, 68, 98
Infinity 35
Ingersoll, R. G. (1833–1899) 213
Initiation(s) 55, 114, 116, 137, 169, 173, 207, 312
 Heart 309
 Pure Love 387–393, 395, 397–400, 403
Insanity 179
Inspiration(s) 34, 56, 77, 78, 104, 105, 108, 114, 117, 172, 239, 241, 253, 255, 272–274, 276, 286, 293,

INDEX 475

321, 335, 345, 362, 370, 451
Holy 77, 99, 100, 106, 112, 113, 221, 228, 244
Instruction 200, 389, 434
 spiritual 62, 126, 156, 157, 212, 290, 293, 435
Insulation, spiritual 113, 114, 123-130, 136, 137, 225, 226, 311, 314, 330, 369, 370, 397
Integrity 56, 66, 101, 126, 188-191, 214, 222, 225, 241, 253, 363, 377, 431, 432
Intelligence 140, 152, 168, 201
Intuition 169, 172
Isaiah (c. 760-700 B.C.) 10, 40, 45, 59, 62, 103, 151, 195, 363, 367, 378, 439
Israelites 129

Jainism 30, 42
Jealousy 241, 317, 356, 400
Jefferson, Thomas (1743-1826) 29, 252
Jesus 22, 37, 43, 52, 66-69, 72, 78, 81, 96, 101, 106, 112, 113, 118, 122, 128, 129, 132, 134, 138, 159, 163, 164, 170, 171, 177, 179, 188, 194, 198, 226, 227, 272, 284, 285, 299, 302, 304, 332, 337, 343, 371, 372, 399, 400-402, 406, 417, 418, 424, 427, 440, 448-452, 455, 456
Jewel in the Lotus 98, 99
Joseph 188, 231, 232
Joy(s) 53, 76, 77, 82, 99, 108, 113, 114, 130, 133, 149, 152, 156, 157, 186, 188, 193, 199, 200, 208-212, 214, 216, 218, 224, 226, 228-230, 232-234, 242, 247, 269, 274, 284, 286, 312, 316, 321, 326, 329, 342, 387, 394, 395, 402, 429, 432, 435
Judas 68
Jude, Saint 67, 133, 324
Jung, Carl (1875-1961) 307
Junius 361
Justice 18, 21, 26, 66, 128, 173, 209, 214, 324
Juvenal (c. 54-138) 6

Kant, Immanuel (1724-1804) 37
Karma 60, 129, 357, 358, 368, 446
 Prototypal 394, 397
Keats, John (1795-1821) 378
Kepler, Johannes (1571-1630) 101
Khan, Hazrat, Inayat (1882-1926) 316
Kindness 27, 93, 116, 157, 212-214, 367
Kingdom of God 22, 131, 146, 153, 192, 253, 256, 257, 273, 274, 286, 308, 319
Kingdom(s) of Heaven 53, 73, 129, 325, 332
Kingsley, Charles (1819-1875) 2, 54
Kipling, Rudyard (1865-1936) 158, 335
Knowing 43, 168
Koran (see Muhammad)
Krishna 8
Kundalini 307-313, 347, 348
Kwang-Tze (399-295 B.C.) 220, 384

Lao Tzu (604–531 B.C.) 17, 42, 54, 173, 184, 236, 296, 357
Lawrence, Brother (1611–1691) 405
Law(s) 85, 99, 105, 107, 114, 130–132, 217, 237, 239, 242, 246, 247, 249, 250, 251, 253, 266, 275, 276, 287, 288, 313, 321, 326–329, 332, 338, 340, 343, 345, 347, 348, 364, 366, 376, 377, 396, 401, 402, 416, 417, 429, 435
  of attraction 58, 216, 217, 229, 351, 357, 395, 398
  of cause and effect 60
  of karma 446
  of reincarnation 62, 63, 149, 417, 418, 444–446
  of sowing and reaping 60, 173
  of suffering 428
  of tithing 126, 218, 239, 303, 354, 446
Leadership 425, 432, 458
Learning 147, 262, 267, 268, 409, 414–417, 420, 423–425, 427, 429
Liberty 222
Life Cycle 42, 312
Lincoln, Abraham (1809–1865) 180, 181, 223, 233, 360, 442
Literature 28
Lives, Past (see Past Lives)
Logic(s) 8, 35, 40, 42, 55, 77, 126, 137, 146, 153, 165, 169, 171, 172, 183, 304, 308, 311, 348, 356, 357, 414, 417, 420, 423, 442–447, 452–455.
  Great 357, 369, 442–447

Logos 293, 350
Longfellow, Henry Wadsworth (1807–1882) 38, 63, 248, 374
Lord's Prayer 271
Love 2, 4, 5, 37, 58, 81, 86, 91, 108, 139, 155–160, 195–201, 208–213, 239–249, 256–260, 308–314, 380, 381, 387–410, 428, 447–458
  Commandments of 126, 239, 303, 329, 377, 380, 445, 446
Loyalty 18, 209, 214, 274, 304, 310, 380
Lunar Cycles 122, 142, 231, 379–385, 401
  Eclipse 372
Lust 86, 139, 179, 193, 208, 228–231, 241, 309, 315, 317, 318, 320, 322, 342, 395, 400, 424
Luther, Martin (1483–1546) 43, 186, 193, 204

Madison, John 180
Magic, black 241
Magnanimity 151
Magnification 76, 126, 127, 129, 152–155, 157, 190, 240, 241, 248, 277, 382, 440
Mahabharata 8, 30, 32, 176, 296, 316, 331, 334, 361, 436
Malachi (400 B.C.) 103, 220, 340, 439
Mantra 273, 275, 367
Mantrams 273, 275, 399
Marriage(s) 2, 26, 34, 61, 62, 127, 148, 179, 204–233,

245, 247, 321, 352, 353, 363, 390, 395, 449, 450
Anointed   208, 209, 232
Divine   111, 116, 122, 126, 127, 128, 132, 139, 177, 196-199, 207, 209, 224, 240, 244, 245, 266, 318, 348, 363, 370, 445, 448-450
Martyrdom   64-73, 150, 424
Mary   152, 170, 187, 188, 231, 232, 284, 406
Mary Magdalene   194, 434
Masterbuilder(s)   129, 274, 410
Masculine polarity   127, 131, 132, 135, 138, 139, 318, 346, 427, 433
Masefield, John (1878-1967)   324
Mathematics   94, 116, 135, 142, 151, 171, 306, 307, 415, 416, 420, 434
Maundy Thursday   122
Mediation   133, 145, 146, 177, 191, 195, 376, 400
Mediation-Host   53, 84, 113, 243, 260, 272, 279, 284, 285, 406, 408, 409
Meditation   15, 16, 53, 57, 82, 86, 99, 105, 113, 122, 157, 171, 183, 218, 229, 236-262, 273, 275, 307, 309, 311, 321, 333, 339, 342, 345, 346, 349, 367, 381, 399, 410, 418, 429, 430
Meekness   13, 43-45, 107, 193, 453, 457
Memory   52, 53, 67, 122, 140, 141, 147-155, 169, 171, 317, 329, 339, 340, 373, 417, 423, 429
  Gene   314, 319

of God   150-152, 157
of Nature   150-152
of the Soul   140, 147-155, 160
Mencius (372-289 B.C.)   6
Mercy   93, 150, 184, 217, 324, 325, 333, 427, 458
Mercy of God   106, 113, 151, 173, 179, 196, 200, 276, 277, 283, 286, 324-345, 362, 364, 371, 373, 376, 378, 394, 401, 402, 404, 426, 431
Messiah   302
Metaphysics   19-21
Michelangelo, Buonarroti (1475-1564)   43, 109, 447
Midrash   14
Milarepa (1100-1135)   116, 358
Milky Way   35, 40, 41, 261, 414, 415
Milton, John (1608-1674)   28, 29, 85, 374, 379
Miracle(s)   43, 76, 113, 134, 148-150, 156, 164, 166, 167, 173, 177-179, 230, 242, 245, 272, 276, 285, 302, 306, 326, 330, 338, 341, 345, 362, 366, 371-373, 376, 388, 391, 398, 400, 404, 405, 409, 456, 457
Mirth   158
Mishnah   13, 14
Moderation   182-184
Modesty   335, 403, 404
Montaigne (1533-1592)   214
Moon   41, 47, 108, 116, 122, 141, 142, 146, 231, 260, 298, 299, 300, 307, 312, 378-386, 388, 394, 396,

397, 401, 407, 416, 421, 427, 446, 458
Cycles 231
Full 59, 122, 372, 382
New 59, 122, 372, 382, 393
Morality 37, 56, 187-191, 193-195, 201, 211, 212, 217, 218, 224, 226, 231, 239, 306, 308, 329, 352, 367, 371, 377, 432, 445, 446
Moses (c. 1200 B.C.) 10-12, 37, 129, 440
Moslems 61
Mother, Divine 123, 227-233, 319
Mountain of Illumination 4, 239
Movement 142
More, Thomas (1478-1535) 334
Muhammad (570-632) 26, 31, 39, 43, 74, 107, 110, 140, 162, 176, 213, 264, 277, 286, 296, 324, 326, 331, 360, 361, 374, 386, 392, 406, 412
Music 19, 28, 78, 167, 253, 273, 274, 293, 305
Mysticism 19, 27

Nation(s) 4, 10, 29, 34, 43, 44, 57, 58, 61, 62, 67, 94, 103, 148, 166, 167, 173, 179, 180, 184, 190, 192, 198, 200, 222, 248, 267, 312, 321, 355-357, 382, 388, 417, 426, 432, 433, 458
Nature 9, 47, 52, 145, 146, 261, 298, 318, 421, 447
Memory of 150-152

Nehemiah (Active 445-432 B.C.) 50
New Covenant 260, 261
New Moon 59, 122, 372, 382, 393
New Testament 22, 23, 68, 169
Nirvana 103, 104, 130-132, 234, 238, 358
Points 130-132
Niscience, Age of 43
Noah 129
Norden, John (16th Century) 267

Obedience 91, 92, 113, 126, 194, 244, 252, 288-291, 366
Obsession 179, 183, 400-402
Old Testament 10-14, 42, 169, 369
Omnipresence 47, 114, 116, 137, 138, 142, 146, 154, 201, 231, 253, 254-258, 262, 270, 273, 277, 291, 347, 355, 377, 388, 390, 393, 399, 401, 408, 409, 435, 441
Origen (185?-254?) 386
Osler, Sir William (1849-1919) 374
Ovid (43 B.C.-18 A.D.) 4, 226, 249, 412

Pain 52, 53, 61, 66, 156, 229, 284, 288, 331, 358, 429
Palladius (c. 368-died before 431) 236
Parable(s) 98, 100
Paracelsus (1493-1541) 175, 386
Paradox 257, 449
Past Lives 51-53, 55, 122, 136,

INDEX 479

148, 149, 151, 152, 154,
160, 168, 169, 198, 199,
217, 230, 231, 312, 314,
317, 319, 321, 322, 338,
345, 351, 357, 362, 364,
367, 368, 371-373, 375,
377, 379, 385, 394, 398,
402, 417, 423, 431, 445
Patanjali (dates vary from 200
  B.C. to 700 B.C.) 16, 17,
  79
Path, Eightfold 15
Path of Virtue 3-6, 51-53,
  80-84, 99-106, 123-130,
  139, 144, 148, 154, 164-
  166, 177, 179, 239, 245,
  284, 291, 320, 326-330,
  343, 362-373, 428, 434,
  441
Patience 94, 210, 227, 230,
  247, 256, 381, 446-448
Peace 76, 130, 193, 229, 239,
  242, 248, 256, 262, 314,
  321, 335, 342, 381, 382,
  397
Penance (see Restitution)
  326, 361
Penn, William (1644-1718)
  29, 59, 116, 204, 446
Pentecost 121, 122
Perfection 73, 456-459
Pericles (495-429 B.C.) 32, 43
Perseverance 101
Persistence 322
Perversion (see Homosexuality)
Petition 271, 281-283
Petrarch (1304-1374) 430
Phaedrus (5th Century B.C.)
  233
Philo of Alexandria (20 B.C.-40
  A.D.) 63, 187, 188, 233
Philosophers 4, 28, 343
Physics 21, 308
Planet(s) 41, 47, 108, 116,

141, 142, 146, 260, 298-
300, 379, 382, 388, 393,
407, 416, 427, 440, 446,
458
Plato (427-347 B.C.) 19-21,
  25, 30, 32, 38, 45, 74,
  109, 110, 145, 147, 316,
  318, 412
Plautus (254-184 B.C.) 72,
  192, 226
Plotinus (205-270) 19, 25
Plutarch (50-120) 24, 25, 32,
  95, 140, 175
Po Chu-I (800 A.D.) 414
Poems 100
Poets 4, 28
Polarity(ies) 123, 127, 128,
  131, 132, 139, 318, 319,
  346, 368, 402
  Feminine 131, 132, 135,
    138, 139, 318, 346, 348
  Masculine 127, 131, 135,
    138, 139, 318, 346, 348
Polarization 112, 138, 347,
  348
Polybius (205?-125 B.C.) 193
Pope, Alexander (1688-1744)
  29, 223, 252, 278
Possession 179, 400-402
Poverty 354
  Holy 91, 155, 448-451
  Lady 72, 73
Praise 271, 279-283, 287,
  336, 340, 350
Prayer(s) 26, 53, 58, 82, 86,
  98, 99, 113, 122, 126, 136,
  145, 150, 151, 157, 173,
  176, 179-181, 183, 218,
  228-230, 240, 242, 247,
  253, 254, 264-294, 309,
  311, 321, 327, 331, 333,
  339, 345, 346, 349, 362,
  363, 367, 373, 376-378,
  381, 383, 395, 399, 401,

402, 404, 410, 418, 430, 435
Before Teaching 293
Dedicated Creativity 273, 274
Dedication of the Day 270-272
Fasting Dedication 178, 179
Gratitude 283-287
Guidance 287, 288
of Confession 402, 403
of Repentance 376-378
Petition 281-283
Praise 279-282
to Overcome Faults 278, 279
Prejudice(s) 112, 139, 198, 208, 314, 330, 356, 380, 402, 425, 433
Presence of God 34, 41, 76, 77, 83, 102, 106, 108, 111, 117, 127, 183, 211, 224, 356
Pride 13, 85, 179, 208, 241, 317, 320, 322, 333, 342, 381, 395, 424, 425, 432
Principle(s) 99, 107, 131, 138, 198, 212, 226, 257, 304, 306, 329, 349, 397, 399, 418, 421
Adversary 425
Christ 395
Father 123
Mother 123
of Expansion 256, 257
of Pulsation 256, 257
Probation, Period of 125, 126, 197, 198, 364
Probationer 251, 417
Procreation 144, 204, 215, 216, 229, 309, 317, 353, 431

Prophecy(ies) 77, 117, 162-179, 338, 341, 417, 422, 424, 444, 452
Archetypal 164, 167-173, 395
Gift of 83, 93, 135, 167
Prophet(s) 106, 165, 167, 168, 173, 180, 200, 239, 301, 331, 387, 410, 457
Fast 179
Prototypal Illuminations 389, 393-398, 403
Prototype(s) 337, 377, 379, 394, 397, 398
Zodiacal 107, 337, 380, 381, 388, 398, 399, 401-403, 407
Prudence 184
Ptolemy (Flourished 139 A.D.) 39
Punctuality 289-291
Pure Creation(s) 58, 76, 86, 117, 118, 126, 211, 212, 243, 253, 273, 274, 321, 382
Pure-Love Initiations 387-393, 395, 397-400, 403
Purification(s) 105, 176, 195, 241-243, 247, 348, 382, 393, 399, 424
Purity 86, 193, 199, 225, 232, 241, 252-254, 273, 316, 321, 353, 392, 398, 404, 449
Pythagoras (582-507? B.C.) 19, 20, 32, 34, 42, 296

Quickening(s) 42, 57, 106, 111, 121, 126, 133, 134, 170, 176, 177, 197, 199, 240, 243, 246, 251, 253, 282, 297-302, 311, 324, 347,

INDEX 481

372, 408, 409, 417, 418, 428, 444, 445, 454
Image-of-God 297-305, 308, 455
Quintilian (42-118) 6, 252

Rabelais, Francois (1494?-1553) 233, 447
Race(s) 4, 10, 44, 57, 58, 67, 94, 167, 179, 198, 267, 299, 321, 356, 382, 388, 415, 417, 426, 433
Rajas 313
Ramakrishna, Sri (1834-1886) 28, 206, 207, 215, 227, 329
Realization(s) 77, 99, 100, 105, 106, 112-114, 122, 172, 198, 239, 241, 244, 262, 276, 332, 333, 345, 371, 375
  Christ 132, 251
  God 5, 128, 132, 251, 290, 304, 332, 336, 457
  Self 251, 434
  Soul 251, 434
Reincarnation 149, 320, 412-435
  Cycles 353, 356, 357, 390, 402, 413-435, 445, 446
  Law of 62, 63, 149, 417, 418, 444-446
Religion(s) 4, 10, 25, 44, 56-58, 61, 67, 75, 77, 94, 111, 112, 114, 165, 167, 179, 180, 188, 194, 198, 200, 248, 284, 299, 318, 351, 353, 356, 357, 382, 388, 417, 425-427, 429, 430, 433
Renunciation 77, 155
Repentance 14, 136, 151, 154, 180, 188, 194, 198,

216, 230, 231, 242, 276, 312, 318, 321, 322, 325-329, 332, 336-340, 345-347, 358, 361, 362, 365, 366, 369, 371-373, 375-378, 394, 401, 426, 430-432
Responsibility, Sense of 210, 214, 215, 431, 445
Restitution 82, 127, 128, 136, 138, 151, 180, 198, 199, 217, 230, 231, 243, 253, 276, 312, 318, 321, 322, 347, 360-378, 394, 395-398, 402, 424, 425, 430-432, 450
Resurrection 61, 73, 452, 454
Retardation(s) 145, 317
Revelation(s) 77, 82, 93, 99, 100, 105, 106, 108, 110-117, 131, 164, 172, 173, 244, 255, 262, 276, 338, 345, 348, 372, 394, 395, 397, 410, 417, 422, 440, 444
  Gift of 83, 115, 135, 177, 178
Revelator(s) 95, 106, 165, 168
Reverence 13, 18, 41, 46, 48, 52, 54-58, 61, 62, 75, 78-82, 104, 107, 108, 111, 113, 116, 126, 131, 143-145, 173, 176, 179, 189, 200, 216, 218, 228, 229, 231, 239, 241, 244, 247, 253, 254, 257, 272, 273, 277, 289, 293, 306, 309, 321, 338, 348, 353, 355, 362, 366, 377, 432
Righteousness 37, 40, 45, 57, 66, 80, 98, 102-106, 108, 114, 117, 119, 120, 124,

127, 130, 131, 134, 135, 150, 167, 192, 198, 212, 230, 253, 257, 261, 262, 268, 270, 275, 304, 308, 309, 311, 314, 315, 338, 339, 362, 363, 368, 392, 394, 417
Ring-Pass-Not 112
Rousseau, Jean Jacques (1712-1778) 186, 213
Rumi, Jalalud-din (1207-1273) 2
Ruskin, John (1819-1900) 194
Ruysbroeck, Blessed John (1293-1381) 27, 105, 120, 394

Sabbath 11, 59–64, 176, 212, 218, 271, 275, 293, 329, 367, 377, 397, 445
  Day Commandment 59–64, 239, 329, 350, 351, 368, 446
  Cycles 41, 59–64, 122, 218, 397
Sacrament(s) 76
  Baptism 240
  Betrothal 211
  Cycles 41, 228
  of Communion 80–82, 228, 367
  of Procreative Love 317
Sacrament-Degrees of the Virtues 76–84, 94, 127, 132, 135, 138, 139, 155, 216, 283, 286, 306, 419, 426
Sacrament-Light of the Soul 75–84, 131, 159, 160, 168
Sacrifice 66, 77, 82, 138, 150, 158, 201, 219, 314, 331, 335, 356, 364, 366, 367, 383, 395, 398, 425

Saint(s) 4, 27, 37, 66–72, 75–85, 96, 111–116, 126, 133, 157, 159, 165, 170, 176, 177, 200, 212, 227, 232, 239, 240, 266, 279, 284, 285, 301, 311, 318, 364, 371, 376, 390, 393, 404–410, 424, 425, 448, 449, 454
  Proteges of 75–77, 114, 148, 149, 156, 226, 266, 346, 364, 390, 404–410
Saint
  Agatha 70
  Agnes 71
  Ambrose 81
  Andrew 67
  Anselm (1033–1109) 74, 282
  Augustine (see Augustine)
  Barachisius 71
  Bartholomew 67
  Basil (Martyred 316) 213, 406
  Bernard (see Bernard)
  Blase 70
  Blasius (died c. 316) 96
  Catherine of Genoa (1447–1510) 387
  Catherine of Siena (1347–1380) 97, 98
  Dionysius (6th Century) 68, 96, 187
  Dorothy 70
  Ephraem the Syrian (c. 306–373) 280
  Felicitas 70
  Francis de Sales (1567–1622) 80, 95
  Francis of Assisi (see Francis of Assisi)
  Fulgentius 70
  George 315

INDEX 483

Gregory of Nyssa (331?-396?) 420
Ignatius 68
James 67, 264, 331, 333, 368, 373
Jerome (340-420) 223
Joan of Arc (1412-1431) 71
John Chrysostom (c. 345-407) 71, 283, 287, 360
John of Damascus (700-760) 74, 118, 454
John of the Cross (1542-1591) 2, 174, 236, 413
John the Beloved 2, 32, 40, 50, 74, 103, 163, 172, 196, 199, 341, 343
Jude 67
Julia 71
Lawrence 71
Loyola, Ignatius (1491-1556) 155, 283
Lucian 69
Luke 68
Mark 68
Matthew 67
Matthias 68
Patrick (389?-461) 287
Paul 68
Peter 67
Philip 67
Polycarp 69
Richard 105
Sebastian 69
Simon 244
Teresa of Avila (1515-1582) 281, 334, 422
Thomas 67
Thomas á Kempis (see á Kempis)
Thomas Aquinas (1225-1274) 74, 282, 292, 318
Venantius 69, 70
Victor 71
Vincent 69
Vitalis 71
Sallust (86-34 B.C.) 438
Sanctuary(ies) 58, 62, 150, 212, 218, 219, 275, 351
Satan 91, 268
Sattva 313
Savonarola 71
Schweitzer, Albert (1875-1965) 78, 79, 327
Science 19, 43, 44, 167, 169, 201, 427, 451
Scientist(s) 21, 35, 170, 343, 440
Scriptures 34, 35, 85, 98, 122, 129, 147, 156, 169, 177, 194, 212, 238, 241, 249, 273, 275, 291, 399, 408, 418
Sealing 81, 106, 111, 116, 117, 126, 133, 197, 198, 420
Self-Control 262, 305, 313
Self-Denial 77, 81, 82, 155
Selfless(ness) 81, 86, 93, 102, 104, 127, 129, 131, 138, 142, 154, 157, 208, 282, 310, 345, 347, 356, 367, 383
Self, Higher 102-104
Self-Mastery 296
Seneca (4 B.C.-65 A.D.) 24, 31, 32, 74, 183, 186, 209, 214, 226, 252, 296, 330, 341, 383
Senility 145
Senses 298, 348, 370, 399
Serenity 241, 321, 343
Sermon on the Mount 113, 218, 239, 250, 300-304, 308, 369-372
Sex 183, 207, 208, 211, 229, 231, 309, 317-319, 353

Cycles 228
Pre-Marital 210, 230
Shakespeare, William (1564–1616) 28, 335, 360
Shelley, Percy Bysshe (1792–1822) 38, 109
Sikhism 31
Silence 236, 238–244
Simon Zelotes 68
Simplicity 91, 240, 246–249, 328
Sincerity 56, 101, 114, 126, 129, 191, 198, 199, 225, 253, 268, 274, 327–330, 332, 338, 339, 356, 366, 372, 375, 402, 426, 431
Sin(s) 61, 136, 180, 194, 198, 199, 211, 217, 230, 231, 238, 242, 243, 253, 310, 312, 314–322, 324, 325, 331, 334, 336, 338, 339, 341, 342, 345, 352, 355, 357, 358, 360, 361, 364–367, 371–373, 375–377, 381, 395, 396, 398, 400–402, 424, 425, 430, 431, 434, 445
  Remission of 154, 365, 366
Six 343–348
Sleep 53, 247, 254
Snowflakes 343–345
Socrates (469–399 B.C.) 20, 110, 327, 384, 441
Solar Cycles 41, 122, 142, 381
  Eclipse 372
Solar System(s) 94, 98, 116, 146, 170, 171, 195, 201, 248, 255, 261, 266, 288, 298, 300–302, 306, 308, 376, 388, 406, 410, 416, 419, 420, 425, 428, 429, 452–456
Solomon (reign 993–953 B.C.?) 2, 10, 32, 42, 46, 103, 109, 140, 189, 190, 199, 206, 213, 215, 222, 233, 234
Songs, New 100
Sophocles (496?–406 B.C.) 213
Soul(s) 52–55, 61, 62, 75–84, 93, 97, 117, 129–160, 167, 168, 176–178, 195, 201, 208, 228, 230, 231, 242, 246, 248, 250–255, 261, 262, 268, 283, 285, 301, 306, 310–312, 321, 329, 330, 335–340, 343, 345, 352, 357, 364, 369, 372, 379, 380, 382, 385, 390, 394, 397, 400–402, 405, 408, 409, 414, 420, 422
  Candelabra of the 159, 160
  Covenants 413–435
  Cycles 41, 141, 142, 209, 379
  Gifts 40, 108, 111, 155, 166
  Grace 59, 76, 127, 209, 242, 243, 274, 289, 346, 350, 381
  Great (See Great Souls)
  Memory of the 140, 147–155, 160
  Realization 251, 434
Sowing and Reaping, Law of 60, 173
Space 35, 43, 80, 81, 83, 165, 168, 169, 230, 246, 255–259, 261, 369, 396, 441, 455, 456
Spinoza (1632–1677) 438
Spirit of God 55, 56, 62, 100, 108, 111, 113, 114, 116, 123, 127, 137, 142, 146, 167, 168, 196–200, 221, 242, 256, 258, 272, 273
Spirit of Truth 30, 117, 167, 318

INDEX 485

Star(s)   33-42, 47, 54, 55, 80, 82, 98, 137, 141, 142, 164, 165, 170, 201, 248, 255-261, 285, 298, 300, 306-308, 311, 312, 379, 382, 407, 408, 410, 414, 416, 421, 440, 441, 453-458
Statesmen   29
Steadfastness   380
Stealing   353, 354
Stevenson, Robert Louis (1850-1894)   226
Stewardship   124, 144, 199, 210, 224, 289, 364
Study   13, 20, 122, 127, 152, 191, 194, 210, 212, 216, 266, 271, 273, 275, 347, 399
Subconscious   112, 217, 231, 242, 243, 314, 315, 317, 321, 322, 330, 347, 370-373, 381
Suffering   61, 66, 200, 230, 243, 317, 318, 396, 422, 428, 429, 431
Sufi   280
Suicide   179, 188
Sun(s)   40, 42, 47, 108, 116, 131, 142, 143, 146, 147, 258-261, 298-300, 312, 372, 379, 381, 382, 386, 388, 393-397, 416, 421, 427, 440, 446, 458
   Sign(s)   390-396
Swedenborg, Emanuel (1688-1772)   186
Symbol(s)   107, 172
Synesius (4th-5th Century A.D.)   433
Syrus, Publilius   330, 447

Tacitus (c. 55-117)   74, 183
Tagore, Rabindranath (1861-1941)   107, 248
Talent(s)   127, 148, 155, 277, 445, 446
Tamas   313
Talmud   13, 14, 30, 32, 222, 236, 316
Talmud Torah   13
Tao   17
Taylor, Jeremy (1613˙-1667)   287
Teacher(s)   4, 56, 106, 108, 114, 122, 126, 127, 129, 151, 166, 177, 196, 208, 239, 250, 266, 268, 275, 277, 284, 285, 290, 291, 305, 306, 308, 326, 327, 335, 337, 365, 366, 380, 388, 404, 446
   Anointed   240, 417, 418, 429
   Great (see Great Teachers)
Telepathy   157, 241, 255, 273
Temperance   249
Ten Commandments   10-12, 62, 126, 210, 218, 239, 242, 250, 300-304, 349-355, 369-372, 377
Ten-Year Cycles   121-130
Tenderness   427
Tennyson, Alfred (1809-1892)   64, 296, 334, 374
Terence (185-159 B.C.)   184
Testament
   New   22, 23, 68, 169
   Old   10-14, 169, 369
Tester   223-226, 425
Thackeray, William Makepeace (1811-1863)   189, 233
Thanksgiving   283, 286, 287, 350
Theophrastus (279 B.C.)   32
Thomas, Gospel of   138
Thoreau, Henry David (1817-1862)   48, 248

486   INDEX

Tibet 98
Time 32, 35, 44-48, 60, 80, 81, 83, 123, 134, 135, 165, 168-170, 217, 230, 246, 255-258, 261, 289-291, 306, 369, 380, 396, 441, 455, 456
  Cycle(s) 39-48, 59, 62, 63, 122, 172, 288, 312
Timelessness 44, 168-170, 456
Timothy 68
Tithe(s) 150, 212, 216, 219, 228, 253, 354, 367, 397, 445
Tithing, Law of 126, 218, 239, 303, 354, 377, 446
Tobacco 401
Tolstoy, Leo (1828-1910) 374
Traherne, Thomas (c. 1637-1674) 28, 85, 96, 286
Tranquility 342
Tree of Knowledge 164, 416
Tribes 167, 267, 299
Trust 58, 81, 209
Truth 45, 71, 81, 102, 117, 127, 149-151, 205, 209, 252-254, 277, 348, 408, 409
  Spirit of 30, 117, 318

Understanding 93, 114, 116, 155, 157, 211, 274, 279, 321, 340, 409, 428
Upanishads 2, 4, 7, 8, 50, 74, 110, 115, 118, 123, 237, 250, 262, 379, 428, 443

Vedas 6, 7, 48, 50, 174, 265
Venereal Disease 430
Vice(s) 85, 95, 156, 313, 317, 321, 341, 385
Virginity 187, 188

Virtue(s)
  Androgynous 138, 139
  Anointed 159
  Anti- 85, 86, 88-90, 133, 179, 229, 314, 317, 322, 393, 395, 400, 401, 409, 423-425
  Apostolic 398
  Bodhisattva 398
  Clusters 54-57
  Diamonds 86, 133-138
  Illuminations 55, 83, 84, 111, 142, 160, 166, 268, 389, 417
  Initiations 116, 168, 169
  Messianic 301
  Petals 305, 306
  Sacrament Degrees of 76-84, 94, 127, 132, 135, 138, 139, 155, 216, 283, 286, 306, 419, 426
  Sanctified 62
  Yogic 399
Virtues and Anti-Virtues, Table of 85-90
Vows 176, 232, 350
  Marriage 212

Washington, George (1732-1799) 176, 186, 252
Water 107
Webster, Daniel (1782-1852) 64, 442
Wedding Ceremony 211, 224
Whitman, Walt (1819-1892) 38, 48, 248, 419
Whittier, John Greenleaf (1807-1892) 156
Wilcox, Ella Wheeler (1850-1919) 213
Will(s) 125, 145, 153, 155, 179, 251, 268, 380, 400, 401, 423, 426

Word of God   150, 219, 266, 293, 367, 377, 382, 398
Wordsworth, William (1770-1850)   214, 335
Work   128, 232, 289
World Conscience   67, 168, 200
Worship   22, 28, 50-64, 75, 82, 96, 99, 106, 108, 114, 126, 127, 138, 144, 149-154, 163, 176, 190, 191, 195, 201, 210, 212, 215-219, 224, 226, 228, 232, 254, 256, 259, 261, 268, 273-275, 285, 288, 289, 304, 311, 313, 314, 321, 329, 332, 339, 349, 351, 366, 367, 371, 377, 397, 418, 429, 430, 445

Cycles   41, 53, 59, 60, 122, 152, 183, 194, 218, 228, 273, 333, 347, 397

Yang   123, 128, 132, 135, 346
Yin   123, 128, 132, 135, 346
Yoga   105, 274, 399

Zechariah   115, 236, 291
Zend Avesta (see Zoroaster)
Zeno (335-263 B.C.)   109
Zenophon   436
Zephaniah (c. 625-608 B.C.)   45
Zodiacal Prototype(s)   107, 337, 380-382, 388-399, 401-403, 407
Zoroaster (c. 600 B.C.)   16, 30, 42, 186, 283, 326, 392

BOOKS BY JONATHAN MURRO

    GOD-REALIZATION JOURNAL
    THE PATH OF VIRTUE

BOOKS BY ANN REE COLTON

    KUNDALINI WEST
    WATCH YOUR DREAMS
    ETHICAL ESP
    THE JESUS STORY
    THE HUMAN SPIRIT
    PROPHET FOR THE ARCHANGELS
      (Co-Author, Jonathan Murro)
    THE SOUL AND THE ETHIC
    THE KING
    DRAUGHTS OF REMEMBRANCE
    MEN IN WHITE APPAREL
    THE VENERABLE ONE
    THE LIVELY ORACLES
    ISLANDS OF LIGHT
    PRECEPTS FOR THE YOUNG

For information regarding the books, cassettes, and home-study lessons by Ann Ree Colton and Jonathan Murro:

              write

Ann Ree Colton Foundation
336 West Colorado Street
Post Office Box 2057
Glendale, California 91209